PAUULU'S DIASPORA

UNIVERSITY PRESS OF FLORIDA

Florida A&M University, Tallahassee
Florida Atlantic University, Boca Raton
Florida Gulf Coast University, Ft. Myers
Florida International University, Miami
Florida State University, Tallahassee
New College of Florida, Sarasota
University of Central Florida, Orlando
University of Florida, Gainesville
University of North Florida, Jacksonville
University of South Florida, Tampa
University of West Florida, Pensacola

PAUULU'S DIASPORA

Black Internationalism and Environmental Justice

QUITO J. SWAN

University Press of Florida

Gainesville · Tallahassee · Tampa · Boca Raton

Pensacola · Orlando · Miami · Jacksonville · Ft. Myers · Sarasota

25 24 23 22 21 20   6 5 4 3 2 1

Library of Congress Cataloging-in-Publication Data
Names: Swan, Quito, author.
Title: Pauulu's diaspora : black internationalism and environmental justice
   / Quito J. Swan.
Description: Gainesville : University Press of Florida, 2020. | Includes
   bibliographical references and index.
Identifiers: LCCN 2019054900 (print) | LCCN 2019054901 (ebook) | ISBN
   9780813066417 (hardback) | ISBN 9780813057507 (pdf)
Subjects: LCSH: Kamarakafego, Pauulu. | Black nationalism. |
   Blacks—Southern Hemisphere—History. | African diaspora. |
   Pan-Africanism. | Internationalism.
Classification: LCC DT16.5 .S93 2020 (print) | LCC DT16.5 (ebook) | DDC
   304.8096—dc23
LC record available at https://lccn.loc.gov/2019054900
LC ebook record available at https://lccn.loc.gov/2019054901

The University Press of Florida is the scholarly publishing agency for the State University System
of Florida, comprising Florida A&M University, Florida Atlantic University, Florida Gulf Coast
University, Florida International University, Florida State University, New College of Florida,
University of Central Florida, University of Florida, University of North Florida, University of South
Florida, and University of West Florida.

University Press of Florida
2046 NE Waldo Road
Suite 2100
Gainesville, FL 32609
http://upress.ufl.edu

To the best parents in the universe, Lorraine and Sinclair Swan

CONTENTS

FIGURES

ACKNOWLEDGMENTS

Thinking, dreaming, researching, and writing this book has been a tremendously challenging but richly rewarding journey. Some years ago, I told students in one of my classes at Howard University that this acknowledgements section would be difficult to write. Little has happened since then to ease my doubts about being able to adequately address all of the debts that I have incurred while completing this project. Indeed, the list of the individuals, communities, and institutions that supported my research journey across the Atlantic, Pacific, and Indian Ocean worlds is *longer than rope.*

Sincere gratitude goes out to my incredible editor Sian Hunter and her colleagues at the University Press of Florida, including Richard Feit, Marthe Walters, and Amanda Price. Sian was unbelievably patient in ushering me toward the finish line. Iconic scholars Gerald Horne and Akinyele Umoja somehow found the precious time to read the manuscript; without question, their constructive feedback made this book stronger. Thanks also to Ellie Camlin and Melissa Hyde for proofing and indexing the work.

A number of fellowships, grants, and awards facilitated research across the United States, Bermuda, London, Kenya, Australia, Fiji, Papua New Guinea, and Vanuatu. A 2004 Sasakawa Foundation Peace Fellowship sponsored time at London's National Archives. A 2013 library fellowship at Indiana University was essential for the Liberia chapter—thanks to Verlon Stone, Valerie Grim, and John and Judy Gay for their precious assistance. A 2013 Andrew Mellon summer fellowship supported research at Howard's Moorland-Spingarn Research Center; thanks to the Center's Joellen Elbashir, Ishmael Childs, Alhaji Conteh, Howard Dodson, Richard Jenkins, Ida Jones, Lopez Matthews, Kenvi Phillips, and Sonja Woods. A 2014 Howard University Faculty Senate Scholarship and Creativity award helped facilitate travel to East Africa.

A 2014 Project for African Decolonial and Indigenous Knowledges (PA-DIK) intensive writing fellowship at Kenya's Jomo Kenyatta University for Science and Technology (supported by Kansas State University and Kenya's African Institute for Capacity Development) allowed me to conduct research in Kenya's National Archives. I am truly gracious to PADIK's Tushabe wa Tushabe, Tinu Maduagu, Besi Muhonja, Mickie Mwanzia-Koster, and Cheikh Thiam for the wonderful opportunity to workshop parts of the manuscript—*majekobaje.*

A 2014 National Endowment for the Humanities Fellowship for University Faculty supported months of fieldwork across Oceania. Sincere thanks goes out to the helpful curators, archivists, librarians, administrators, and staff at Fiji's National Archives and National Library, the libraries of the University of the South Pacific (Suva and Vila), Vanuatu's National Archives (particularly Anne Naupa) and National Library and Museum, Australia's National Archives (Canberra), National Library, and State Library of New South Wales, the Australian Institute of Aboriginal and Torres Strait Islander Studies (particularly Michael Dodson and Russell Taylor), Papua New Guinea's National Archives and National Library, and the archives of the University of Papua New Guinea.

Elegba meets Muai. In Fiji I was hosted by Lea Lani Kinikini and Salesi Kauvaka, two incredible activist scholars from Tonga. Captain Huey, although we did not complete the journey from Fiji to Vanuatu, I learned much as a deckhand on your yacht. Vanessa Griffen and Claire Slatter, I cannot express enough gratitude and admiration for your years of activism and for my warm reception in Suva; you both gave far much more than I could have asked for.

In Vanuatu, Rose Coung and Baizum Kamarakafego graciously allowed me to stay in their wonderful home. Special thanks are due to Dominique Hoa Cuong and Leitong Coung and the extended family of Mele village; that includes Chris and Adi Sokomanu. Hilda Lini infallibly chaperoned me across Pentecost, Santo, and Ambae. Daniel Nato hosted me in Malekula. Thanks to the Vanua'aku Pati for providing access to its archives, to BUZZ FM Radio's Morning Show, and to Edison Mala, Kalkot Mataskelekele, Ati George Sokomanu, Peter Taurakoto, and Barak Sope for the remarkable interviews.

In Australia, special thanks are due to Gary Foley, Jenny Monroe, the Redfern Tent Embassy family, DJ K-Note, Patricia Korowa, Kim Kruger, John Maynard, Emily Nicol, and the late Sol Bellear. Patricia, I cannot thank you enough for looking out for me in Sydney. Gary, in my next (next) trip I promise to spend more time in Melbourne. Alex Carter's generous sharing of primary documents and timely introductions were essential in helping me to navigate Australia's labyrinth of archives and libraries—*much respect*.

A 2016 Harry Ransom Center Research Fellowship in the Humanities at the University of Texas-Austin, supported by the Dorot Foundation Postdoctoral Research Fellowship in Jewish Studies, facilitated research for chapter 10. A 2017–18 American Council of Learned Societies Frederick Burkhardt Fellowship at Harvard University's Radcliffe Institute for Advanced Study provided time and resources for completing the second half of the book. I do not know how I would have survived that year of working on two book projects without the exceptional comradeship of Erica R. Edwards, Steffani Jamison, Deborah Vargas, Quincy Flowers, and Maceo the Titan. Special thanks go out to the Radcliffe's African-American studies working group—Erica R. Edwards, Francois Hamlin, Shireen Hassim, Steffani Jamison, Chad Williams, Patricia Williams, and Leah Wright Rigueur provided critical feedback on chapter 7 (and beyond). Thanks also to my Radcliffe co-fellows, floor mates, administrators, support staff and student research partners, including Doohwan Ahn, Amahl Bishara, Sharon J. Bromberg-Lim, Dean Lizabeth Cohen, Julie Guthman, Jonathan Guyer, Rebecca Haley, Sophie Hochhäusl, Bouchra Khalili, Jodie Mack, Camilo Mendez, Samantha Power, Jackson Gates, and Oya Gursoy. I would also like to thank the staff at the Schlesinger Library, specifically its Curator for Race and Ethnicity, Kenvi Phillips. Thanks also to archivists across Harvard's Houghton library, UMass-Boston's Healey library, and David Hale, Associate Archivist and Historian at Goddard College, Vermont.

Research conducted during a 2018–19 fellowship at the Wilson Institute for International Scholars, Washington, DC, provided critical sources for chapters 5 and 6. Special thanks to Lindsay Collins, Kimberly Conner, Ruslan Garipov, Jane Harman, Robert Litwak, Natalie Ruiz Morato, Brad Simpson, Janet Spikes, and Yinuo Wei.

In Bermuda, Kim Dismont-Robinson, Heather Whalen, and the Department of Community and Cultural Affairs have provided me with platforms to share my work. Thanks to the staff at Bermuda's National Archives and the Bermuda National Library's Joanne Brangman. Thanks must also be extended to Nelson Bascome III, Latoya Bridgewater, the late Walton Brown, Colwyn Burchall, Lauren Francis, Iman Gibbons, Max Hull, Tonisha Key-Holmes, Sofia Mohammad, Sherri Simmons, Vejay Steede, Delight Vickers, Lucinda Worrell, and the Pauulu Kamarakafego Grassroots Collective (PKGC) for our collective conversations about Kamarakafego's significance to Bermuda and the world. David Tesfa Chapman provided timely feedback on chapter eleven. Former Bermuda Premier Ewart Brown's generous material support allowed me to launch the Pauulu Project in 2013, which supported travel and the gathering of primary documents for the book.

I have benefitted from having strong mentorship, tough love, and a plethora of support from several remarkable individuals. The short list of those who need to be thanked include Gerald Horne, Charles Jones, Franklin Knight, John Maynard, Yvette Modestin, Merle Brock Swan Williams, Akinyele Umoja, Michael West, and Ben Vinson III. Joseph Jordan had faith that I could complete this project even before I did—his vote of confidence mattered much.

Much of the ideas for this book were conceived, rinsed, and rehearsed during my time in Howard's Department of History. To the late Selwyn H. H. Carrington, my dissertation advisor, *you were right and you are missed.* Over the years, I enjoyed the benefits of sharing an office with Emory Tolbert, whose wise counsel and friendship encouraged me to be both a better scholar and person. Elizabeth Clark-Lewis consistently provided me with always welcome and always honest advice—*medase.* Jeanne Maddox Toungara taught me how navigate the university as an institution. Jean-Michel Mabeko-Tali, thanks for constantly reminding me to stay focused on the project. At the *Mecca,* I had the greatest of colleagues. Special thanks are due to Clement Akassi, Ana Cardoso, Greg Carr, Alem Hailu, Haile Gerima, Jim Harper, Daryl Harris, Joseph E. Harris, Bessie Hill, Charles Johnson, LaShawn Harris, Azaria Mbughuni, Ethelbert Miller, Msomi Moor, Lorenzo Morris, Tonija Navas, Nikki Taylor, and Noelle Trent. Several of my former students (and now often colleagues) informed this project in a variety of ways. These include TaKeia Anthony, Adisa Beatty, Marcus Bellamy, Jocelyn Imani Cole, Loren Collier, Alhaji Conteh, Justin Dunnavant, Lora Hargrove, Araba Evelyn Johnston-Arthur, Kimberly Monroe, Christopher Shell, Latif Tarik, Neil Vaz, Benjamin Woods, and Students Against Mass Incarceration (SAMI).

Chocolate City (Washington, DC) you are missed. Acklyn Lynch, you have been a rock and a true elder—I truly miss our conversations. My brothers Jared Ball, Mark Bolden, and Todd Burroughs, it is always love. Mention must be made to Obi Egbuna, LaTanya Brown-Robertson, Eddie Marshall Conway, Shirikiana Gerima, Tarica June, Diarra Robertson, Chess Girls DC, Chaundi Randolph, Sankofa Bookstore and Cafe, the Sankofa Home School Collective, LAMB PCS, the late Baba Agyei Akoto and Nation

House, Mwiza Munthali and James Pope of *Africa Now!*, Juan Daniel Mo-rocoima, Dominique Stevenson, *We Run Tings,* and WPWF radio.

The gratitude list stemming from my ASALH, NCBS, ASWAD, and AAIHS families is a long one. Warm shout outs are due to Maria Hamil-ton Abegunde, Leslie Alexander, Curtis Austin, Monique Bedasse, Richard Benson, Keisha Blain, Stefan Bradley, Ashley Farmer, Jonathan Fenderson, Ibram X Kendi, Minkah Makalani, Jeffrey Ogbar, Russell Rickford, Robyn Spencer, and Jakobi Williams.

Thanks to all of Kamarakafego's family members and close comrades who I was able to meet, talk to, and work with, especially Rronniba and Baizum Kamarakafego. Rronniba, my thanks to you does no justice to the level of support that you have granted me. Baizum, *bonafide,* you are my brother for life. Suzanne Darrell, our meeting in Lahey was short but meant much. Sincere thanks to all those who gave their time, documents, photographs, phone conversations, emails, and interviews. In this regard, thanks to Mama Farika Berhane, Courtland Cox, Sylvia Hill, Jimmy Garrett, John Bracey, and Jeanna Knights. Distinctive thanks are due to Michelle Khaldun, who first introduced me to Kamarakafego in the summer of 1997 in St. George's, Bermuda.

Indeed, I have had special help on this journey. *Mojuba Oludamare, Elegba, Obatala, y Ogun. Seeknfind.* My *divine dictionary* guided me through new words and ways to think about this book and I will always be grateful for that. Baba Kwao, *forty days!* Marcus Bellamy drove hours with me to see Kamarakafego while he was hospitalized in Massachusetts; somehow the closure of writing the draft of this book also took place there. Louis Woods, our conversations are always grounding. Glenn Chambers, you are the truth brother—keep showing us how to do it. Maryam Sabur—uncon-ditional thanks for your years of labor. Iyelli Ichile—my twin sister—your words and strong medicine always bring me clarity. Furqan Khaldun, hail up Socrates for me; bring the ion cannon and head to the vault. Theodore Francis, give thanks for all the laughs, the reasons, and the prayers—build studio!

I have the honor of having the best parents and wisest siblings in the world. Mom and Dad—Lorraine and Sinclair Swan—you have always been there for me. Niqué, Tamisheka, and Kashima, I love you lot! Momma Phyl-lis Basden, it is always love. Natalie and Jerodd you have adding so much to our family with your love. The memories of Madge Swan, Kingsley Swan Jr., Sherlyn Swan Caisey, Sherlene Swan, and Walter Brangman live closely with us. Tiante, Tomei, Adanna, Jalen, Jamison, Jordyn, Sabian, and Sebastian, you all know what it is! Akinwunmi, Ifasadun, Ayah, Mariama, and Kairos, you are truly loved and are very special. Ifa and Ayah, your dazzling input was essential to conceiving chapter eight as "Minecrafting a Black World." Now, who wants some *injera*?

AUTHOR'S NOTE

Members of Aboriginal and Torres Strait Islander communities are advised that this book contains names and images of deceased people.

ABBREVIATIONS

6PAC	Sixth Pan-African Congress
7PAC	Seventh Pan-African Conference
AAL	Aborigines Advancement League
ACM	Afro-Caribbean Movement
ALSC	African Liberation Support Committee
AME	African Methodist Episcopal
AOSIS	Alliance of Small Island States
ASCRIA	African Society for Cultural Relations with Independent Africa
ASIO	Australian Security Intelligence Organization
BCO	British Colonial Office
CAM	Caribbean Artist Movement
CAP	Congress of African Peoples
CBE	Center for Black Education
CFTC	Commonwealth Fund for Technical Co-operation
CIA	Central Intelligence Agency
CIO	Congress of Industrial Organizations
CIT	California Institute of Technology
CRC	Civil Rights Congress
CSD	Commission on Sustainable Development
CUAS	Committee for Universal Adult Suffrage
FBI	Federal Bureau of Investigation
FCAATSI	Federal Council for the Advancement of Aborigines and Torres Strait Islanders
FCO	Britain Foreign and Commonwealth Office

FEANF	Black African Students Federation in France
FED	Forum for Energy and Development
IEC	Intelligence Evaluation Committee
INSNI	International Network of Small Island Developing States, NGOs, and Indigenous Peoples
IRD	Information and Research Department
MCP	Member of Colonial Parliament
MIT	Massachusetts Institute of Technology
MOSOP	Movement for the Survival of the Ogoni People
NAACP	National Association for the Advancement of Colored People
NBPG	Niugini Black Power Group
NHNP	New Hebrides National Party
NJAC	National Joint Action Committee
NOI	Nation of Islam
NYU	New York University
OAAU	Organization of Afro-American Unity
OAU	Organization of African Unity
ODECO	Organization for Ethnic Community Development
ONECA	Organización Negra Centroamericana
OVD	Office of Village Development
PAPO	Pan-Afrikan People's Organization
PLP	Progressive Labor Party
PNC	Peoples National Congress
PNG	Papua New Guinea
PPM	People's Progressive Movement
PWC	Pacific Women's Conference
SCSC	South Carolina State College
SIDS	Small Island Developing States
SNCC	Student Non-Violent Coordinating Committee
SPATF	South Pacific Appropriate Technology Foundation
SSTAD	Society of Scientists and Technologists for African Development
TANU	Tanganyika African National Union
UBAD	United Black Association Development

UBP	United Bermuda Party
UCA	United Caribbean Association
UCPA	Universal Colored People's Association
UEA	University of East Africa
UFC	United Fruit Company
UN	United Nations
UNIA	Universal Negro Improvement Association
UPNG	University of Papua New Guinea
USP	University of the South Pacific
UWI	University of the West Indies
WCAR	World Conference Against Racism, Racial Discrimination, Xenophobia, and Related Intolerance
WCC	World Council of Churches
WSSD	World Summit on Sustainable Development

Introduction

It was May 1975, and Bermudian Black Power organizer Pauulu Kamara-kafego had just arrived in Port Vila, Vanuatu. It was not the environmental activist's first visit to the political condominium then known as the New Hebrides, which lay some thousand miles east of Australia. As an architect of Tanzania's Sixth Pan-African Congress (6PAC), Kamarakafego had passed through the joint British and French colony the year before to organize a black delegation from Oceania. Seeking black internationalist support in their bitter anti-colonial struggle, the New Hebrides National Party (NHNP) sent representatives to the 1974 Congress. While in Dar es Salaam, the party invited Kamarakafego to Vanuatu to conduct political education among its rural indigenous masses, a black Melanesian people known as the Ni-Vanuatu. Numbering about 100,000 people, they represented 85 percent of the total population and formed the political base of the NHNP. He accepted this invitation without reservation.[1]

But after Kamarakafego gave speeches to rural audiences of about two hundred people, British and French colonial administrators moved to deport him from the 4,739 square mile archipelago for "propagating Black Power doctrines."[2] From the state's perspective, his other "crime" was developing environmental projects that enabled the Ni-Vanuatu to make key commodities from natural resources, such as natural soaps from lye, oil from coconuts, salt from the ocean, sweeteners from sugar cane, and cement from calcium carbonate deposits and clay. As a result, their communities could avoid having to buy these products from European and Australian multinational companies.[3]

British officials recommended using a joint Anglo-French military force to extract Kamarakafego if he forcibly resisted arrest. The British resident minister stressed that the operation needed to be "clean and effective" and that it would require "the total strength available" to handle a possible crowd of five hundred party supporters. They hoped that French gendarmeries could be placed on standby, and they considered flying in British troops stationed in Singapore or Fiji or Gurkhas from Hong Kong.[4]

However, Kamarakafego's capture was timed to take the party by surprise, and it occurred with little incident. Placed on board a small plane piloted by an Australian official, Kamarakafego was taken to a deserted airstrip. The strip's surrounding sea, forest, and hills were full of aging Coca-Cola caps and bottles and discarded US weaponry—corroded grenades and bazookas, rusty helmets, and algae-attracting tanks—all lingering reminders that the airstrip had been built by the US military during World War II. Flanked by the British police commissioner and five Ni-Vanuatu officers, Kamarakafego remained here for most of the day. In between verbally dressing down the pilot and police commissioner about their colonial white privileges, he pressed the Ni-Vanuatu officers about their rights for self-determination. Why was the commissioner a person of British descent and not a Ni-Vanuatu? he asked. Why did the country need Australian pilots? He detailed his ability to fly the aircraft as an example of how indigenous New Hebrideans could technologically administer their own country. To the chagrin of the commissioner, this five-foot-six, muscularly built man completely enthralled the officers.[5]

Kamarakafego was eventually flown to Vanuatu's main airport in Port Vila, where he was to be quickly switched to a commercial flight headed to the United States. This time it was the party's turn to use surprise. As Kamarakafego's plane was taxiing to the back of the other aircraft, twenty-six NHNP members "caught the police on their wrong foot." These protestors drove onto the tarmac, parked, and locked their cars in front of his aircraft. Shouting "Black Power!" they tossed away their car keys. Clashes with police broke out, arrests were made (conveniently, at nightfall), charges were filed, fines were levied, and Kamarakafego was sent on his way back to Bermuda.[6]

However, with the help of two African American women, he miraculously evaded his FBI escort in the Los Angeles airport. Undaunted, he soon obtained a new passport from one his contacts at an African embassy. With the financial help of black activists and artists such as Jeff Donaldson, Mari Evans, Gwendolyn Brooks, Lerone Bennett, Elizabeth Catlett, and Ademola Olugebefola, he headed back to Oceania—this time to Fiji and then to newly independent Papua New Guinea as a rural development consultant for its government.[7]

In the words of Kamarakafego's political mentor, C. L. R. James, this account may seem "beyond belief."[8] How did a devout pan-Africanist environmentalist from some nine thousand miles across the Atlantic Ocean end up embroiled in a black indigenous struggle for decolonization in Oceania? And why did his presence—and the ideas of Black Power—twist the proverbial knickers of the British and French governments? Remarkably, for Kamarakafego, such improbably wide-ranging, multidimensional, and potent engagement was typical. His fascinating sojourn throughout the African Diaspora is the heart of this book.

Born in the segregated British colony of Bermuda in 1932, Kamarakafego lived an epic life of global activism. He survived demonstrations against Cuba's United Fruit Company and bouts with the Ku Klux Klan as a student activist in South Carolina's black freedom struggle. Between 1959 and 1966, he taught biology and environmental studies at Liberia's Cuttington College and University of East Africa's campuses in Kenya, Tanzania, and Uganda. He also co-organized Bermuda's Committee for Universal Adult Suffrage (CUAS, 1961) and became a member of parliament for the island's Progressive Labor Party (1968). Kamarakafego is perhaps best known for his leadership roles in organizing Bermuda's First International Black Power Conference (1969) and 6PAC. His versions of Black Power and pan-Africanism included appropriate technology, sustainable development, and environmental justice. As such, his most lasting contribution as a black internationalist was in his dual political and environmental advocacy across the Global South.

Pauulu's Diaspora explores how Kamarakafego fused his political worldview with his technical expertise in the service of black self-determination. In Vanuatu, Papua New Guinea, and Liberia he launched rural-based projects that built sustainable homes and water tanks from bamboo. Between 1959 and 1977, he wrote nine structural engineering manuals—*How to Build a Watertank from Bamboo and Cement*, *Rural Agricultural Irrigation with Bamboo Tanks*, *Rural Electrification*, *A House for Every Family*, *Making Oil from Coconut*, *Making Soap*, *Rural Sugar Factory*, *Integrated Coconut Factory*, and *Back a Yard Garden*. Into the twentieth-first century, his international posts included coordinator of the International Network of Small Island Developing States, NGOs, and Indigenous Peoples (INSNI); United Nations consultant on rural development and renewable energy sources; cofounder of the Southern Caucus of NGOs for Sustainable Development; and Consultant on Global Sustainability to the European Economic Community and the Commonwealth Fund Rural Development Program.

Chapter 1 unpacks Kamarakafego's upbringing in Bermuda, where myths of white supremacy, British colonialism, de facto segregation, black disenfranchisement, labor exploitation, West Indian migration, black culture, and his family's Garveyism fueled his political development. By the time Kamarakafego reached secondary school, he often thought about how to best help his family, school, and community. His first foray into direct political action occurred in Cuba, where summer visits to family exposed him to both the Spanish-speaking black world and the exploitation of black migrant laborers working the sugarcane fields in the province of Central Chaparra. He entered the United States to attend New York University well aware of the international scope of racism and segregation.

Chapter 2 spans his time as a college student at Orangeburg's South Carolina State College, Durham's North Carolina Central University, and Pasadena's California Institute of Technology between the years 1954 and 1959. It is focused on radical memories of armed self-defense and political activism in South Carolina. As a college student, Kamarakafego read newspapers and watched news broadcasts about the "injustices and suffering of the people in Africa." He would ask himself, "How can *Me One* help to solve the injustices and suffering in Bermuda, Africa, and the world?"[9] He was eventually expelled from South Carolina State College as a result of his involvement in a 1954–55 citywide boycott organized by the local National Association for the Advancement of Colored People (NAACP) chapter against White Citizen Council racial violence. This chapter challenges scholarship that has tended to render invisible South Carolina's black freedom struggle of the mid-1950s.

Chapter 3 explores Kamarakafego's political activities between the years 1959 and 1961. This was a particularly intense period for him, both politically and personally. He completed his college studies, traveled to Africa for the first time, got married, buried his father, and cofounded Bermuda's CUAS. While he had been "wearing Africa on his back" for much of his life, his time on the continent was transformative. According to Kamarakafego, he was ceremoniously given the name Pauulu Kamarakafego, "brown-skinned son of Chief Kamara," while visiting Kpelle relatives in Liberia.[10]

In 1961, he joined a major labor strike in Liberia, forcing him to flee to Ghana. Here, Kwame Nkrumah urged him to continue on to Kenya, where Kamarakafego lived from 1963 to 1967. Chapter 4 explores his time in East Africa, where he assisted Jomo Kenyatta's new government in "Africanizing" its national science and education programs. While teaching across the University of East Africa, he wrote his first manual on building water tanks with bamboo and cement.[11] In Kenya, he joined an African American expatriate community that included women such as Catherine Mbathi, Ruth Stutts

Njiri, and Ernestine Hammond Kiano. A fateful 1964 meeting in Kenya with Malcolm X led him to join the Black Power Steering Committee upon his return to the Americas. This chapter also details his involvement in party politics in Bermuda and on the Black Power conferences of Philadelphia (1968) and Bermuda.

Kamarakafego's Black Power politics were charged by the major political trends sweeping Africa—decolonization, sustainable development, liberation struggles, neocolonialism, sustainable development, universal adult suffrage, and pan-Africanism. Chapters 5 and 6 demonstrate his growth into a leading coordinator of Black Power in the Caribbean. In particular, these chapters detail state repression of the movement in the region and Kamarakafego's botched efforts to organize a 1970 Black Power conference in Barbados.

While thwarted in the West Indies by government forces, the Black Power Committee decided to hold the Congress of African Peoples (CAP) in Atlanta, Georgia, in 1970; Chapter 7 focuses on Kamarakafego's significant roles in these talks. In 1969, Melbourne's Aborigines Advancement League invited him to Australia to support its Black Power struggle, which referred to land rights, self-reliance, and sovereignty for indigenous Australians. In return, he invited Bob Maza, Bruce McGuinness, Patsy Kruger, Jack Davis, and Sol Bellear to the talks. This chapter highlights the relationships between Kamarakafego and Australia's delegation to explore CAP's international dynamics.[12]

Chapter 8 is focused on Kamarakafego's significant role as a catalyst for 6PAC. While held in Tanzania from June 19 to 27, 1974, the organizing of the congress was a monumental five-year process that began as early as Bermuda's 1969 Black Power conference. Kamarakafego's environmentalist background was stamped on 6PAC's tangible aim to establish a pan-African science and technology center in Africa. His global network of black organizers were essential to the congress; through his relationships with activists from Oceania, leaders of Vanuatu's NHNP participated in the talks.

The congress solidified the deepening linkages between Africana liberation struggles and decolonization in Oceania. Chapter 9 explores Kamarakafego's involvement in the NHNP's liberation movement, his deportation from the condominium, and his return to Oceania—this time to Fiji. In Fiji, he forged relationships with activists Vanessa Griffen and Claire Slatter; these women were leaders in the Nuclear Free and Independent Pacific movement, the Pacific Women's Conference, and the Pacific People's Action Front.

Kamarakafego did not return to Vanuatu until after it achieved political independence in 1980. Chapter 10 details how Griffen and Slatter helped to get him established in Papua New Guinea as the government's rural development officer. From Papua New Guinea, he became a conduit for global representations of the Black Pacific. His experiences in Melanesia definitively marked his environmental and political work across the Global South for the rest of his career.

The final chapter spans Kamarakafego's return to the Americas, where he worked extensively as an environmental activist within the framework of the United Nations Commission on Sustainable Development. It details his advocacy of Small Island and Developing States, his coordination of INSNI, and the pan-African movement, and his work around renewable energy, climate change, and sustainable development. By this time, he had returned to Bermuda, where he continued to mentor generations of organizers, artists, and students.

Interventions

Pauulu's Diaspora makes a number of critical historiographical, theoretical, and methodological interventions to the disciplines of African American, Caribbean, US, and African Diaspora history, and Africana, environmental, and Pacific studies. Kamarakafego remains conspicuously absent from book-length historiographies on global Black Power, pan-Africanism, and CAP.[13] Some studies briefly mention his involvement with the 1969 Bermuda conference, 6PAC, and decolonization in Oceania.[14] A few notable works seriously engage his global activism, including James Garrett's illuminating *Black World* article, "The Sixth Pan-African Congress" (1975), Tracey Banivanua Mar's pathbreaking *Decolonization and the Pacific* (2016), and my own *Black Power in Bermuda* (2009).[15]

This unique project uses a conceptual framework of what I am calling *Radical Black Diaspora*, which is centered on global black freedom traditions of struggle, power, and self-determination. It engages the interdisciplinary methodological tools of African Diaspora studies and Africana/African American studies. This includes what Joseph E. Harris calls *trans-Africanism*, and his approach to studying the Diaspora from a pan-African perspective centered on dialectic relationships between global black spaces. It also centralizes the praxis and calls for a sense of urgency in using radical narratives to defend exploited communities of color within and beyond academia.[16]

Elegba, too, makes history. *Radical Diaspora* is particularly focused on black movements that have been marginalized by scholarship. It particularly looks for black Diaspora linkages in unexpected crossroads, including spaces of supposed disconnect between black communities. It borrows from Pacific studies scholar Lea Kauvaka's notions of "berths," which she describes as being "real spaces influenced and constrained by geography, holding real memory of journeys, departures, homecomings, and crossings." For Kauvaka, berths are not roots or routes, but "spaces of reciprocal exchanges that signify, create, and maintain relationships over distance and across time."[17]

Radical Diaspora engages but expands upon Cedric Robinson's concept of the black radical tradition, particularly in the areas of black women's activism, non-Anglophone movements, and the Black Pacific. It does so largely through the theme of black internationalism, a term attributed to Jane Nardal's classic 1928 political essay "Internationalism Noir." Writing from black Paris, Martinique's Nardal called for the cultural rise of Afro-Latin and Francophone "New Negro" artists and writers, who, inspired by the New Negro movement, would study the history of the black race. Jane and her sister Paulette Nardal were among the pioneers of Negritude, that powerful black Francophone cultural and political anti-colonial movement of the 1930s.

Since that time, writers—Merz Tate, W. E. B. Du Bois, and Kwame Nkrumah, for example—have long since described black internationalism as an *idea*—often through the lens of pan-Africanism, Garveyism, socialism, and Black Power. However, the past few decades have witnessed a striking growth of studies implicitly framed under the banner of black internationalism. This scholarship continues to expand the conceptual, spatial, and temporal discourses on black internationalism beyond both the twentieth century and the Atlantic rim, describing how black communities vibrantly raised questions of struggle beyond the boundaries of European colonial and nation-states.

Radical Diaspora embraces West, Martin, and Wilkins's notion of black internationalism as being historically rooted in struggle. Furthermore, it is interested in its routes across a radicalized Global South, or as Tate argued in 1943, the "darker peoples of the world" who questioned the reality of white superiority. Tate's "darker peoples" included not only the "millions of Negroes" in the United States, the Caribbean, and Central and South America, but also the inhabitants of Africa, Asia, Malaysia, Polynesia, and Melanesia.[18]

Kamarakafego was very much a part of *this* radical diaspora. A political Anansi, he weaved diverse streams of black consciousness into his efforts to help himself, his family, his community, and African people worldwide. Even as a child, he was a quintessential trickster who consistently outwitted his foes with wit and a wisdom that belied his young age. Much like a spider moving across a web, he traversed along the longstanding networks of black internationalism. But in Kamarakafego's world, British West Indians in the early twentieth century not only migrated to the familiar nodes of black Diaspora, such as London, Harlem, or Colón. They also unpredictably traveled, like Kamarakafego's parents, from St. Kitts and Nevis to smaller Atlantic outposts like Bermuda.[19]

In *Pauulu's Diaspora*, the Atlantic, Indian, and Pacific Ocean worlds are shown to be and to have been in constant dialog. As Kamarakafego sojourned through southern hemispheric port cities, archipelagos, and travel spaces he forged concrete relationships with artists, exiles, laborers, students, and activist scholars of similar passage. From Bermuda, Kamarakafego and other activists organized 6PAC. Fiji played a similar role for his network in Oceania. Ships, airports, villages, immigration depots, buses, trains, classrooms, railway stations, and street corners linked the Diaspora through crossroads such as Hamilton, Dar es Salaam, and Suva. In these hubs of travel, boundaries of race, power, class, (de)colonialisms, identity, culture, (inter)nationalisms, gender, and ethnicity could be intensified and also transformed. *Pauulu's Diaspora* shows how these "mobile metropoles," berths, and border spaces have historically functioned as dynamic sites of knowledge production, political transformation, black internationalism, and Diaspora creation.

The book presses beyond a conceptual cartography of Africana scholarship and popular memory that has explored pan-Africanism as largely an Atlantic world experience, told through the lens of conference resolutions, speeches, arguments, and debates of heads of state—Africa's "Big Men." It recalibrates these boundaries, showing how pan-Africanism was also a grassroots movement that diversely impacted Africa and the Indian and Pacific Ocean worlds.[20]

Scholarship on pan-Africanism and twentieth-century repatriation to Africa has placed most attention on Ethiopia and Ghana. Given the conceptual and political space that both countries have long occupied in the pantheon of pan-Africanism, this is certainly understandable. Harmonized by the pulsating chords of reggae music, Rastafari's global trod has ensured that somewhere across the world, the sun is shining on a brightly waving red, green, and gold flag of Ethiopia. Ghana's Black Stars are arguably the Diaspora's favorite African nation to root for during FIFA's world cup—bested perhaps only by little Nigeria (Brazil). But Kamarakafego's time in Africa demonstrates how countries like Liberia, Kenya, Uganda, and East Africa *beyond* Ethiopia were also significant sites of twentieth century pan-Africanism.[21]

Overshadowed by Liberian president William Tubman's challenges to Nkrumah's pan-African vision of a United States of Africa, Liberia is not typically viewed as a crossroads for pan-African activity in the era of African independence movements. However, Kamarakafego's experiences show that pan-Africanism on the continent was also the muse of students, women, scholar activists, migrants, artists, and working-class laborers in urban and rural spaces. His return to Africa also reminds us how Africa's children have "reversed sails" and returned to the continent in diverse capacities such as technicians, scientists, revolutionaries, lawyers, doctors, educators, and artists.[22]

Pauulu's Diaspora brings necessary attention to 6PAC, which in many ways was a complicated manifestation of decades of organizing by Black Power, pan-Africanist, and Civil Rights activists. In addition to serious ideological differences, other divisive issues plagued delegates as well—egoism, pettiness, and sexism. The interpersonal fallouts that emerged from 6PAC endured for a very long time, as old and new wounds alike were both opened and healed.

Scholarship has largely marginalized the congress's focus on science and technology, ignored its impact on decolonization in Oceania, only hinted at Kamarakafego's extensive involvement, and minimized the centrality of black women in the talks. Primarily engaging the perspectives of dissatisfied African American visitors to Tanzania and West Indian activists who were wrongly denied participation, the congress has been projected as a collective failure that did little to transform the political landscapes of the United States and the Americas. This view rightly holds some currency. But this vision of 6PAC has been dominated by the loudly masculinist voices that wrote their oft legitimate and oft unfair critiques of the congress with lyrical wit, in bold fonts, and in all capitals. This includes Amiri Baraka, who denounced the early efforts of the Washington, DC, organizers as abstract "airplane PanAfrikanism" and lambasted Haki Madhubuti for sliding around Tanzania like a reactionary "liberal phantom pouting about being black." Yet Baraka counted himself among the outnumbered progressive factions who won out at 6PAC through its final declaration to end neocolonialism.[23]

Pauulu's Diaspora is more concerned with highlighting the experiences of black women and men whose extensive and global efforts to organize 6PAC have been rendered largely invisible. It echoes emerging scholarship that explores the impact of 6PAC through lenses such as gender, return movements, Tanzanian politics, and state surveillance.[24] It unpacks Kamarakafego's involvement with 6PAC to explore the relationships between pan-Africanism, appropriate technology, and decolonization in Oceania. In addition, it reveals how governments of the United States, Australia, the West Indies, France, and Britain monitored and harassed its organizers in a collaborative effort to curtail the congress's global impact. Furthermore, it demonstrates the networked and international relationships between the Pan-African and Black Power movements.

Black women like Sylvia Hill, Geri Augusto, and Australia's Roberta Sykes were central in organizing 6PAC. These women established their own "networks within networks" to circumnavigate the bureaucracies of male chauvinism. Throughout his life, Kamarakafego formed political and personal relationships with women of such ilk. In addition to the aforementioned women, this global roll call includes Modjeska Simkins, Sonia Sanchez, Septima Clark, Mary M. Townes, Hilda Lini, Patricia Korowa, Queen Mother Audley Moore, Thais Aubry, and Lois Browne Evans. This speaks to the centrality of pan-Africanism's ideological "daughters" and "mothers"—organizers, theorists, and martyrs alike—on historic black internationalism, Black Power, and the global black radical tradition.[25]

Pauulu's Diaspora is in conceptual conversation with an emerging subfield of Black Pacifics that is expanding the discourses of the black Diaspora beyond the Atlantic. While not in inherent opposition to the notion of the Black Atlantic, Black Pacifics interrogates the black world's engagement with Oceania, Asia, and the Pacific coast of the Americas. This is clearly one future of Africana studies.[26]

Kamarakafego's pioneering roles in the areas of sustainable development, appropriate technology, and environmental justice makes a critical contribution to scholarship that demonstrates the intersections between Africana studies, Black Power, and environmental justice. This includes his manuals, conference papers, resolutions, and proposals on environmental justice that collectively span social activism, science, environmental racism, renewable energy, food security, the "NGO industrial complex," reparations, and political sovereignty. *Pauulu's Diaspora* thus offers much for contemporary green movements for environmental and social justice across the Global South.[27]

Kamarakafego's political significance as an environmental activist can be contextualized in the work of Africana environmental activists such as Kenyan Nobel Prize winner Wangari Maathai and her Greenbelt movement, Amilcar Cabral and the African Party for the Independence of Guinea and Cape Verde, and Ken Saro-Wiwa of Nigeria's Movement for the Survival of the Ogoni People (MOSOP). A brilliant writer, Saro-Wiwa outspokenly denounced the environmental exploitation of Ogoni lands and waters by multinational petroleum companies like Royal Dutch Shell. He was captured and executed in 1995 in a military operation led by Nigeria's Rivers State Internal Security Task Force (RSIS). In May 1994, the RSIS noted that Shell's economic operations would continue to be impossible unless "ruthless military operations [were] undertaken" against MOSOP to allow "smooth economic activities to commence." The RSIS's strategies to eliminate Saro-Wiwa included "wasting operations" during MOSOP gatherings, "wasting targets" that cut across various communities and leadership cadres (especially "vocal individuals"), the deployment of four hundred military personnel, "psychological tactics of displacement," the restriction of visitors—particularly Europeans—to the area, the disbursement of fifty million naira as advanced allowances for officers and logistics, and the pressuring of oil companies to make "prompt regular [financial] inputs." According to the chairman of the RSIS, surveillance, ruthless operations, and high-level authority were necessary for the effectiveness of the operation, which was to continue until "full economic activities commenced."[28]

Black Power

Black Power was a global phenomenon. It shouted at both imperialism and its own contradictions in many different languages, mother tongues, *lingua francas*, and *slungs*—including Bislama, Kiswahili, English, Ebonics, Patois, Pidgin, French, Yoruba, Creole, Spanish, Kikongo, Tok Pisin, and Portuguese. It grew locks, fades, and Afros and donned dashikis, *ilekes*, and *khimars*. Black Power was black and brown. It sometimes smoked peace pipes, sometimes drank rum, and regularly made love, fought wars, broke hearts, birthed children, built villages, and raised families. It coped with dysfunction. It simultaneously frightened and intrigued white allies. Black Power read books, penned memoirs, loaded Kalashnikovs, shut down universities, set cities on fire, grew food, and painted pictures of liberation. It poured libations, raised hell, called on God, built shrines, portrayed Jesus as black with locks, hailed Haile Selassie, gave *ebo* to ancestors Orisas, Abosua and Laos, and ate "soul" foods, ital meals, *laplap*, codfish and potatoes, and yams and *fufu*. Black Power was emotionally intelligent and possessed the logical impatience of young men and women who believed that tomorrow was not promised for the African world.

Black Power was public enemy *numero uno*. It burst through the airwaves of imperialistic radio stations with the musical scores of Bob Marley, Miriam Makeba, Fela Kuti, Peter Tosh, Steel Pulse, Ilê Aiyê, and Nina Simone. These tracks were stained with the blood of Walter Rodney, Fred Hampton and Mark Clark, Erskine "Buck" Burrows, George and Jonathan Jackson, Beverly Jones, Patrice Lumumba, Steve Biko, and Amilcar Cabral. In response, state intelligence agencies relentlessly infiltrated Black Power groups like cancerous attacks on the blood cells of Fanon, Marley, Nkrumah, Ture, and Kamarakafego.

But what are the roots of the Black Power movement? Are sovereign, historic African nations such as Kush, Kemet, Ghana, Mali, or Great Zimbabwe examples of Black Power? In the afterword to *Black Power* (1992), Kwame Ture asserted that the mass movement emerged in the 1960s "because of centuries of struggles by Africans everywhere, and that is why it affected Africans everywhere."[29] If we follow this line of reasoning—that Black Power was forged within a global tradition of African resistance to the ilk of white power (slavery, colonialism, and racism)—are not revolts by the enslaved or maroon communities examples of Black Power? Should not the roll call of the movement include the Amistad uprising, the Haitian Revolution, Bermuda's Sally Bassett, Jamaica's Nanny, Brazil's Palmares and Zumbi, Mexico's Gaspar Yanga, and Venezuela's José Leonardo Chirino and Macuquita? This was the position of Guyana's Walter Rodney, who located the roots of Black Power in African struggles against slavery.[30]

What do we make of Edward Blyden's nineteenth-century call, "We need some *African power*, some great center of the race where our physical, pecuniary and intellectual strength may be collected"?[31] What of the radicalism in David Walker's *Appeal*? Paul Bogle's 1865 charge to "Cleave to the Black"? Ida B. Wells's position on armed self-defense? Menelik II and Taitu's 1896 victory over Italy at Adwa, Ethiopia? Jane Nardal's 1928 "Internationalisme noir?" Aimé Cesaire's *Discourse on Colonialism*? Claude McKay's *If We Must Die*? Where do black political organizations like Cuba's Partido Independiente de Color, the Universal Negro Improvement Association (UNIA), Brazil's Frente Negra Brasileira (Black Brazilian Front), and the African Blood Brotherhood fit within the genealogy of Black Power?

Is it possible to speak of *black power* in a general sense, but also give agency to the Black Power *movement* that emerged in the 1960s? Would it be appropriate to follow St. Claire Drake's suggestion for pan-Africanism—that is, to speak of "Black Power" as a movement and "black power" to describe ascendants to the movement more broadly?[32] This is more than an exercise in nomenclature. For while black struggles against white hegemony since the era of slavery were struggles for power, some recognition should be given to the generations of the 1960s that were politically transformed by Black Power's symbolism and agenda. After all, many of these freedom fighters still suffer from political repression for their efforts—Assata Shakur and Pete O'Neal are still "at large" in Cuba and Tanzania, respectively, and Mumia Abu-Jamal, Leonard Peltier, Jamil Al-Amin, Sundiata Acoli, and Mutulu Shakur all remain political prisoners.

The mid-1990s to early 2000s witnessed a proliferation of academic scholarship about the Black Power and Black Arts movements; studies on these themes continue to grow in exciting directions.[33] Arguably, this initial thrust was largely the work of diverse scholars who were responding to myriad historical, social, genealogical, political, and cultural stimuli from within and outside of the academy. A fruitful project would be to delineate the broader contexts in which this community emerged. Collectively, this group had been engaging the ideas of Black Power at variant degrees for decades—via family and community members, educators, political prisoners, and Black Power activists themselves.

But whether raised in the movement or not, these scholars were tremendously influenced by the publication, recirculation, popularization, and active study of Black Power literature in the late 1980s and 90s, some as high school and undergraduate students. These books included Horace Campbell's *Rasta and Resistance* (1985); Amy Jacques Garvey's *Marcus Garvey's Philosophy and Opinions* (1986); Assata Shakur's autobiography (1987); *The Autobiography of Malcolm X* (1987); Black Classic Press's editions of Bobby Seale's *Seize the Time* (1991) and George Jackson's *Blood in My Eye* (1996); and Walter Rodney's *Groundings With My Brothers* (1990). This occurred in a context of thriving black book stores, screenings of Julie Dash's *Daughters of the Dust* (1991) and Haile Gerima's *Sankofa* (1993), bootleg VHS copies of Sam Greenlee's *The Spook Who Sat by the Door* and *The Battle of Algiers*, study groups around the writings of bell hooks and Cornell West, the health and self-care regimen of Dr. Africa's *Nutricide*, ital food, Queen Afua and Dr. Sebi, community organizing around police brutality and mass incarceration (Rodney King and Amadou Diallo), Africana studies prison programs, African dance, drum and Capoeira Angola circles, Farrakhan mix tapes, Sizzla's *Praise Ye Jah* (1997), Sister Souljah and Khalid Muhammad on the Donahue Show, African street festivals, the writing and reading of letters from political prisoners, poetry collectives, demonstrations against apartheid in South Africa, questions of the US invasions of Grenada and Panama, the threat of nuclear war, popular culture (Hip-Hop's Dead Prez, X-Clan, and Nas; Neo-Soul's Erykah Badu; Reggae's Buju Banton, Garnett Silk, and Capleton; and Dancehall's Supercat, Lady Saw, Beenie Man, and Bounty Killer), immigration discrimination, black heritage tours to Kemet, the war *with drugs* against black and brown communities, student campus activism, the O. J. Simpson verdict, the Afrocentric movement's lecture circuits, VHS cassettes and CDs, the refashioning of locks and wearing of natural hair, the reinvigoration of traditional and transformed Africana spiritual systems (largely Rasta, Christianity, Islam, Nation of Gods and Earths, Lucumi, the National of Islam, African Hebrew Israelites, Ifa, Vodun, and Akan traditions), the braids of Venus and Serena Williams, Tiger Wood's "Cablinasian" comment, Brazil's FIFA 2002 World Cup victory over Germany, the 1995 Million Man and subsequent Women and Family marches, September 11 and its political and social aftermaths, and political comedy expressed through HBO's *Def Comedy Jam*, *Martin*, BET's *Comic View*, and Comedy Central's *Chappelle's Show*. These broader phenomena influenced how this generation's ideas about Black Power eventually turned into term papers, theses, dissertations, articles, and now award-winning books. This was certainly the context in which I met Kamarakafego in Bermuda in 1997.

The immense personal, political, and community investment in these relationships by academics has led to important and contentious definitional debates about the movement from what appeared to be two distinct but certainly overlapping orientations—mainstream academic and activist scholar. The mainstream approach is based on ideological inclusion, in which Black Power represents a wide spectrum of black politics from the conservative to the radical, all placed into a political calabash of "black people wanting the same thing but by different methods." But in this light, then, Black Power, very much like putty, can be molded, shifted, and baked to suit the needs, ideological positions, and perspectives of the writer, discipline, and contemporary politics. This certainly helped give Black Power academic and professional currency, and scholarship on the movement has been uncomfortably in vogue for some time. Still, as historian Brenda Plummer warns, "If Black Power is to mean anything, it cannot mean everything."[34]

Indeed, there is something to be said about Black Power's conceptual flexibility that facilitated its wildfire-like spread across the world. However, one could argue that its global advocates were endeared to certain fundamental ideas: black political and economic self-determination, global south solidarity, a revolutionary agenda, the legitimization of armed self-defense, pan-Africanism as an identity, embracement of political culture, environmental justice, a class analysis, freedom for political prisoners, and the overthrow of white power, capitalism, imperialism, and empire.

In contrast to inclusion, these "fundamentals" form the bedrock of activist scholar approaches to studying Black Power. These perspectives caution against the marginalization of Black Power discourses on revolution in favor of its supposed more "pragmatic" aims. This includes questioning attempts to link the movement to individual black-progress narratives within systems of white power. Concerned with the relevance of Black Power to contemporary brown and black movements, activist scholar approaches are particularly sensitive to the mainstream expansion of COINTELPRO-like surveillance and the plight of political prisoners. Whether appropriate or not, the activist-scholar approach is also suspicious of Black Power writers who appear to have little personal commitment to the movement's tenets or to social justice in general.

The battlefront for some of these tensions occurred within Black Power studies, which historian Peniel Joseph founded as an academic subfield of American and African American history circa 2001. Among other concerns, the subfield's US-centric framework largely dismissed an existing and growing canon of literature on Black Power's global dimensions. Its argument asserting Black Power's "deepening of American democracy" actually encouraged myopia in regard to the movement's diasporic influences, indigenous stimuli, critical moments, key personalities, questions about gender, organizations, repression, challenges, pitfalls, successes, and legacies.[35]

This book is in conversation with existing and emerging projects on global Black Power that, intentionally or not, challenged this conceptual invisibility. In 2007, V. P. Franklin edited a *Journal of African-American History* special edition on New Black Power studies, which sought to address the national, international, and transnational perspectives of Black Power. In 2009, Bermuda's Pauulu Kamarakafego Grassroots Collective held a conference to honor the fortieth-year anniversary of the 1969 Bermuda conference. In 2010, the University of the West Indies, St, Augustine, held an International Black Power conference in Trinidad. A year later, the Association for the Study of the World Wide African Diaspora (ASWAD) held a conference on African liberation and Black Power at the University of Pittsburgh. Exploring Black Power as a global phenomenon, ASWAD sought to interrogate the antecedents of Black Power from the seventeenth century and spanned questions of culture, sexuality, environment, and ideology across Africa, the Americas, the Middle East, Europe, and Asia.[36]

Pauulu's Diaspora defines Black Power as a global, black internationalist, anti-colonial, inherently pan-African, and revolutionary movement that sought political, economic, and cultural self-determination from systems of white hegemony such as (neo)colonialism and imperialism, even when these systems were represented by black heads of state. It shares this perspective with Kwame Ture, who stressed that black visibility in political offices was not Black Power. He connected Black Power to Global South liberation struggles, defining America's black community as being an internal colony of the United States. His mentor Nkrumah defined Black Power as being "part of the vanguard of world revolution against capitalism, imperialism, and neo-colonialism." Writing in 1968, Amy Jacques Garvey linked the movement to Marcus Garvey and the UNIA of the early twentieth century. Rodney saw Black Power in the West Indies as representing a "break from imperialism," the "assumptions of power by the Black masses," and "the cultural reconstruction of the islands in the image of the Blacks."[37]

This is in contrast to Peniel Joseph's *Dark Days, Bright Nights*, which asserted that Barack Obama's presidency was an "example of black power once thought inconceivable." However, from a global perspective, Obama's presidency reflected a very familiar political situation that Black Power had in fact rebelled *against* across the world. This included clashes with neocolonial black leaders, heads of state, police officers, and soldiers in the Caribbean and Africa (and in the United States). Joseph also portrayed the political agitation of both Ture and Malcolm X as a "pragmatic" attempt by Black Power to transform American democracy. But this is problematic, because for the wider Black Diaspora, Malcolm X and Ture largely represented black revolution *against* American imperialism.[38]

Pauulu's Diaspora cautions against "US-centric" appraisals of Black Power that render its global spread as either a hodgepodge of sporadic, fractured, and inevitably failing moments or a collection of loose appropriations of Black Panther symbolism. Such conceptual invisibility surrounding Black Power's global roots and routes means that all too often, explorations of Black Power's internationalism only go as far as the travel logs and intelligence documents of US-based activists and organizations take them. But this book hopes to go further than this. It calls for a paradigm shift in the study of Black Power. The global narratives of Black Power should not be "stuffed" into a US framework; Black Power in the United States should be read within this global context. Put another way, the book's critical intervention is that the movement must be globally contextualized to holistically grapple with and understand its collective challenges, international criminalization, and aborted transformative possibilities to the (post) colonial state worldwide.

Kamarakafego's deportation by the French and British governments from New Hebrides is an apt example of how state hostility to Black Power needs to be understood beyond the conceptual boundaries of the desks of J. Edgar Hoover, his "look out fetishes," and the US Federal Bureau of Investigation's (FBI) COINTELPRO. It is a story that includes the offices of the United States Department of State, National Security Agency, and Central Intelligence Agency (and its domestic programs like Project Merrimack and Project Resistance); Britain's Foreign and Commonwealth Office (FCO), M-15, M-16, and Scotland Yard; Australia's Security Intelligence Organization (ASIO); the Canadian Royal Military Police; France's Direction Générale de la Sécurité Extérieure; and the Caribbean's Special Branches. Along these very lines, *Pauulu's Diaspora* examines the role that US, British, Canadian, Dutch, French, Australian, and West Indian governments played in the surveillance and suppression of Black Power. Supported by a body of work about the repression of Black Power, it suggests that we internationalize our studies of COINTELPRO to better understand the repression of Black Power within a context of the global suppression of black radicalism.[39]

Kamarakafego's Black Power politics of the late 1960s were precluded by years of agitation against segregation, racism, labor exploitation, and (neo) colonialism across Africa and her Diaspora. As such, *Pauulu's Diaspora* engages literature on Black Power that has redefined perspectives that suggest that where and when the Civil Rights movement ends, Black Power begins. While Sundiata Cha-Jua and Clarence Lang demonstrated the pitfalls of this symbiotic long view approach, this study is informed by works that locate the routes of Black Power with black internationalism of the interwar era and post–World War II African American engagement with Global South anti-colonial struggles. For example, David Austin, Kenyatta Hammond Perry, and Robbie Shilliam demonstrate how Black Power was globally connected with black Diasporic migration to Canada, Britain, and New Zealand, respectively.[40]

While *Pauulu's Diaspora* clearly intersects with Black Power across the Americas, Oceania, Africa, and Europe, it is not a complete narrative of the movement. To tell this massive story of an unapologetic global black rebellion that torched the world would be a daunting but fruitful task. While the most ambitious and far reaching attempt appears to be Rhonda Williams's groundbreaking *Concrete Demands*, the writing of such a monograph is well overdue.

Kamarakafego's time in Africa only hints at the full scope of Black Power in the continent. This would certainly include its dynamics in Algeria and Tanzania, Stephen Biko and South Africa's Black Consciousness movement, Amilcar Cabral's fight against Portuguese colonialism in Guinea-Bissau and Cape Verde, and Nkrumah's time in Guinea. As in the Caribbean, it was often fallaciously claimed that African countries with African leaders *was*, in fact, Black Power. For example, in Mobutu Sese Seko's neocolonial Zaire in 1974, one billboard in Kinshasa boasted, "*Le pouvoir noir se cherche partout, mais il s'exerce effectivement au Zaire*"—Black Power is sought everywhere, but it is already realized here in Zaire. Yet in Africa, Black Power reflected a struggle against neocolonialism. Fela Kuti, who became a Black Power advocate after being introduced to black radical literature by African American Sandra Isadore, decried the colonial mentality of African leadership. Kuti, whose music referenced Black Power, referred to the Nigerian government's attacks on himself, his mother, and his comrades against South African apartheid.[41]

Mapping Kamarakafego's evolution into an international Black Power organizer raises fundamental questions about the movement's definitions, temporality, and geographic scope. It gives us some sense of how Black Power organically filtered throughout the world, convincingly demonstrating that the movement globally was more than just a sidebar of the US-based movement. It shows how Black Power's global emergence was more than a spontaneous response to television broadcasts of Black Panthers—it was impacted by local, national, regional, and international factors, such as Global South liberation struggles in Africa, Asia, the Americas, and Oceania. Physical contact between intentional conduits of Black Power—often from the Caribbean—facilitated the movement's growth and spread of ideas, literature, and material culture. Kamarakafego's transcontinental activism dating back to the early 1950s helps to reposition the movement's roots before the 1960s. He served as a direct bridge between elder pan-Africanists—such as Nkrumah, Amy Jacques Garvey, and C. L. R. James—and an emerging generation of Black Power organizers; this demonstrates the relationship between Black Power and the pan-African movement. His involvement in decolonization movements—as in Oceania and Bermuda—highlights the movements' anti-colonial nature. Kamarakafego's understanding of Black Power reflected praxis of ecological self-determination. His environmental activism well into the 1980s reveals another intersection of the movement, asking, What can we learn by analyzing the relationships between sustainable technology and environmental justice across the Diaspora?

Methodology

Pauulu's Diaspora is constructed via the exhaustive worldwide trail—paper, phonetic, and technological—that Kamarakafego left, both consciously and unwittingly, of his global experiences. This includes an immense trove of interviews, correspondence, photographs, newspapers, print and digital media, oral testimonies, books, scientific manuals and proposals, organizational reports, conference proceedings, and government surveillance. Numbers of Kamarakafego's communities, comrades, friends, and family members recall his political and environmental work across the Global South. His physical footprint remains in places such as Vanuatu, where a few of his water tanks and a home that he built (albeit no longer functional) are still standing in Mele and Pentecost Island.

Despite his relative invisibility in scholarship on Black Power and pan-Africanism, Kamarakafego was quite visible to the state authorities that kept tabs on his activities across the world. This included the US Justice Department Intelligence Evaluation Committee's 1972 report on the "Interrelationship between Black Power Organizations in the Western Hemisphere," which considered Ture, Kamarakafego, and Rosie Douglas to be the most significant coordinators of Black Power across the Caribbean region.[42] A 2013 Freedom of Information Act request revealed that the FBI holds approximately 1,500 pages of surveillance documents related to Kamarakafego, who also shows up notably in the archives of the CIA, Britain's FCO, ASIO, French and British residencies in Vanuatu, Bermuda's Intelligence Committee, and the State Department of the United States.

Gerald Horne has long since called for scholars of African American history to adopt a "transnational research agenda," one that utilizes archives across the globe. Indeed, Horne's prolific body of work has singlehandedly demonstrated the far-stretching reach of black internationalism across the world.[43] Ambitiously following his charge, this project required travel to national, local, and private archives and special collections located in the United States, Bermuda, Canada, Britain, Australia, Vanuatu, Kenya, Papua New Guinea, and Fiji. It was an unforgettable challenge to conduct research in Oceania. Traveling by fishing boat, yacht, microbus, eight-seat prop plane, and on foot, a 2014 National Endowment for the Humanities fellowship allowed me to conduct extensive interviews with villagers, artists, family members, scholars, musicians, and political leaders who had close relationships with Kamarakafego.

Kamarakafego's invaluable autobiography, *Me One: The Autobiography of Dr. Pauulu Kamarakafego*, is the only full-length work based on his life. It was indispensable in completing the current text, which is also buttressed by formal interviews that I conducted with Kamarakafego in 2004, numerous conversations that we had between 1997 and 2007, and personal recordings of his lectures in Bermuda and Washington, DC. Much of my time writing this book was spent clarifying and painstakingly reconstructing Kamarakafego's political life from *Me One's* plethora of uncaptioned but telling photographs, imprecise dates of events, and references to scores of individuals, political movements, and geographical spaces that scholarship deems to be obscure. For sure, this colossal task has certainly produced its own imprecisions.

Indeed, despite its heavy use of "the imperial archive," *Pauulu's Diaspora* is in consistent conversation with and critique of Kamarakafego's radical memories of his upbringing in Bermuda in the 1930s until his passing in 2007. These are largely told through *Me One*. As in the case of his involvement in South Carolina's black freedom struggle in the 1950s, these memories often clash with narratives mined from traditional archives. But how do we find balance between truths, experiences, and reality?

All that being said, this book is *not* a biography. Kamarakafego crossed paths and formed relationships with global trailblazers similar to himself, indicating how black internationalism functioned within a globalized, multigenerational, networked, gendered, and often contested ideological space, replete with black women and men who traversed the Diaspora as activists, revolutionaries, cultural workers, students, teachers, scientists and even agents provocateurs. Oftentimes, Kamarakafego drops into the background of the text as other political personalities and movements that he engaged move to the forefront. This is intentional. In essence, the book is a political narrative of twentieth-century black internationalism logistically anchored by Kamarakafego's globe-trotting activism. It is a journey that begins in Bermuda.

I

Corner Stones

Hamilton, Harlem, and Havana

It was December 1928, and Bermuda's beautiful skies were dark, deep, and expectant with rain. In what was perhaps the stormiest night of the year, the island's torrential winds gave birth to muddy, slippery lanes throughout "Back-of-Town's" Angle Street. Still, crowds of black people braved the drenching downpour to reach Alexandrina Hall, headquarters of a local black Friendly Society. They came by horse, by push bike, by carriage, and by foot, on their way to listen to a lecture by the Universal Negro Improvement Association's (UNIA) Amy Jacques Garvey.

Garvey's husband and UNIA president, Marcus Mosiah Garvey, had been scheduled to speak. Yet having been marked as an "undesirable alien" by British colonial authorities in the island, he had been denied entry into Bermuda. From the deck of his ship, he waved at uniformed members of the UNIA's Bermuda Division—women, children, and men—who waited on the docks of Hamilton harbor in anticipation of the arrival of their "Black Moses." Refusing to be moved, they held steady the red, black, and green flags of African liberation that snapped in the gusty winds of Hamilton's Front Street.[1]

The turbulent weather might have seemed a divine manifestation of Jacques Garvey's charge to look for Marcus in the "whirlwind and the storm." Yet Jacques Garvey was no mere substitute for her husband. At age thirty-three, she was a seasoned pan-Africanist, a veteran journalist, and a masterful orator. She weaved her words between the mercurial rumbles of Shango's thunder and the lightning flashes of Oya. The audience was electrified by her "moving address." Here she was, in the "South Africa of the Caribbean," under the close watch of British authorities, unflinchingly telling black Bermuda about political turmoil in Europe, global violence against black people, and the virtues of Garveyism.[2]

This was the world of Roosevelt Nelson Browne, who would later become renowned as the Black Power activist and environmentalist Pauulu Osiris Kamarakafego. Young "Roose," as local friends and family would affectionally call him, was born in Bermuda on November 28, 1932. By the time he had celebrated his fifth birthday, Marcus Garvey had already been denied entry into Bermuda on five separate occasions. Kamarakafego was raised in a world marked by British colonialism, pan-Africanism, Italy's 1936 invasion of Ethiopia, West Indian migration, racial segregation, environmental injustices, and black resistance to white violence. His political consciousness was woven of the fabric of these racial, cultural, political, and economic contradictions of a majority black society that was dominated by a minority white elite.[3]

Kamarakafego's parents, John Horatio Brown and Henrietta Brown, had migrated to Bermuda from St. Kitts circa World War I with the thousands of West Indian laborers who sought work in the island. They would meet in Bermuda, marry, and have six children. Horatio's father had traveled to St. Kitts to work as a locomotive driver. A mechanic, he also operated a sugar cane mill there. Kamarakafego's paternal roots lay in Liberia and Nigeria; his mother was of East Indian descent. Teenage travels by boat took Horatio from Basseterre to the Dominican Republic, to Brazil, and to relatives in West Africa. He would learn many things in these years away—speaking Spanish and Portuguese, doing masonry and carpentry, and driving a locomotive among them. By 1920, he had found work as a mason in in Bermuda's dockyard.[4]

Strikingly beautiful and industrious, Henrietta Brown arrived in Bermuda with her parents and three siblings around 1917. She knitted sweaters and worked as a seamstress at the Trimingham's Company, owned by one of Bermuda's oldest white oligarchs. Her father, Joel Brown, was an agricultural worker and machine mechanic who worked on Bermuda's tugboats. Her mother, Ruth-Ann Nesbitt, was from Nevis.[5]

The Browns and their six children lived in the Middletown (Back-of-Town) area of Hamilton, Bermuda's capital, in the proximity of the Pembroke Glebe Lands. According to Bermuda's assistant colonial secretary F. G. Gosling, many of these homes remained "mere shacks and without proper tanks for drinking water or sanitary conveniences." The land was "thickly covered with one hundred and ten of these houses" and "considerably overcrowded at night." The bishop felt that there was a danger that if an epidemic disease broke out in the densely populated area, it would "menace" the whole island; for years he had been pressing the government to take over the area and create a new housing scheme there. The rectors were criticized for these lucrative arrangements, which netted them £300 a year via annual rents of between 30s and £3.[6]

It was here that Kamarakafego spent countless hours in the kitchen of his grandmother, whom he remembered as being a quiet, very dark-skinned, "African looking" woman. The smells, sights, and tastes of traditional bush teas and spicy West Indian foods made from yams, taro, ado, jelly coconut, saltfish, dumplings, salt pork, salt beef, and warm Johnny bread enthralled him. Nourished physically and culturally, his childhood was marked by close relationships with his maternal grandparents.[7]

From the kitchen to the back yard to the Glebe lands of Pembroke, Kamarakafego was raised in a very African-centered space. Africa and the wider West Indies were rich, living spaces to him, brought alive by folklore told to him by his well-traveled family members. This certainly helped to buffer him from the plethora of negative stereotypes about Africa and the black world that were popular in those times. Bermuda's black community collectively remembered Africa through oral traditions, Gombey practices, folklore, culture, and song. Scholar Babacar M'Baye argues, for example, that two stories recorded by black Bermudians in 1925 had parallels in Africa. The first, "What Darkens the Hole," featured a wolf trickster who enters a hole, consumes food, and forgets to leave. M'Baye connects its plot to Anansi tales found in African and Caribbean stories. The second, "Playing Godfather," was essentially a Tar-Baby narrative, which, featuring the theft of butter, was a typical theme in African American folklore and an extension of West African tales.[8]

Perhaps most importantly, Kamarakafego's grandfather, father, and uncle were staunch Garveyites. They frequently spoke about "Black Moses," the Black Star Line, and UNIA schools. Perhaps they participated in UNIA activities, joined one of UNIA's Bermuda chapters, or frequented its headquarters at E. B. Grant's Church of God on Hamilton's Angle Street. They certainly would have known of Jacques Garvey's 1928 lecture, and they would have had much to say about the British government's repeated refusal to allow Garvey to enter Bermuda.

From his family, Kamarakafego learned much about the world. His great-aunt May lived in Nigeria from 1937 to 1950 and "kept the lines of communication with Africa open." This unsung pan-Africanist taught him to speak some Kpelle, Ibo, and Yoruba. Countless stories about the West Indies and the wider world, told to him by his great uncle Nesbitt, introduced him to the capital cities of the world. He also listened to world news broadcasts from his father's shortwave radio about wars and the suffering of the masses from diseases such as tuberculosis and measles. Even at a young age, global issues moved him.[9]

As a child, Kamarakafego began to harness a wide range of skills that would help him survive and thrive in a world grafted on the oppression of people of color. The knitting he and his siblings learned from his mother, for example, helped support him through his college years, with spending money earned selling handmade sweaters.

Kamarakafego embodied all things beautiful and creative in African culture. He grasped early a dynamic and compelling sense of fashion, inherited from both his mother and father. His mother "dressed up" whenever she left the house, and she taught him how to coordinate colors. From his father, he learned the art of accessorizing his clothes with shoes, ties, and cufflinks.[10]

Kamarakafego's father danced Gombeys and played the fife and guitar. This exposure to music helped instill in him a deep love, respect, and appreciation for the musical diversity of the African world. Furthermore, his embracement of dance and sound allowed him to build cultural relationships with black societies across the globe. Kamarakafego's father was a social anchor of the black community. His cultural makeup combined African and West Indian traditions with knowledge of Spanish and Portuguese, and he was outfitted with a strong sense of social justice. Living "up the country," where he settled after he and Henrietta eventually separated, Brown raised a farm with cows, goats, ducks, dogs, horses, chickens, pigs, and rabbits. A generous provider, Brown often gave away his produce; when he slaughtered an animal, he distributed the meat among their community. He charged little for his services and sent barrels of goods back to their family and others in the West Indies.[11]

Brown also practiced traditional medicine. Almost daily, he prepared cornmeal, oatmeal, or cream of wheat porridge with pimento leaves and goat's milk. Kamarakafego and his siblings consumed Johnny cake and bush tea made from herbs such as lemon grass, sweet marjoram, mint, father john, cattle tongue, and fennel. This was perhaps a driving force behind Kamarakafego's very personal engagement with the earth. In many ways, he was becoming a "scientist." Like many children in tropical places like Bermuda, he collected lizards, bugs, toads, berries—cedar, cock, and spiceberries—prickly pears, and bay grapes. He made rudimentary "banger" fireworks and bows and arrows from tree branches and fishing line.[12]

It was from his father that Kamarakafego learned how to wield profanity like a weapon and also how to fight white men and racism. Once, when

Kamarakafego was still a child, a white man demanded that his father not build a home on what was his father's own property. His father chased the man out of his yard, swinging at him with an ax. Kamarakafego laughed at the incident. Another incident occurred while his father was preparing to put down a sick horse. A white man suddenly approached his yard, instructing his father that he would need to pay for eliminating the horse, despite his father's lament that money was scarce and times hard. In front of the man, his father hammered the horse over the head a few times, after which it fell into a hole that he had dug the previous day. After the man threatened to report him to the Society for the Prevention of Cruelty to Animals, his father cursed, hit, and chased the man out of his yard.[13]

Of course, Bermuda's blacks often "wore their insolence on their sleeves." Anthropologist Clews Parsons claimed to have observed "Negro uppishness" among "hack drivers and waiters" who sometimes bullied white tourists. Given white American racial attitudes, it was strange to witness a hotel starter holding up carriages with white passengers. In one case, Parsons overheard a starter chief say to a white lady, "No, you cannot have that carriage, I am going to use it for myself." It was even "more bizarre to see a crowd of whites at the dining room entrance waiting eagerly on the waving hand of the black overlord who assigned places at the crowded tables." For Parsons, this was "reconstruction unresented since unrecognized." She was stunned at the agency of blacks in Bermuda, who seemed to demand respect from white tourists. According to one of her "Negro informants," there was often "more race prejudice in Bermuda than even in the Southern States, only it is not expressed."[14]

Kamarakafego's recollections of his childhood are strewn with personal experiences with segregation, environmental injustices, and racism. Regular train rides between the homes of his parents featured black drivers and the white conductors who collected money. His mother often took him to football matches that were occasionally played between white and black soldiers. His primary-school days were filled with joy, learning, and, perhaps most cherished of all, childhood mischief.[15] At the age of eight, he attended the segregated Central School, which, in 1935, the Garveyite newspaper *Bermuda Recorder* chided for its "dreadful conditions." Central was "built in pond land, below a hill and next door to the parish dump heaps." According to the paper, any of these three factors alone should have sufficed to disqualify the site. To add insult to injury, the "stench and smoke" enveloped the school building by day. Windows had to be kept closed even on the hottest of days to keep the "atmosphere suitable to human comfort." How, the

Recorder asked, could boys and girls be expected "to become thrifty and take pride in their surroundings when we send them to mud holes and municipal dumps?"[16]

Kamarakafego had his own issues with the school. A teacher who decried his strong St. Kittian accent and his troubles with reading often beat him. He felt intimidated, and as a result of continual fights, he was labeled a "rude boy." Put in the slow-learner's class, Kamarakafego marked these school experiences as being significant to his political development. He would sit by himself "and think about how he could best mess with someone if that person messed with [him]." From putting tacks in the chairs and frogs and lizards in the lunch bags of teachers who mistreated him, Kamarakafego waged a quiet war against Central. On one occasion, while his mother held him down, the school's principal, Victor Scott, put soap powder in his mouth for using profanity in school. In retribution for this and other indignities—Scott had also severely caned Kamarakafego—he slashed the principal's bike tires.[17]

Always good at mathematics, Kamarakafego passed a dockyard apprenticeship scheme exam at the end of primary school. This would have allowed him to enter a trade such as electrician or shipbuilding. Yet the board suggested that he was too small and too young to enter the program, which sent students to England for further training.[18]

While he may have been small in stature, Kamarakafego was a juggernaut. Physically fit, he lifted weights with Pond Hill's Nick Swan, played football, ran track, and was a Boy Scout. While on school holidays, he worked construction with his father, where he learned masonry, carpentry, and landscaping, as well as the rudiments of architecture—reading house plans, creating house profiles, and developing engineering concepts and architectural designs. It was on the quarry that he first developed an awareness of the colonial exploitation of the black laborers who arduously cut limestone (a skill he also learned while on the job) for little pay. His conclusion was clear: "People work hard in all colonies and reap very few benefits."[19]

Decades earlier, William Drysdale informed the *New York Times* about his disgust in witnessing blacks "lazing" about a Bermudian stone quarry. "There are fifteen or twenty darkies in the quarry, at a dollar a day for the best of them down to fifty cents or less for the poorest. . . . Half the darkies are standing looking at the stone." The other half stood examining a truck and "holding the poor little horses that are only too glad to stand still." Drysdale heard them speak, "Heah, you dar, git hold ob sid rope; don' be stan' dar restin' yourselves; you heah?" "We's can't hist dat big stone on dat truck, jes' us few. Tink we's hosses, you man?" "Gabble, gabble, gabble like a party of monkeys up a cocoanut trees," complained Drysdale, "every man telling the others what to do and no man lifting a pound."[20] Kamarakafego's own experiences challenged this racist idea.

The lessons that he learned from his family formed the cornerstone principles that informed his commitment to struggle for the African Diaspora. His mother, father, uncle, and cousins collectively taught him that whatever knowledge he had "acquired from society did not belong to [him]" and had to be given "back to [his] family." As he aged, this sense of responsibility was extended "to community to country to Africa and to the world." His "philosophy in life" was that "one should always give back to society wherever we are—be it Bermuda or some other place in the world."[21]

Kamarakafego's road to adulthood was paved with clashes with racism. More times than not, he chose to fight back; in light of his upbringing, it would have been surprising if he had not. In this way, he was certainly "his father's son." Once, while working as a dishwasher in the Belmont Hotel, Kamarakafego was kicked in the backside by a white manager. In reply, he hit the manager across the back of his head with a shovel, as hard as he could. Upon being told what happened, his father responded, "That's good."[22]

Among Kamarakafego's most impactful experiences were his conversations with black laborers who had been incarcerated on Bermuda's Nonsuch Island, which is now a nature reserve. Technically a "junior training school," in reality, it was a harsh and brutal penal outpost. The island had once been used as a quarantine station. Black boys were regularly sent to the island for the smallest of infractions, often for several years. Stories of the prison "made his blood boil." He recalled a boy of eight who had gone to visit his mother, a domestic worker for the Conyers family in the white enclave of Fairylands. After eating a grapefruit that the boy found on the ground, he was attacked by Conyer's dogs, arrested, and sent to the island for eight years. According to Kamarakafego, most of these men returned as mere shells of themselves, having suffered verbal abuse, hunger, and violence while on the island. In the 1990s, Kamarakafego spoke with several returnees who suffered from serious mental and physical trauma as a result of their experiences.[23]

The positionality of Kamarakafego's family within a black internationalist network that extended far beyond Bermuda forged his long-term relationships with renowned activists. Guyana's Ras Mokennen, host of the 1945 Fifth Pan-African Congress, once stayed with them. In 1945, Trinidadian pan-African stalwart C. L. R. James visited Bermuda, where he was denied lodging in Bermuda's segregated hotels. James was a friend of Dr. Edgar Fitzgerald Gordon, known as Bermuda's Father of Trade Unionism. Also hailing from Trinidad, Gordon arranged for the Brownes to host him. Kamarakafego remembered James, who would become Kamarakafego's life-long mentor, as being a "very tall man with a wide-brimmed hat."[24] Such budding relationships helped Kamarakafego develop a worldview based on the shared history of Africa's diasporic peoples in the Caribbean, the Americas, and Asia.

Kamarakafego turned nineteen in 1951. This was a challenging time for him. Elliot Skinner, the principal of his beloved high school, Howard Academy, had died and had just been buried. Kamarakafego, who expressed an affinity toward him and the school, decided not to return to his studies. Instead, he obtained a job as a bellman at the exclusive Mid Ocean Club in Tucker's Town. The stint did not last long. Three weeks into the job, he threw his white steward—who had wrongfully struck him—into the bar's shelves. The steward was cut and bruised, and Kamarakafego was fired. Disgusted with this racist incident and upset over Skinner's death, Kamarakafego felt the need to get away from Bermuda, if only for a short while. He was fully prepared to go to school in the United States that coming fall after having been accepted to attend North Carolina's Kittrell College, a historically black college associated with the African Methodist Episcopal Church. Still, his need to clear his head was more immediate, and he told his father that he wished to go to the West Indies before the start of the semester. Only days before, his father had received a letter from his brother, Philip Dublin, who lived in Cuba. Dublin had lived in Chaparra since 1917. His father asked Kamarakafego if he wanted to go visit his uncle, and soon thereafter, Kamarakafego was on a Reina Del Pacifico passenger ship on his way to Havana. This would be a life-changing experience.[25]

Cuba

Kamarakafego arrived in Havana in March 1951 with one small suitcase and only a smattering of Spanish. His uncle, the only soul in Cuba Kamarakafego knew, had been unaware of his arrival and was not there to greet him. Fortunately for him, a curious young Afro-Cuban named Gus approached and asked him about his destination. To Kamarakafego's reply that he was heading to Chaparra, Gus retorted, "That's a long way from Havana"—seven hundred and six kilometers to be exact. Gus took him to the bus station. Learning that the next bus would not leave until 11:30 p.m., some six hours

FIGURE 1. Pauulu Kamarakafego (*second from left*) in Bermuda with brother, father (John Horatio Browne), and friend. Photo courtesy of Rronniba Kamarakafego.

later, Kamarakafego's new *amigo* offered to take him to his own home to wait. There Kamarakafego met Gus's mother and had his first meal in Cuba. Gus's father was a wealthy white Canadian owner of a sugar plantation. His mother was of mixed racial heritage, and her phenotypically black features were shared by her son. Gus insisted that Kamarakafego return to his house at a later date, offering to teach him how to fly his father's small seaplane. Kamarakafego enthusiastically agreed before leaving.[26]

The bus left Havana at night as expected. Exhausted, Kamarakafego woke to the morning sun and a beautiful Cuban countryside. The land revealed its past and present through seemingly endless stretches of sugar plantations, tobacco fields, pineapple orchards, orange groves, banana patches, and cattle ranches. Along the road, the architecture of small towns and friendly people welcomed him to Cuba's black belt, the Oriente.[27]

In the early twentieth century, Chaparra had been the "grandest sugar mill in the world." Situated in Cuba's Oriente province, Chaparra was distinguished by "large scale US investment, ultramodern machinery, massive landholdings, and an integrated system of production that included ports, railroads, and easy access to food, work animals, and sugarcane." This "super-plantation" was Cuba's first of its kind and one of the world's largest sugar factories. In 1899, the Cuban American Sugar Company constructed the Chaparra mill on sixty-six thousand acres of land in Puerto Padre. Machinery was supplied by New Orleans– and Philadelphia-based firms. In 1914, Chaparra produced over half a million bags of sugar in a single crop, setting a world record for sugar production. The United Fruit Company (UFC) followed on its heels, with its own purchase of 240,000 acres for its neighboring Preston plantation.[28]

To be a sugarcane laborer on the Chaparra, however, was not so grand—as could be attested to by any of the hundreds of thousands of black Caribbean workers who had come to Cuba to do just that. The UFC imported nearly two hundred thousand workers from Haiti and eighty thousand from Jamaica over the next decade to service its sugar operations.[29] Chaparra became a magnet for West Indian laborers. In the late 1800s, several St. Kittians traveled to Cuba on shipping lines that went there directly. In 1912, the non-violent protests of the Afro-Cuban Independent Party of Color were violently crushed by the Cuban government and US forces. British West Indians were among those repressed in the Oriente during other rebellions in 1917.[30] According to historian Lara Putnam, migration in the inter-war Caribbean created a "West Indian-centered black internationalist" world "accentuated by critiques of imperial and colonial power." Packed in the luggage of these individuals and family units came "social networks, formal institutions, and cultural consumption."[31] Kamarakafego was a part of this world.

Kamarakafego arrived in Chaparra at sunset. Before long, passersby directed him to his uncle's residence. Although they had never met Kamarakafego, Dublin and his four children welcomed him into their home with open arms. The very next morning, Kamarakafego met his first love, Rosita, just a few months younger than he, as she helped her mother deliver milk to the Dublin household.[32]

Though Rosita was one of the Oriente's thousands of Afro-Cuban peasants, in the sultry summer evenings when he and Rosita found themselves together, hers was the only deep brown face that Kamarakafego noticed. It might have been the deafening and hypnotic drumming that had drawn him into the festive streets of Chaparra, but it was his cousin Victoria who pulled him into the circle to dance with Rosita. With his limbs already well tuned to the rhythms of Calypso, it was not long before he found his groove within the pulsating, Afro-Cuban rumba. So while Kamarakafego and Rosita did not exchange a single English or Spanish word that evening, they did dance. "And so passed that night."[33]

A long three days followed before he saw her again. This time, she was wearing a long sundress that flowed to her ankles. Her scarf covered her hair, which was almost long enough for her to sit on. She had gone to cut sugar cane, and she could have been gone for weeks in the vast fields surrounding the Chaparra sugar mill. Upon her return, she offered to show him the fields. They walked for what seemed like miles, beyond the sounds of the other British West Indian and Afro-Cuban cane cutters. Rosita not only showed him the process for planting and cultivating cane, but also introduced him to the different species of plants that grew abundantly in the area. Between intimate moments, she cut his name into a piece of sugar cane with her well-sharpened machete. For him, it seemed that this moment would last forever.[34]

But their moment was fleeting, passing as quietly as the cool winds blowing through the plantations. Before arriving in Cuba, Kamarakafego had never heard the word "peasant"; for him, Rosita was "just as much a person" as he was. But in their world tensioned by the lines of race, class, ethnicity, and power, their social and cultural differences inexorably divided them—she was a peasant and he the visiting nephew of a West Indian migrant laborer from St. Kitts. He would soon leave, and she would stay. Furthermore, his letters to her would not be forwarded by his uncle.[35]

About two weeks later, Kamarakafego headed back to Havana to see Gus, with whose family he stayed for the next two and half months. In that time, he learned much about race and class in Cuba. For example, unlike Kamarakafego, Gus did not expect to attend college; this was a luxury reserved for the upper classes, and despite his father's wealth, the fact that his father and mother were unmarried effectively banished him from those echelons of society. If he wanted to attend university, he felt that he would have had to leave Cuba to do so. And he did not want to leave his mother. As promised, Gus gave Kamarakafego daily flying lessons in his father's seaplane.[36]

Kamarakafego returned to Cuba the next summer. In May 1952, he attended a Boy Scout Jamboree in Jamaica for about two weeks. As a scout, Kamarakafego explored far more than tying knots and reading maps; over the years, his travels as a scout introduced him to race across the Global South. For example, during his trip to the 1949 Australian World Jamboree, he first met Indigenous people of Oceania. In 1953, he traveled across England, Switzerland, and Denmark with the Boy Scout association, meeting pen pals and swapping gifts. In September of that year, he left Liverpool for Bermuda on board a Reina Del Pacifico steamship, traveling third-class passage.[37]

The 1952 Jamaica Jamboree hosted 1,100 scouts from seventeen Commonwealth countries. "Those Jamaicans drove us crazy," remarked one scout from the United States. "They'd swap anything from jewelry to underwear, and they hung around our camp until all hours. We finally had to rope off our kitchen to get any work done." Yet their kitchen was not off limits to Jamaican girls, who showed them how to cook Jamaican dishes. On their way home, the American troupe traveled through Cuba, where they found themselves "sandwiched between Batista and his armed guard."[38] Backed by the United States government, dictator Juan Batista had just returned to political power through a coup on March 10, 1952.

Kamarakafego was not among this group, but it would soon be his turn to meet Batista's soldiers. His passage to Cuba was not by plane but by a Pacifico ship. He headed directly to Chaparra, longing to see Rosita. Once there, he was told that she had moved to Havana. He felt that she had done so to seek fortune, break free of her own poverty, and become "more than a peasant." However, for those from the rural areas, particularly young women, "things ended up quite badly" in the city. He feared that the cycle of poverty and prostitution that had overcome so many peasant girls in Cuba would overtake her as well. He scoured the streets of Havana for her, but to no avail. He would never see her again.[39]

He sought out Gus at one of the latter's favorite spots. On the way, he stumbled across "a very large crowd of high-spirited, mostly young demonstrators," protesting at a town square in Old Havana. No one was empty handed—they all carried something with them—women in sundresses with babies in their arms, elderly widows donning black headscarves and shawls, "shabbily dressed plantation workers in broad straw hats," ragged youths with their shoeboxes, and angry youngsters with a list of grievances against Batista and his soldiers. Those who had only voices to wield shouted "Down with Batista!" The crowd carried placards stating, "United Fruit Company get out" and "Batista Dictator government."[40]

As Kamarakafego joined the onlookers, he remembered the issues that he had heard among Chaparra's villagers. They lamented Batista's "blatant punitive atrocities" and his soldiers' disregard for their rights and property, briefly surrendering "their pain in a litany of well-rehearsed complaints" and "slowly shaking their bowed heads in despair." Their sullen voices "soon revived a false, frail façade of contentment, for so great were the dangers of being labeled a troublemaker." Seemingly paranoid from the unpredictable presence of Batista's informants, this was a real concern. They complained about rampant prostitution, venereal diseases, gambling, rape, poverty, racism, illiteracy, educational discrimination of blacks and the poor, elitism of the Catholic Church, money laundering, the dangerous lifestyles of the US Mafia, and theft by US troops and Batista's Guantanamo-trained troops.[41]

While watching the protest, all these ideas came together for Kamarakafego, who recalled, "At an early age, I had learned from my father and my mother's uncle that all people have rights and that I should not just stand by while other people were denied their rights. I had to make the wrong, right. For me, the battle lines were instantly drawn, and I was on the right side. I joined in the demonstration."[42]

The group marched through Old Havana, on its way to the government capital. Suddenly, Batista's soldiers appeared, jumping from army trucks armed with rifles and attacking the demonstrators. Shots rang out, the crowd scattered, and a bullet pierced Kamarakafego's leg. As he hopped away, an elderly Afro-Cuban woman beckoned him up the steps to her one-bedroom apartment, where she nursed his wound. He was lucky, she said, as the bullet had traveled straight through his leg. She patched his wound with some "good old country traditional medicine." The smell was strong, but it worked. A cup of herb tea and fifteen minutes later, soldiers banged on her neighbor's door. She hid him under her bed, and when they came to her apartment to ask if anyone had entered her place, she argued with them until they left. After a meal of black beans, rice, pig's feet, and ginger beer, Kamarakafego slept. It would not be the last time that a black woman would rescue him from imminent danger.[43] He would retell this story often over the course of his life.

Kamarakafego later found Gus, and his flying lessons continued. Eventually, he could fly as far away as Santo Domingo and Miami. By the end of the summer, he had obtained a pilot's license. This qualified him to fly an air-taxi service on small planes like Canadian chipmunks and Cessnas.[44]

It is significant that Kamarakafego's first involvement in an organized protest against discrimination took place in Cuba. His "young demonstrators" were likely students, who were among the first groups to protest Batista's coup. Inspired by José Martí, students from the University of Havana had been protesting since March. This included Cuban women like Angela Elvira Díaz Vallina, a student leader of the Federación de Estudiantes Universitarios, and those of the Martí Women's Civic Front. Fidel Castro, who was practicing law at the time, was planning to run for elections as a member of the Partido Ortodoxo (Eduardo Chibás's Cuban People's Party) in June 1952.[45] He had also formed the clandestine group the Movement, which published the underground newspaper *El Acusador*. By the time Kamarakafego left Cuba in August, the movement had begun a massive recruitment drive to arm and train anti-Batista recruits across Havana.

New York

Kamarakafego loved to exercise. As a young person, he played soccer and cricket, did gymnastics, developed some martial arts skills, lifted weights, ran track, and swam. As such, it came as a great surprise to him when Bermuda's medical examiner, W. H. C. Masters, declared him to be medically unfit to attend college in the United States. This was late July 1951, and he would never make it to Kittrell. Angry and annoyed by this unfair denial, Kamarakafego continued to have racial altercations in Bermuda. In October 1951, his godmother approached his parents about having him visit New York for a few days. Concerned that he would only get into more trouble if he remained in Bermuda, they agreed.[46]

He had been in New York for three days when he began to badger his godmother about going to school. One day while shopping in New York's garment district, she discovered that New York University (NYU) was close by. They paid a visit to the school and were informed by the registrar that classes were closed for the fall semester. "You're late, and you do not have any transcripts, I cannot help you." Persistence being half the battle, Kamarakafego refused to go back to Bermuda. His godmother succeeded in enrolling him in evening classes with the understanding that he would start full time in the spring. He stayed with his godmother's sister in East Orange, New Jersey, and for the rest of the year, he took courses in biology, chemistry, and English. He loved these classes, and he enthusiastically read the glossaries of his science books before the rest of the text, a study technique he successfully utilized throughout his university years.[47]

Kamarakafego joined New York and New Jersey's thriving community of black Bermudians, which had long since been a part of the West Indian cultural fabric of Harlem. The Bermuda Benevolent Association, which had been formed in Harlem in 1898, maintained a long-standing relationship with Harlem's Abyssinian Baptist Church. In 1954, the church's reverend, David Licorice, and its young adults sponsored an "Evening in Bermuda" forum. In September 1955, the church hosted a student delegation from Bermuda's Church of God, which also attended a BBA forum. Hilton H. Tobitt, founder of the Bermuda division of the UNIA, was an honorary member of the association. In August 1954, Tobitt assisted Licorice in conducting funeral services for BBA members. Kamarakafego also spent time at Abyssinian. In 1952, he attended a lecture there by C. L. R. James, who at the time was facing deportation from the United States."[48]

New York expanded Kamarakafego's fast-growing world of black internationalism. In a "special corner" of NYU's cafeteria that was "reserved" for black students, he began to meet others like himself. It was there that Bermuda's Clovis Scott sought him out. Scott studied library science and sociology at NYU from 1953 to 1957. A poet, Scott published articles in the *Bermuda Recorder*. His poem "Islander," which described Bermuda as the "tightest of cages," denounced colonialism, segregation, and racism in the island.[49]

In 1952, Kamarakafego joined NYU's active Student Government Council as a foreign student representative. In the spring of 1951, the council's School of Education wing had attempted unsuccessfully to bring W. E. B. Du Bois to campus to give a talk for Negro History Week.[50] The council held rallies in support of the legalization of prostitution in New York City. They argued that this would lower venereal disease rates as sex workers could be regularly monitored by the city's Health Department. When their demonstrations attracted the police, scuffles broke out. As expected, they were labeled as Communists.[51]

In Harlem, Kamarakafego encountered, embraced, and fell in love with black culture in the United States. He loved to dance, and he spent weekend after weekend dancing to the mambo, meringue, cha-cha-cha, pachanga, and bossanova. This took him to nightspots such as the Savoy Ballroom, the Palladium, and the Apollo Theater. The concerts of Duke Ellington and Count Basie were infectious spaces of black social life that Kamarakafego could not ignore.[52]

In fact, it was almost too much for the nineteen-year-old budding revolutionary. After a five-week dancing binge, a fellow student reminded him to tend to his academic responsibilities—he had not been in the lab or cafeteria in some time. She also invited him to a political meeting, held by the Civil

Rights Congress (CRC). Kamarakafego went and subsequently attended regularly. He realized that he would have to balance his time to include school, socializing, and CRC meetings.[53]

He soon met William Patterson, Communist Party stalwart, veteran lawyer, and CRC executive secretary. In 1951, Patterson filed a genocide petition, *We Charge Genocide: The Crime of Government Against the Negro People*, with the United Nations General Assembly of Paris. *We Charge Genocide* declared that the racism inflicted on African Americans by the US government violated the UN Genocide Convention. Patterson's network included the Council of African Affairs's Du Bois, and Paul and Eslanda Robeson. Paul Robeson, who had been denied a passport to travel with Patterson to the convention in France, felt that "the struggles of the Negro people for full citizenship" in the United States were "linked with the struggles of colonial people for independence." For him, this environment of racism was based on "the fiction of white supremacy," which was "the legislative premise of South African apartheid laws" and "the postulate of White Citizens Councils of Mississippi." It was the cornerstone of colonialism in Africa, and in the US South, it was "employed to deny Negroes the franchise, to deprive Negro children of education, to discriminate, segregate, oppose and persecute in a thousand shameful ways."[54]

Kamarakafego became good friends with Patterson's daughter, Mary Lou Patterson. Moving in these circles, he became acutely aware of the US government's attacks on West Indian activists, who were often charged with being Communists.[55] This included Jamaica's Ferdinand Smith, founder of the Communist-supported National Maritime Union. Smith, who participated in both the National Negro Congress and the Negro Labor Victory Committee, was deported in 1951. Communist Trinidadian Claudia Jones suffered a similar fate. From New York, she wrote extensively about the "triple oppression" of black women, which was "a barometer of the status of all women." Her 1949 "An End to the Neglect of the Problems of the Negro Woman!" argued that the "bourgeoisie" was "fearful of the militancy of the Negro woman." For once black women took action, "the militancy of the whole Negro people, and thus of the anti-imperialist coalition," would be greatly enhanced. This was because the "Negro woman" had historically been the guardian and protector of the "Negro family." Furthermore, "as mother, as Negro, and as worker, the Negro woman [fought] against the wiping out of the Negro family, against the Jim Crow ghetto existence which [destroyed] the health, morale, and very life of millions of her sisters, brothers, and children." As such, it was not accidental that the "American bourgeoisie" had particularly intensified its oppression of "Negro women." In 1948, Jones was found to be in violation of the McCarren Act, which required members of Communist organizations to register with the US attorney general. In 1951, she was convicted of "un-American activities." The thirty-six-year-old was imprisoned in Ellis Island. Suffering numerous health challenges—she had a heart attack in prison—she was deported to England in 1955.[56]

During the summer of 1955, Kamarakafego worked at the Blythedale Children's Hospital in Valhalla, New York. As a recreation officer, his job was to teach joint disease rehabilitation clients how to swim. Here he learned a great deal about "people and suffering because of their disabilities through no fault of their own." He respected them for "showing him respect, love and commitment to life."[57]

Kamarakafego enjoyed his time at NYU. Putting the lie to those who had once declared him medically unfit, he was awarded a swimming and track scholarship. In 1954, he represented the school at the Penn Relays. Given the extent of his academic activities—he studied biology and took post-graduate courses on human physiology, protozoology, and taxonomy—Kamarakafego was surprised to find that he had not taken enough electives to graduate. Refusing to take American history, he signed up for sociology instead in the spring of 1955. He had an eventful semester, traveling to Bermuda and returning to New York via Idlewild airport (now JFK) in February.[58]

Kamarakafego was the only black person in the sociology class of seventy-two students. During the semester, students were required to give presentations on pamphlets about segregation in the United States South. During his presentation, he complained that as southern blacks had written none of the materials, the body of articles did not provide a true picture of segregation. His professor argued that because "learned scholars" had written them, they were as close to the truth as possible. Kamarakafego asked to see versions written by black people. His professor responded, "What version? You know they haven't done much writing." Kamarakafego knew that this was untrue. After all, he had been regularly attending CRC meetings. He was also well aware of segregation in Bermuda. The two began to argue. Kamarakafego peppered him with expletives and was told to leave the class. That he did, but not before passing on choice words to the entire class. He did not return to the course, but he continued to run track and swim. At the end of the semester—May 1955—he received a letter from NYU informing him not to return to the university.[59]

While studying in NYU's library shortly afterward, he met Mattie Pegues, director of Orangeburg's South Carolina State College's (SCSC) Department of Home Economics. At the time, Pegues was completing a master's degree in home economics at NYU.[60] She was also the founder of the New Homemakers Association, a national organization that established home economic programs for black girls. Kamarakafego informed her of his issues, prompting her to suggest that Kamarakafego continue his studies at SCSC, a historically black college that was less expensive than NYU. With his father's support, he did just that.[61]

Kamarakafego's resistance to segregation in the United States was an extension of his dealings with racism in Bermuda and Cuba. In Bermuda, racial segregation was not always formally legislated; in many instances, it was codified within the island's social and economic culture, including the tourist industry. Legislation was implemented loosely enough to allow segregation to exist. However, Kamarakafego would soon understand firsthand how it manifested itself within the context of the United States.

Orangeburg

Kamarakafego left New York for Orangeburg by train. His passage reflected a very transnational black experience of traveling through a world contoured by the cryptic desires of white supremacy. The ride to Washington, DC, was one of relative comfort. The seats were clean, and he sat where he wanted to. However, after changing trains in the nation's capital, he was verbally ushered to the segregated "colored section." From there, the cars that he sat in were unkempt and foul. With no dining service, black travelers carried their own meals. Segregation took no break at the rest stops and their bathrooms and diners. As the train snaked through the cotton fields of the American South, Kamarakafego movingly remembered the days of slavery, with heavy images of African people toiling across acres and acres of plantations. Countless conversations with black passengers ran together like one long soliloquy of suffering. They were bound together—much like the strips of string that wrapped their parcels of food—by common themes of "hard times, money problems, racism, segregation," and the lack of "justice and equality." He reached Columbia, spent one night there, and continued to Orangeburg.[62]

When Kamarakafego arrived in the summer of 1955, Orangeburg's humidity was not the only thing that reminded him of his island home. Segregation in the city reminded him of Bermuda's racial conditions. With an uncanny knack for crossing paths with black radicalism, he had arrived at a critical moment in South Carolina's black freedom struggle. The year 1955 was marked by a climate of white violence and terror stimulated by resistance to the *Brown v. Board of Education* Supreme Court decision that declared racial segregation in public schools to be unconstitutional.

The experience and activism of Joseph DeLaine was emblematic of those times. Based in neighboring Lake City, Methodist reverend Joseph DeLaine worked with Thurgood Marshall and Modjeska Simkins on the 1952 Supreme Court case *Briggs v. Elliot*. Challenging segregation in Clarendon County's school system, *Briggs* became the first of five cases that would form *Brown v. Board*. DeLaine and his family were violently harassed for these efforts. DeLaine's mortgage was foreclosed, and rotten vegetables, beer cans, and whiskey bottles were thrown at his parsonage window. His home in Summerton, his St. James African Methodist Episcopal (AME) church, and his funeral home were all burned down.[63]

One of numerous death threats that he received read, "Several hundred of us have had a meeting and pledged ourselves to put you where you belong . . . I wonder if you ever heard about the Negro postmaster that was sent to Lake City and notified to leave. He refused. However, he left in a coffin. So we have decided to give you ten days to leave . . . rather than let you spread your dirty filthy poison any longer, we have made plans to move you if it takes dynamite to do so. This is final."[64] The letter referred to Frazier Baker, who, along with his infant daughter, Julia, was lynched in Lake City in 1898. A mob of three to four hundred persons surrounded, set fire to, and shot at his home, seriously wounding his wife and three other children.[65]

The *Bermuda Recorder* reported that in September 1955, every window in DeLaine's house was "smashed by bottles and stones" thrown by a passing caravan. He filed a charge with the FBI, which officially agreed with white claims that his church members had burned the church down for insurance purposes. Bureau director J. Edgar Hoover informed DeLaine that his case was outside of the bureau's jurisdiction and that he should rely on local law enforcement.[66]

One night in October 1955, a black police officer telephoned DeLaine, asking him to come to the police station to meet a black man who was allegedly waiting for him. Wisely suspecting foul play, DeLaine refused to go. Later that evening, several bursts of gunfire were fired at their parsonage. His wife, Mattie DeLaine, observed that a car had driven past their home in several intervals. Reverend DeLaine stood guard, shotgun in hand. An hour later, Ku Klux Klan nightriders drove by and fired shots at his house. DeLaine fired back "in the name of Jesus," wounding and hospitalizing two of the four occupants. DeLaine later stated that he had been trying to mark the car. According to activist Septima Clark, the owner of the car later suffered a severe heart attack and had become speechless as a result. Whites now murmured, "You better let that preacher alone. . . . He'll pray you."[67] DeLaine himself might have added, "God is good, all the time."

After awaiting the police for an hour, DeLaine drove to his brother-in-law's house in neighboring Florence. He woke the next morning to find the incident on the news. The report stated that he was "armed and dangerous" and was to be apprehended on sight. To avoid arrest, DeLaine headed to New York.[68] Police questioned Mattie DeLaine at length about the whereabouts of her husband, his firearms, and their children. "All I need is the Lord," she declared, and positively identified the shooter as being white.[69]

South Carolina's Democratic governor George Bell Timmerman Jr. sought to have DeLaine extradited from New York, charging him with "assault and battery with a deadly weapon." In response, Modjeska Simkins proclaimed on a Columbia radio station, "DeLaine was not running from justice but from injustice."[70]

DeLaine received strong support from New York's black community, including the Abyssinian Baptist Church. The city's leading black radio station, WLIB, received over ten thousand post cards, letters, and telegrams denouncing the governor. DeLaine told audiences in the city that shooting at the car was "the crowning moment" of his life and that he was forced to do what a police officer should have done. Bermuda Benevolent Association president Elmore Bean was among those at Harlem Bethel AME who heard him state that he had "shot in the name of Jesus." "The Klan has a new name," he told audiences: the White Citizen Council (WCC). He informed a Brooklyn College audience that these councils had created a "climate of fear through thought control" enforced "by financial sanction." He compared their actions to that of Nazi Germany and racism in South Africa.[71]

Black South Carolina's resistance was grounded within the black community's longstanding understanding of its right to use arms to defend itself from white violence. In 1936, one Mary Anis had informed Charleston's police chief that Marcus Garvey had taught black people to "buy up and lay by all the firearms that they could handle." They hid these weapons in their meeting places and lodge halls. The community called "their meeting palace the UNIA" but had "the NAACP fight for them in court." They raised young people to do "mean things" because they were "too young to go to prison."[72]

According to Simkins, as had been conceded for generations, a man had a right to defend his castle. Blacks in the state were ready to bring "tea for the fever." According to one Clarendon resident, "The WCC say they that they will cause no violence. Hell, I am not going to cause any either. I don't believe in it. But I've got my powder dry and my 'irons' oiled and shiny. I am not looking for any trouble, but I am going to stay ready in order not to have to get ready."[73]

"'NUFF SED!" responded Simkins, who was secretary for the South Carolina chapter of the NAACP (National Association for the Advancement of Colored People). After all, she was one among several NAACP leaders whose homes were attacked and shot at in 1955, a group that included James Hinton, Baptist minister and president of South Carolina's NAACP chapter. The funeral home of DeLaine's nephew, Bill Fleming, had twice been the target of nocturnal gunmen; on September 16, it was struck by three loads of buckshot. The Klan also burned a cross across the street from the home. An Executive Committee member of Clarendon's NAACP, Fleming had armed himself with "several guns." "Fleming Ain't Scared of Nothing!" reported the *Pittsburgh Courier*.[74]

Elloree's Lee Blackman was also one of the fearless. Located some twenty miles from Orangeburg, the city had a population of about 1,127. Seventy years old, Blackman joined the NAACP in 1924 and had been president of the city's chapter since 1950. In December 1955, some sixty Klansman staged a cross burning and rally near the edge of the town's "black section." There were about fifteen cars, most bearing North Carolina and Georgia plates.[75]

Blackman could hear the loudspeaker's blare from home. Friends stopped by to tell him that his name was being called at the rally. As Elloree mayor W. J. Deer would later confirm, the speakers ordered Blackman to leave, urging that the black community force him out. Blackman's friends suggested that he go to the rally, saying, "We'll back you up." The "we" was a "pretty well armed group." They went to the meeting, and from the back of his friend's truck, Blackman declared, "I'm here in Elloree, I've been here for seventeen years, and I have no idea of leaving." Klan leaders urged him to "come out into the light" to state the NAACP's agenda. Blackman held his position under the cover of the dark. A "moment of uneasiness ruffled the Klansman," who "shifted about nervously" and soon disbanded.[76]

Over one hundred black people were also present. They were quite aware of the event, as the Klan had placed leaflets advertising the "display-for-terror" all across Elloree. They recognized a number of local whites who were there, including a magistrate. "We just laughed and booed at what the speakers said," said one black spectator. "The Klansmen acted like they were scared. Lots of us had our pistols in our pockets. Guess those Klansmen figured we were ready."[77]

For months afterward, Elloree's black community did not allow Blackman to sleep alone, and over that time, he spent the night in several "well-fortified" homes. Said one resident to the *Afro-American*, "If the white people so much as talk hard to Mr. Blackman everyone of us is going to . . . give them the worst time that they ever had."[78]

Kamarakafego soon discovered that to be black in South Carolina was to be treated like a non-citizen. It meant inheriting the status of a colonized subject. It was to be disenfranchised behind the social and political barbwire of one of many threads of environmental racism—in South Carolina, this manifested itself as segregation. It was to be lynched by white men who could admit to doing so and find themselves celebrated instead of being criminalized. In Bermuda, it was de facto colonialism. This was not an imagined experience. This was an unfortunate reality of blackness. This is why the interlinked questions of citizenship, racism, and sovereignty were critical to blacks in both locales. And it was *this* familiarity with colonialism and longing for self-determination that Kamarakafego would find across his travels across the black world.

But for Kamarakafego, the local was also the international. He had come to South Carolina charged with political experiences learned in Bermuda, Cuba, and New York. He would carry his memories of South Carolina with him across the black world. These very local experiences of Orangeburg would become part of his political identity as well as his larger global narrative of diaspora. For him, Orangeburg *was* Hamilton, Havana, and Harlem. In due time, it would become Monrovia, Accra, and Melbourne.

2

Twenty-One-Gun Salute

Armed and Dangerous in Orangeburg

Kamarakafego's well-traveled shoes touched the scorching pavement of South Carolina State College (SCSC) in the summer of 1955. His first task was to find Mattie Pegues, who would help him check in to his all-male dorm. When asked by football players if he was interested in playing sports, he declined. Entering as a sophomore, Kamarakafego wanted to get down to the study of biological sciences in pursuit of a major in physical therapy without the distraction and time commitment that college sports would require. Still, he did find time in his studies to take part in SCSC's National Boy Scout Week ceremonies, which was presided over by the college's president, B. C. Turner.[1] Both he and Turner were likely unaware that their relationship would soon become a most tenuous one.

Kamarakafego quickly made friends. Student journalist Rudolph Pyatt found him to be a good guy and fun to be around. As he socialized and studied between the neighboring campuses of SCSC and Claflin University, Kamarakafego was referred to as "Bermuda"; as he walked through the fence that bridged both schools, one could hear "Ber-moo-da!"—his "praise name"—being bellowed. Kamarakafego joined Pyatt on SCSC's student council as a student representative. His main responsibility on the council was to assist transfer students like himself to adjust to school. However, he would soon find out that the council's most critical task was to join in the perilous fight against white violence.[2]

South Carolina's white-run state and local legislatures were staunchly committed to maintaining segregation. This was certainly the case in Elloree, where, in the summer of 1955, thirty-seven black parents petitioned the city's school board to immediately take concrete steps to eliminate segregation in public schools. Fifty-seven black parents of Orangeburg County followed suit. Drawn up and circulated by the local NAACP, the petition

FIGURE 2. Kamarakafego, South Carolina State College, 1955. Photo courtesy of Rronniba Kamarakafego.

FIGURE 3. Kamarakafego (*first row, fourth from left*) and sophomore class, South Carolina State College, 1956.

represented a cross section of the black community, including sharecroppers, lawyers, farmers, teachers, business owners, domestic workers, and students like Kamarakafego.[3]

In response, at a rally that drew a crowd of three thousand, whites across Orangeburg County formed a local chapter of the WCC, a network of white supremacist organizations that grew like weeds across the South in the wake of *Brown v. Board*. Participants included blueblood attorneys, bankers, religious leaders, publishers, and representatives from Mississippi's WCC headquarters. The WCC, which was seen by many black citizens as little more than "the Klan without robes," claimed that race relations in Orangeburg had excelled for decades and that "outside Communist agitators" were responsible for the black community's dissatisfaction with segregation. The group was determined to resist this "clear and present danger" that threatened the "principles of constitutional government, racial integrity, and state sovereignty." The WCC pledged "to make every legal and moral effort to save" segregated public schools.[4]

The WCC devised a cruel campaign of economic coercion against the petitioners. Its leadership included the city's mayor, sheriff, clerk of courts, and solicitor, as well as several state legislators. Also among its ranks were members of SCSC's all-white board of trustees, such as the president of S.C. National Bank, Wallace C. Bethea, and Elloree's former mayor. These men used their social privilege to terrorize the black community. Orangeburg mayor and WCC member Robert Jennings, who owned the Coca-Cola franchise, the Paradise Ice and Fuel Company (producers of Paradise Ice Cream), and the Palmetto Baking Company (makers of Sunbeam Bread), refused service to businesses owned by petition signers, including the gas station of Orangeburg NAACP treasurer James Sulton. Jennings told one NAACP official, "Go and crack your whip and then take it up with our company's attorney."[5]

According to the NAACP's Modjeska Simkins, the WCC used "every device and subterfuge . . . to starve and persecute Negroes . . . into economic and educational enslavement." It possessed "no qualms of conscience in firing parents of helpless children" and denied them bread, milk, and medicines. According to the outspoken journalist, the inhumane WCC prepared to "employ any heathenish scheme . . . to widen its . . . sadistic prowl." Simkins compared its actions to Hitler's Nazi Party; its "Gestapo strategy" included offering ten thousand dollars for the purchase of the NAACP membership list—which the NAACP burned in response, disconcerting at least one "Black Judas."[6]

Simkins suggested that the WCC merchants had become "business suicidal maniacs" in their frantic zeal to "squeeze" Negroes and to discredit and destroy the NAACP. Coble and West End Dairies refused ice cream and milk deliveries to the petitioners. Raleigh's Taylor Biscuit (distributors of Lay's products), Augusta's Claussen Bakery, distributors for Pepsi Cola, Dr. Pepper, and Royal Crown Cola, and Crum Brothers, which owned a General Motors franchise and sold Frigidaire appliances and Pontiac and Buick cars, all participated in the WCC "squeeze."[7]

Roy Wilkins, NAACP's director, felt that Orangeburg's black citizens were "being forced to choose between their employment, food and shelter, and their rights as American citizens." Whites were discharging petition signers from their jobs, evicting them from rental housing, refusing deliveries from black retailers, and calling in farm, home, and business mortgages and loans. Indeed, the squeeze was more than a question of biscuits and bread; it was an assault on black humanity and the idea of citizenship. As educator and civil rights activist Septima Clark would assert, "I am a Negro. Born black in a white man's land. . . . I am a teacher. I have spent nearly all my adult life teaching citizenship to children who really aren't citizens."[8]

The squeeze was backed by white violence, whether from the WCC or the reinvigorated KKK. Elloree's mayor promised to fight the NAACP "from ditches to fence posts to keep Negroes out of white schools." A Clarendon County NAACP leader was told by the Klan that he would be "kidnapped and horse-whipped," and an armed guard maintained "vigil over his home." In reference to the WCC, he declared, "The Klan has been born again. They have adopted a new name."[9]

In October 1955, Elloree's Blackman and a group of four others investigated the burning of DeLaine's church. The group, disguised in "poor farming attire," included Albert Redd, executive director of South Carolina's NAACP chapter, and *Jet* magazine journalist Simeon Booker. Visibly moved, Booker suggested placing an advertisement in *Jet* to ask for aid those being squeezed by the WCC.[10]

An October 1955 *Jet's* exposé, "South Carolina's Plot to Starve Negroes," reported that a new danger threatened thousands of African Americans in South Carolina's cotton and tobacco lowlands. The "vicious hate boycott" aimed to starve some three thousand blacks, who could not get as much as a shoelace. The WCC had forced the withdrawal of credit in downtown stores for an estimated two thousand possible NAACP members. In Clarendon County, notes due were issued on their tractors, mules, fertilizers, seeds, and farms. The county's 2,800 black farmers needed about $250,000 to buy fertilizer and seeds for planting for the next year. Some were denied facilities to gin their cotton or sell peas and corn. They could not get loans to buy milk or clothing, pay medical expenses, or get supplies for the upcoming planting season. One Helen Thompson was fired from her $55-per-week laundry job, leaving her unable to care for her sick husband.[11]

The NAACP documented over forty families in need in Summerton. Fired from her job, Annie Gibson sought clothing for her two children; she was told that she had to remove her name from the NAACP petition or leave her rented property by the end of the year. Rose Lee MacGainey had been refused credit since she signed the petition; with four children, she sought food. Masie Solomon had been fired from her job, and the WCC gave her sixty days to move or to remove her name from the petition; she needed bedding and clothing. James Tindel had one mule, two boys, and no money, and his landlord had taken all of his cotton and was threatening to remove his corn; his employer refused to help him as he had signed he petition. The backbone of the Summerton community was seventy-year-old land renter Gilbert Henry; ill, Henry was forced to pay his medical bills well before they were due. The pressure caused some fourteen petitioners to withdraw their names, with some claiming that they were not aware of what they had signed.[12]

Simkins and Blackman established a supply drive to support such families. From her years of NAACP activism, Simkins perhaps knew more black South Carolinians than any other woman who was not a professional politician. Within a week, money, clothing, and canned foods by the ton were sent to her residence. She drove truckloads of donated goods to Blackman's home in Elloree. He distributed clothing, canned food, and over a hundred pairs of shoes to some 250 black families. This prompted Adam Clayton Powell to invite Simkins to give a talk at Harlem's Abyssinian Baptist Church, which sent relief materials. New York's Sojourners for Truth and Justice organized a canned food drive. Reverend Leon Sullivan, the "Lion of Zion," of Philadelphia's Zion Baptist Church raised support. Baptist churches in Philadelphia donated $1,800 and six thousand pounds of food.[13]

Financial assistance was funneled through deposits placed in the Victory Savings Bank of Washington, DC, which was owned by Simkins's brother-in-law, Henry Montieth. South Carolina's Palmetto Education Association made substantial deposits. The national office of the NAACP deposited $20,000 through Victory bank. A farmer from Quito, Ecuador, sent a financial donation. In May 1956, Bermuda's Hilton Hill, of Hilton Travel, held a raffle for a free trip to Haiti, with proceeds going to the NAACP. Supporting the NAACP's "Fighting Fund for Freedom," the 50¢ raffle tickets raised about $5,000. According to Orangeburg NAACP leader Reverend McCollum, about $40,000 had been made available for loans to blacks affected by the squeeze. The National Council of Churches and the Congressional Christian Church both donated $5,000, which helped avoid foreclosure on the mortgages of three farms.[14]

While not officially placed by the NAACP, the *Jet* ad asked for help from members of the association. This angered the NAACP's Wilkins, who called Simkins to express his displeasure, interrupting her Sunday dinner with her mother. "The NAACP is not a relief organization," he chastised, "and we just [will] not have it. And any money that you have, you send it back, every penny of it, to whoever sent it." Simkins raised hell:

Now Roy, I am not going to send back a damned cent to anybody ... These people are under pressure. You all asked us to get these petitions signed ... We have an obligation to these people. Now, you all sit up there and drink all the Bloody Marys and eat all your big sirloin steaks and drink your Scotch and milk, but we are down here under the pressure. And we've got the load on us, and we're going to handle it.[15]

Yet South Carolina NAACP leaders responded by saying they were not facing wholesale starvation—clothing and foodstuffs were secondary to the need for money contributions. The community was asking for loans to sponsor farm families.[16]

With Christmas came further insults for blacks in Elloree. In past years, black youths followed the Santa parade and, along with white children, received sacks of fruit, candies, and nuts. This year, Santa brought smiles and waves but nothing for the black youth; there was "no Santa Claus for a n@gger."[17] Meanwhile, a white police officer told the black kids that "Big Red" had not come for Negroes, and he ran them "from the streets when Santa" passed through. According to Blackman, "It was the most touching and pitiful sight I've ever seen. They gave every little white child his present, but passed over all our children." Yet through donations, Redd was able to distribute three bushels of oranges, apples, and tangerines, four boxes of candy, and toys for three hundred and fifty black children on Christmas Eve.[18]

Buckras, Tallows, and Student Boycotts

Black South Carolinians refused to see themselves simply as victims. Simkins felt that their "fortitude and persistence was almost above description." They were undergoing, with astounding humility and forbearance, "the chance to fight and to suffer for our children and our rights." Summerton's Hessie McBride was self-employed with four children. Her family needed clothing and $20 for winter seed. Yet she stated that she would die before she took her name off the petition. Sixty-four-year-old Ladson Stukes refused to take his name off the list until "Thurgood Marshall came down and told him to do so."[19]

The collective response to the WCC "buckras" was swift and remarkable. The community organized cooperatives to purchase foods, fertilizers, groceries, and farm machinery for rural and urban families. Some items were purchased through mail-order catalogs. The purchase of luxuries was limited. The NAACP organized a "restricted buying campaign" against businesses owned and supported by the WCC. "Anywhere the councils get ready to put on the squeeze," said Simkins, "we stand ready to put on a boycott." This needed to be done until the "fight for full citizenship" was "properly regarded by those who would starve us into enslavement." Blacks were encouraged to buy as little as possible in and as far away as possible from Orangeburg. They carpooled to cities like Augusta, Charleston, and Columbia to shop, and they bought food from towns fifty to seventy miles away. The campaign served pace on the shelves of Coble Dairy, Coca-Cola, Sunbeam, Kirkland's Laundry, Lane Electric Company, Horne Motors-Ford Dealers, Edisto Theatre, Becker's Women's Apparel, Paradise Ice Cream, and Esso products. One petitioner promised to drink "molasses water" before he took "another drop of Coca Cola." One woman used to drink a least bottle of Coke a day, and did not think that she could "do without its refreshing build-up." But Mayor Jennings's comments got to her: "It was hard on me the first day. But I am definitely off of Coca Cola."[20]

Simkins mimeographed a list of twenty-three businesses or products to be boycotted. These were cut into strips, distributed across major black venues, and placed under windshields at the big football games in Orangeburg. These would have included SCSC's home matches, played in its new $170,000 stadium, against Allen, Claflin, Ft. Valley, and Morris Brown. Such games were hubs of black southern culture—local newspapers even covered SCSC's football *practices*. South Carolina's Colored Fair was another such site. Held in Columbia in October 1955, the fair was organized by the New Farmers and Pegues's New Homemakers Associations. Attended by over ten thousand spectators overall, its football game between Benedict and Claflin drew thousands.[21]

In the summer of 1955, NAACP treasurer James Sulton calculated that several firms owned by WCC leaders were dependent on the patronage of Claflin and SCSC students. It was expected that the arrival of new college students, like Kamarakafego, could further drive their push. In September 1955, he approached Fred Moore, president of SCSC's student council, to garner student support for the boycott.[22]

This was a brilliant move, as the council enthusiastically joined the boycott. This included Kamarakafego, who strongly supported the broader black community's belief's that the NAACP would assist them in stating their grievances, fighting for fair employment practices, and gaining justice. Kamarakafego, along with most students on campus, became actively involved in the strike.[23]

However, SCSC's administration did not support its students. In fact, when Moore approached President Benner C. Turner about supporting the boycott, he was swiftly reprimanded. Turner warned Moore not to get involved in civic matters, claiming that the university was "separate and

distinct" from the community. Septima Clark closely followed and commented on the student body's actions at SCSC. She was certain that Turner
had "no spine in [his] backbone," as he had told Moore that if he called a
meeting on campus, he would be expelled.[24]

Turner's response did not surprise Clark. As SCSC had been developed
with the explicit purpose of maintaining segregation in higher education,
the all-white board of trustees made it clear that they did not want a college
president sympathetic to desegregation. In a 1950 meeting in the office of
Governor Strom Thurmond, the board selected the conservative Turner as
SCSC's president. In an earlier incarnation as the South Carolina Agricultural and Mechanical Institute (before becoming the Colored Normal Industrial Agricultural and Mechanical College of South Carolina), SCSC was
housed within Claflin until 1895. As such, by the 1950s, Claflin was structurally and politically distinct from SCSC. Founded in 1869, it was South
Carolina's oldest historically black college. It was a private Methodist school,
and its administration advocated desegregation.[25]

As such, Claflin students could organize in ways that those at SCSC could
not. The school's administration had supported the founding of Claflin's
NAACP chapter as being "a good and noble cause." Its chapter spoke before civic organizations, churches, and parent-teacher groups, including in
Elloree. Newspaper boys delivered their mimeographed materials discussing voting and civic rights. The actions of these students pressed the local
NAACP chapter beyond negligence and into further activism, particularly
in the aftermath of *Brown v. Board*. As such, when Orangeburg's NAACP
chapter pushed the school board to integrate, this only added "fat" to an
already "stirring fire" of community organizing.[26]

In the spring of 1955, Claflin's NAACP president Willis Goodwin and
faculty advisor Ezra J. Moore represented Claflin at the NAACP's National
Youth Legislative Conference in Washington, DC. Since "scheduling issues"
prevented the conference from being held at Howard University, American
University hosted eight hundred attendees on the theme of "Youth and the
Challenge of Integration."[27]

In the absence of an NAACP chapter, SCSC's student council drove support for the boycott. Kamarakafego recalls how Coca-Cola was sold in the
campus canteen. Sunbeam bakery made all the bread used in the dining
hall and cafeteria. The council decided that they should push the school to
boycott these firms. It took about three weeks to educate the student body
about doing so. Soon, drinking Coca-Cola and eating Sunbeam bread were
things of the past on both campuses.[28]

FIGURE 4. Kamarakafego (*fourth from left*) and student representatives, SCSC, 1956.

The students largely refused to consume any products or patronize businesses that were on the NAACP's list; this included a women's apparel store, a television firm, a motor company, a theater, an auto parts stores, a grocery, a laundromat, a butcher, and several hardware stores and bakeries. Kamarakafego and the council organized hunger strikes in the school dining halls, mass meetings, and freedom marches. According to Simkins, "the young people [were] doing a wonderful job. They [were] not attending theatres nor patronizing any white stores."[29]

Black women were central to the boycott's success. The *Afro-American* reported how black house wives fueled the campaign through telephone calls, club meetings, and social gatherings. In September 1955, black women teachers, students, and staff at SCSC, Claflin, and Orangeburg public schools were "fighting mad" about a WCC-supported women's apparel store. The credit of one Alba Lewis had been discontinued since she and her husband had signed the petition. Their white physician also threatened to withhold their son's medication that he needed for a rare blood condition; a "staggering medical bill" demanding immediate payment followed. The group canceled their accounts at the store. This business did not survive the boycott.[30]

There was no need for a student boycott at Claflin. In October 1955, Claflin dean L. L. Hayes told students that he would obtain for them "any and all items of clothing" from outside of Orangeburg. They were "free to leave classes at any time" to organize. For Hayes, this protest was as important to the educational process as was "textbook material." One professor affirmed that "as a matter of Christian practice," the school would not conduct further business with the WCC firms. "Claflin does not patronize these people," said one SCSC student. "Why should S.C. State?"[31]

High school students also joined in the struggle. This included those at the Wilkinson, a Catholic school located in the vicinity of the colleges. Wilkinson had been purchasing about $450 worth of milk for its lunch program. In September, the priest in charge refused a delivery and closed the account.[32]

At the South Carolina NAACP's annual meeting at Allen University in Columbia, delegates mapped out such strategies as teacher and financial security to handle the squeeze. Kamarakafego, who had returned in time for the meeting from a 1955 trip to Bermuda, was stirred by Thurgood Marshall's keynote address there. Marshall expressed outrage at the threats, intimidations, and murders aimed at blacks, but he saw no reason "to let anti-integration southern forces determine the future." In an iconic moment captured by the camera of Cecil Williams, the civil rights lawyer also spoke at an NAACP meeting at Claflin's Seabrook Auditorium. According to the student paper the *Claflin Panther*, Marshall discussed "Negro rights" before an audience of 1,500.[33]

By mid-October, the *Afro-American* reported that the squeeze was "flunking." One owner of a motel was told that his meat, soft drink, and foodstuff deliveries would not supply him with products if he did not keep a certain waitress employed. Another white merchant believed that a 90 percent effective boycott would close 80 percent of white businesses. To the idea that some white business owners did not truly support the WCC, one black man's response was, "So be it. The tallow has to go with the hide."[34]

The black community's countermeasures of withdrawing their spending power from white businesses extended into 1956. This powerful cross section of black activism was altogether too much for the WCC, which had attacked the black community through the media, firearms, burning crosses, insults, firings, and economic intimidation. Its attacks would continue through the mechanisms of the state and would directly target SCSC's students.[35]

In the spring of 1956, South Carolina's legislature, under the auspices of Governor George Timmerman and legislator Jerry Hughes, passed fourteen pro-segregation measures. In March 1956, its resolution—H-2100—called for the US Attorney General to classify the NAACP as a subversive,

Communist-affiliated organization. The resolution called for the NAACP to be kept under surveillance so that all citizens of the United States could have "ample warning" of the danger that it posed to their "way of life."[36] A concurrent resolution was passed in support of the WCCs. It claimed that the purpose of the WCCs was: to maintain proper relations between all races; to oppose the use of force by radicals and reactionaries who attempted to disrupt the peace; to make every legal and moral effort to maintain segregated public schools; to develop ways and means to provide adequate education for children of all races; to acquaint public officials about the impossibility of integration in South Carolina; and to demonstrate that the majority of whites and blacks preferred segregation. The General Assembly commended the councils and encouraged other persons to form more.[37]

A subsequent bill, H-1998, declared it unlawful for the state and any school district, county, or municipality to employ NAACP members. This prompted boards of education across the state to include questions such as, "Are you a member of the NAACP?" and "Do you believe in integration?" on teaching applications and affidavits. In Elloree, thirty teachers were given the choice of filling out the affidavit or signing a prepared form of resignation. Eighteen teachers and a principal were dismissed after signing the form. Parents in Elloree charged the board of education with damaging academic freedom.[38] Another bill, H-1900, called for the investigation of NAACP activity among SCSC students, faculty, and administrators. It stated that the NAACP's major objective was to foment bitter feelings of unrest and unhappiness among African Americans. The investigation was conducted to decide if the NAACP was "misleading the Negro citizens" and to determine if its activities were detrimental to the welfare of the college, its students, and South Carolina.[39]

New York's *Amsterdam News* urged "every Negro and fair-minded American" to stand with the NAACP against these unconstitutional moves. W. E. Solomon, executive secretary of the Palmetto Education Association (PEA, an alternative professional organization to the white-only South Carolina Education Association), challenged claims by the South Carolina legislature that most of the 7,500 teachers in black schools were NAACP members. The PEA had been formed in 1900—almost a decade before the NAACP—as the South Carolina Education Association barred blacks from joining. Solomon felt the state's notion that there was an NAACP branch at SCSC was laughable; in reality, the college was often chided as being apolitical for *not* having one. Individual students joined though Claflin or directly through the NAACP's national office.[40]

Meanwhile, the state did not halt the Klan's threats against the black community. In March, the Klan had held two major rallies that were attended by crowds of 1,500–2,000. On March 3, two thousand attended a Lake City rally. In May, a thousand rallied in Williamsburg County. Florence drew eight hundred in May, including Imperial Wizard E. Edward of Atlanta and Grand Kleagle J. Bickley of Marion. Cross burnings on historically black colleges and universities (HBCUs) occurred regularly. This occurred at SCSC in August 1956. On a Saturday night, several white college students in three cars were speeding through the campus and "hurling racial epithets at summer school students." A campus patrol officer arrested and ticketed two of the drivers for speeding. They returned that evening and burned a cross on the school's campus. A black campus patrolman, B. E. Evans, spotted the perpetrators. As they sped off, he chased them for twenty minutes "through a maze of suburban streets." Evans was credited with the first arrest of cross burners in decades. Police officials claimed that the burning could have been in "sympathy" for the ticketing, and denounced suggestions of any "Klan theory."[41]

On a rainy evening in early February 1955, the Klan held a rally in Orangeburg. El Paso's *Herald Post* reported that some fifty-five robed Klansmen and women held their meeting in a field "bordering a Negro residential area." The *Afro-American* detailed how the Klan motorcade paraded through the campus of SCSC's campus. The group proceeded to the city's limits, about six minutes away. After the black community was tipped off about the rally, a group decided to attend. They drove about a dozen cars to join the twenty-car procession, which was led by a vehicle marked with a lighted cross. The *Afro-American* sarcastically lambasted the "integrated cross-burning." The dozen robed and unmasked figures huddled near the "smoking cross," as Atlanta's imperial wizard urged the blacks in attendance to withdraw from and attack the "communist fronted" NAACP. According to one black witness, he "begged" them to accept segregation." "Oh no! We were not scared," said another. "If the weather was not so bad, we'd had more people out. We knew they would not start any stuff around here." Alabama's *Anniston Star* reported that the Saturday night Klan rally drew so much "Negro interest" that most of the crowd was black.[42]

In *Me One*, Kamarakafego states that he and other male students decided to challenge the Klan's repeated "unchecked visits" to campus. He recalls being seriously injured and hospitalized as he attacked one such group on his own. He was knocked out, a rope was put around his neck, and he was dragged. Fortunately, some students rescued him, overturning the car in process. However, his neck was permanently injured from the affair. Although a mining of archival sources have not been able to confirm this incident, Kamarakafego would retell this story several times over the course of his life. At a 1969 meeting in Australia with members of the Aborigines Advancement League, he showed his Black Power allies the scars from the rope burns on his neck and the bullet wound in his leg that he sustained in Cuba. Australia's Security Intelligence Organization claimed that he told his audience that the students killed the Klansmen who had harmed him. Vanuatu's Rose Cuong recalled how in the 1980s, Kamarakafego sometimes wore a neck brace while sleeping due to pain related to the injury.[43]

Memories do not live like people do. Kamarakafego also describes how he suggested that students arm themselves in preparation for Klan attacks on campus with rifles secured from SCSC's reserve officer training corps (ROTC) armory. As it was mandatory for all male freshman and sophomores to join the ROTC, Kamarakafego's collective would have had little trouble gaining access to the firearms, which they were able to retrieve—to the chagrin of the ROTC director. He asserts that they fired warning shots over the heads of a group of Klansmen that passed through the SCSC campus. The cross burners returned later as the National Guard, fully geared with trucks and military jeeps with mounted submachine guns. Soldiers searched their dorms for firearms and maintained a military presence on the campus for two weeks.[44] It is likely that Kamarakafego was referring to the aforementioned Klan rally in February 1955, which occurred during the state's heightened attacks against student activism at SCSC. His depiction of the National Guard is a reference to the presence of state troopers and South Carolina's State Law Enforcement Division (SLED), which the governor sent to campus in March 1956 to suppress further student demonstrations.

In March, SCSC students increased their demands that the school's administration "cease and desist" from patronizing products provided by WCC firms. On Friday, March 23, an anonymous resolution denouncing segregation was distributed among SCSC faculty, staff, and students. The document also expressed support for the NAACP and decried the state's investigation of SCSC. One hundred and seventy-six of its 190 members unanimously denounced the attack on their academic freedoms. They argued that if SCSC was inimical to the interests of South Carolina, the school should be disbanded and its entire student body admitted to PWIs—predominantly white institutions—across the state. The resolution was eventually supported, signed, and adopted by 99 percent of faculty and staff.[45]

According to a related report by Turner to the board of trustees, on this same day, writings on the sidewalks of the school opposing the college's use of Sunbeam bread, Coble Dairy milk, Coca-Cola, and Curtis candy. The following Sunday, Kamarakafego and about five hundred others rejected their noon meal at the college dining hall. They poured water on the bread (Sunbeam), refused to drink the milk (Coble Dairy), and "mixed their plates" so that the food could not be used again. However, that afternoon and evening, food was delivered to the students at their dormitories by sources and persons unknown to Turner. During the vesper services that evening, Turner addressed the students and faculty. He implored them to respect law and order and stated that the college would not enter into "economic warfare or boycott" and would honor its contracts. He called for the students to select seven representatives to meet with him about their grievances. During his address, students repeatedly scraped their feet on the floor in unison, "punctuating . . . his remarks," a gesture they called "sanding the floor" and "Uncle Toming."[46]

On Monday, approximately 150 students marched on Turner's campus residence at 7:30 a.m. Kamarakafego was one of the more vocal leaders of the protest. This involved a complaint against a matron who had struck a female student who was delivered dinner the night before. The students were grappling with whether they should remain non-violent, given the violence used against her. According to Kamarakafego, they also wanted to know how the administration planned to respond to the state's pending probe. Turner agreed to meet with a smaller committee, and he held a hearing in his office about the striking incident. Six students testified that they witnessed the matron hit the student, and she was shortly dismissed.[47]

The students also produced an underground newspaper, the *Free Press*. Initially a one-page mimeograph, the paper listed products that were not to be consumed and businesses not to be patronized, and it encouraged students to join the NAACP. It read, "Eat no Bress products from the Dining Hall, Student Center, Cafeteria and Webber's Soda Shop. Change no Linen Tonight!! Drink no Cokes!! Check the Master Lists . . . Join the NAACP now! They are walking and dying for us elsewhere . . . Let's do something for ourselves . . . Don't let Emmett Till die in vain." They also distributed a "Bird Breast list" that contained the names of "stool pigeons."[48]

Meanwhile, Turner discussed the resolution with SCSC's board of trustees, which instructed him to continue the school's contracts with Sunbeam, Paradise Ice Cream, and Kirkland's laundry services. He maintained that the students were being "exploited by outside forces." The following day, a committee of seven students met with Turner. Over a three-hour-long meeting, he reiterated his comments at the vesper services while also expressing his authority over what could be printed in the student newsletter.[49]

With Good Friday and Easter break approaching, the students intensified their efforts. On Thursday, March 29, they hung Turner and Hughes in effigy before the dining hall. The next day, the campus awoke to "a blanket of slogans" scribbled along the sidewalks, written in chalk and black crayon. These strokes of creative genius included statements such as "Paradise Lost," "Here lies Coke and Jennings," "Be a Man or get the hell back to Georgia," and, according to the *Baltimore Afro-American*, words that the paper deemed unprintable drawn in front of Turner's campus residence. One statement denounced two faculty members—"TMJ is a handkerchief-headed chief" and "Turner is a tyrant." Extensive efforts by the college police, administrators, and others to discover the perpetrators of these acts were unsuccessful. The next day, Turner gave notice to the students that these acts were considered "lawless and intimidating."[50]

By the following Tuesday, some students were receiving food from other sources, including their families. When they left school on Wednesday for spring recess, they agreed to return with enough linen to avoid having to use the WCC-affiliated laundry.[51]

Reporting for the *New York Post*, Murray Kempton traveled to campus. He claimed that one "backward student who ordered a ham sandwich was told that he could have the ham but not the sandwich." The students were using home-cooked biscuits, cornbread, and crackers instead of Sunbeam. For Kempton, it had been difficult to measure the success of Orangeburg's boycott of WCC's squeeze, but it was now clear that they were joined by SCSC's 1,400 and Claflin's 500 students, with "devastating effect."[52]

Students across the campuses of Claflin, Allen, Benedict, and Morris supported the SCSC demonstrations. During the effigy hanging, Claflin students cheered from across the fence. On Good Friday, some dozen Claflin students established a picket line in Orangeburg's business section, carrying signs suggesting that observers join the NAACP and the selective buying campaign. They protested the treatment of the SCSC students and reiterated their calls to have the school sever ties with WCC establishments. Claflin had suspended financial relations with these businesses in the fall of 1955.[53]

During a Claflin student field trip in downtown Orangeburg, five women and one male student were arrested and held until trial after a scuffle occurred with a white man. According to the *Afro-American*, a white insurance agent intentionally walked between the women, "maliciously elbowed one of the girls in the breast and knocked her into the street." While doing so, he "uttered some profanity about niggers." A Claflin male struck the white man with his umbrella. They were chased by other white men and subsequently charged with "assault and battery of a high and aggravated nature." Claflin launched its own counter charges.[54]

During spring break, Governor Timmerman publicly claimed that SLED had received information about subversive elements at SCSC. He was aware that the students had "rioted and burned in effigy representatives." As such, he was sending in the division and local police officers to monitor the situation and arrest law violators.[55]

By the time of their return to campus on April 9, the students received word that county, city, and SLED officers were patrolling the campus. In response, nearly the entire student body of SCSC refused to go to class during a weeklong strike. This included the entire student body of 1,172 undergraduates, reflecting the exceptional organizational abilities of the council. Some students informed the *Pittsburgh Courier* that they were afraid to leave the dormitories because of the governor's orders to arrest all violators. "This is not a mental . . . nor a penal institution," student president Moore informed the press. SCSC was "an institution of higher learning, attended by free people in a free land." The students voted against returning to class as long as the SLED police force was on campus. By midweek the campus looked deserted.[56]

Local white papers chastised the protests. The *State* claimed the students had exchanged textbooks for comic magazines and were enjoying card games rather than attending classes. In contrast, African American papers unabashedly defended them. The student paper *Free Press* continued to circulate. "Don't weaken!" it encouraged the students. "In unity there is strength. The cops are still outside. We noble citizens will stay inside." The *Voice*, another underground mimeograph, reminded students that the Student Center was off limits. It claimed that Governor Timmerman was sending Wings over Jordan (South Carolina highway patrolmen) to campus. But "the road to freedom" awaited the march of the students, who had victory in their grasp. The "blood of their forefathers" pleaded for them to "join the NAACP NOW!" "Turner is not with us," the *Voice* proclaimed. "He is the most erratic problem we've faced in this entire matter." He had screamed at the students, reminding them that they were going to get "all of us in a lot of trouble."[57]

The students resented the police presence. The *Baltimore Afro-American*'s John McCray wrote that "unidentified white men had driven through the campus several times on Sunday and Monday." It was alleged that the police

had taken "strategic positions" around and off campus. One police lieutenant admitted as much, informing the *Afro-American* that there would
be "no further forays" through the campus by local police. The *Pittsburgh
Courier* described how several cars of whites patrolled SCSC. A *Times and
Democrat* reporter recognized a SLED agent driving through the campus
on Easter Sunday. The *Times* stated that the sheriff's department frequently
sent several cars through the campus and that all police agencies were to
"arrest immediately any law violators."[58]

Turner claimed that SCSC's board had requested the police presence.
In uptown Orangeburg, whites believed that the SCSC students were now
"heavily armed and might break out . . . in a 'shoot em up' demonstration."[59]
Could this have been a reference to Kamarakafego's account of shooting at
the Klan?

Turner refused to negotiate until the students returned to classes. They
did so on Friday, April 13, but Moore called a student-only meeting in the
chapel that morning. Faculty members as well as a "curious campus policeman" were not allowed to participate. Of the 716 students at this meeting,
614 gave Turner a vote of no confidence, and only two voters expressed
confidence in the president. Turner had subjected them to abuses such as
"threats, widespread investigations, and other kinds of indignities and in-
quisitorial procedures." They had now reached the point where they felt that
their "minds and spirit" were "being suppressed beyond containment."[60]

The students compiled a list of twelve grievances, which centered on two
main concerns—the criminalization of the student body and Turner's leadership. One demanded that the administration desist in using police forces
against them. Another called for Turner to refrain from "handling disciplinary problems . . . in a courtroom of inquisition," where students were
"treated as criminals" and "given sentences or punishments." This included
his handling of the school paper. The president was asked to declare his position on the faculty/staff resolution, and to explain why the college continued
to purchase products from the WCC's firms. They also wanted "unequivocal
assurance that no reprisals" would be used against the protestors.[61]

They refused to leave the chapel until Turner agreed to give them an
audience. Turner did not meet with them, but instead sent out a notice
that advised students to resume attending class. Claiming that they were
accumulating "academic deficiencies" from unauthorized school cuts, he
gave them ultimatums—return to class, withdraw from the school, or suffer disciplinary action and expulsion. He also threatened that because of
the class absences, the trustees might need to consider closing the school.

They replied, "If you close down our school you will have nine hundred Autherine Lucys knocking on the door of the University of South Carolina and Clemson," referring to the activist who was the first black student to attend the University of Alabama. They resented the notion of going to "classes at gunpoint" and decried being criminalized. "Call off Timmerman's cops and we'll go back to classes," they responded.[62]

The students eventually returned to class after Turner promised that there would be no reprisals. This was not to be so however, and the students were further attacked. WCC leader and board of trustees secretary Bethea expressed that the board would not "put up with any such insurrections."[63]

The board moved to punish any students found guilty of "violence, disorder, insult or intimidation." On Wednesday, April 25, supported by state forces and the white media, SCSC's board expelled Moore, denounced the "unwise" resolution of the faculty, and praised Turner's "sane" leadership. The *Afro-American*'s Louis Lomax found that the board had expelled Moore for "bad conduct, bad influence and violation of college rules and regulations." The school claimed that the "student insurrection was organized both on and off the campus," and it continued to persecute its leaders. In the over eight-hour meeting, the board unanimously resolved that "any student who engages in any future student insurrection or other form of defiance of authority shall be expelled from the College" and any faculty members who encouraged such insurrections would be immediately dismissed. Interestingly, the board used a National Defense Act to appoint a military property custodian who would be responsible for safekeeping of arms, ammunition, equipment, and SCSC supplies.[64]

Students rallied around Moore. Along with Claflin students, they gave him "thunderous applause." After a day of fasting and prayer in protest, they jeered and demonstrated in front of Turner's campus residence. They wore signs on their back reading, "Am I Next?" The *Free Press* declared, "The spirit of Fred Moore will never die." It instructed students to boycott the dining hall and cafeteria and to hold prayer meetings three times a day. They were urged to "be ashamed to die until [they had] won some great victory for humanity." A student statement charged Turner with a "breach of faith." They protested this denial of their right to protest as "American citizens to peaceable and freely assembly."[65]

Moore, the left side of whose body had been permanently injured by polio, appeared at an evening prayer meeting like a victorious prizefighter. Standing at the head of a motorcade, his presence electrified the group. Scores of Claflin students dashed over the fence that bridged both campuses, joining SCSC faculty, students, and staff. While some wept, others cheered wildly.[66]

Protests continued for days. Near Turner's home, students wrote on the concrete in black paint, "This way to Uncle Tom's Cabin." A drawn arrow pointed toward his house. Similar wordings were written on placards dangled from trees, continuing to his doorstep. Students canceled the annual spring fraternity and sorority dances and other social activities, choosing instead to use these funds to support Moore.[67]

The administration unsuccessfully attempted to ban further meetings by SCSC students. In early May, students attended Sunday services at an Orangeburg church where Moore was the guest speaker. Women students complained that a matron had tried to prevent them from going. They were among several hundred who were unable to get inside the over-packed church.[68]

The board was not finished. Kamarakafego was among the fifteen members of the student government and others who were instructed not to return in the fall as a result of their leadership in the strike and the "disorder" that occurred in response to Moore's expulsion. The contracts of three faculty members were not renewed, others were forced to leave, and two staff members were fired, among whom was Florence Miller, who had been editor of the *Collegian* when Pyatt wrote a pro-integration article. Turner called them "on the carpet" and ordered all subsequent articles to be inspected by him before publication.[69]

Twelve of the fifteen students were women. One was twenty-one-year-old Vivian Lennon, daughter of Adam Clayton Powell's confidential secretary, Acey Lennon. Powell held a press conference in New York in which he lambasted the SCSC board of trustees as being members of the WCCs and Turner as a "captive" of the board. Lennon completed her studies at Baltimore's Morgan State University.[70]

Many others also raised their voices in support of the students. College faculty and staff were proudly jubilant at the actions of the SCSC students. Clark felt similarly. Three days after Moore's expulsion, she spent time with the student leaders. "All Saturday night," she recalled to Judge Julius Waties Waring, "I spent with the boys from State College. They have shown tremendous tact and strong leadership keeping 1,200 students under control. . . . With such thinkers the future holds much. I have been disgusted with the grown ups but the youth have given me great inspiration to fight on."[71]

Clark was not surprised by the board's actions to expel the students. In June, she wrote to Roy Wilkins, "The time has come that I anticipated." In fact, she had actively sought to secure enrollment for the students at other institutions even before they were expelled. Her experiences in doing so highlight the gendered tensions surrounding the NAACP's handling of the situation. Clark had some hope in the common folks of the organization but less faith in its national leaders like "timid-souled" Wilkins.[72]

Since May, Clark had been urging the NAACP's male leadership to contact the presidents of denominational schools so that expelled students could immediately enroll in them tuition free or with financial support. This they did not do, and their "round about circle and the world go cautiously" approach infuriated her. She questioned the need to wait in giving the students financial support when they needed to secure lawyers and make trips and telephone calls. Clark pushed Wilkins and James Hinton to stir the local NAACP clubs into action. These children had "fought long and hard" and were due legal protection, financial security, and assistance to get into other schools. She pleaded with Wilkins to give her "a word of encouragement" to pass on to them.[73]

Clark's own case was "a baffling one." She was one of the NAACP-affiliated schoolteachers in South Carolina whose contracts were not renewed for the fall of 1956. In a letter to Elizabeth Waring, she remarked, "I anticipated this long ago. I can easily take it on the chin. No shock. No surprise." She was more concerned about the welfare of the students. By March 1957, she felt that the "only thing left" was "to go to jail." For Clark, "the spiritual power working for us" was the only reason that the "Klan did not kill Blackman." Most of the twenty-four teachers from Elloree were "still out of work, losing homes, and other possessions."[74]

Eventually the NAACP found colleges that would admit "the boys." Kamarakafego and Moore were to enroll in Chicago's Roosevelt University. Clark's friend Maude Veal, wife of Allen University president Frank Veal, helped him and eleven other ousted students get enrolled in Allen.[75]

From North Carolina to California

By July 1956, Kamarakafego was living in Brooklyn, New York. Interviewed by the *Amsterdam News*, he stated that he was seeking assistance from New York–based groups to find another school to attend in the fall. With the help of Brooklyn NAACP lawyer Paul Gibson Jr., he hoped to continue at an institution in the South.[76] Eventually, the NAACP helped to get him enrolled in North Carolina College (NCC), Durham's heralded HBCU. Upon his arrival on campus, Kamarakafego met with its president, Alfonso Elder, and dean of biology, John Stewart. They talked about the demonstrations at SCSC and their expectations for him at NCC.[77]

Kamarakafego's time at NCC was both fruitful and short-lived. Here he met his first academic mentor in ecology, biology professor Mary J. McLean Townes. Townes arrived at NCC in 1950 with an MS degree in public health. Decades later, she would serve as chair of its biology department and dean of both graduate students and the College of Arts and Sciences. She bequeathed $1 million to NCC at her death in 2003, and the university science complex now bears her illustrious name.[78] However, in 1956 she was a temporary instructor of biology, and her time at NCC was full of uncertainty.

In 1953, Townes was awarded a fellowship from the general education board to pursue an MS degree in zoology at the University of Michigan. She returned to NCC in 1954 while completing her PhD dissertation in zoology. When she left, she was a full-time instructor with an annual salary of $3,000. During her leave, she married Ross E. Townes, an NCC professor of physical education and recreation and an assistant coach of the school's football team. Upon her return, President Elder denied her being hired on a full-time basis, maintaining that it was against school policy to employ "husband and wife in two major positions." However, he informed her that occasionally, wives of professors could be employed as part-time instructors. Townes pushed back, asserting that a she had served and enjoyed the privileges of a full-time faculty member. She unsuccessfully argued for a faculty status and salary consummate with her training and experience. Eventually, she accepted the part-time position, which came at a decreased salary of $124 a month per course.[79]

Kamarakafego learned much from Townes, and they had "very serious and stimulating conversations." Under her tutelage, his interests in ecology and the environment "went through the roof." He enrolled in her graduate course on invertebrate zoology, which "seemed to bring everything together in the whole environment." The course dealt with the ecological succession of protozoa, which he would study at the graduate level beyond NCC. Kamarakafego also assisted her in her lab and collected specimens for her research.[80]

After visiting an NCC football practice, Townes's husband asked Kamarakafego to join the team as a punter, which he did. The team was certainly in need of serious help. In dire need of equipment, they found themselves renting equipment from high schools just to practice. The situation was so acute that the following semester's match against undefeated juggernaut Florida Agricultural & Mechanical University was canceled.[81]

When Kamarakafego traveled with the team to Raleigh to scout a competitor's game, things got testy, and an altercation at the football game led to a fight with a white police officer. According to Kamarakafego, the officer reached for his gun after Kamarakafego swept him off of his feet. Kamarakafego stepped on his hand to stop him from raising the weapon. He was soon arrested by other officers and spent the night in jail.[82]

The next day's light revealed that he was not in his cell alone. Surrounded by a group of black inmates, they began to share stories. Given his accent, they believed him to be from Charleston; none had ever heard of Bermuda. They taught him a card game called "coon can," which they played all day. Kamarakafego was supposed to have stayed overnight in Raleigh with his teammate, John Baker Jr., who would later play professional football. As fate would have it, John's father, Sergeant John Baker Sr., was Raleigh's first African American police officer. Later that day, Baker Sr. realized that Kamarakafego was to stay at his home. He retrieved him from jail and warned him not to say anything about the incident. Kamarakafego did just the opposite and was pressed by an NCC law professor to charge the police with unlawful arrest. His case was eventually thrown out.[83]

In the meantime, Kamarakafego continued his activism. He traveled back to Bermuda around Easter weekend. The only Bermudian on his flight, he returned to the United States on April 21, 1957. Shortly afterward, he involved himself in black Durham's efforts to desegregate a number of facilities in the city, including the Carolina Theater, tennis courts, the Long Meadow Park swimming pool, the public library, and the Durham Athletic Park. In May, 150 black protestors refused segregated seating at the Athletic Park during the opening game of the Carolina baseball league. According to the *New York Times*, a team had withdrawn from the league the year before because of segregation. Reverend Douglas E. Moore pressed Durham's city council to end racial segregation at the theater and library. On June 23, he led a group of African Americans in an attempt to desegregate the Royal Ice Cream parlor; the "Royal Seven" were arrested and charged with trespassing on the all-white side of the parlor.[84]

Like Moore, Kamarakafego was denied entry into the theater after refusing to sit in a segregated section. A subsequent scuffle with the police landed him not back in jail but in Elder's office. He was eventually asked to leave NCC because of the "negative publicity" that it received regarding such efforts. It was once again time to move on.[85]

Kamarakafego arrived in Bermuda on March 23, 1958. He listed his US address as NCCU, Durham. He spent the summer with his father, and while he remained passionate about studying ecology, he worked in construction building homes. During this time, he suggested to his father that he wanted to study in a warm climate, such as California. His father suggested he visit a Dr. Bowman, a gynecologist at Pasadena's California Institute of Technology (CIT); his father had built Bowman a home in Barbados. One flight and a three-day Greyhound bus trip from New York later, Kamarakafego reached California and informed Bowman that he wanted to study biology.[86]

Bowman spoke with his colleague, Albert Tyler, CIT professor of biology and renowned expert of embryology. They agreed that Kamarakafego should take a status examination, which he passed. Apparently with enough credits to enter graduate school, he was awarded a fellowship to work with Tyler on a project of "immunology and fertility." This research dealt with sterility, estrogen, and hormone balancing. His thesis proposal was the "ecological succession of two protozoa and the environmental factors of their habitat."[87]

Kamarakafego's time at CIT was "one of the high points of [his] academic life." Tyler's pathbreaking studies on fertilization included the "expansion of classical experimental embryology into modern developmental science," with an emphasis on genetics and molecular biology. Kamarakafego benefited from his research, which applied "modern physiological and biochemical methods to the study of development." He collected specimens for Tyler's work in embryogenesis in sea urchins by scuba diving in the waters off Santa Monica.[88]

Kamarakafego spent countless hours in one of CIT's air-conditioned labs, where he worked with sophisticated equipment. This included his first experience with a computer—a tricarb scintillation counter that was a loud, bombastic, twelve-foot machine. He worked with ultra-centrifuges, ultra-microtomes, and a ceiling-high electron microscope, doing his best to learn the functions of their moving parts. He also conducted two five-week field trips in Florida that were directly related to ecological engineering and land management, during which he worked on landfill, drained swamp areas, and participated in field studies of housing and fish farming.[89]

He also earned occasional spending money by knitting and selling sweaters. He somehow found time to play percussion in a highlife band with

Kenyan, Nigerian, Congolese, and Gambian musicians. Engaging in soccer and cricket with other international students helped satisfy his recreational needs but also helped him forge long-lasting political relationships.[90]

At CIT, Kamarakafego grappled with the intersections between radical politics, environmental justice, and science. One day, Linus Pauling, CIT biochemist and anti-nuclear activist, joined him in the cafeteria. In 1954, Pauling had won a Nobel Prize in chemistry, an accolade he would follow in 1962 with a Nobel Peace Prize. Kamarakafego and Pauling continued to have numerous conversations about W. E. B. Du Bois, the peace movement, global politics, and the Cuban revolution.[91]

Pauling certainly knew Du Bois. In 1949 they were vice-presidents of the American Continental Congress for World Peace. Pauling was a member of the Federation of Atomic Scientists, which, chaired by Albert Einstein, argued that the atomic bomb was the most destructive force known to mankind. He also signed an appeal by American scientists urging for an international agreement to stop nuclear testing.[92]

Continually attacked by the US government and mainstream media, in 1952 Pauling had been denied a passport to travel to a conference in London. In 1956, he asked the question, "How many . . . significant discoveries has the attack on scientists kept from being made. How many scientists have trained themselves to suppress unconventional thoughts?" Charged as a communist, CIT's administration expressed concern about his social and political interests and pressured Pauling to cease his public denouncements against nuclear testing. This drove him to step down as chair of the university's chemistry program in 1957. According to Pauling, CIT's focus on science and engineering marked it as being more conservative than universities with humanities structure.[93]

In Pauling, Kamarakafego had a living example of how the worlds of science and political activism intersected. Kamarakafego talked with Pauling extensively about his own visions for environmental justice, which, as the next chapter shows, included political activism in Bermuda and his yearning to travel to Africa.[94]

3

Liberia

First-Class Africa

Kamarakafego's political activities between the years 1959 and 1961 formed a particularly intense period for him, both politically and personally. He completed his college studies, traveled to Africa for the first time, got married, buried his father, and played a leading role in Bermuda's Committee for Universal Adult Suffrage (CUAS). While he had been "wearing Africa on his back" for much of his life, his time on the continent was transformative. He was electrified by the major political trends sweeping Africa at the turn of the decade—decolonization, sustainable development, African liberation struggles, universal adult suffrage, and pan-Africanism. Wherever he found himself, he sought to utilize the political lessons of the African Diaspora , a reminder of pan-Africanism's dogged attempts to engage both the grassroots and global concerns of the black world. By the end of this two-year span, his transformation was nearly complete—Roosevelt Browne had become Pauulu Kamarakafego.

Kamarakafego completed his studies at the California Institute of Technology (CIT) in 1959. No longer "limited by the bounds of university life," he felt that he "could finally be a real engineer." Politically inspired by the Cuban revolution and Bermuda's 1959 Theatre Boycott, he sought to transform his "thoughts and initiatives into innovative schemes that would help people." Although he had received a contract from CIT to continue his research, he wanted instead to visit his family in Liberia. Pauling and Bowman advised him best on how to do this. During this time, he also met the soon-to-be Betty Browne, a Canadian Afro-Indigenous Cayugan. A descendant of Harriet Tubman, she also had family in Liberia. They were married in a traditional ceremony and set their sights for West Africa.[1]

Founded in 1847, Liberia occupies a prominent place in the collective consciousness of the African Diaspora. Originally a colony of the American

Colonization Society, it was formed via the repatriation of formerly enslaved black people from the United States. For many white supporters, African repatriation was a convenient way to free America from what they believed to be a menace—quasi-free blacks. For the approximately fifteen thousand returnees who resettled in Liberia up to the outbreak of the US Civil War, Africa seemed a better alternative than American racism. These Americo-Liberians developed a stratified society in which indigenous African ethnic groups resented the political and economic power embedded in the former.

Still, in a twentieth-century world full of European imperialisms, to speak of *any* "sovereign" Africa country was to inspire hope across the African Diaspora. There was Ethiopia (as in Adwa, Taitu, and Menelik II) in the east and Liberia in the west. Pan-Africanists conceptualized Liberia in their concrete plans for pan-Africanism. Marcus Garvey told the black world that princes would come forth from Ethiopia, but the Universal Negro Improvement Association's repatriation project included Liberia. This was a blunder, as the Liberian government's allegiance was to foreign capital—including rubber companies such as Firestone and Goodrich. Quiet reports of Du Bois's active role in the sabotage of these plans still linger, but his scything 1933 critique of imperialism bears repeating:

> [Liberia's] chief crime is to be black and poor in a rich, white world; and in precisely that portion of the world where color is ruthlessly exploited as a foundation for American and European wealth. The success of Liberia as a Negro republic would be a blow to the whole colonial slave labor system. Are we starting the United States Army toward Liberia to guarantee the Firestone Company's profits in a falling rubber market or smash another Haiti in the attempt?[2]

During World War II, the African American press was highly critical of this relationship between rubber, American capital, and Americo-Liberian elites.[3] But by the time Kamarakafego reached Liberia, it was no longer the country of E. W. Blyden, Du Bois, or Garvey. In many ways, it was the backyard of William Tubman, president of Liberia since 1944. His leadership has been defined as many things—authoritarian, omnipresent, shrewd, omniscient, and strong-willed. Tubman wielded his political, kinship, military, and economic clout to keep his European and African enemies at bay for most of his almost thirty years in political power. In 1960, he informed the US ambassador that he felt that the US government was handling him "like a child." According to E. Frederick Morrow, the first African American to hold an executive position in the White House, Tubman was left to conclude

FIGURE 5. Kamarakafego, Liberia, 1961. Photo courtesy of Rronniba Kamarakafego.

that the United States was no longer interested in Liberia as a friend, and that perhaps he needed to seek technical assistance from the Communist bloc.[4]

As leader of the Monrovia group, Tubman was the key antagonist to the pan-Africanist aims of his political neighbors Kwame Nkrumah in Ghana and Sekou Touré in Guinea. Amid proclamations of African unity, Tubman opened Liberia even wider to foreign investment, enforcing a "stability" that would protect his own interests and the interests of his benefactors. In 1960, the National Security Council argued that US influence on the policy and attitudes of emerging West African governments was facilitated through its close connection with Liberia, marked by a 1959 Agreement of Cooperation. This "open door" policy attracted $100 million in US investments to Liberia. Between 1960 and 1963, US expenditures in Liberia were projected to total $9.6 million. Liberia was the only West African country receiving US military aid, which aimed at improving its internal security capabilities through a training mission and financing arms and equipment. These relationships led to public silence from US officials regarding Tubman's personal expenditures. For example, in 1962, as the United States government was financing a $4.5 million high school in Monrovia, Tubman was constructing a new home for $16 million.[5]

Penny Von Eschen describes Tubman's 1952 inauguration as an example of the celebratory reporting of the African American press in contrast with its critique of US imperialism in the 1940s. The ceremonies were attended by an aging Mary McLeod Bethune. The prominent black activist, philanthropist, and stateswoman watched Tubman take to his knees in the midst of thousands and "petition God for wisdom and guidance." Deeply moved, Bethune thought, "This is Africa."[6] Bethune's wanting to *feel* Africa contrasted with her legacy of anticolonialism. Still, for people of the Diaspora, the physical return to Africa can often be driven by such politics of emotion. Put another way, for this community, any return to Africa can feel like a political act in and of itself.

Kamarakafego was more ambitious. He returned as an environmentalist with both tangible memories and imagined futures. The stories of his Liberian relatives were passed down to him from his father and his Aunt Mae (who lived in Africa from 1937 to 1950). Kamarakafego's desire to return to Africa was also very much grounded in his experiences across the Americas. He felt that in Africa, he would be "able to put into practice at the rural level" skills that he had learned from his parents, uncle, grandfather, and educational institutions.[7]

The Brownes boarded a Norwegian West Africa Barbara Line for Liberia in the late summer of 1959. They were dismayed that the ship did not head directly east, stopping instead in Connecticut, Boston, and then Halifax before heading across the Atlantic. This reminded Kamarakafego of how enslaved Africans "made the long journey on those slow ships under such inhumane conditions." They eventually docked in Freetown, Sierra Leone, in the dark hours of early morning. Seasick and with child, Betty stayed on board. Kamarakafego did not stop to kiss the soil; he hit the streets as soon as he could, and he hit them *hard*. His ears caught the pulsating sounds of a nearby nightclub—Palm Wine music, perhaps, for it reminded him of Calypso. Kamarakafego entered the club and joined the jumping crowd moving to the infectious rhythms. For him, they "sounded like West Indians."[8]

Two days later, they were on their way to Monrovia, Liberia. Here, the country's ethnic and class dynamics where pronounced. Kamarakafego took note of the political position of Americo-Liberians, Lebanese-owned stores, and Dutch control of the country's diamond industry. Closely tied to the US dollar, Liberia was a magnet for West Africa's diamond industry.[9]

Kamarakafego may have had family in Liberia, but Betty actually knew people there. She carried with her a letter from her father addressed to a distant relative, President Tubman himself. Four months pregnant, she was concerned about Kamarakafego's lack of employment. Still, a problem is not a dilemma. Within two weeks, they had both found jobs at Cuttington College and Divinity School, located some two hundred miles from Monrovia in Suacoco, Bong County. Betty, a licensed nurse, found work as an administrator of Cuttington's clinic. Kamarakafego claimed that he taught biological science, coached the football team, advised a student council, and oversaw the college's physical plant. He also taught science courses at Sierra Leone's Fourah Bay College. This he did by putting to good use the pilot's license that he had obtained in Cuba. As there was a shortage of pilots, he occasionally air taxied himself and other passengers the five hundred kilometers between Monrovia and Freetown.[10]

In the early spring of 1960, a seven-months-pregnant Betty contracted malaria. Tragically, she lost their child. Three months later, expecting again, she decided to return to Canada to have the child. This was a life-changing situation for the couple, as she was aware that Kamarakafego was determined not to live in North America. They returned to Canada, where immigration officials gave him a hard time about entering the country. Given a temporary visa, he stayed there for only five days.[11]

Passenger records suggest that Kamarakafego landed in New York on

May 20, 1960, on an Air France flight from Paris, perhaps on his way to Canada. On his immigration card, Kamarakafego initially wrote that he boarded in Monrovia, Liberia, but this was scratched out and Paris written in instead. Given a visa of five days, he claimed that he was in transit to Bermuda. Kamarakafego used his time in New York to visit John Henrik Clarke and Yosef Ben-Jochannan. Knowing of his interest in Cuba, the two prominent scholars and historians informed him that the Fair Play for Cuba Committee had just been formed that April. After meeting with the committee, he headed back to Liberia.[12]

African Students and Grassroots Pan-Africanism

In April 1958, Ghana hosted the Conference of All Independent African States, and in December, the historic All African People Conference. The latter conference represented twenty-eight African countries and an illustrious political delegation from across the black world. Sandwiched between these two critical moments of African nationalism was the First Pan-African Student Conference of July 1958. Held at Makerere College in Kampala, Uganda, the talks were attended by forty students from thirteen African countries along with African student groups from Europe and India. Edwin Munger, a visiting lecturer in geography at CIT, attended as an American University field staff member. His report of the talks overemphasized how delegates had to survive "extraordinary" cultural, racial, political, and emotional tensions, noting how Anglophone and Francophone students clashed around parliamentary procedure, "tea breaks," and political experience.[13]

In this era, pan-African conferences were not simply spaces of revolutionary rhetoric. They were crucial sites where the ideas of African liberation could be developed, contested, and internationally coordinated. This process was particularly significant for emerging activists from diverse linguistic, ethnic, and political backgrounds.

The Black African Students Federation in France (FEANF) made a critical impact on the Kampala talks. Formed in 1950, the federation included poets, playwrights, filmmakers, novelists, and scholars, such as its spokesperson, Cheikh Anta Diop. It published books—including Diop's own *Nations Nègres et Culture* (1954)—and a periodical, *L'Étudiant d'Afrique Noire* and *Présence Africaine*. Joe Van Den Reysen, editor of *L'Étudiant d'Afrique Noire* and secretary of FEANF, represented the group at the conference. Hailing from the Republic of the Congo, Van Den Reysen was "bitterly critical of the French murderers" in Algeria and Cameroon. Distributing

FEANF materials, he was outspoken in his call for the conference to heed the anticolonial path of Bandung, Accra, and Cairo.[14]

The keynote speaker was Kenya's Tom Mboya, who aroused delegates with "thoughts of a new Africa." Mboya stressed that pan-Africanism was changing the "arbitrary and often illogical boundaries set up by the colonial powers." Africa would create a new society, conditioned to its own circumstances and history but enriched by a synthesis of what was good from other systems. For Mboya, the youth needed to be in the vanguard of Africa, because there were "no elderly . . . experiences on which to lean." Drawing wide applause, Mboya pressed that the fight for freedom would continue as long as any part of Africa remained under European colonial rule or settler domination. He criticized those who preached democracy and Christianity but refused to practice or live it.[15]

Mboya expressed similar views during a visit to Cuttington College in May 1960. Since its founding in 1889 by the Episcopal Church of the United States, the Cuttington campus had been a site of local, national, and continental political concerns. In meetings with students and staff, Mboya suggested that Africa needed to ask if the church stood for what it preached. He called on Africans to "test all Christian missions" about their support for colonial rule. As he toured the campus, male and female students flanked him carrying signs such as "Africa Unite, and Total Liberation of Africa Now." As did Julius Nyerere for Tanganyika, Mboya formed agreements with Cuttington to train Kenyan students.[16]

Nkrumah also toured the college while in Liberia for Sanniquellie 1959 Community of Independent African States meeting. This summit between Nkrumah, Tubman, and Touré was based on the "objectives of freedom, independence and unity of the African personality." However, it also provided Tubman the opportunity to demonstrate his political superiority over his younger counterparts. One of its resolutions was that each member of the community would "accept the principle of non-interference in the internal affairs of any other member."[17]

Tubman was also not particularly enthused about the spread of pan-Africanism in Liberia or at Cuttington, which hosted students from Kenya, Tanganyika, Rhodesia, Sudan, Swaziland, South Africa, Ghana, Nigeria, Cameroon, and Sierra Leone. American Missionary John Gay served as dean of instruction at Cuttington and taught there from 1958 to 1974. According to Gay, this multinational, pan-Africanist student body helped make the school "an exciting place to teach and learn." It allowed faculty to implement a curriculum in history, philosophy, and religion that was "broadly pan-African."[18]

A group of Tanganyikan students were particularly outspoken. After attending the 1958 All-African People's Conference in Accra, they continued on to Cuttington. There on scholarships, they were excellent students and "influential radicals." Identifying with Nkrumah and Nyerere, they sought to "join forces with freedom-loving people across the continent to create a single blazing beacon of hope for the world in the United States of Africa." Their apparent "intoxication" with "the promise of a free, united, socialist Africa" was infectious. Gay, his wife, Judy, and other Cuttington faculty strongly believed that they could help these students in building a new society.[19]

Indeed, Cuttington's students were politicized. In 1960, they participated in a workday organized by Gay. This included clearing out a storage shed, followed by a cookout next to a neighboring river. Most students refused to walk to the river and went on strike. They argued that they were being "exploited by the wicked *kwii* foreigners." One rally was presided over by the chairman of Cuttington's board of trustees, African American bishop Bravid W. Harris. Kamarakafego remembers this event somewhat differently. He states that the students were upset about the food choices presented by the college. Furthermore, some did not appreciate being forced to go to chapel on a regular basis.[20]

However, it was not all notebooks and revolutionary placards. Passionate about the game of football, the Tanganyikans formed "the backbone" of Cuttington's soccer team. In 1961, the squad played the University of Liberia at Monrovia's Antoinette Tubman Stadium (named after president Tubman's wife). Even imperialism liked to "kick ball"; the Mobile Oil Company of Liberia sponsored the cup. Supported by photographs, Kamarakafego states that he coached the team, which would have put him contact with these students from Tanganyika.[21]

Nearby the campus lay the Kpelle village of Sinyea. Land had been taken from Sinyea to build the college and grow rubber. Highlighted by Gay's novel, *Long Day's Anger*, this resulted in significant tensions between Cuttington and Sinyea. Sinyea's chief, Sigbe Dorweh, had open disdain for the college over the issue. Furthermore, Sinyea's villagers had been forced to work for *kwii* (coastal peoples or foreigners) as day laborers. The chief's radical sentiments resonated with the Tanganyikan students, who made clear efforts to politicize rural Liberians. In the evenings, they offered night-school classes in Sinyea, seeking to bring "political radical/liberal ideas to an oppressed Liberian populace."[22]

Kamarakafego also visited Sinyea between 1959 and 1960. In fact, he asserts that it was here, during his first Christmas in Africa, that he became "Pauulu." His Aunt Mae had told him since childhood that his family was Kpelle, a historically rice-cultivating Mande-speaking people and Liberia's largest ethnic group. In *Me One*, he recalls being reunited with members of his family in a Kpelle village near Cuttington. During a ten-day period of celebrations, which included the slaughtering of a cow, drumming, palm-wine drinking, and the eating of monkey and rice, the elder of the village, Chief Kamara, welcomed him as a son. Kamarakafego states that it was here that he was ceremoniously given the name Pauulu Kamarakafego, "brown-skinned son of Chief Kamara." During his time there, he used local materials to design and build a water tank, a village school, and a health-aid post. He claims that the chief of Sinyea lamented about how young men from the village were being routinely rounded up at night by soldiers, taken to plantations, and forced to tap rubber. After witnessing this himself, village elders allegedly asked him to assist them in stopping the practice. Kamarakafego's account gives plenty of room for pause. According to Gay, in 1959, the chief of the Sinyea was named Sigbe Dorweh, not Kamara. In addition, Sinyea is a Kpelle village, but Kamarakafego is a Malinke name. Still, Malinke traders had been migrating to Liberia for centuries and had married into Kpelle families. If things did occur as Kamarakafego has suggested, it is likely that they did not all take place in Sinyea. For example, a village school was built in 1959.[23]

Violent forced labor in Liberia is a well-documented practice. Kamarakafego's possible conversations with Dorweh may have included some of these historic occurrences. This would have deeply touched Kamarakafego, who was particularly sensitive to the relationships between labor, land, and environmental justice. Across Bermuda, Cuba, and South Carolina, he witnessed black communities being exploited in the production of limestone, sugarcane, and cotton; now in Liberia, it was rubber. For Kamarakafego, *this too* was Africa. But Bermuda was calling again.

Bermuda and the Committee for Universal Adult Suffrage

While in Liberia, Kamarakafego kept abreast of things in Bermuda, both political and of personal interest. This included correspondence about the 1959 Bermuda Theatre Boycott organized by the clandestine Progressive

Group, which led to desegregation of the island's theaters, hotels, and restaurants. In August 1960, Kamarakafego returned to the island because his father was ill, remaining there for the next six months.

The most pressing concerns facing black Bermuda in the 1960s were arguably segregation, political and economic disenfranchisement, and colonialism. According to one black member of Colonial Parliament (MCP), Donald Smith, the "irksome" restricted franchise was "designed particularly against colored people." Smith was absolutely correct. The question of the franchise was connected to broader issues of race, segregation, and political power. Since the abolition of slavery, Bermuda's white elite had implemented voting restrictions to maximize their vote, while disenfranchising blacks, poor whites, and white women.[24] In 1958, voting eligibility on the island was based exclusively upon property ownership. Voters were required to own property accessed at more than £60; officials of the British Colonial Office (BCO) admitted that assessments bore little relation to market values and that the vote was "restricted to those owning considerable property." The election system itself was based on plural voting, which allowed voters to cast ballots in every parish in which they owned land. This practice enabled Bermuda's white oligarchy and wealthy landowners to sway election results in multiple constituencies. In 1961, only 6,603 of Bermuda's citizens were registered to vote. Bermuda's population stood at around forty-five thousand—sixteen thousand whites and twenty-nine thousand blacks. Under the property-ownership requirements for eligibility, there were four thousand eligible white voters and three thousand eligible black voters. Plural voting, which allowed several whites to vote across all of the island's nine parishes, increased the impact of the white electorate to five thousand votes—a situation that the BCO was well aware of.[25]

Bermuda's black community had long since raised its collective voice against the biased franchise. The BCO noted that over the past three decades, a black "politically conscious minority" had unsuccessfully agitated for the extension of the franchise. This included the Bermuda Worker's Association, whose 1941 demonstrations led to modest reforms in 1948. A few years later, Hilton Hill led a delegation from the Amalgamated Parochial Political Association to meet with Bermuda's governor in complaint of the franchise.[26]

These acts pushed the government to form a 1958 Select Committee on the franchise. It was led by "politically moderate" W. L. Tucker, who was one of a few economically independent black MCPs. In 1960, the committee proposed abolishing the plural vote, changing the land qualifications to measure by area instead of by assessed value and extending the franchise to renters of homes with property valued of £240 or more. It advocated gradual extension, as plural voting was indefensible and called for one man, one vote.[27]

In May 1960, Bermuda's majority-white House of Assembly stood in approval of the committee's majority report. Unsurprisingly, most white MCPs were against universal adult suffrage in Bermuda, reflecting their collective position in support of segregation, white supremacist ideas, and patriarchy. Henry Vesey claimed Bermudians were well off and "by and large happy." H. T. Watlington felt that property owners were "more responsible" then leasers, and he wanted to know how many voters would be added with the extension. Remarkably, Earl Outerbridge felt that the current franchise was already "pretty universal," as "all real Bermudians" were homeowners or hoping to be so. Colonel Brownlow Tucker favored plural voting because he had big investments in several parishes. C. V. Burch felt that universal suffrage was inevitable and that it would come about either by revolution or by evolution. In this "revolutionary age," young folks wanted revolution and rock 'n' roll. They did not want to become "apprentices before demanding pay as full-fledged artisans; they wanted to pass from childhood to adulthood without going through adolescence."[28]

Speaker of the House Sir John Cox referred to universal adult suffrage as "government by kindergarten." He argued that the report's eight-year plan for universal suffrage would destroy "much that had been built up." He argued that Bermuda's franchise had worked well, claiming that there had been "general freedom from oppression" in Bermuda. As such, it was "claptrap" for some to complain about disabilities. He claimed that just because some people (read, *black* people) did not have the franchise, it did not mean that they were not as free as others across the world. Cox exclaimed that he had property in various parishes and felt that he should have a right to say who should represented him in each district.[29]

Edmund Gibbons claimed that plural voting had created a government of the best men from each parish. Hailing from one of Bermuda's oldest slaveholding white families, he put forth a minority report that advocated dividing each parish into two racial electorates. Referred to as the "wealthiest man in the Commonwealth," he saw Bermuda's government as the "envy of the world," suggesting that it would be dangerous to play with it. In terms of splitting up the parishes into two electorates, he remarked that "when he took a friend fishing, he did not give him all the bait." He shared it. There were two groups in play—the "colored group" and "those who did the plural voting." "One group was trying to get power, while the other was trying to hold onto it. . . . If you control the bait, each one group would protect the interests of the other. It would bring about a balance, and it is the safest and soundest method."[30] Gibbons spoke for the white oligarchy. Indeed, in a world of increasing black and brown militancy, a system of white minority rule that was militarily supported by British colonialism in an ecological island paradise like Bermuda perhaps *was* the envy of the white world.

The unquestioned leader of the white oligarchy, banker Henry J. Tucker, had much to say. He felt that the removal of plural voting would make a substantial difference in the next election. In seven out of nine parishes, there would now be a black majority. Abolition of the plural vote was inevitable, but if the "colored people" would "apply themselves" to Bermuda's economic woes then "there would be no trouble." If they realized that they had not produced enough able people "to take over all facets of life," they would continue to vote for the most qualified man. Tucker feared that universal suffrage would lead to racial party politics. He was against shifting political control from one-third of the population to two-thirds. He also decried a "rapid transition from a very conservative to an inexperienced and more radical group." As such, he first wanted to "see the colored people learn how to live with this power."[31]

In contrast, black MCPs Arnold Francis and Walter Robinson vehemently challenged the majority report and called for immediate universal adult suffrage. Despite having met for twenty-two months, Francis likened the committee, which had met for twenty-two months, to an elephant that "went into labor but produced a mouse." Universal suffrage was the only way to prevent the loopholes that could occur with a lease franchise. He also challenged Gibbons's idea to divide each parish into two electorates.[32]

Robinson wanted to "see every citizen of this country have the right to vote." He saw the report as a "political abortion" and a "charter for oppression." In introducing the report, Tucker stated that the franchise had worked well. "For whom?" Robinson asked. The present electoral system had been determined through the "manipulations of the nine parish vestries and a group of assessors." Now the committee advocated putting the electorate in the hands of five thousand landlords. This, in essence, "was a charter for more oppression." The only positive element was its suggestion to remove plumping, syndicate, and plural voting, a "steamroller of rich people casting their votes."[33]

Concurrent with the debate, the *Bermuda Recorder* reported that posters in support of universal adult suffrage were being circulated across the

island. Reminiscent of those used by the Progressive Group during the Theatre Boycott, they read "One Man One Vote" and "Law-Abiding, Peaceful,
Non-Voting Citizens. Bah!" Most of them were spread across the colony's
public utility poles. Police officers busily removed them from the poles of
the Electric Light and Telephone companies.[34]

The racial implications of the franchise were no secret. Disenfranchised
blacks wanted change; whites who had reaped the political benefits from the
status quo did not. Officials of the BCO repeatedly referenced "an element
of racial prejudice in the situation." They argued that there was "a *natural* re-
luctance on the part of the [white] oligarchy which has dominated Bermuda
since the earliest times to share political responsibility with the descendants
of their family slaves."[35]

Yet they also claimed that it was easy to exaggerate the grievances against
the franchise and to "oversimplify the issue of typical racial discrimination
of a white minority with vested interests denying political rights to a black
minority." They denied that there was a popular demand for universal franchise. They marginalized the island's advocates of change as a small group
of "colored intellectuals, mostly professional people, doctors, lawyers and
schoolteachers." In contrast, Bermuda's black population was "politically
apathetic" and interested in "making money and enjoying a high material
standard of living than agitating for intangible political benefits."[36]

This denial of collective black political agency in Bermuda was typical of
Bermuda's white elite. This perspective refused to recognize how disenfranchisement intersected with a myriad of racial assaults on black humanity
in Bermuda—second-class citizenship, segregation, unfair labor practices,
sexism, and colonialism. This environment of racism was quite clear to the
organizers of CUAS, who called for complete adult suffrage based on citizenship with a voting age of twenty-one.[37]

Since June 1960, founders of what would become CUAS had circulated
a petition seeking the immediate extension of the franchise to people at
least twenty-one years of age. It found that select committee's recommendations on the franchise to be too restrictive. Signed by "local citizens of Her
Majesty," it had gathered a few thousand signatures. Among the signatories
were members of the Progressive Group, including Edouard and Rosalind
Williams, whose home had served as the base of boycott. Supplies, such as
copying equipment, were hidden in the ceiling of their kitchen. The location
of the copying machine engenders our spatial imaginations about *where*
black resistance has historically occurred. It is not supposed to exist in the
kitchen, but it has.[38]

The Williamses were active members of St. Paul's African Methodist Episcopal (AME) church. Circa 1957, African American minister and civil rights organizer Wendell Foster was posted to the church. Hailing from the Bronx, NY, Foster quickly built a reputation for activist ministry. He reinvigorated St. Paul's young-adults program, which hosted discussions about segregation in Bermuda and the United States. It was through spaces such as this that Rosalind, who had studied in Canada, sharpened her public speaking skills and eventually joined the Progressive Group.[39]

In the summer of 1960, Kamarakafego attended a discussion at St. Paul's young-adult program on the extension of the franchise. Here he spoke with the Progressive Group's Florence Maxwell and Edwena Smith about popularizing the idea of universal franchise. Later that evening, he thought about voting rights in Africa, Cuba, and the United States. He felt that the extension of the franchise would be the most efficient way to push for democracy in Bermuda, as it "lacked rural areas to wage a revolutionary struggle" and blacks were a demographic majority. He agreed with Nkrumah's popular axiom, "First seek the political kingdom." This would require political education at the grassroots level. Kamarakafego then gained the support of the Howard Academy Ex-Student Association to hold debates about the franchise under its name.[40]

This was the birth of CUAS, which blossomed into an extremely efficient grassroots organization through overt and covert tactics. Its leadership involved veteran and burgeoning activists, artists, educators, and politicians. Strategy sessions for CUAS occurred all across the island, including in the Williams's home. Kamarakafego himself held smaller meetings "on the seashore rocks" with people like veteran activist Wilfred Allen. He also met with executive members of the island's Workmen's clubs, which were significant hubs of intra-local cultural, sports, and community interests.[41]

From September to November 1960, CUAS held seventeen meetings across all of Bermuda's nine parishes. To maximize black participation, the discussions were held at local institutions such as the Devonshire Recreation Club. Kamarakafego chaired and organized the meetings, which intentionally included black and white speakers, parliamentarians, community leaders, youth, and franchise supporters, and non-supporters. The first meeting, held on September 5, 1960, at St. George's Richard Allen AME church, featured MCP Robinson, future premier of Bermuda John Swan, and two white MCPs from St. George's, A. D. Spurling and Brownlow Tucker.[42]

While Kamarakafego assured white MCPs that their voices would be heard at the talks, his hope was that those who were against universal adult suffrage would publicly commit "political suicide." The tactic worked. When asked difficult questions, these detractors exposed themselves as being "arrogant, egotistical, shallow, racist, fascist, supremacist, and mentally bankrupt individuals." They raised hypocritical questions about if mixed race people, the formerly incarcerated, or those born of wedlock should have the right to vote.[43]

The meetings were lively affairs. Some two hundred people attended a September talk, which included the afore mentioned Rosalind Williams as a speaker. Williams told the audience that universal suffrage was a human right deserved by Bermudian citizens. Furthermore, she asserted, the government had not "educated its people politically, socially and spiritually."[44]

Country wisdom tells us that when one throws a stone, the dog that barks is the one who got hit. In this case, white MCP Sir Bayard Dill played the hound. He remarked that it was important to look for "intelligence and stability" in voters and that land ownership was a measure of stability. He disputed Williams's notion that adulthood or citizenship signified readiness to vote. Just as doctors needed to meet requirements to practice medicine, one needed to meet "certain requirements of citizenship." Furthermore, he felt that the larger the electorate, the "lower its average of intelligence became." Given Bermuda's prosperity, he felt that Bermuda was not ready for universal franchise.[45]

Panelist Leon Williams challenged Dill. If Bermuda's current electorate were responsible citizens, he asked, then why were the majority of the representatives white and not reflective of Bermuda's racial demographics? For Williams, the franchise had nothing to do with "intelligence or responsibility," but rather with land ownership. Amid applause, he declared that universal suffrage would make it possible for all people to live daily with self-respect."[46]

Dill's counterpart, white MCP John Cox, found it absurd to say that one only needed to be twenty-one years of age to be eligible to vote. According to the *Recorder*, Cox proclaimed that in his mind, "universal franchise was the best way to ensure the deterioration of the government." Drawing cynical laughter from the crowd of some two hundred, he claimed that the present system had enabled the election of the "cream of the community." There was no question in his mind that universal suffrage would lead to "a less efficient government" than what Bermuda currently had.[47]

Seventeen-year-old Stuart Hayward brought Cox "obvious discomfort" with two brilliant questions: If Bermuda's government was so good, then why had they not taken steps to wipe out racial discrimination? And if segregation had been eliminated, why was there a need for a discussion on the franchise?[48]

Also sharing the stage was MCP Robinson, who asserted that land ownership was not a sign of stability. In fact, the "little fellow with land was swamped out by the plural vote." Robinson wanted to vote because he lived and was born in Bermuda. It was a question of what was "morally right and politically wise." It was "only just, honest, and right that all people in Bermuda" could vote. He defied anyone to tell him that he was not qualified to vote unless he owned property. "What makes it so special that these people are stable because they have land? How can you say the government has worked well when the basic requirement for government—freedom to vote—is denied?" From the audience, white historian William Zuill asked if lunatics should be given the vote. Robinson rolled up his fists, stating that if he were near Zuill he would be tempted to give him "some physical chastisement."[49]

W. G. Brown read from the United Nations Declaration of Human Rights, asserting that Bermuda needed to recognize the UN as the supreme authority. He suggested that people who wanted the right to vote should consider using the tactics of the theater boycotters. English schoolteacher Colin Benbow asked why those who wanted universal adult suffrage did not vote its supporters into Parliament. Robinson's response was that those who wanted it were the ones who were disenfranchised.[50]

One October meeting packed Warwick's Samaritan Hall to capacity. As crowds stood outside, white MCP Dudley Butterfield claimed that Negro crime and illegitimacy proved that "colored" people "were not ready for universal suffrage." He cited statistics and a murder case from the year prior to argue his point. Butterfield claimed that CUAS was stirring up "discord between the races" for political gain. He pleaded with the audience not to do anything that would be detrimental to all. Drawing from the master patriarchal narrative, he claimed that the races had for years "lived side by side in harmony," white women ran the island's charities for the benefit of "colored" people, and that universal suffrage would upset this spirit of cooperation. To ask for universal suffrage was to address the needs of blacks and not whites. He decried that universal suffrage had made the "vote of an illiterate farmhand" equal to the vote of Mr. Macmillan.[51]

In a poignant response, panelist E. Smith contended that Butterfield's statistics were an indictment of the very government that he alleged was so wonderful. The Berkeley Institute teacher and Progressive Group member refuted Butterfield's claim that universal adult suffrage was just about black people, asserting that the fight was for everyone. Panelist Hilton Hill felt similarly. He dismissed Butterfield's comments about black crime, stating that they were "irrelevant" to the discussion of the franchise. He felt that adults who could not vote could not be considered citizens of any country. As such, as long as Bermuda's franchise was based on land ownership and plural voting, many people in the island would not be citizens. Yet, he argued, if blacks in Bermuda were to suddenly disappear, universal suffrage would be granted within twenty-four hours. The issue was racial because "everything in Bermuda was predicated on the fact that there are too many dark-skinned Bermudians."[52]

A talk at Trinity Hall featured a panel of all women. The meeting of over five hundred people was a heated one. Speakers included R. Williams, Marva Stovell, and two white women, Lady Conyers and Humbert Parker. After Kamarakafego closed the meeting, a heated exchange erupted between Parker and audience member C. V. Burch about a woman who the former said was in Bermuda taking the jobs out of the hands of Bermudians as a result of government irresponsibility.[53]

In November, CUAS met at Hamilton's Leopard Club. The audience stood in support of Kamarakafego when they heard that he had received threatening phone calls. Someone with a "rather cultured English accent" had called and warned them that he and Kingsley Tweed were "going to get what's coming to them." The caller had suggested that they "go back to Africa," likening Kamarakafego to the Congo's Patrice Lumumba.[54] Kamarakafego was likely flattered by this comparison.

Tweed was secretary-general of the Bermuda Industrial Union. A brilliant speaker, he had electrified crowds during the Theatre Boycott. As a panelist at a Vernon Temple AME meeting, he stated that if Bermuda did not get universal suffrage peacefully, they would get it in the same way that the cinemas were integrated.[55]

The tactics of mobilization used by CUAS included the use of political culture—poetry, sound, print media, and song. According to the *Recorder*, political poetry was one of the committee's weapons in its "island-wide fight for the vote." It distributed mimeographed flyers with limericks underscoring the issues of the franchise. Most of these poems were witty plays on nursery rhymes, such as the following: "Baa Baa little sheep, have you got a vote. No sir, No sir, none that you can note. There's one for the master, and one for his spouse, but none for the man who hasn't a house." The committee ran newspaper ads such as "Bermuda Sleeps! Awake to Your Political Rights. Demand the Vote. Be Free by Sixty Three."[56]

At the home of Coleridge Williams, CUAS recorded a Calypso song, "Hear the Talk in Town, the Government Turned the Franchise Down." Sung by artist Reuben McCoy, the song's political use contrasts the perception of Calypso as a non-political art form solely used to serve Bermuda's tourism industry. Using loudspeaker vans, CUAS broadcast "Hear the Talk" and other political messages through the streets. As occurred during the Theatre Boycott, CUAS effectively used speaker systems and microphone to galvanize support. These political chords broadcast beyond Bermuda's shores. For example, the Scottish newspaper the *Scotsman* decried such "quiet ferment" among Bermuda's "Negroes." For the paper, CUAS's vans patrolled the streets "drumming up support" for the franchise with "speeches and doggerel set to calypso music." Bermuda's Negroes, it argued, enjoyed a better standard of living then Negroes across the world. Yet since racialism had appeared in Bermuda's theater boycotts, blacks had been fighting for equal rights. With a new Africa rising in the east, African American protest to the west, and Caribbean struggles to their south, blacks in the colony of Bermuda were now reappraising their situation.[57]

During the public meetings, CUAS distributed a pamphlet to audience members titled "Bermuda and Its Social Problems." Written anonymously by a core of activists in the 1950s, the document decried the limited franchise, discrimination, and racial prejudice of Bermuda's white oligarchy, whom black Bermudians colloquially referred to as the Forty Thieves. The pamphlet chided Bermuda's housing shortages, racist tourist industry, inadequate and overcrowded schools, hand-to-mouth existences, disproportional rent relative to salaries, lack of government social security, poor prisons, substandard mental health institutions, delinquent children organizations, lack of parks, playgrounds, and cultural centers, and underdevelopment of Bermudian culture. It argued that films that depicted black people as being happy-go-lucky and dimwitted "spades, n-ggers, and darkies" buttressed Bermuda's myths of black inferiority.[58]

"Bermuda and Its Social Problems" laid out a program for addressing Bermuda's ills. This included complete universal adult suffrage and the criminalization of segregation, sexism, and racial discrimination. It argued that the power of Bermuda's "vested interests" was "founded on their wealth and not on their numbers." The document called for a "broad public movement" to eliminate discrimination and segregation, to extend the franchise, and establish wage, price, and rent legislation. According to Kamarakafego, the document was outlawed. However, at the time of CUAS, he received copies of it in a wrapped package.[59]

In early November, CUAS held its final indoor rally. Held at Hamilton Hall, this was the first time that Kamarakafego had to pay for a meeting space (the cost was £55). This was testimony to the community support of the franchise—all of the other venues were operated by black organizations. In contrast, the corporation of Hamilton, which was firmly controlled by Bermuda's "vested interests," owned the Hall.[60]

About 1,200 people, including the US Consul George Renchard, a member of Britain's colonial secretariat, and "a few plains clothes detectives" attended this meeting. Speakers included R. Williams, Russell Pearman, and Mansfield Brock. No white MCPs attended. Speaker L. Williams questioned the absence of white MCPs, particularly those who had been talking about marginality and illegitimacy. "I want to know where the bastards are tonight!" Robinson called for the whole population to march for universal suffrage.[61]

Williams's fluent forty-minute address garnered a roaring standing ovation from the audience. Kamarakafego spoke next: "What we mean by Universal Adult Suffrage now . . . is the right to vote tomorrow, or at the latest by the next General Election of 1963." The committee had requested that the governor hold an island-wide referendum on universal adult suffrage. Kamarakafego informed the audience that Britain's governor of Bermuda, Julian Gascoigne, had "flatly rejected" this demand and would not take any action while the legislature was considering the franchise.[62] During the meetings, Kamarakafego had stated that the talks were only the first of six steps in their agitation for the franchise, a comment that generated considerable noise in the media. Now, stated Kamarakafego, as a result of the intransigence of the governor, CUAS was being forced to engage in their "next step," which he refused to reveal publicly.[63]

In response to the governor's refusal to call a referendum, CUAS organized a mammoth rally in December. The event, to be held outdoors at the Devonshire Recreational field, promised to be "stimulating, educational and entertaining." Participants were asked to come to the Friday evening event dressed as if they were "going to a good night soccer game." They planned for motorcades to drive to the field from Somerset and St. George's. A dynamic mystery guest speaker was set to attend, but Kamarakafego refused to divulge the person's name. At the end of the meeting, Hill congratulated Kamarakafego on his "brilliant planning and foresight, and dynamic leadership in getting the movement started." One Solomon Kawaley hoped that the talks signified "the nucleus of United People's Party."[64]

Second-Class Government

Black political agency was of grave concern to Bermuda's white community. For example, the Church of England's *Churchman* claimed that it could not understand why the "race question" had entered the debate, as the issue of land qualifications had nothing to do with complexion. It called for a fine to be levied on those who raised the issue of race over the next year, as to do so was "a quirk, or obsession, or a neurosis."[65]

Governor Gascoigne felt it unwise to introduce universal adult suffrage for Bermuda's 1963 elections. Such was the case even as he admitted that the current franchise allowed "a lot of people—nearly all white—to vote in all of Bermuda's nine parishes." He feared that "on a wave of emotion a predominantly colored House would be elected," leaving Bermuda even more racially divided than it currently was. He further supposed that a "colored" majority with "leftist and do-gooder views" might be spendthrift and seriously harm the tourist industry. He expressed concern that Kamarakafego was going to petition the British secretary of state, who would receive pressure from Britain's Labor party to support CUAS's calls. He wrote Britain's undersecretary of state for the colonies, Sir Hilton Poynton, remarking that conservative whites regarded the plus vote as a safeguard. He did support extending the franchise to leaseholders.[66]

Colonial secretary J. W. Sykes disagreed with Gascoigne, arguing that the franchise would be "a potential source of agitation and unrest" until granted. He was inclined to believe that it would be better if "it were freely granted now by the dominant white oligarchy rather than being conceded reluctantly and under pressure later." He also did not share the view that it would lead to a "predominantly colored and irresponsible legislature." He was "favorably impressed by the standard of intelligence" of Bermuda's "colored community," in particular the younger and "better educated ones." Under universal adult suffrage, many "prominent and intelligent white leaders" would still be elected. Conversely, he felt that some of the "irresponsible crackpots" of both races would not be. But regardless of the governor's concerns of irresponsible government, universal franchise was accepted as "the basis of a democratic state." If it could be granted "freely to peoples in West and East Africa," it was difficult for him to see why Bermuda was not ready for it.[67]

The BCO sided with the governor. Ambler Thomas, assistant undersecretary of state for the colonies, felt that to extend the franchise would be putting "the cat among the pigeons." In response to Sykes, he conceded that universal adult suffrage had been granted in the West Indies and West Africa. However, in East and Central Africa, the Colonial Policy Committee steered development away from universal adult suffrage for Africans. This was their policy in places with multiracial problems—as Bermuda.[68]

Gascoigne's local Intelligence Committee placed CUAS under surveillance. The committee reported that attendance at the sixteen meetings ranged between one hundred and seven hundred people, noted Kamarakafego's bias toward the franchise, and detailed that hardcore of advocates for immediate universal suffrage attended each meeting.[69]

In October 1960, Gascoigne reported to London that "undoubtedly" the most important political events of recent months had been the political emergence of Kamarakafego and CUAS, whose public discussions were influencing the House's debates on the franchise. In a meeting with Secretary Sykes, Kamarakafego had stated that the main purpose of the talks was to "educate the people" to the limits of the constitution; the governor believed that they were having some success. Kamarakafego and his "group of coloreds" were attracting interest via the press and gaining larger attendances at their meetings. Along with their petition on universal suffrage, they were creating broad calls for extending the franchise. Kamarakafego ran the meetings sensibly, enlisting panels of five people or so drawn from various classes and ethnicities—"white, Portuguese, and colored."[70]

In October 1960, Gascoigne requested to see Kamarakafego, who reluctantly went. Seated across from each other at the governor's mansion, Gascoigne threw a copy of "Bermuda and Its Social Problems" onto the table. When the governor exclaimed, "You have been breaking the law by giving this book out in public," Kamarakafego remained silent. Gascoigne then demanded to know what the other five steps were. Kamarakafego again did not respond. Irate, Gascoigne remarked, "I think you are a damn silly fellow!" Kamarakafego pointed at his face, responding "I think you are a f—king a—!" The meeting was over. Gascoigne stormed out the room, his monocle swinging from side to side.[71]

Gascoigne's subsequent report about their ninety-minute meeting unflatteringly referred to Kamarakafego as an "unattractive little colored man." The governor remarked that he had spent a "checkered career" at South Carolina State College, North Carolina College, and, allegedly, American University. He seriously doubted that Kamarakafego had received a degree in biology. He stated that he had been teaching at Liberia's University of

Monrovia in return for a yearlong scholarship that allowed him to complete his degree through the University of America or Washington. He noted that he had been expelled from both SCSC and NCC for "taking a leading part in the activities against the white people on behalf of the NAACP."[72]

Gascoigne felt that the opinions on suffrage at the meetings and in the press ranged from "dire forecasts of utter disaster" to pronouncements that it was the key to making Bermuda a heaven. In the eyes of Kamarakafego, he argued, it was "essential to human dignity" and would make all "wonderful in the garden." Yet, he claimed, Kamarakafego knew nothing of the economics of the island, and that he made statements such as "We must have men like Mr. Tucker and Mr. Pearman and men like that to run the tourist industry for us." For Gascoigne, Kamarakafego was either being "ingenuous, ignorant, unscrupulous or a mixture of all three."[73]

The police monitored Kamarakafego's activities. One of his neighbors informed him that officers hid in the trees close to his residence. The press also described him as being many things—Communist, non-Bermudian, and an agitator who should return to Africa. The vested interests bought pressure on his parents; both were told to tell him to cease his activism with CUAS. But Kamarakafego was firmly backed by the black community, which occasionally gave him funds to live on as he could not find employment in the island. In November 1960, Kamarakafego's attempt to travel to New York to petition the UN Committee of Twenty-Four on Colonialism on Bermuda's behalf was foiled after he got into a physical scuffle at the airport when an immigration officer told him that they knew how to deal with n-ggers of his ilk in his town.[74]

Other members of CUAS were also harassed. In December, F. Maxwell was fired from her teaching job at the Central School. Her husband, Clifford Maxwell (also of the Progressive Group), was head of the Bermuda Union of Teachers. MCP Robinson questioned if she had been fired because of her political views.[75]

According to the governor's Intelligence Committee, Bermuda's white elites were seriously concerned about these discussions around the franchise. Led by Henry Tucker, the "leader of the conservative whites," this group of vested interests believed that the opening of the franchise was inevitable. However, they would only agree to immediate suffrage with a guarantee of white representation in the House of Assembly proportionate to the white population. Put another way, they would only concede to a black majority in the House if white minority representation was secured via amendments to Bermuda's constitution. This was "one of the boldest proposals for constitutional advancement" that the committee had seen in Bermuda.[76]

In his October 1960 intelligence report, Governor Gascoigne informed Britain's secretary of state for the colonies, Iain Macleod, of Kamarakafego's statement that if he rejected CUAS's request for a referendum, the group would shortly take other measures. This came on the heels of a visit to Bermuda by a security intelligence advisor, who advised the governor to concentrate his attention on matters of major political and security interest, namely CUAS. Gascoigne agreed. White conservative leaders Tucker, Cox, Gibbons, and Watlington met with him to discuss their concerns about the extension of the franchise. As stated, they sought to secure guarantees of white representation before they agreed to universal suffrage and called for the governor to arrange for London's secretary of state to receive them on the matter.[77]

Assistant Undersecretary Thomas advised Macleod to discourage the proposal for the delegation's visit. He thought that it would not be in the interests of white Bermudians to polarize "conservative whites and extremist coloreds" over the issue. Furthermore, the delegation's plan to create additional districts would expose them to the charge of gerrymandering in the interests of white representation. In response, Thomas traveled to Bermuda to meet with this collective. He also met with Kamarakafego, who advocated the immediate enactment of universal suffrage followed by a three-year period of civic education before the next election.[78]

Thomas attended a meeting at Bermuda's House of Assembly, noting that he felt as if he had "stepped straight into the eighteenth century" given its "low standard of debate." He found Watlington to be "muddled and rather stupid." More so, MCP Outerbridge informed him—incredibly—that he had heard that he was "going on to the n-ggers in the south."[79]

Thomas had dinner at the Coxes, where they were joined by Tucker, Watlington, Pearman, Gibbons and their wives. Flanked by the house's old furniture and the seal of the American confederacy, they discussed in length the "burning question" of the franchise. Tucker exclaimed that white opinion had hardened and was "not prepared to make any advance without safeguards for their rights." He favored a "package deal" that would accept universal adult suffrage, implement a "Cox scheme" of racially dividing the parishes, and guaranteeing extra white seats in constituencies where they might be left "seriously underrepresented." Thomas thought Tucker's suggestion that the British government should impose such a solution via an act of Parliament was inconceivable. Pearman felt that the Cox scheme would be seen for what it was, that universal franchise was bound to come, and that the white community should gradually make concessions "and seek to stave off black predominance as long as possible." Cox decried this "hope for the best" approach, arguing that they would lose an opportunity to introduce safeguards to white minority rule.[80]

British colonial officials shared an affinity with Bermuda's white elite, perhaps none more so than Gascoigne. His superiors were concerned with curbing the white nationalism of Bermuda's vested interests only to the extent that this would minimize and not further radical black protest. Macleod instructed Gascoigne to "keep up a head of steam sufficient to move the white population in the right direction fast enough to give reasonable satisfaction to the colored people and to maintain the position of the responsible and moderate colored leaders in command." He felt it important not to press the white population too hard and drive them into "stubborn opposition." This would be troublesome, as the "coloreds" would react by "throwing over their present leaders and turning to extreme, and possibly violent, expedients to gain their ends."[81]

The BCO recommended that a covert "memorandum on systems of minority representations adopted elsewhere" be used as "guidance" for Bermuda's government and for white Bermudians only—perhaps later this could be shared with black Bermudian leaders. Largely a blueprint for white minority rule, the lengthy memorandum detailed the franchise and minority representation across the Federation of Rhodesia and Nyasaland, Northern Rhodesia (whose voting system was also based on property qualifications), Uganda, Zanzibar, Somaliland, Tanganyika, and Kenya. It noted that the plans by Bermuda's white MCPs to geographically divide the electorate would essentially create one white and one black constituency in each parish. This would ensure that at least half the seats in the House were structurally secured for white representatives. But under universal adult suffrage, this could only occur through gross inequalities in the remapping of the electorate. Ironically, BCO officials claimed that the memorandum demonstrated that the global tide of constitutional and political racial equality implied that the days were past when even Britain's oldest colony could practice Canutism—holding back the tide of political change as eleventh-century King Canute allegedly claimed he could do.[82]

W. Tucker was one of the BCO's preferred moderate leaders. Over the summer, he attended a Commonwealth parliamentary conference in Uganda. In the aftermath of the meeting, he traveled to London to meet with Macleod. Meanwhile, the governor was sure that the petition for universal suffrage would be turned down in the House of Assembly.[83]

Tucker returned to Bermuda in February 1961. He had spent months away, on business and recovering from illness. Eva Hodgson argues that he had been politically transformed by his time in Africa. One could quibble over this, but Tucker had made some interesting observations while in Uganda and Kenya. He noted that Europeans controlled the civil service, Asians dominated economics, and the "African was on the bottom rung of the ladder." He also spoke of unrest, Jomo Kenyatta's incarceration, and white fears of Kenya's Land and Freedom Army, the Mau Mau. He also met numbers of people who were aware of Bermuda's racism.[84]

Kamarakafego left for Africa just as Tucker returned to the island. The *Recorder* reported his travels across the world, noting that he worked for Liberia's government. The political work of CUAS continued in his absence. For example, in February 1961, Rosalind Williams gave a thought-provoking address at the Allen Temple Youth Center. Sponsored by the Allen Temple's board of religious education, the church sought to hold monthly forums for free expressions of progressive ideas.[85]

The government moved to halt CUAS's momentum. Well into the summer of 1961, the House debated the election bill. Three CUAS members were invited to informally study the question of the franchise with H. Tucker and six other members of Parliament. In June 1961, this legislatively formalized Select Committee on Universal Adult Franchise voted in support of immediate suffrage.[86]

Gibbons challenged this vote and forwarded a minority report as "protection for the white people." This report proposed restricting voting to people over twenty-five years of age across thirty-eight electoral districts. This excluded more than five thousand Bermudians—namely black and between the ages of twenty and twenty-five. Yet Gibbons moved to give the vote to all British people in the colony regardless of their status as Bermudian, adding another 1,500 voters.[87]

The *Recorder* denounced this and encouraged its readers to examine Kenneth Robinson's thesis, "Class, Caste, and Education in Bermuda," which argued that Bermuda's Parliament had been a "pseudo-democracy" since 1620. According to Robinson, property requirements for voting had created a "hereditary class" that was convinced of its "destiny to govern."[88]

In a four-hour-long debate in June, W. Tucker reviewed the thirty-six-page bill for forty-five minutes. Rather lukewarmly, he suggested that "some good" had come out of Kamarakafego's agitation around CUAS. Bermuda needed to move with the times. There had been white fears about desegregation and the restaurant bill, and afterward, there would be fears about the integration of schools. Yet the people were happier after the theater boycotts. Bermudians were intelligent enough "not to upset a good pail of milk" and the government had to "maintain a state of happiness and do nothing" to upset the "economic equilibrium of the country." By lowering the voting age to twenty-one, this would increase the electorate from 5,500 to 23,000 people. Tucker said that he would be "the last person to want to see a black House of Assembly," for white representation was as essential to the country as was tourism. To deny the vote would drive "intellectuals into more radical camps." Dividing the island into racial camps would create large blocs of extremists. Furthermore, he argued that Gibbons's minority report "smacked of gerrymandering."[89]

In response, H. Tucker claimed that the minority report would not create racial cleavage. He denied that the report would create artificial districts or that it was gerrymandering. He was certain that racial feelings had improved immeasurably over the past three years. "Nothing would be worse for the white people than not to have reasonable representation in the House, and nothing would be worse for the colored people if we do not have such representation. . . . We must do it together."[90]

Black MCP E. T. Richards felt that racial harmony needed to be maintained, and the minority report called for just the opposite. The proposal to change the boundaries was a charged "political bomb . . . You are putting constitutional matters on a racial basis and creating black enclaves and a white one."[91]

Member of Colonial Parliament George Rattery was proud to have signed the majority report. He added that the committee's "about face" on the issue was the result of "a man named Roosevelt Browne," who publicly galvanized the issue and had since returned to teach in Africa. He thanked CUAS and Kamarakafego as being responsible for the storm that had blown onto the political aspects of the community.[92]

In July 1961, the House of Assembly moved to give the vote to British people in Bermuda (around 1,500 individuals) but still denied it to Bermudians under the age of twenty-five. W. Tucker saw this as a move to "offset" Bermuda's black majority. Francis questioned that if these Britishers were West Indians, would Gibbons, who proposed the bill, be supportive of extending the franchise to them.[93]

In an August letter to the Recorder, W. G. Brown argued that Kamarakafego's efforts around the suffrage had been admirable. However, he felt that CUAS lost its prestige when his associates compromised with the government. In June 1961, CUAS sponsored a public meeting to clarify why they had went behind the scenes" to talk with the "other side"—the "Henry Tucker Unofficial Franchise Committee." Held at Devonshire Recreational Club, this included L. Williams, Robinson, and Francis.[94]

L. Williams claimed that prior to the CUAS lectures, there had been much apathy in the black community regarding the extension of the franchise. Kamarakafego had attempted to get the support of all the black MCPs, but this had not happened. This was also a slight toward W. Tucker, who claimed that CUAS had "worked out a deal" with H. Tucker. Williams found it unfortunate that those who had not assisted were now "the most vociferous" in showing them "where and how we went wrong." He found it "sickening to hear people" claim that they were "striving for personal power and gain." Rather, they felt they now had "new power" to elect people. The committee had come to the conclusion that there were two courses of action left in October—to "either talk or walk down Front Street and crack heads."[95]

Bermuda's House of Assembly finally passed a version of the franchise bill in December 1962. It granted voting rights to all adults over twenty-five, and to property owners who held more than two thousand square feet of land, it granted an extra "plus" vote. According to the Intelligence Committee, this likely gave as many additional votes to black residents as it did to white. In addition, it increased the voting districts from thirty-six to thirty-eight.[96] The Forty Thieves had had their day.

The Committee for Universal Adult Suffrage reflected Bermuda's political and racial climate over the duration of the long sixties. It also showed how the questions of race, citizenship, segregation and decolonization were interlocked issues. Kamarakafego might have left Bermuda, but he faced these similar issues in Africa.

4

Kenya

All of Africa Is on Our Backs

Pharaoh Alymphaa Nkongo was in clear and present danger. It was March 1966, and the twenty-six-year-old could find no escape from the "unmentionable sufferings" of African people. To hear him tell it, the situation at the hands of the "white destroyers" had become unbearable. Internal conflict, external oppression, poverty, confusion, white violence, the shattering of black families, miscegenation, and "hypocritical black women" who helped whites by "draining the life-blood" of black people—all these things had brought him to the doorstep of hell. Nkongo felt the heat but remained a man of faith, even if misguided. Hedged between the nefarious exploits of "white-devils" and black ministers alike, the Howard University alumnus found it a miracle that he had "escaped the clutch of the white look." He had called on his ancestors to rescue his people from the "death chamber." His many libations had been spilled to the Gods of the Earth, the Seven Seas, tidal waves, oceans, lightning, thunder, fire, earthquakes, cyclones, hurricanes, tornadoes, storms, wildernesses, and reptiles. Now, from his apartment in Brooklyn, New York, he penned a prayer to former political prisoner and now president of Kenya, Jomo Kenyatta. On behalf of forty million people of African descent, Nkongo sought immediate help from his *Negos Negosti*. This Pharaoh of New York was on a mission to return and save his people. But he needed Kenyatta's assistance to travel back to Africa.[1]

Nkongo's prayer speaks to the myriad ways in which the black world engaged Africa in meaningful, fascinating, and personal ways. It is unclear if his letter and its attached photo reached his East African father, but it did reach Kwame Nkrumah in Conakry, Guinea. Still, it tugs at the political and cultural significance of Kenya for conceptions of the African Diaspora.

Kamarakafego's own experiences in Kenya between 1962 and 1967 unravel this idea further. While there, he witnessed the republic's emergence out of British colonialism. His time in East Africa greatly affected his ideas about decolonization, environmental justice, and black power. Across the campuses of the University of East Africa (UEA) in Tanganyika, Uganda, and Kenya, Kamarakafego launched his lifelong career of activism in sustainable development and appropriate technology. These experiences would fuel his transformation into a Black Power activist upon his return to the Americas.

Liberia

Kamarakafego returned to Liberia from Bermuda in February 1961. Now based in Monrovia, he served as a rural development volunteer. He continued his relationships with students from Cuttington, who were enraged about the recent assassination of Patrice Lumumba that January, and helped them organize a demonstration at the US embassy.[2]

Months later, Kamarakafego joined a small group of Liberians, Ghanaians, and Nigerians who were agitating against the economic exploitation of Liberia's working class, decrying the low wages, long hours, and terrible working conditions across the country. After starting as a protest among laborers in the rubber economy, the strike spread to longshoremen, dockworkers, and other sectors of the workforce. The group sought to stimulate industrial action through the unions, but they faced a major roadblock: the president-general of Liberia's Congress of Industrial Organizations (CIO) was President Tubman's son, William Tubman Jr. To circumvent this potential obstacle, the collective decided to take action while Tubman was out of the country celebrating his recent marriage in August 1961.[3]

On Monday, September, 11, over fifteen thousand workers launched a general strike in Monrovia, the largest in Liberia's history. Their demonstration began at Tubman Stadium. According to the *Liberian Age*, this was the city's "greatest display of labor force," and never before had the city been in "such an uproar." Marchers protested in the streets. All shops were closed, building projects ceased, and activities at the Free Port were put on standstill. Monday's usual calm had been purportedly interrupted by pandemonium. The "seemingly leaderless and not well organized" demonstration turned into a "mass stampede." Thousands advanced to the executive mansion. Bayonets drawn, mansion guards drove the crowd away, injuring a few strikers in the process. Two soldiers were disarmed and their rifles broken into pieces.[4]

Liberia's *Listener* reported that the labor outburst had "paralyzed all businesses, houses, industries and building projects" in Monrovia. Tubman unsuccessfully ordered the strikers to return to work; strikers were now protesting the arrests of two CIO officers, whose detentions only served to increase tensions. Management had refused to meet with labor leaders over disputes for some time. For example, workers had made appeals to Firestone to increase wages for months. The *Liberian Age* claimed that on the way to the stadium, "the power of mobocracy went to the heads of some and lawlessness became rampant." Workers were "dragged out of their working places, citizens . . . molested, private property molested," and taxi drivers forced out of their cars. The "mobocracy was traveling in its only direction—terror." To curtail such "hooliganism" and to protect public lives and private property, the government deployed soldiers and police to the stadium. Special service troops fired tear gas into the crowd.[5]

About one hundred workers at the magnificent Ducor Palace Hotel went on strike. Overlooking Monrovia Harbor, the Ducor was heralded as "Africa's Waldorf Astoria." Only months before it had hosted Tubman's Monrovia conference and was lauded as Africa's *Palais des Presidents* and the "landmark of African Unity and Solidarity." Its laborers, who put in ten to twelve hours a day for meagerly monthly stipends of between $25 and $30 while their white counterparts earned "soaring salaries," thought otherwise.[6] They demanded better wages and an end to the discriminatory practices inflicted upon them by white managers. Tubman called off the two-hour strike after "establishing a basis for negotiation."

One employee of the Liberian Mining Company complained of having made 49¢ an hour since 1951, though he taught foreigners to operate machinery. Workers at the United States Trading Company's garage, a subsidiary of Firestone and one of Liberia's largest wholesalers and importers, had already been on strike for about a week. The company distributed American vehicles, soft drinks, and even Liberia's staple food, rice; decades before, Du Bois had decried its connection to Firestone.[7] According to Martinus Johnson, "historians have yet to explain Firestone's role as the dominant employer for many decades, the degrading and inhumane lease agreement and its devastating effect on the lives of hundreds of thousands of Liberians who worked for twenty-five cents per day." For Johnson, such conditions hastened "the call for revolt." The US trading company ran two sections, one for native Liberians and one for Americans. The inequalities were visible in housing, where "white employees lived in beautiful red and white bungalows, while local employees lived in brick huts" with squatting toilet facilities.[8]

In response to the strike, the *Liberian Age* questioned if "communism

had arrived." At a labor conference, President Tubman listened to the grievances of the strikers and promised to establish an arbitration commission
through which labor could express its grievances for the best interests of "all
parties concerned." He urged the strikers to return to work, claiming that
their action was "an outrage of decency and disregard for law and order by
officers and members of the CIO." He stressed that the government would
not permit "lawless citizens" to do so.[9]

Power is predictable. As Tubman was promising labor a venue to express
its concerns, the legislature was simultaneously moving to restore an emergency power act targeting antigovernment conspiracies that would suspend
habeas corpus and allow arrests without warrants and detentions without
bail. The act also declared any activity organized by Liberians or foreign
nationals to disturb the socioeconomic stability of Liberia by influencing
or inciting strikes or violence to be a felony.[10] Tubman, meanwhile, promised his civil servants priority in raises over other groups of employees. At
a rally, he proclaimed that "95 percent of the population is in favor of our
policy" and stated that he would not be deterred by a "small dissident group
of ingrates and malcontents." Africa was facing a "day of resurrection," he
proclaimed, and he would not permit dissidents to alter Liberia's course.[11]
While assuring workers that their grievances would receive due consideration, Tubman ordered soldiers to arrest the leaders of the union, and he
armed his military machine with more troops and weapons.[12]

The year 1961 saw more strikes in Liberia than in all years prior. At least
thirteen persons were arrested in a supposed plot to overthrow the government and establish a communist regime. Tubman claimed that a communist "underground movement" was organizing the strikes. He declared
that Liberia had been infiltrated by "organized underground experimental
movements designed at subversion, sedition, and treason with intent to undermine and overthrow the Government by craft, artifice and subversive
anti-Liberian activities." He further asserted that the strikes were instigated
by "a small dissident group of malcontent citizens," including students and
foreigners.[13]

The government blamed the strike on two different plots. A Booker T.
Bracewell was found disguised as a woman and arrested. The Liberian Secret
Service claimed that he had tried to obtain $1 million from the Soviet Union
to establish a communist regime in Liberia. He was caught allegedly trying
to escape to Conakry, Guinea.[14] Another group was said to have been organized around a secretary of the Ghanaian embassy, J. A. Boateng. Boateng
had supposedly indoctrinated the group with the idea that "indigenous

tribes" were the "real owners of Liberia" and that the Americo-Liberians were the same as white colonialists and needed to be expelled. Boateng reportedly offered the group assistance in getting to Ghana, where they would be given passports to travel to Moscow to be trained in guerilla warfare. This was to enable them to return to Liberia to "stage a revolution to take over the government." Another Liberian, William Appleton, had already escaped to Moscow.[15]

Given Kamarakafego's account, it appears that he was affiliated with Boateng's group. He states that Tubman issued arrest warrants for the Liberians who had organized the strike, who were to be captured "dead or alive." As the strike organizers fled the country, Liberian soldiers fired upon them in pursuit. In one tense moment, a bullet grazed Kamarakafego. Traveling primarily by foot, they were certainly grateful for the two rides they were able to secure—one by truck and the other by donkey cart. Eventually, they reached neighboring Côte D'Ivoire.[16]

According to Gay, the group of Tanganyikan and Southern African students also fled Liberia through Guinea. They had come to the country to "find freedom, but had found instead a severely undeveloped neo-colonial Liberia run by an old-line capitalist president with strong American ties." Eventually, they went to various universities in the Soviet Union and neighboring satellite countries.[17]

Two weeks later, Kamarakafego's group reached Ghana. While there, Kwame Nkrumah hosted them at his residence. He had first met Nkrumah, along with journalist and author George Padmore, in 1953 at C. L. R. James's residence in London. In Ghana, he met political luminaries such as Du Bois, Shirley Graham Du Bois, and Nelson Mandela.[18] Following Nkrumah's advice, Kamarakafego continued on to Kenya.

The Black World Needs a Mau Mau

Gerald Horne's *Mau Mau in Harlem* demonstrates the significance of the Mau Mau (Kenyan Land and Freedom Army) uprisings in the conceptions of African American liberation struggles in the 1950. It also highlights the colonial violence that the British inflicted on Kenya's African population through violence, political imprisonment in its gulags.[19] The Mau Mau uprisings also inspired black political struggle in the Caribbean. For example, Horace Campbell's *Rasta and Resistance* argued that Jamaica's Rastafari community grew locks after seeing photographs of Mau Mau guerillas, such as Dedan Kimathi, donning them.[20]

Kenya and the Mau Mau were no strangers to Bermuda. In 1952, the *Bermuda Recorder* refused to believe that the Mau Mau was a "murderous anti-white African movement" and denounced their sensationalism in the Western press. The paper saw the stories as being "encouraged by white settlers" to "distort the true situation and smash any movement for African progress." The world, stated the *Recorder*, was "asked to believe that 30,000 Europeans" lived in terror. It questioned if the special powers against uprisings and the ruthless internment of the Mau Mau were necessary. For A. B. Place, editor of the *Recorder* and former member of the UNIA, the answer was not repression, but black self-government.[21]

The *Recorder* also noted that numbers of Kikuyu, who had initiated the Mau Mau movement, were arrested, while blacks in South Africa were being shot and killed by police. By late 1952, the Mau Mau uprising was front-page news, but the *Recorder*'s perception of the movement was less than flattering. One article characterized the movement as being fundamentally atavistic and a primeval, superstitious, barbaric cult that was not only anti-white but also anti-twentieth century and dedicated to destruction. Interestingly, the piece was actually written in defense of uprisings in South Africa in denouncing a report comparing such "riots" to the Mau Mau.[22]

In 1953, the *Recorder* printed an article about a thousand Kikuyu women who had petitioned Queen Elizabeth to preserve their rights as women and whose husbands and sons were now being arrested and placed in forced labor camps that had been set up to fight the Mau Mau rebellion, where police were brutalizing them. Such coverage continued into the 1960s. The *Recorder* specifically marked the activities of Thomas Mboya, Kenyatta, and the Kenyan African National Union (KANU). In April 1961, it reprinted a *New York Herald* article in which Mboya denounced Kenyatta's imprisonment, racism, and British colonialism.[23]

Bermuda also "consumed" Kenya and East Africa through movies like *Simba* (1954) and *Safari* (1956), which were based on the Mau Mau uprising. Both films featured the island's own Earl Cameron, who played a Kikuyu doctor (in *Simba*) and a Mau Mau leader (in *Safari*). The *Recorder* covered Cameron's role in *Simba*, which was filmed in Kenya, purportedly during an actual military operation against the Mau Mau. In the summer of 1957, *Safari* played in Bermuda's Island Theatre and New Opera House. In 1960, Cameron acted in the movie *Killers of Kilimanjaro*, set in Tanganyika, which was also shown in Bermuda.[24]

Beyond these media representations, Kamarakafego reflected a direct linkage between Bermuda, Kenya, and East Africa. Recall that it was

Nkrumah who had suggested that Kamarakafego head to East Africa to help the region in "its struggle against imperial powers."[25] Kenyatta arrived in Kenya in 1962, only a year after having been released from political imprisonment, where he then led KANU to victory in the national elections in 1963. Kenya proclaimed political independence months later.

According to Ruth Stutts Njiiri, Kenya's "freedom from colonialism brought forth the need for a new racial composition in Kenya's Civil Service." This process of decolonization was driven by what Kenyatta called an unapologetic process of Africanization. An extension of KANU's manifesto, this "vitally urgent" process involved the government's displacement of non-Kenyans by qualified Kenyans in the public service. This "great transformation" required the training of as many young Kenyans as possible.[26] As such, Kenya became a critical space from which national questions of indigenous education, decolonization, science and technology, pan-Africanism, sustainable development, and self-determination were being raised in Africa. The UEA played a central role in this process. Founded in 1962, the university was federated with satellite campuses across Kampala, Uganda (Makerere), Dar es Salaam, Tanzania (University College), Nairobi, and Kenya (University College).[27] The challenging work of these institutions included the production of schoolteachers across disciplines.

To be an educator of African descent in Kenya was to be a "sufferer." Such teachers had long launched complaints about teaching conditions. In the early 1950s, the British colonial administration government garnered 7.5 percent of the pay of African teachers to ostensibly provide them with housing. The Nyanza African Teachers Union challenged this, noting that this had a negative impact on African education. In urban areas, African teachers also paid rent to landlords in addition to the house rent. Such policies directly impacted local interest in becoming a teacher.[28]

In 1960, the United Nations Educational, Scientific, and Cultural Organization (UNESCO) produced a telling report on the teaching of science in Kenya. It noted that secondary education was compulsory until the age of fifteen for all European and Asian children (not African) in Nairobi and Mombasa. Kenya had different directors for African, Asian, and European education. Uganda's Makerere College was the only center that trained secondary-school science teachers. This program ended in 1963, and it was left to Kenya's Ministry of Education to train its science teachers. In 1962, the Ford Foundation agreed to fund short courses to upgrade teachers who were willing to teach science. Refresher courses in biology, chemistry, and physics were also being offered.[29]

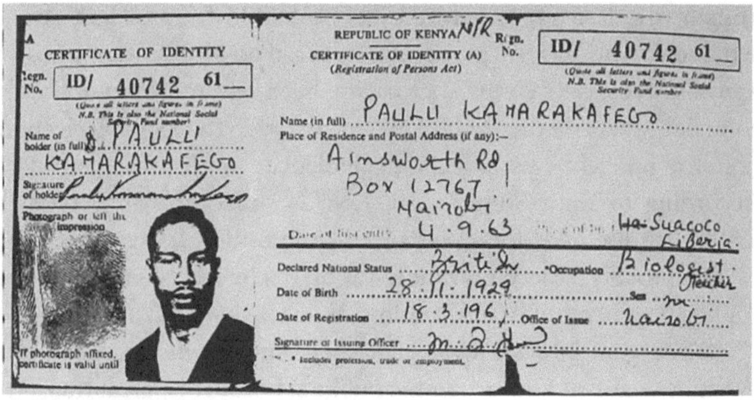
CERTIFICATE OF IDENTITY
Regn. No. ID/ 40742 61
Name of holder (in full) PAULU KAMARAKAFEGO
Signature of holder
Photograph or left thumb impression
If photograph affixed, certificate is valid until

REPUBLIC OF KENYA NFR
CERTIFICATE OF IDENTITY (A)
(Registration of Persons Act)
Regn. No. ID/ 40742 61
Name (in full) PAULU KAMARAKAFEGO
Place of Residence and Postal Address (if any):— Ainsworth Rd, Box 12767, Nairobi
4.9.63
Suacoco Liberia
Declared National Status British
Occupation Biologist. Teacher
Date of Birth 28.11.1929
Sex m
Date of Registration 18.3.196
Office of Issue Nairobi
Signature of Issuing Officer
* Includes profession, trade or employment.

FIGURE 6. Kenya ID card, 1963. Photo courtesy of Rronniba Kamarakafego.

It was also hoped that Nairobi's newly established Royal Polytechnic would be able, with Ford funding, to train students to be artisans and craftsmen through its applied science departments. The school was being supported by a special UN fund after UNESCO reported that the number of science teachers was inadequate. In European schools, there were thirty-seven graduates, in African schools, forty-two graduates, and in Arab and Asian schools, ninety-two graduates. The UNESCO report claimed that little had been done to "popularize science in Kenya," where "the desire for knowledge for its own sake was yet to be achieved." Still, the author claimed that science should not be presented as being alien to any culture and that it should have been projected as being "relevant to the life of the people" and "not as an example of twentieth century magic."[30] For someone like Kamarakafego, whose political and scientific pursuits were interlinked, all this made Kenya an ideal location in which to work.

True to form, Kamarakafego had friends in Kenya. This included Philip Githinji and Gikonyo Julius Kiano, whom he had met in California while he was studying at California Institute of Technology (CIT). Githinji earned a BS in mechanical engineering from CIT in 1961 and was Kenya's first indigenous professor in mechanical engineering. He also studied at Baltimore's historic black university, Morgan State University. Storied nationalist Julius Kiano was Kenya's first PhD—awarded in political science at the University of California, Berkeley in 1956—and was a lecturer at the University of Nairobi. He had also studied at Antioch College, where he dated Coretta Scott (later, Scott King).[31]

Kamarakafego was met at Nairobi's airport by Githinji, with whom he stayed for several weeks. The families and communities of these men introduced Kamarakafego to Nairobi's social, political, and cultural worlds.[32] This included a community of African American women like Catherine Mbathi, Ernestine Hammond (wife of Kiano), and Ruth Stutts Njiiri. Kamarakafego would later befriend the pioneer of African Diaspora studies, professor Joseph E. Harris, who codified the Diaspora as a field of study at Tanzania's First International Congress of African Historians Conference in 1965. In 1972, Harris was a visiting professor and head of the University of Nairobi's History Department. Here he taught classes on Africa and the African Diaspora, particularly in the Middle East. Kamarakafego met and spent a lot of time with Harris, his wife Rosemarie (Pressley), and their children in Kenya; the two became lifelong intellectual comrades. According to Harris, Kamarakafego expressed concern that US authorities had placed him under surveillance; this he sought to address by communicating with Harris through cryptic messages, secretive phone calls, and discreet meetings.[33]

Kamarakafego's hosts played key roles in Kenya's liberation struggle. Kiano was Kenya's first minister for commerce and industry. Along with Mboya and Oginga Odinga, he had formed and led the Kenyan Independence Movement (KANU's precursor). Radicalized by politicized Kenyan veterans of World War II, Kiano entered the United States committed to challenging colonialism. At the University of California, Berkeley, he studied comparative colonial liberation in Asia and Africa. To the chagrin of British administrators, in the United States, he was a vocal advocate of the Mau Mau uprisings. Kiano conducted political education across the country. For example, in 1958, he debated white political leader Michael Blundell in front of a rural audience of about 250 Kikuyu farm laborers. He informed them that Africans should lead Kenya, and he demanded universal suffrage for all individuals. He argued that the white-dominated highlands needed to be opened to Africans but not necessarily to Asians. Garnering much applause from his audience, he exclaimed in Kikuyu that Africans had a special right to land. Next to Kiano was his wife Ernestine Hammond Kiano.[34]

Hammond Kiano was a thriving entrepreneur. A former nurse in the United States and organizer of the YWCA, in 1964 she became the first Kenyan-based US citizen to renounce her citizenship. She and Kiano had married in the United States, and her time in Kenya was full of opportunities and challenges. Tall, brilliant, striking, and fearless, Hammond Kiano decried the racism and segregation that awaited them in Kenya. In 1963 she organized an "emancipation of Kenyan woman" seminar that called for increased political rights for Kenyan women. She bought 176 acres of land in Kabete as British settlers departed the country. She was also the business manager of the Competent Commercial College, which taught shorthand, typing, office administration, and English. Hammond Kiano then transformed the college into a private school.[35]

In 1961, Ralph Bunche visited Nairobi after attending Tanganyika's independence celebrations. According to the US officials based in Kenya, Bunche met with the Kianos and agreed to help raise funds for the college. By 1962, the school was renamed as the Ralph Bunche Academy. In 1962, the US Department of State reported that G. Kiano had left Kenya for New York as a guest of the American Society of African Culture. He was there to raise money for the academy.[36]

Ernestine Hammond's relationship with Kiano would not last. After a number of public personal clashes—one in which she hurled her shoe at Kiano when she found him having a drink with an attractive woman at the pristine Nairobi club—she was deported from Kenya. The *Kenya Gazette* simply read: "Ernestine Hammond Kiano had shown herself by act and speech to be disloyal and disaffected towards Kenya."[37]

In the summer of 1963, Kamarakafego passed through Bermuda with his wife, Betty Brown. According to the *Recorder*, he was "going by a tongue twisting African name that he did not want publicized." Kamarakafego informed the paper that he did not want to be and was no longer a Bermudian—"I am an African now." He told the *Recorder* that he was heading back to Kenya to take over as principal of the Ralph Bunche Academy. Like Hammond Kiano, he planned to give up his British passport when he got there. He was traveling with a reference letter from the aforementioned CIT professor of biology, Albert Tyler, addressed to Kiano at the Academy.[38] The letter primarily spoke to his research at CIT, stating that he had "learned many new chemical and biological techniques" for research in chemical biology. According to Tyler, this showed that Kamarakafego, whose work included protein synthesis and tumor development in the development of animal eggs, was capable of advanced scientific work. With all of Kamarakafego's potential, Tyler regretted that the couple had left California.[39]

Hammond and her close friend Stutts Njiiri were intricately involved in the Kenya airlifts program that brought Kenyan students to US colleges and universities between 1959 and 1961. Stutts Njiiri served as secretary to Reverend James Robinson, the founder of Operation Crossroads Africa. She was married to Kenyan political leader Kariuki Karanja Njiiri, who forfeited his parliamentary seat to allow Kenyatta to join Parliament. She then worked as Kenyatta's personal secretary throughout the 1960s. Her 1974 dissertation, "Kenya and North America: Educational Comparisons of their Black

Populations"—completed in the Education Department of the University of Massachusetts Amherst—was based partly on these experiences. Stutts Njiiri would later work for the Phelps-Stokes Foundation, where she directed its International Education Program.[40]

Stutts Njiiri invited Kamarakafego and Nairobi's small community of black repatriates to a meeting with Malcolm X on October 22, 1964. This was Omowale's second trip to Africa, and he was traveling through Nairobi on his return from making Hajj in Mecca, Saudi Arabia. In Nairobi, he also sat with Kenyatta and Vice President Oginga Odinga, whose international anti-imperialism caused grave concern among US officials.[41]

The group met at the home of Cathy Mbathi, African American wife of Titus Mbathi, permanent secretary of Kenya's Ministry of Economic Planning and Development. The Detroit-born Mbathi was a gospel singer who had been a featured artist with Mississippi's Cotton Blossom Singers. In Kenya, she produced a gospel album—*Cathy Mbathi Singing Your Favorite Negro Spirituals*, recorded in Kiswahili with Kenya's Rift Valley Academy Chorale. She also regularly performed in concerts and appeared on Nairobi television and radio.[42]

Kamarakafego had first met Malcolm X in California in the fall of 1958, when he attended one of the minister's speeches at Los Angeles City College. In 1957, Malcolm had founded the Nation of Islam's Temple No. 27 in Los Angeles. He frequently held meetings at Normandie Hall, some five miles from the City College. Kamarakafego went to the lecture with three of his City College friends who hailed from Kenya, Zaire, and Uganda. They briefly conversed with Malcolm X after his lecture. Kamarakafego informed Malcolm X of his studies at CIT. Malcolm X responded, "That's good. . . . We need science people." Kamarakafego was certainly inspired by his vote of confidence in his focus on science.[43]

Now in Kenya, Malcolm remembered Kamarakafego from this brief meeting, remarking kindly, "You are a far way from where you were." According to Kamarakafego, Malcolm X asked him if he wanted to address a Black Power conference that he was planning with Adam Clayton Powell. Kamarakafego declined, but the Black Power movement was certainly in his future.[44]

Malcolm X was keen to meet with Nairobi's black repatriate community. The US Central Intelligence Agency (CIA) monitored this assembly. Noting that there were about twelve persons in attendance, an agency report of the event corroborates Kamarakafego's accounts that Malcolm X discussed his current clashes with the Nation of Islam, his newly formed Organization of Afro-American Unity (OAAU), and the civil rights struggle. The CIA claimed that Malcolm X informed the group that he was trying to modify his public image as a "racist" and now maintained that white persons were not inherently evil. In addition, the OAAU would cease its public attacks on "moderate" black organizations in an effort to achieve greater racial unity. He rejected nonviolence and passive resistance as being ineffective and incapable of halting racial discrimination in the United States. As such, he advocated greater reliance on violence as a means of self-defense against white bigots.[45] Significantly, Malcolm X also encouraged African Americans in Nairobi to organize themselves "into a militant pressure group" and to speak out "publicly about the lack of real progress in eradicating prejudice" against African Americans. This, he argued, was because the United States could be embarrassed abroad for its racial troubles. Such embarrassment might lead to greater efforts to abolish racism domestically.[46]

The CIA shared this report with the FBI, which described Malcolm X as an anarchist who could not look beyond "the struggle and chaos that he desired." Malcolm reportedly said that all efforts to give blacks in the United States more access to courts were hypocritical and designed to give black people a false sense of progress. He spoke "charitably" of the violence used by younger blacks against police brutality. Similarly, he expressed great admiration for the Mau Mau uprisings, whose boldness he contrasted with the "feebleness" of black movements in South Africa. His affinity toward violence stemmed from his "deep feeling for the suffering and lack of human dignity of the twenty-two million Negroes in the United States."[47]

As Kamarakafego would recall, Malcolm X informed the group that he had left the Nation of Islam and that he no longer had infallible faith in Elijah Muhammad. Still, he maintained that Islam was a building force for African people. Malcolm X also talked about Rastafari repatriation to Africa. One version of the CIA report states that he *rejoiced* over the movement; another version asserts that he *rejected* it. The report also claimed that he challenged the idea of partitioning America into white and black regions. His purpose for the trip was to seek the support of African leaders, but he insisted that African Americans "had become completely different from Africans in Africa" and needed to be judged in isolation.[48] Problems aside, this report speaks to the international surveillance of Malcolm X and black freedom movements.

Malcolm X's speeches upon his return to the United States speak to his experiences in Kenya. In December 1964, he introduced Fannie Lou Hamer to a New York audience. He began by praising the Student Nonviolent Coordinating Committee's (SNCC) Freedom Singers performance of the song "Oginga Odinga." He also described Kenyatta, Odinga, and the Mau Mau as perhaps being the "greatest African patriots and freedom fighters that that continent" would ever know.[49]

He continued:

> You and I can best learn how to get real freedom by studying how Kenyatta brought it to his people in Kenya, and how Odinga helped him, and the excellent job that was done by the Mau Mau freedom fighters. In fact, that's what we need in Mississippi. In Mississippi we need a Mau Mau. In Alabama we need a Mau Mau. In Georgia we need a Mau Mau. Right here in Harlem, in New York City, we need a Mau Mau.[50]

These kinds of political experiences in East Africa were transformative for Kamarakafego. While witnessing Kenya's mass movement for independence, he also experienced the lingering legacies of colonialism. Being harassed by white and black policemen while smelling flowers at the elite Nairobi club reminded him of Bermuda's own segregated yacht club. Githinji then suggested he get an identity card, including a photograph and fingerprint; this reminded him of South Africa's ID passes for blacks.[51]

Kamarakafego was moved by how closely racism in Kenya resembled his experiences in Bermuda. Whites represented less than 1 percent of Kenya's population but had over eight secondary schools; Kenyans had access to only three.[52] He sought to make change in Kenya by pushing for racial change and self-determination through its education system.

In Kenya, Kamarakafego's work-related activities were multifaceted. He led annual orientation programs for Peace Corps science teachers, and he organized yearly track meets for the Kenya Secondary School Sports Association, taught science part-time in secondary schools, and organized annual science exhibitions. When Kamarakafego first arrived in Kenya, Githinji was a lecture in thermodynamics at the University of Nairobi. Through Githinji's advice, Kamarakafego applied for and received a three-year lectureship in biological science and ecology there. As part of the ecology program, he conducted research in one of Kenya's game parks.[53]

At UEA, Kamarakafego designed and introduced a PhD program in ecology. While there, he also became involved in UNESCO's efforts to establish an East African environment program. Kamarakafego became a UN consultant on the environment, a hat he would wear in various capacities throughout the rest of his life.[54]

Kamarakafego joined the Curriculum Development Center for Science

Teaching, which was formed in 1961. He joined a team of science teachers who were rewriting O and A levels syllabi in physics, chemistry, and biology for East African secondary schools. These curricula had been decidedly colonial. Through the aforementioned Ford Foundation program, he organized ecological workshops and refresher courses for science teachers. He also taught biology, created teaching aids, apparatus, and instructional materials, and rewrote a biology syllabus for a new East African certificate of education.[55]

In 1966, the Center for Science combined with its English and mathematics counterparts to create a Curriculum Development and Research Center. In 1966, these merged into the Kenya Institute of Education, which, according to Stutts Njiiri, developed new methodologies for teaching (such as in mathematics) while also advising the government on Africanizing the curriculum. This was critical, as colonial education had not focused on arts, history, music, and science for African students. There remained a heavy demand in Kenya for engineers, surveyors, teachers, and technicians.[56]

Just after independence, the Kenya Education Committee produced a critical report on education. Led by Simeon H. Ominde, the committee was charged with developing a curriculum that "appropriately expressed the aspirations and cultural values of an independent African country." It pushed for policies that would appraise historical facts and history from an African perspective. Essentially, it was to find a balance in African education between modernization and "the assertion of the African character." Its curriculum was also to be based on national unity instead of separation and segregation—a far cry from colonial policies that had distinct tracks for African, Asian, Arab, and European students.[57]

Kamarakafego became involved in this process. In 1966, he advised Kenya's minister of education, Jeremiah J. M. Nyagah, in the government's efforts to develop its public education system. A critical issue was that the three segregated secondary schools that were preserved for black Kenyans could not absorb the thousands of African children who graduated from primary schools. Kamarakafego's recommendations included allowing Kenyans into all schools and to build new high schools. He pushed Nyagah to focus specifically on the production of black science teachers, prodding him with the following question: What would be the logic of Kenya gaining independence and inviting the colonial master back to run the country" because it had no "scientific technocrats?" He suggested that Kenya establish a teacher's science college.[58]

This last effort was not in vain. In 1966, Kenya and Sweden (through a Swedish foreign aid program, the International Development Authority) built the tuition-free Kenya Science Teachers College. Kenyatta laid the foundation stone of the college, which was to "train men and women—irrespective of race, color and creed—as secondary school teachers in science subjects," particularly in math, physics, chemistry, biology, and geography. The college's initial teachers were all Swedish, with the idea that it would eventually transition to being run by Kenyan faculty.[59]

Kamarakafego's technological expertise blossomed in Kenya. While lecturing at UEA, he completed his manual on building water tanks using bamboo and cement. The tanks were designed to be constructed in three days. Kamarakafego's main aim was to assist as many people as possible—particularly those living in rural areas—to gain reserves of fresh water. The manual's second edition was published in various languages through the UN Development Program and eventually globally distributed free of charge.[60]

Kamarakafego understood access to fresh water as being essential to life, environment, personal usage, and development. He had begun development of the water-tank design while in Liberia at Cuttington. For him, the harnessing of fresh water was connected to questions of black self-determination. Kamarakafego's sustainable water-tank design spread across the Global South through reprints of the manual and rural technology workshops that he launched across the Americas, Asia, and the Pacific. He argued that "the young people and particularly women throughout the world in rural areas of Africa, Asia, South America, the Pacific, are usually the fetchers and carriers of water." As such, he stressed that women should always be involved in rural technology workshops.[61]

Back to Bermuda

During Kamarakafego's time in Kenya, the era of party politics had been born in Bermuda. In 1963 the Progressive Labor Party (PLP) was founded as the mainstream embodiment of the political desires of the black working class. In response, Henry Tucker and Bermuda's white oligarchy formed the United Bermuda Party (UBP) in 1964 to protect its interests.[62]

The soon-to-be leader of the PLP was Kamarakafego's cousin, Lois Browne-Evans. Browne-Evans's interests in African freedom were self-evident. In 1963, she had traveled to Nigeria to celebrate its independence. Kamarakafego visited her in London for a Nigerian Independence Day party. In the summer of 1967, Kamarakafego received calls from Browne-Evans and PLP stalwart architect Wilfred Allen encouraging him to return to Bermuda to assist the party in the upcoming 1968 elections—the first to be held in Bermuda based on universal adult suffrage. After some thought, he agreed to do so. Browne reached Bermuda in August 1967.[63] Shortly after his arrival, he informed the *Bermuda Recorder* that he was ready to stand for the PLP. When asked about his political philosophy since his time in Africa, Kamarakafego stated that he believed that Bermudians needed to work together for the benefit of Bermudians. Bermuda had always had a "superficial harmony," which he called crocodile grinning and "show-case integrating."[64]

In September, Kamarakafego was elected as a branch leader of the PLP. In October, the PLP announced that he had been appointed as organizer of the party, suggesting that he was responsible for the creation of universal adult suffrage in the island. He became heavily involved in the PLP's grassroots election campaign. In September, he spoke at an outdoor rally. There he commented that future rallies would deal with the issue of victimization, particularly around the government's attacks on PLP supporters. This rally, he asserted, would take place "within earshot of the Government House." Unfortunately, Governor Martonmere would be away; had he stayed, Kamarakafego promised, "he would hear a thing or two."[65]

The PLP's 1967 political platform included full political independence, economic empowerment for the people of Bermuda, and a free medical and healthcare scheme. In February 1968, Kamarakafego formed the PLP Youth Wing in an effort to further politicize Bermuda's radicalized black youth. In this era, these youth were beginning to challenge racism, police brutality, and colonialism through the language and aesthetics of the Black Power movement. In April 1968, after being racially discriminated against and denied entry into a fair, youths from the "Back-of-Town" area of the capital city, Hamilton, spontaneously clashed with the majority British Police Force. This swiftly transformed into a weekend-long organized uprising through urban guerilla warfare and arson attacks on white establishments. The British government sent a company of 180 Royal Inniskilling Fusiliers to suppress the rebellion, marking the first in a number of occasions between 1968 and 1977 when British troops were sent to suppress Black Power–related incidents. Even as Kamarakafego and Browne-Evans took to the streets in an effort to calm things down, the PLP was blamed for uprisings.[66]

Kamarakafego convinced some of these "Back-of-Town" youth to join the PLP Youth Wing. While the party did not win the May 1968 elections, he was elected as a member of Parliament (MP) in the constituency of Pembroke East. Along with PLP leaders Arthur Hodgson, Elvina Warner, and

Freddy Wade, he actively supported Black Power's growth in the island. In 1967, PLP leaders attended the Second National Black Power Conference in Newark, New Jersey.[67]

In 1968, Kamarakafego attended the Third National Black Power Conference in Philadelphia, whose organizers included Chuck Stone and brothers Benjamin and Nathan Wright. Malcolm X had previously informed these men about Kamarakafego's work in Kenya, which prompted them to ask Kamarakafego to address the conference. He was introduced by Zambia's Isaac Monday as "Theodore Brown," an organizer for Bermuda's all-black PLP. Stating that the British government had sent troops to Bermuda during the recent election, Monday noted that he was fighting against white minority rule in the island.[68]

Kamarakafego was not one for speeches. He greeted the audience with "a salaam alaikum," stating that he did not like to talk much but liked to "do things." He brought greetings from the black people of Bermuda, remarking that a Black Power conference would be held in the island in 1970. Kamarakafego stated that such talks were necessary to help black people across the world become aware of their similar problems with white oppression. He also warned that "whether whites were communists, capitalists, or other oppressors," whenever they gave black people freedom they always "left [behind] some people" who would continue to enslave blacks "to perpetuate the white man's way." He was also placed on the advisory board for a 1969 national conference on Black Power. According to both the British Foreign and Commonwealth Office (FCO) and the FBI, "extremists" at the conference gave instructions in urban guerilla tactics, the manufacture of explosives, incendiary bombs, and booby traps." Officials of the FCO also noted that Kamarakafego was nominated to be the Caribbean's regional Black Power organizer.[69]

In January 1969, National Black Power Conference leaders announced that Kamarakafego would host the first international Black Power conference in Bermuda that following summer. In a lengthy press conference, Kamarakafego informed the *Bermuda Recorder* and the *Royal Gazette* that he was a member of the committee and that the conference would include Black Power representatives from across the Atlantic. In Bermuda, he stressed, Black Power was an anti-colonial movement. Bermuda could not remain a colony forever under white domination or British exploitation; Blacks in Bermuda had a right to self-determination. He drew on his experience in East Africa, stating how in Kenya it had taken the Mau Mau uprisings to force the colonial whites to recognize that Africans meant that they intended to rule themselves. In Detroit, Watts, Newark, and Harlem, it took "Burn, Baby, Burn." What would it take in Bermuda?[70]

Kamarakafego was publicly and politically harassed for his Black Power advocacy. At Bermuda's annual Speaker's Dinner, for example, an event that included an address by Bermuda's governor, Kamarakafego wore the gown of a Liberian Kpelle paramount chief rather than the traditional tuxedo. A black UBP MCP, Quinton Edness, asked him where he was going in his pajamas. Kamarakafego's retort has provided the title for this chapter: "Let me tell you something, all of Africa is on my back and all of you should be f—king lucky that I wore this to a dumb a— event like this."[71]

As evidenced in my book *Black Power in Bermuda*, the British, Bermudian, Canadian, and US governments collaborated in an attempt to sabotage the Bermuda conference. The US State Department noted that Kamarakafego's had a large following among Bermuda's black youth and that he was "actively recruiting" black radicals from the United States.[72] The FCO and its Information and Research Department (IRD) sought information from Britain's MI5 and MI6 and US officials about "Black Power organizations, advocates, and activities in the Caribbean and US." With the assistance of the FBI, Bermuda created a stop list of black radicals to prevent them from entering Bermuda.[73]

Lord Malcom Shepherd, British minister of state for foreign and Commonwealth affairs, informed the British governor of Bermuda, Lord Martonmere, that the British Defense Department would happily "arrange" for a vessel to have "engine trouble" off Bermuda during the conference. British troops were stationed on the island, and the Canadian government placed two warships in Bermuda's waters during the talks. News of this spread far and wide; for example, Russia's daily newspaper *Izvestia* noted that the British frigate was there to patrol the conference.[74]

At the behest of the FCO, the UBP implemented a Race Relations Act to attack the Black Power conference. During the debate over the bill, Kamarakafego was suspended from Parliament. While speaking in defense of the conference, UBP MPs disrespectfully told him to "shut up and sit down." Kamarakafego refused to be silenced, retorting, "Which one of you bastards is going to sit me down?" He looked at Henry Tucker, who stood over six feet tall, and said, "Are you going to sit me down, an old shriveled up bastard like you?" As he recalled:

When [Henry Tucker] . . . looked challengingly at me, I put my fist in his face and he ducked under the desk. Moving from desk to desk, I asked several people the same question. No one said anything. Then I went to where the mace was and knocked it off the desk.[75]

When recalling this story in 2002 to students at Bermuda's Cedarbridge Academy, Kamarakafego added that Tucker's size meant little to him. "You could be as big as a house, it makes no matter to me." The Speaker of the House asked him to leave. On his way out, another white MP said, "Look at him, that arrogant thing swearing in the Queen's House." Kamarakafego then exclaimed, "F*** the Queen, that syphilitic whore!"[76]

Held July 10–13, the Bermuda conference aimed to formally launch the Black Power movement in the Caribbean. It also sought "to help Black people achieve political, economic, educational, and cultural Black power" across the world. After canvassing across seventeen countries for the talks, Kamarakafego expected the international conference to attract participants from the Caribbean, the United States, Canada, the United Kingdom, and elsewhere.[77]

The talks also demonstrated the genealogical intersections between the Black Power and Pan African Movements. Veteran pan-Africanists like C.L.R. James, Queen Mother Audley Moore, and Kwame Nkrumah supported the talks. Moore led a workshop on Black women. Despite the implementation of immigration restrictions to sabotage the conference, well-known activists like Acklyn Lynch, Florence Kennedy, Fernando Henriques, and Yosef Ben-Jochannan managed to participate.[78]

In front of a crowd of some two thousand at the Pembroke Hamilton Club's football stadium, James opened the conference with a ringing speech. James placed Black Power within an internationalist framework of Global South struggle. He contextualized the Movement within a global, masculinist framework of a "mighty struggle against the forces of American imperialism" and the revolutionary world of Asia's Vietnam, the Caribbean's Cuba, and Africa's Tanzania. James asserted that he was not born into the world of Black Power. Rather, he came of age in the days when leaders like Lenin, Mao Zedong, Mahatma Gandhi, George Padmore, and Kwame Nkrumah forced the militaries of imperialism into retreat. He saw Black Power as being marked by the significance of political thinkers such as Fidel Castro and Julius Nyerere, whose political ideas were "second to none." [79]

For James, Black Power was one of the greatest political slogans of the twentieth century; he asked his audience not to misunderstand it. Defined by Kwame Ture in 1966, Black Power was intricately linked to the struggles of the Global South and meant the complete overthrow of the global system of capitalism. Embodied in the slogan, he asserted, were the past two hundred years of insurgency against capitalism, slavery, and racism.[80]

Black Power meant power to the people, to *black* people. In the Caribbean, the movement was marked by demographics of a black majority. Yet Black Power was not only a reference to skin color; several black leaders in the Caribbean and Africa were hostile to the concept because it meant power to *the people*. Even more significantly, because colonialism had increased in strength since political independence in the Caribbean, Black Power *had* to be anti-colonial.[81]

James saw black people as being in the forefront of the fight against imperialism. He challenged black youth to not "play with revolution," arguing that mobilization of the masses was the only way to successfully resist imperial intervention after a revolution. He told his young audience that they should be prepared to "speak to the people and then go out and fight the police," as these were revolutionary and political acts.[82] Demonstrating Black Power's relevance to the Global South were the many communications sent to Kamarakafego from groups across the globe, including the Palestinian Liberation Organization, North Korean organizations, the North Vietnamese, the Japanese Red Army, the United States Black Student Association, Guyana's People's Progressive Party, the United States Black Panther Party, the South African National Liberation Front, the Cuban Revolutionary Committee, and Oceanic struggles in Tahiti, New Caledonia, and the Solomon Islands further.[83] Haitian exiles in Montreal denounced Duvalier and his Tontons Macoutes as being "enemies of the Haitian Revolution." They called for the release of Haitian political prisoners, chastising Duvalier as a supporter of American imperialism even though he proclaimed being a champion of black people. Similarly, the Ethiopian Student Association in North America and World-Wide Union of Ethiopian Students referenced to the "persecution of Ethiopian students."[84] These critiques of class and imperialism were particularly important in the context of the Caribbean and Africa.

Kwame Ture wrote in support of the conference. Quoting Nkrumah, he stated that Black Power was the "struggle for the possession of economic, cultural, social and political power which [black people] in common with the oppressed of the earth" needed to have to "overthrow the oppressor." This could only be achieved through pan-Africanism.[85]

Ture sent the cable from Conakry, Guinea, where he was studying with Nkrumah himself. "Osagyefo" also telegrammed "revolutionary greetings" to Bermuda. He informed the brothers, sisters, and comrades of the Black

Power movement that Bermuda's "historic Black Power meeting" was part of "the world rebellion" of the "exploited against the exploiter" across Africa, the Americas, and "wherever Africans and people of African descent" lived. Black Power's fight was against imperialism, international and domestic (neo)colonialism, and racism, against which blacks should unify in armed struggle. For Nkrumah, the total "unification of Mother Africa" was the prerequisite to black survival.[86] Black Power activists in Bermuda agreed.

Bermuda's Black Beret Cadre

The Bermuda conference signified the emergence of Black Power in Bermuda and the broader Caribbean. It was officially sponsored by the PLP's Youth Wing, which implemented some of the resolutions of the conference. In its aftermath, Youth Wingers formed the Black Beret Cadre, which quickly established itself as Bermuda's vanguard of Black Power.[87]

Led by its chief of staff, John Hilton Bassett Jr., the cadre called for a total revolution in the island, advocating revolution by any means necessary, including armed struggle if called for—"Peace if possible, compromise never, freedom by any means necessary."[88] Through political education, its Mark Albouy [Malcolm X] Liberation school, survival programs, publications, demonstrations, rallies, and low-scale urban guerrilla warfare, Berets clashed with the island's security forces. The group formed relationships with the US Black Panther Party.[89]

The Cadre's 1970 manifesto called for a revolution to end white supremacy, colonialism, and oppression, recognizing that colonialism was designed to benefit the Forty Thieves and Britain, not the black masses of the island. Based on the study of revolutionaries and black political thinkers such as Malcolm X, Huey P. Newton, Frantz Fanon, Lerone Bennett, Eldridge Cleaver, and Bermuda's Eva Hodgson, the manifesto argued that black women were historically revolutionaries, as was evidenced by the activism of such notable figures as Sally Bassett, Harriet Tubman, Kathleen Cleaver, Angela Davis, and Palestinian Leila Khaled. As such, the vanguard needed to combat male chauvinism and male superiority. It called for the development of revolutionary culture through art and literature and the mobilization of the community. It also expressed support for Third World (colonized) struggles across Latin America, Africa, Babylon (America), and Asia.[90]

The Cadre's biweekly newspaper, the *Black Beret*, was replete with political art, essays, book reviews, poetry, news, and political commentary.

Labeled the Voice of the Revolutionaries (People), the publication, which was the Cadre's primary point of contact with Bermuda's black community, included poetry and letters of students in the group's Liberation school.

As he had done for the Progressive Labor Party Youth Wing, Kamarakafego was an advisor to the Cadre. He attended meetings, participated in Beret functions, and critically encouraged the group. He also pushed for the Berets to make international connections. In February 1970, for example, he attended a Cadre seminar on community education and communication. Additionally, in April 1970, he co-organized a Black People's movement rally that included some thirty students from the Cadre's Liberation school. Kamarakafego had concerns about the tactics of the Berets. He felt that they should be more discreet and that they needed to avoid publicizing their plans, as this would alert the authorities. His approach was "If you are going to do something, just do it."[91]

Kamarakafego also reminded the group that geographically and politically, Bermuda was *not* Cuba—it did not possess a mountainous landscape like Cuba's Sierra Maestra from which to successfully wage a guerilla war. He suggested that they build a wider political base among Bermuda's masses (as James had suggested) as opposed to taking direct military action against the establishment.[92] But despite these tactical disagreements, he formed long-lasting relationships with Berets, among whom were Michelle Khaldun and Jeanna Knight, who, as high schools students, were both PLP Youth Wingers. At age fourteen, Knight attended the Bermuda conference with her labor-activist uncle, George Desilva. She was moved by veteran activists like Queen Mother Moore as well as by younger visitors. The talks triggered her political self-awareness. She saw Moore speak several times in New York, where she visited Black Power organizations such as the East. Knight was one of a few black high school students at Mt. Saint Agnes Academy—a private, Catholic, and very much segregated school. Having first met Kamarakafego at the conference, she respected him for never biting his tongue. She soon joined the PLP Youth Wing and learned much from Kamarakafego's leadership style as a "quiet giant." He never diminished them as youth, but rather engaged and encouraged them to take on leadership roles. In April 1970, she went with Kamarakafego as part of a Youth Wing delegation to meet with Bermuda governor Martonmere. Driving his green sports car, he picked her up from her school.[93] The group raised a number of concerns with the governor, who concluded that their platform contained "some really dangerous stuff." He also claimed that Knight remarked, "We don't want trouble and bombings, but if we want to get something done, what else can we do?[94]

In 1970, the CIA noted that the Berets blew up a church and set fire to government buildings in the 1970 uprisings. The agency was also aware that Beret Ottiwell Simmons Jr. (Chaka) was in communication with Sam Napier, who organized the national distribution of the Panther paper. Napier was assassinated in 1971.[95]

In April 1970, British FCO officials declared Black Power in Bermuda to be a rapidly expanding and dangerous movement. They argued that while Black Power could not be "eradicated," "its evil influences" needed to be "retarded." The FCOs Intelligence Committee led the attack on Black Power. It included Bermuda's attorney general, British police commissioner George Duckett, the head of Special Branch, a Bermuda regiment official, an army intelligence officer, UBP and government leader of Bermuda Tucker, Governor Martonmere, and the head of the FCO's West Indian Department, A. J. Fairclough.[96] Their key target was the Cadre, which they attacked via harassment, police brutality, infiltration, surveillance, and an extensive propaganda campaign.

The FCO's IRD mounted a "sustained counter propaganda" campaign against the cadre. E. Wynne, an IRD officer, reported that the Cadre had triggered a daily philosophy of "permanent protest" among Bermuda's black youth. He noted that the UBP refused to address genuine issues affecting blacks like police harassment, racism, and economic discrimination. Still he called for the committee to use propaganda to isolate the Cadre from the black community.[97]

By June 1970, Bermuda's Special Branch claimed to have infiltrated the Cadre. They knew that the Berets were planning a public burning of the British flag. In April, the FCO stationed a frigate in Bermuda in anticipation of a demonstration planned by Kamarakafego and the Berets in response to the trial of H. Rap Brown.[98]

On August 8, 1970, Berets burned the Union Jack on the steps of Hamilton's City Hall. This took place during a rally on a crowded Saturday afternoon. They burned the flag in indignation at Britain's proposed sale of arms to South Africa, to commemorate the 1960 Sharpeville Massacre, and to protest the connections between South African apartheid and colonialism in Bermuda. The Cadre released a statement to the *Bermuda Recorder*, demanding that Bermuda's government denounce these arms sales as these weapons could be used to further repress black southern Africans. "Should the Government fail to do this," they warned, "we will be relentless in our efforts to see that the Government receives a political consequence."[99]

Expecting to be attacked by the police, the Berets had stockpiled weapons, including wooden handles from shovels, axes, and tools; these were transported by car to the City Hall parking lot, where the car was parked and the weapons then hidden under the car. The plan was that if the police approached, the driver would pull away, exposing the hidden cache. The Berets were to then move to the spot, arm themselves, and fight back. [100]

The police, however, had plans of their own. In anticipation of the demonstration, Bermuda's government passed an Offensive Behavior Bill. Bassett was targeted; though he did not burn the flag, he was later arrested, tried, and imprisoned for offensive behavior. The Crown's key witness was a British police officer who stated that he had not seen Bassett burn the flag but would have been "offended" if he had. The months leading up to Bassett's trial were replete with clashes with police and arson attacks. Bassett was sentenced to six months imprisonment.[101]

After the Cadre denounced Bassett's arrest through the *Beret*, members were charged with breaking the Prohibited Publications and Seditious Intentions Bills that had been recently implemented specifically to attack the group. Jamaican lawyer and senator Dudley Thompson defended Bassett in court. For the veteran pan-Africanist, Bermuda's promising black youth were frustrated with the island, which remained "socially and politically" in the eighteenth century.[102]

Dressed in all black, Knight was at the flag-burning protest. Police detectives later showed up at her school, demanding to speak with her about the event. Knight had become an outspoken and significant Beret organizer; she spoke at one of the cadre's first public rallies, held in Victoria Park. Along with Khaldun, Jennifer Smith, Wanda Perinchief, and Beverly Lottimore, she established and coordinated the Liberation School. Held on Saturdays, the school hosted at least twelve young activists weekly. The group taught them liberation songs and black history and helped them with their homework. Occasionally, they sang their songs during group walks throughout Hamilton.[103]

The FCO used an ostensibly non-partisan and community-membered Race Relations Council to target the Cadre. In the spring of 1971, Tucker requested that the chair of the council, Reverend George Buchanan, meet with himself and Bermuda's attorney general to discuss the appointment of an ombudsman. But during the meeting, Tucker and the attorney general asked Buchanan to have the council investigate and prepare papers on the

Cadre, its manifesto, the Liberation School, and the PLP's newsletter, *Party Line*.[104]

The council discussed the manifesto for months, concluding that the Berets falsely imagined they were in a struggle against colonialism. It also claimed that the manifesto was factually inaccurate, had more in common with African American freedom struggles, was thus not relative to Bermuda, and was likely written by outside persons. It argued that the manifesto ideologically bordered on Communism and used race to appeal to the "unenlightened masses." In a report to Tucker, the council deprecated the document's supposed "apartheid philosophy." The government had seemingly "overestimated the intelligence of the masses," and needed to "combat the Berets."[105]

Over the entire year of 1971, the council had not made any progress in its moves against the Liberation School; Knight skillfully kept the council at bay. Still, in August, the council advised Tucker not to take any action against the Cadre, as it felt that they were on the way to being "converted" via regular and fruitful meetings. Council members claimed to have gained the confidence of the Cadre and would be "damned as government stooges and narcs" if the group were attacked. In December, the council suggested that the government use its official resources to investigative the group, as opposed to using the council for that purpose. Buchanan still advised against action that might drive the Berets further underground.[106]

In August, Buchanan felt that the Berets were being influenced by Black Panthers in Britain and the United States, who were prioritizing community programs over revolutionary rhetoric. Yet the council was concerned that with the recent release of Bassett from prison, they might have called for more violent action. In 1972, the council pushed to have an open forum with Bassett and the Cadre. It was then decided that a closed meeting would be better than an open discussion where the Cadre could air its views. The council suggested that they add a Beret as a member. Tucker had serious reservations about that because he felt it might grant official recognition to an underground organization.[107]

Meanwhile, the Cadre and its nearly seventy-five members dubbed Kamarakafego its "elder statesman."[108] They respected him, even if they had tactical disagreements. In contrast to their distrust of the council's members, Kamarakafego was a bona fide and international Black Power organizer who respected their political agency. While he was not right about everything, Kamarakafego was correct about the colonial state's apparatus and agenda to suppress Black Power.

The US State Department claimed that it was Kamarakafego's leadership that also drove the PLP's strong themes of black solidarity between 1969 and 1970. In the latter part of 1970, however, Kamarakafego became less conspicuous in the party. This coincided with his activities abroad. He was the sole PLP incumbent who did not stand for the 1972 elections, and the PLP announced its regret that they had lost his services as a result of his international responsibilities. The State Department also believed the PLP's involvement in any international or regional Black Power activities was the result of Kamarakafego's work.[109] Having traveled across the black world—Africa, Oceania, Cuba, and the United States—Kamarakafego was clear about the global potential of Black Power. In organizing the Bermuda conference, he was fast becoming a regional Black Power leader in the Americas. As the next chapter demonstrates, this only increased the state's harassment of him.

5

Anansi's Revolution

In March 1970, the *Bermuda Recorder* reported that detectives had confiscated three books being shipped through Queen's Warehouse in Kingston, Jamaica. These texts were the *Autobiography of Malcolm X*, Elijah Muhammad's *Message to the Blackman*, and Stokely Carmichael and Charles Hamilton's *Black Power*. The owner of such prohibited Black Power literature was twenty-one-year-old Fitzroy Griffiths, who had just returned home from college in England. Affiliated with London's Black Panther Party, twenty-four of Griffiths's five hundred books had been seized by immigration officials. Not taken was Frantz Fanon's *African Revolution*, which the *Recorder* promptly reviewed as an "itinerary of a mind in constant revolution." Six months later, the Nation of Islam's Elijah Muhammad was refused entry onto the island.[1]

These incidents hint at the global criminalization of Black Power. State-sponsored tactics to suppress the movement included political assassinations, infiltration of Black Power organizations, military attacks, police brutality, incarceration, immigration control, and the prohibition of Black Power paraphernalia. Across the world, colonial and neocolonial governments alike banned the leaders and literature of the movement. This included Kamarakafego, who played a critical role in coordinating the movement at the international level.

This chapter explores Kamarakafego's Black Power activities in the context of the Caribbean. It canvasses Black Power's massive impact, transnational scope, and political potential in the West Indies. Further, it demonstrates the movement's threat—real or perceived—to (neo)colonialism, capitalism, and minority white and black elite rule. British, US, Caribbean, Dutch, and Canadian security forces saw Black Power in the region as a threat to their geopolitical interests. They beleaguered the movement via collaborative, international networks of intelligence and repression. These dynamics are reflected in the bulk of this chapter's primary sources, which are largely drawn from state intelligence documents. One problematic issue embodied in this method is that state surveillance was largely gendered and tended to focus on black men rather than black women, not to mention that it was also often inaccurate.

Black Power was akin to a political Anansi, spreading across the world in ways both predictable and unexpected like the quintessential trickster hero of West Africa and her diaspora. Caribbean Black Power traversed along the long-standing webs of historic black internationalism, such as black nationalism, pan-Africanism, *Negritude*, civil rights, black women's feminism, *cimarronaje*, Africana liberation struggles, and Global South revolutionary praxis. It drew inspiration from a deep well of global radicalism. This included Black Power in the United States and the Caribbean's long-standing traditions of protest. Across the region, Black Power was written with the words of Marcus Garvey and the memories of maroons like Jamaica's Nanny. Born from the Haitian and Cuban revolutions, Black Power was a political, economic, and cultural rebellion against the region's "Afro-Saxon" leadership.[2]

From the fibers of these battle-tested forms of protest, Black Power spun new networks of global radicalism. Like Anansi, our proverbial spider, the movement wove a tapestry of ironic possibilities that linked the black world sometimes through contradiction, coincidence, and intentionality. It was in the red, black, and green wristband wiping the sweat from the brow of Viv Richards. It was a stepping razor that would have walked into Rome and started a fire—if only it could have gotten off the Vatican's immigration stop list.

Like Anansi's web, Black Power was fundamentally grounded in the principle branches of black self-determination yet elastic enough to have global relevance. And this is what made the movement a serious threat to a world order of white power, capitalism, and colonialism. But what manner of axiom was this that could torch the hearts of the world's sufferers and strike fear in the minds of the benefactors of world imperialism? Western governments saw Black Power as a two-legged infestation that needed to be stamped out. Agents armed with x-amounts of insecticide-like propaganda used prisons, bribes, vacuums, spells of Gargamel, bombs dropped from police helicopters, visas, sedatives, laws, bullets, and malice to destroy this powerful Anansi. But Black Power never licked marbles with John Crow—there was no killing what could not be killed.

From Bermuda to Barbados

According to the US Department of Justice's Intelligence Evaluation Committee (IEC), Bermuda's Black Power Conference was "a vehicle for promoting [Kamarakafego's] political stock as both a national (Bermudian), regional (Caribbean), and international (pan-African) leader." Indeed, between 1969 and 1970, Kamarakafego extensively toured the Americas while organizing the Bermuda conference and a subsequent Black Power meeting in Barbados. These travels took him across Anguilla, Antigua, Australia, Cuba, Guyana, St. Kitts, Guadeloupe, Barbados, Trinidad and Tobago, Grenada, Venezuela, Curaçao, Martinique, St. Vincent, Mexico, Canada, Jamaica, the Bahamas, and the United States. As he did so, US, British, Australian, and Caribbean governments monitored and hindered his movements. Indeed, Kamarakafego was denied entry into Anguilla, the Cayman Islands, and St. Vincent.[3]

To be sure, Kamarakafego was not the only "undesirable" Black Power activist in the Caribbean. In 1970, St. Vincent's "prohibited immigrants" list of Black Power advocates included Antigua's Kensington Soares; Barbados's Bobby Clarke; Bermuda's Arthur Hodgson, Leonard Wade, and Kamarakafego; Dominica's Roosevelt Douglas and Michael Pollydor; Grenada's Kennedy Frederick; Guyana's Walter Rodney and Eusi Kwayana; Jamaica's Peter Phillips; Trinidad and Tobago's Pat O'Daniel, Clive Nunez, Makandal Daaga, and Kwame Ture; and St. Lucia's Leroy Butcher, Peter Josie, and John Primus. In March 1985, the "Daily Latin America Report" of the CIA's Foreign Broadcast Information Service noted that St. Vincent and the Grenadines had finally lifted the fifteen-year ban on these activists.[4] While conspicuously comprised of only men, this list still speaks volumes about the scope of and resistance to Black Power across the region.

In 1968, the CIA's Office of Current Intelligence began to earnestly document black radicalism in the Caribbean. Its emphasis was on determining the political potential of black nationalism in the region and its threat to the security of Caribbean states. It also aimed to detail Ture's travels outside of the United States after he had dropped out of public view. In the aftermath of Bermuda's 1969 conference, United States president Richard Nixon called for a formal investigation into the relationships between Black Power in the United States and black militancy in the Caribbean. This prompted the Special Operations group of the Office of Current Intelligence to produce a telling report titled "Black Radicalism in the Caribbean (August 6, 1969)." This document was repeatedly updated throughout the mid-1970s.[5]

"Black Radicalism in the Caribbean" described Caribbean Black Power as a "home-grown phenomenon." However, it contended, the Bermuda conference led to serious efforts to increase ties to the movement on the US mainland and to establish a regional network of West Indian radicals. Furthermore, the conference symbolized "a real and growing, albeit still relatively ill-defined, interest in the potential of Black Power as a political and social force in the Caribbean."[6]

Kamarakafego was on the CIA's radar. It was aware that he had lived in Kenya, had traveled to the "Far East," and had a relationship with Kwame Nkrumah. It believed that the coordination between Black Power organizations in the Caribbean was, to a major degree, a result of Kamarakafego's activities and his extensive connections with "extremists" across the Americas. This included Amiri Baraka and brothers Benjamin and Nathan Wright.[7] The CIA also noted that Kamarakafego had exerted "much effort and some money to drum up support" for the conference across the region, but the agency was still unsure of the source of his resources. It noted that during the conference, considerable focus was placed on establishing "international coordination of the Black Power Movement." This enthusiasm led to plans for a subsequent 1970 Black Power conference in Barbados.[8]

Interesting to note, presidential counselor Patrick Moynihan, author of the controversial and racially problematic *Negro Family*, thought well of the report. The memo stated that "neither political independence in Guyana, Trinidad-Tobago, Jamaica, and Barbados" or internal autonomy in other territories had transformed the fundamental racial and socioeconomic structures of these countries. The colonial social patterns of the plantation economies remained. "The bulk of the lower classes" were comprised of black people and the small middle classes were largely "mulatto," "colored," and admixtures of East Indians, Chinese, and whites. "A small white or near-white elite" occupied the "apex of the social and economic pyramid." Furthermore, white minorities and foreign-based companies controlled "a highly disproportionate share of the agricultural estates, businesses, commerce, banking, and industry."[9]

The CIA would later state that the Caribbean's "Afro-Saxon leadership" had largely embodied a white and European educational and cultural orientation. Black revolutionaries were calling for the removal of this leadership.

In educational institutions like the University of the West Indies (UWI), there was renewed interest in Afro-Caribbean culture linked to the black arts movement in the United States.[10]

Significantly, Britain's Foreign and Commonwealth Office (FCO) felt that Black Power in the Caribbean was approaching the momentum "of 1960s African nationalism." The movement addressed the needs of the "unemployed, discontented, and unfulfilled youth" and targeted foreign white capitalist control of the region and black politicians who profited from this system. Black Power pushed for a "Black Caribbean nationalism that would transcend . . . national barriers," imagining a region-wide nation led by Black Power sympathizers backed by popular support. The FCO also felt that if the Black Power were moderate, it could bring political unity and socioeconomic parity in the Caribbean. But it argued that the movement was racist, destructive, "sinister," and "in its more extreme manifestations," inimical to British interests and tourist industries.[11]

In 1972, the IEC argued that while there were a large number of Black Power movements in the Western hemisphere, relatively few had the potential to take state power. Yet it claimed that most of them had the capability to launch acts of terrorism, arson, sabotage, and vandalism. The committee felt that Black Power in the West was being conducted by a relatively small group of people who were primarily from the Caribbean. It felt that the most effective "exploitation" of Black Power was the 1970 Trinidad and Tobago uprisings. It listed Kamarakafego, Dominica's Rosie Douglas, and Kwame Ture as the three leaders largely responsible for the organization of Black Power conferences and civil disorder. These three, they felt, had established themselves as regional or international political figures, and if any one of them were able to carry out a political coup in the Caribbean, then his political influence would be immensely enhanced.[12]

The report distinguished between various Black Power groups in the region. It problematically concluded that outside of the "avowedly Marxist-Leninist oriented" SNCC and the Black Panther Party, Black Power groups in the United States were "ethnocentric and pragmatic." They concerned themselves generally with issues of black people within the United States, lacked substantial interest in ideology, and rejected collaboration with non-blacks. In contrast, the report claimed, the movement's leaders in the Caribbean were power-seeking Marxists who "made common cause" with their ideological allies of any race. They were using Black Power to bring about "fundamental changes in the ideological orientation of their governments." As such, this made them "true revolutionaries" in that they sought "to destroy existing political and economic institutions and replace them with some form of socialisms based on Marxist-Leninist principles." According to the IEC, from St. Croix to Martinique, Black Power groups were emerging in the one of the most "explosive regions in the Americas." This was particularly the case, as in Bermuda, were whites still maintained economic power.[13]

In 1971, Horace Sutton of the *Saturday Review* referred to the movement as a "Palm Tree Revolt." "From Bermuda to the top of South America," he wrote, "the black islands roil with riot, mutiny, and political jostling. Is it an awakening of Black Power or the first radical thrust toward black Marxism?"[14] Sutton was both wrong and right. Black Power in the Caribbean did engross itself in Marxism, but it also emerged from its own black radical traditions.

In Jamaica, Black Power waved an Ethiopian flag and quoted Marcus Garvey's *Philosophies and Opinions*. Rastafari's red, green, and gold fabric wrapped the movement with threads of liberation theology, spiritual militancy, and positive black representations forged from decades of struggle against Babylon. Garvey's ideas of African redemption and repatriation did the same. Rastafari represented the voice of the underprivileged urban youth, the unemployed sufferers, and the grassroots intellectuals. In 1959, Rasta Claudius Henry led a guerilla rebellion in a reported effort to take over Jamaica, turn the island over to Fidel Castro, and repatriate to Africa. Charged for treason, Henry formed the New Creation International Peacemakers Association after his release from prison in 1966. By 1969, the association held over a thousand members. The CIA considered the Peacemakers to be "a racist religious organization" whose revolution aimed to force Jamaica's government to support African repatriation. Edna Fisher, a fish vendor and the wife of Henry, developed the Peacemakers' entrepreneurial ventures. These included a bakery, a church, a school, vehicles, block and tile making works, a farm, a shop, and an electric plant. Her focus on self-reliance was central to "Henry's evangelical Black Power."[15]

The University of the West Indies, with its campuses across Jamaica, Trinidad and Tobago, and Barbados, was a significant hub for Black Power. According to the US State Department, a core of "extreme, left-wing intellectuals" spearheaded Jamaica's movement. This included Guyanese professor of African history Walter Rodney. While at Mona, Rodney famously grounded with students, activists, and the Rasta community about Black Power and African history. He defined Black Power in the West Indies as representing three things: a "break from imperialism," which was "historically white racist"; the "assumptions of power by the black masses"; and "the cultural reconstruction of the islands in the image of the blacks."[16]

The CIA alleged that in a May 1968 meeting, Rodney declared that Black Power sought black rule through violent revolution. Five months later, Jamaica's government claimed to have seized a pamphlet that outlined plans for violence that proved that Rodney was involved in a plot to promote a "Castro-like" revolution. Declared a persona non grata by Prime Minister Hugh Shearer, Rodney was prevented from reentering the island on his return from the October 1968 Montreal Black Writer's Conference. In response to this and to the broader socioeconomic conditions that plagued Jamaica, a UWI student-faculty protest demonstration segued into uprisings across Kingston. Black Power's sentiment could be seen through graffiti sprayed on walls in Kingston, Montego Bay, and Ocho Rios—"Revolution Now! Kill White! Blood Up! Black Power!"[17] This energy was also captured in Prince Buster's 1968 Rocksteady song, "Doctor Rodney (Black Power)."

Shearer claimed that the agitators included Jamaicans and non-Jamaicans, Rastas, university personnel, and known "criminals and political hoodlums." He opined to Jamaica's *Daily Gleaner* that the uprising had "been engaged under the guise . . . of Black Power," which to all well-thinking Jamaicans meant black dignity as opposed to rebellion. Black Power advocates were "subversives" who rallied "popular dissatisfaction."[18]

State pressure was intensified across Kingston and UWI. Jamaica's security forces continued to receive instruction from Britain's FCO. Shearer approved a 25 percent increase in police wages to "build morale and spur recruitment." Additional riot gear was purchased, and raids were launched across Kingston. Activists such as Kwame Ture, H. Rap Brown, and James Forman were prevented from entering the island. University of the West Indies' Guyanese professor of economics Clive Thomas was refused reentry in 1969 after touring Central and South America. He became a leading figure in Guyana's Ratoon Group and was a "cause célèbre" in the Caribbean.[19]

The *Abeng* group emerged in the aftermath of the October 1968 rebellion. Rupert Lewis writes that *Abeng* was a "political matrix" for Black Power, socialism, the trade unionism, Rastafari, and supporters of the opposition People's National Party. The CIA claimed that the group wanted black supremacy in Jamaica both by reform and from a socialist revolution. The CIA incorrectly described this political diversity as an absence of a "coherent plan of action" as opposed to the movement's flexibility.[20]

The group was centered on the publication of its bi-weekly paper, also titled *Abeng*, which was edited by George Beckford, Trevor Munroe, Robert

Hill, and Lewis. The CIA believed that Hill was one of *Abeng*'s more prominent, most radical and influential militant leaders. A quintessential Garveyite, he was intent on forming an international revolutionary movement. For
example, Hill attended the 1968 Montreal conference, where he called for a
"United Black Revolutionary Front."[21]

Abeng reflected the aspirations of Jamaica's politicized youth. It was a
transnational nexus of Caribbean Black Power, pan-Africanism, and Garveyism. The name paid homage to the war horns of Jamaica's Akan and
Twi speaking maroons. *Abeng* printed speeches, letters, and essays by and
about the Black Panther Party, African liberation struggles in Mozambique,
Ghana, Guinea-Bissau, and the Congo, Black Power, police violence, attacks
on Rasta dwellings, the Caribbean Artist Movement (CAM), Prince Buster,
Ska and Reggae, political poetry and artwork, legalization of marijuana, the
New World Group. In March 1969, it printed Rodney's "Rise of Black Power
in the West Indies."[22]

The CIA was concerned about the paper's supposed "violent tone." Indeed, *Abeng* denounced state repression and the banning of Black Power
literature, musical records, and activists. It reported that Jamaica's education
department had warned school headmasters to watch out for Black Power.
Furthermore, distributers of the paper were being harassed across Trench
Town and "Ghost Town." The paper also noted how British troops were
stationed around Bermuda during the 1969 Black Power conference. Yet, it
argued, the British security forces had allowed the conference to proceed so
that immigration officials could compile a list of attendees who would likely
cause future trouble in the Caribbean.[23]

Abeng was a direct link between Black Power and the Universal Negro
Improvement Association (UNIA). The group had direct access to veteran
activists like Amy Jacques Garvey, who viewed the UNIA as being the origi-
nator of twentieth-century Black Power. In May 1969, *Abeng* printed letters
from 1950 written to Jacques Garvey by W. A. Domingo and George Padmore on the suppression of black radical literature. Domingo wrote, "Quite
a formidable list of publications have been banned from entry into Jamaica."
The people should ask, "What are the leaders afraid? To whom is the banned
literature a danger?"[24]

Following Jacques Garvey's lead, *Abeng* defined Black Power on the lines
of Garvey's pan-African vision for African liberation. This included the
struggle for power by "African minorities and majorities" outside of Africa.
As such, it argued, there could be "no talk of Black Power in the Pan-African sense without Africa's liberation." The paper spread beyond Jamaica; for

example, the Barbadian People Progressive Movement's Black Star Bookshop carried it. While holding a circulation of twenty thousand, it was in publication for only fifteen weeks.[25]

The CIA documented the activities of other Black Power groups in Jamaica as well. This included Marcus Garvey Jr.'s African National Union (ANU), the Nation of Islam, Jama-Youth, the African Youth Movement, the Black Solidarity Committee, the Council for Afro-Jamaican Affairs, and the African Revolutionary Movement. Jama-Youth called for race-first socioeconomic change through revolution. The African Revolutionary Movement attempted to "launch a training program for Jamaican revolutionaries."[26]

In August 1970, Roy Philbert announced the official formation of the ANU at a Black Solidarity Committee commemoration of the anniversary of Marcus Garvey's eighty-second birthday in Kingston. Attended by about four hundred people—including Amy Jacques Garvey—Philbert read a statement by Garvey Jr. declaring that the aims of the ANU included to "preach and promulgate" Black Power as this philosophy was "outlined by Marcus Garvey." Concurrently, the first St. Ann Black Power conference was held. It sought to address how to "advance the struggle against the enemy of Black people—American imperialism and its local house slaves."[27]

West Indian communities were critical conduits for the global spread of Black Power's aesthetics, articulations, literature, and protest. In the United Kingdom, John Anthony La Rose, Edward Kamau Brathwaite, and Andrew Salkey founded the London-based Caribbean Artist's Movement in 1968. In July of that year, Salkey led a protest against Jamaica's banning of Black Power literature. Inspired by a visit to Cuba, he argued that revolutionary artists had a responsibility to dismantle the entrenched class-based cultural establishment. In that same month, CAM's Third World Benefit featured steel pan music, poetry readings, and speeches in support of Wole Soyinka, Amiri Baraka, and Obi Egbuna, all playwrights who were facing politically motivated criminal charges in their respective locales.[28]

Black Power in Canada was intricately linked to the movement across the Americas, including the Caribbean. In Montreal, West Indian students from McGill and Sir George Williams universities were the primary organizers of the city's monumental 1968 Congress of Black Writers. Political luminaries who attended the congress included C. L. R James, Michael X, Ted Joans, Guyana's Walter Rodney, Canada's Rocky Jones, Kwame Ture, Jamaica's Robert Hill, Harry Edwards, James Forman, South Africa's Miriam Makeba, Richard B. Moore, Richard Small, Michael Thelwell, and Jimmy Garrett.[29]

Dominica's Rosie Douglas was a key organizer of the congress. Along with Tim Hector (Antigua), Anne Cools (Barbados), Hill (Jamaica), Alfie Roberts (St. Vincent and the Grenadines), and Franklyn Harvey (Grenada), Douglas had been a member of the Caribbean Conference Committee, which for years had organized conferences and seminars focused on issues impacting Montreal's black community and political independence in the Caribbean.[30]

In early 1969, over four hundred students at Sir George Williams occupied the school's computer center for ten days. Led by the likes of Douglas, Cools, and Cheddi Jagan Jr., this was a protest against racism on campus. Eventually, police raided the center. According to the *Bermuda Recorder*, the students were led away from the computer center at gunpoint and taken to a broken-windowed room that stood at a frigid 25°F. One officer pushed a gun in the stomach of one student, stating, "through here you nigger." Forced to stand with their hands outstretched on a wall for three hours, the students were beaten if they could not. One such student was assaulted, spit in the face, and called a bloody nigger. Another suffered a concussion from a beating. One officer took a blanket from a cold female student, soaked it in water, and gave it back to her. Other females were called "negress sluts" and were the subject of "lewd suggestions by policemen." Once jailed, the students slept on the ground for a full day before getting their first meal.[31]

Over ninety-seven people were arrested, forty-two of whom were black. Struck on her head by a baton, Bahamas' Coralee Hutchison died from a brain tumor a year later. When a fire broke out during the arrests, a passer-by infamously shouted, "Let the niggers burn." Eight students were charged, and Cools served four months in prison. Charged with arson, Douglas served eighteen months in prison before being deported.[32]

Bermuda's Black Power conference declared its unconditional support for the arrested students. Its Politics workshop discussed the trial of the students, identified as the February 11th Defense Committee. Committee Chairman, Norman Cooke, planned to speak at the conference but was denied entry into Bermuda as an "undesirable visitor." The workshop condemned the Bermudan and Canadian governments for suppressing "the freedom of travel."[33]

Montreal student leaders Terrence Ballantyne and Pat Townsend conducted a Caribbean fundraiser. Interviewed in Jamaica by *Abeng*, they reported that a revolver had been pressed against Douglas's forehead. For the paper, this event dispelled any myths that Canada was a beacon of antiracism; it also highlighted the relationships between the Canadian military and economic exploitation in the Caribbean.[34]

Douglas traveled across the Caribbean to rally public opinion against Canadian racism. The FCO would later claim that his calls to use violence against Canadian imperialism helped to trigger Trinidad and Tobago's Black Power uprisings. While visiting Bermuda at Kamarakafego's invitation, Douglas gave a press conference that the governor found to be "unfit to present to the public." Placed on the stop list, Douglas left the island before the governor could deport him.[35]

According to the CIA, Ture's 1968 visit to Halifax in the aftermath of the Congress unleashed Black Power activity to "dangerous proportions" among Nova Scotia's "20,000 Negroes." This was followed by visits from US-based Black Panthers. After conversations with the local black community around issues like the razing of Africville, segregation, and labor discrimination, the Panthers suggested that a "Black family" meeting be held. Thus, in November 1968, over five hundred black Nova Scotians met at the Halifax North Memorial Library to discuss black liberation. This meeting, which included "Rocky" Jones and William Pearly Oliver, led to the creation of the Black United Front. Black Power groups also emerged in Toronto, including the Afro-American Progressive Association and its successor, the Black Youth Organization. West Indians such as Jamaica's Horace Campbell, who headed the organization's Black Education Project, led the organization.[36]

Douglas may have been Dominica's most internationally known Black Power activist, but he was not the only one. United States officials claimed that the raised fists of African American athletes Tommie Smith and John Carlos at the 1968 Mexico Olympics "fired up" numbers of Dominica's unemployed black youth to adopt Black Power. While Mexico was an iconic international moment for Black Power, Dominica's movement was grounded within its Black radical tradition.[37]

In the aftermath of a 1969 New World group teach-in, Dominica's United Black Socialist Party was formed. The party "sought radical change in the island's social and economic structure." One of its founders, William Winston, had attended Bermuda's 1969 conference. William Riviere, a UWI lecturer, formed the "Roseau College of the University of Dominica." Roseau College was a "speaker's corner" forum and a site of Black Power politics. Gabriel Christian writes that Black Power countered the "psychic scars lashed into the minds of Dominicans by centuries of Western-taught self-hate and the ridicule lavished upon Africa and people of African descent."

Circa 1970, high school students met at places like the Botanical Gardens' "One Hundred Steps" to debate books on Malcolm X, Che Guevara, and the Black Panthers.[38]

Dominica's urban youth denounced the inadequacies of colonial education and called for Caribbean history and radicalism in Caribbean art and cultural studies through plays, literature, and dance. As street corners and parks became sites of political education and protest, Black Power crowds sometimes reached numbers of between two and three thousand. Audiences could hear speakers like Riviere and Desmond Trotter lecture on Dominican history, Black Power, pan-Africanism, feminism, and economics. One could also hear of the guerilla struggles of Guinea-Bissau's Partido Africano para a Independência da Guiné e Cabo Verde, Mozambique's Frente de Libertação de Moçambique, Angola's Movimento Popular de Libertação de Angola, and the anti-Apartheid struggle in South Africa.[39]

Political films were shown at schools and community halls, and donations were collected for the Organization of African Unity Liberation Committee. In 1972, the Movement for a New Dominica was formed. It raised black consciousness, popularized dashikis, promoted Afro hairstyles, and hosted meetings. Later that year, students at the Catholic St. Mary's Academy held a Black Power demonstration after a teacher punished a student for wearing an Afro. So-called blaxploitation films from America also galvanized this generation.[40]

Black Power was marked by the growth of Rasta communities that were established in the mountains of Dominica. These "modern day maroons" were attacked by the Dominican Defense Force, leading to shootouts. The violence did not cease here. During the Carnival of 1974, white American tourist John Jirasek was murdered. Trotter was found guilty in the highly publicized and polarizing case. Trotter's defense lawyers were Maurice Bishop and Brian Alleyne.[41]

Like Douglas, Antigua's Tim Hector cut his political teeth in Montreal. An astute journalist, Hector's return to Antigua dramatically influenced Black Power's growth on the island. Hector was a protégé of C. L. R. James. He joined the Afro-Caribbean Movement (ACM), which, formed in 1968, transformed into the Antiguan-Caribbean Liberation Movement. By the summer of 1969, he and his comrades, among whom was his wife, Arah Weeks, helped to develop the ACM into what may have been the Eastern Caribbean's "best-organized" and "most vocal" Black Power organization. From the CIA's perspective, it was also the most "outspokenly racist group."

This was in contrast to the Afro-Caribbean Association, which was founded by Mali Olatunji and Robin Bascus, chairman of the ruling Antigua Labor Party. Premier Vere Bird tolerated the culturally focused association but warned it about its political leanings toward Black Power.[42]

Kamarakafego visited Antigua in January 1970, when he delivered an allegedly "highly inflammatory anti-white speech." According to the CIA, he was the "major Black revolutionary impetus to the ACM." While it is not clear if this was so, the ACM sent delegates to Bermuda's Black Power conference. Activists such as Walter Palmer, a Philadelphia-based Black Power activist, visited the group. Palmer also attended the Bermuda conference, where it is possible his connection with Antigua was established.[43]

The ACM organized public seminars, lectures, and film viewings. Its engine was its paper, *Outlet*, a critical regional voice of Black Power. In August 1969, *Outlet* published a letter from Montserrat inquiring how to start a local Black Power movement. In late 1969, the paper released a series of articles denouncing Canadian military exercises in Jamaica. This coincided with visits to ACM by the Montreal student group and a Day of Solidarity for them. Under Hector's leadership, by March 1970, ACM was producing five hundred copies of *Outlet* per issue. Soares passed copies out to tourists off the cruise ships. Subscriptions were purchased from Dominica, Grenada, St. Lucia, St. Vincent, and St. Christopher-Nevis-Anguilla. Kwayana distributed it in Guyana. New York's Literary Book Shop had it on its shelves. In Montreal, copies circulated at George Williams University. Kamarakafego carried the paper to Bermuda.[44]

In November 1971, *Outlet* printed an extensive call by Antigua's Black Power movement for a pan-Caribbean federation to stretch from the "Bahamas to the north to Guyana in the south." Its "Grenada Declaration" declared that the aspirations of Caribbean peoples for political freedom and socioeconomic justice could be "fulfilled through the creation of a West Indies nation" that included the Spanish, French, Dutch, and English-speaking countries. The ACM held Caribbean unity to be self-evident. It called for the creation of People's Assemblies, which were the only way to give power to the people. It saw a federation of Dominica, Grenada, Guyana, St. Lucia, St. Kitts, and St. Vincent as being the first step toward unifying the "whole archipelago." Black people needed to unite globally, and the federation would be the "West Indian contribution to the struggle for the world-wide regeneration of the Black-Man." The call featured an oath that acknowledged Africa as the motherland and every black man and woman as being brother and sister. Respondents were to pledge "the soul, mind and body to the destruction of all obstacles that stood between . . . total Black liberation."[45]

Antigua's summer of 1971 was marked by racially motivated incidents. This included six incidents of petrol bombing at the homes of white Antiguans and English residents. An anonymous pamphlet, *Liberator*, emerged across the island. A Caribbean Liberation Book store was formed. Hector conducted political lectures and organized visits to the island by Black Power activists. Two Antiguan Black Panther Party supporters who lived in the United States ejected two white Canadians from a public forum. According to the CIA, Black Panther Walter Thompson (Baba Odinga) was one of these men; Thompson was one of the "New York 21," the twenty-one Panthers who were indicted in April 1969 for allegedly plotting to bomb public establishments. Antigua's government blamed all of these incidents on the ACM; it banned an Afro-Caribbean Black Power conference that was to be held in Antigua in September 1971.[46] According to David Austin and former Black Panther, political prisoner, and author Eddie Marshall Conway, African American agent provocateur Warren Hart targeted Hector. Hart worked for the US National Security Agency. He was allegedly "borrowed" by Canadian authorities to infiltrate Douglas's circles. He also helped to found the Baltimore branch of the Black Panthers and had been a bodyguard of Kwame Ture.[47]

The regionally based Forum emerged in the aftermath of the Bermuda conference. Grenada's Bishop and Unison Whiteman, St. Lucia's George Odlum and Peter Josie, and Jamaica's Munroe founded the group during a covert Black Power meeting on Rat Island, St. Lucia. The Forum launched groups in St. Lucia, St. Vincent, Antigua, and Guyana.[48]

St. Lucia's Black Power–affiliated Forum was founded by Josie, Odlum, and Hilton Deterville and announced publicly in October 1969. The group denounced foreign capitalism's socioeconomic domination of St. Lucia. St. Lucia's British governor expressed considerable concern with the group's supposed penchant for violence. What was most troubling for colonial officials was that Forum members occupied significant social positions in St. Lucia and the broader Caribbean. Josie was in close contact with Trinidad's Makandal Daaga. Deterville, the organization's "most extreme advocate of violent action," was employed in the Ministry of Trade. Odlum, the executive secretary of the Forum, was its most effective speaker. As secretary to the West Indian Associate Council of Ministers, Odlum openly denounced the repression of Black Power by Caribbean governments.[49]

The Forum sought political power in the island and achieved "remarkable success" in publicizing its views. Visible on television forums and in newspapers, the group had the support of the editor of St. Lucia's principal newspaper. They had even "made themselves the first topic of conversation . . . in cricket pavilions during Shell Shield matches." Their popular urban base was the young, ambitious, and dissatisfied. Odlum had once informed London's Eastern Caribbean Commissioners (who, according to the FCO, wholeheartedly disliked him) that the Forum would continue to attract support from the "thirty and below generation" and that within a measurable time, the existing parties would be seen as anachronisms. This would leave the Forum to run the government. Indeed, it had the support of St. Lucia's Labor Party, which could not agree with the Caribbean's repression of its own people, even if it did not agree with the Forum or leaders like Carmichael.[50]

In March 1970, Forum representatives publicly stated that the group did not preach violence but that "violence might arise" where it was needed. The following evening, St. Lucia's premier, John Compton, denounced the group in a government meeting. He claimed that the Forum contained "a number of misguided idealists" as well as persons who were being used by "outside elements more concerned about East-West struggle" than about the interests of St. Lucia. Their object was to replace government stability with anarchy. Compton also claimed to have proof that Forum members were being funded by external sources. He told the group to "watch it," threating that he would resolutely thwart their ambitions. He chided Forum members who were civil servants, saying that those who did not like the government's edict should "get out and engage full time in politics and not expect the taxpayers to underwrite" their political opposition to the government.[51]

Special Branch could not substantiate Compton's allegation that the Forum was being financed by outside sources. It found this improbable, as many of its members were "relatively well-paid civil servants." One "thoroughly unreliable member" of the Labor Party claimed that the forum had received $12,000 from Communist sources, but the FCO felt that it was more likely that external financial assistance would come from US-based Black Power activists.[52]

D. Kerr, an official of the FCO, felt that Compton's "open attack on the forum" was a "striking change," as his earlier response to the group bordered on "mild approval." This Kerr attributed to the improvement in Special Branch's activities in St. Lucia and its ability to impact "a more realistic appraisal of the dangers presented by the Black Power Movement." The uprisings in Trinidad had also "served as a powerful warning in these islands" and hopefully disillusioned the public about Black Power. However, given its public support, the forum was unlikely to be perturbed by the government's counterattack. Meanwhile, St. Lucia's government continued to try to "refurbish" its radical image.[53]

Kerr hope that the Forum was under the control of "moderates." He cited John Primus's participation in St. Lucia's Carnival with his own band as an example of this. "I doubt many Black Panthers in the United States took part in Carnival. God help us if the extremists ever take over."[54] This misreading of political culture by colonial officials was typical.

Kerwyn Morris led St. Vincent's Educational Forum of the People, which emerged out of a group known as the Bridge Boys and whose leadership was comprised solely of educators. Its political potential rested in its membership of two hundred educated young people who were civil servants. Furthermore, as popular support was relatively balanced between the ruling Labor Party and Opposition Peoples Political Party, they stood to have a tremendous impact on the political future of the island.[55]

Morris was a veteran activist. In 1965, he founded Montreal's St. Vincent and the Grenadines Association. One of its aims was to "work for the greatest good and welfare of Black and/or African people and that of the poor and needy everywhere." In April 1970, Morris and Parnell Campbell—both teachers—appeared before the Public Service Commission to address criticism they had launched at the government during the forum's public meetings. They were not charged, yet the commission proceeded to examine legal means to control public statements made by civil servants.[56]

On April 15, 1970, St. George's radio reported that Trinidad's Daaga and other members of the National Joint Action Committee (NJAC) representatives would soon visit Barbados, St. Vincent, Guyana, and Grenada to spearhead a Caribbean revolution. This prompted St. Vincent's government to covertly release its aforementioned list of Black Power undesirables. According to FCO officials, the control of immigration to St. Vincent was "water-tight." Yet it was "fairly easy to slip through the Grenadines," and those on the stop list could reach the island without much trouble. However, once arrived, they would be easy to spot.[57]

St. Vincent's prime minister, Milton Cato, shared this list with his counterpart in Grenada, Eric Gairy. Gairy's current dilemma was Carmichael's travels through the Caribbean. "If Black Power shows its ugly head in this country," he warned, "they will be meeting brain power. My police force and the effort we are putting into it will be able to fight elements of any evil force here." In early May 1970, Gairy denounced Black Power as being "fraught with hypocrisy." He had no doubt that, as it had done in Trinidad, the movement could do much damage across the region. "One should wet his own house when his neighbor's is on fire." In preparation, Gairy doubled his police force and purchased modern weaponry, but such efforts could not halt Black Power activity in Grenada. The Angel Harps Steel Band had formed an Organization of Black Unity with the assistance of UWI lecturer Patrick Emmanuel. In 1972, Bishop coordinated a covert meeting in Martinique to discuss the creation of a socialist Caribbean society.[58] His New Jewel movement seized state power in 1979. He was assassinated in a coup four years later, shortly followed by the US invasion of the island.

Similarly to the forum, the New World Group established branches on various islands. This critical intellectual voice of Caribbean nationalism published its quarterly, New World, from UWI's (Mona) Institute of Social and Economic Research. It advocated for radical and socialist change and staunchly denounced US imperialism in the region.[59]

The FCO was quite interested in Kamarakafego's activities in Tortola, British Virgin Islands. In December 1969, the FCO was disturbed by a Black Power nucleus on the island. This group met at the home of Sylvester Vanterpool and included lawyer Z. Butler, W. Lindy de Castro, Kenneth Narine, Sydney Brathwaite, Kenneth Smith, and Alfred Creque. De Castro was a member of the Positive Action movement and was accused for instigating cases of arson. Though he was alleged to have brought tear gas into Tortola, police raids of De Castro's home found nothing. Smith had served in Vietnam with the US Army. Narine, a high school teacher, corresponded with Guyana's Cheddi Jagan. His colleague, Elton Georges, was reportedly indoctrinating his students with Black Power ideas. Officials were concerned about the "Tamarind Tree Boys," a reference to a group of "not well educated" young men who congregated at the Tamarind Tree at Road Town Methodist Cemetery. Such men could "be easily influenced by any person or group with ulterior motives" and were linked with Black Power. The Island Sun referenced Black Power elements in the Tortola branch of the Jaycee movement.[60]

In May 1970, Mario Moorhead founded the United Caribbean Association (UCA) of Black People in the US Virgin Island of St. Croix. The UCA included Victor Nurse, Glenn Williams, and Jacqueline Sa botker, who edited its newsletter, UCA Speaks. A schoolteacher, Moorhead studied in Puerto Rico and Washington, DC. The UCA program called for the "unification of all black people of the Caribbean," the removal of all forms of oppression from the Caribbean, and the creation of an atmosphere in which black people could live in harmony rather than in competition. This was particularly important in St. Croix, where in addition to racial tensions between the local black community and the white population (which included mainland white Americans), the black population was often at odds with West Indian migrant laborers on the islands. These included young men and women hailing from St. Kitts, Antigua, Nevis, St. Lucia, Tortola, Montserrat, Trinidad, and the Puerto Rican island of Vieques who came to the island to work in the racially biased tourist industry. The UCA pushed back against these tensions, calling for racial unity against white hegemony—"Why should our Caribbean brothers be more 'alien' to us than a white man from Alabama?" they admonished.[61]

According to the CIA, Moorhead was involved in a series of robberies "with racial overtones directed at white tourists." The agency claimed that Eldridge Cleaver was considering utilizing the UCA in establishing a safe haven in the Caribbean for Black Panthers. In 1970, Cleaver pleaded guilty to a 1967 armed robbery of a Safeway grocery store in Washington, DC, and was sentenced to fifteen years in prison. In April 1970, an armed group robbed a branch of the Virgin Islands National Bank on St. Thomas of $36,255. Eventually, Moses Lewis, UCA's interior minister, was convicted of the robbery.[62]

The United Community of Bahamas, with a membership of about seven hundred, was driven by a blend of "Black Power, idealism, socialism and anti-establishment sentiment." The group included many middle-class youth who pushed the government for socialist reforms in the economy.[63]

In St. Kitts and Nevis, cabinet ministers and leaders of its Trade and Labor Union publicly supported Black Power. In April 1970, Premier Robert Bradshaw told a rally that "Black Power should be used as a vehicle and not as a weapon to improve the Black man's lot." Bradshaw hoped that the movement was not confused about its potential to "foster disaffection" in the island. Of course, there was already disaffection in St. Kitts and Nevis. Eustace Esdaile, a school principle, formed the Black Power Group in February 1969. Though the group focused on educational and cultural questions, the potential for Black Power to challenge the state was highlighted by plans to further develop a regional Black Power organization. This push was being driven from Antigua.[64]

After participating in Atlanta's Congress of African Peoples (1970), Surinamese journalist Cyriel Karg, seeking to develop black consciousness to end institutional racism, formed the Black Power Organization (Afro-Sranan).

The CIA claimed that the organization was patterned after the Republic of New Africa and that Karg had signed an agreement of mutual aid and a solidarity pact with the group.[65]

Black Power was relevant to the non-Anglophone Americas. Writing in 1972, William Lux asserted that Haiti's Francois "Papa Doc" Duvalier used an aberrant form of Black Power to maintain political control of Haiti. Masking his wielding of political violence, this included his embracement of Negritude, his close affiliation with Vodun, and the support from thousands of Vodun priests, or *houngans*. He would exclaim, "Only the Gods can take power from me."[66]

Black consciousness, emanating from black literature, such as *Ebony* magazine, and from Soul and Reggae music, was heavily embraced by Afro-Brazilians. In 1974, influenced by Black Power and African liberation struggles, Antônio Carlos dos Santos Vovo and Apolônio de Jesus formed the African-centered Carnaval group, Ilê Aiyê, in Liberdade, Bahia (Salvador). In 1979, an offshoot of Ilê Aiyê, Olodum, emerged and produced Samba Reggae. In 1980, the Unified Black movement was formed, which was a network of Afro-Brazilian organizations and activists such as Abdias do Nascimento.[67]

Black Power in British Honduras (Belize) challenged British colonialism. The movement was linked to the black radical traditions of its Garifuna community. The United Black Association Development (UBAD) pushed Black Power in the colony. Lilette Nzinga Barkley-Waite, Lionel Clarke, Rufus X, and Evan X Hyde formed UBAD in February 1969. An "agent for Black social and political empowerment," UBAD flourished into a "Black radical" organization under Hyde's leadership. A "disciple" of Malcolm X, Hyde graduated from New Hampshire's Dartmouth College in 1968. As a student, Hyde was heavily influenced by Malcolm X, black nationalism, and the Black Power movement. After Hyde's return to British Honduras, the would-be founders of UBAD attempted to infiltrate Honduras's still-active chapter of the UNIA, seeking unsuccessfully to become officers and to radicalize the chapter "into a Black Power unit." Lionel Clarke believed that as the UNIA was a "long established organization," it would shelter them from attacks by the government. They eventually abandoned this strategy but utilized the UNIA's charter as a template to build UBAD's constitution. They applied its Garveyism—African consciousness, race pride, and a struggle for political rights—in an effort to mobilize the colony's Black majority. United Black Association Development was also heavily influenced by the Nation of Islam; both its secretary/treasurer, Ismail Omar Shabazz (George

Tucker), and its minister of lands and war, Charles X. Eagan, were members of that organization.[68]

For Hyde, Black Power was "not confined to those of African descent but also to the peoples of the black nations of Latin America and Southeast Asia." He hoped to bring Black Power to Belize "to unite the black people of Southeast Asia, Latin America, the United States, and Afro Hondurans." Black Power aimed to neutralize white power and to fight against American, Russian, and British white imperialism.[69]

On January 1, 1969, UBAD launched its first public act, a three-to-four day demonstration against the showing of the imperialist film *The Green Berets*. In a town hall meeting, Hyde stated that the Vietnam War was "one more example of U.S. global racism against black, brown, red and yellow people. The same man killing the Vietnamese people was the same man brutalizing the Black people in Amerikkka was the same man starving us in Belize. *The white man-the Caucasian*." In the summer of 1969, UBAD launched its newspaper, *Amandala*, named after the South African word for power, *amandla*. It also launched a free breakfast program. Primarily run by women, UBAD also established a bakery called UBAFU, a Garifuna word for "power."[70]

In May 1972, UBAD's secretary general, Norman Fairweather (also head of the Afro-Honduran Liberation Committee), was arrested during Pan-African Liberation Week. What began as a parade turned into an uprising that targeted government office buildings. Fairweather denounced British colonialism for having done nothing "but remove vast amounts of mahogany" from Honduras. UBAD wanted self-rule and "compensation from Britain for raping" the country to eliminate governmental corruption, inadequate housing, overcrowded cities, and coastal erosion. During an African Liberation Day event, UBAD treasurer Shabazz was found guilty of illegal possession of firearms and of keeping ammunition without a license.[71]

In 1972, the Garinagu Dangriga Cultural Association came to the attention of the British colonial authorities as a result of its Black Power and Marxist leanings. Publicly focused on creating programs of "educational and cultural activity, arts and crafts for the benefit of black people," British colonial officials determined that it sympathized or was affiliated with UBAD in opposition to the Establishment. According to Special Branch, UBAD officials were mainly farmers and teachers, and its eighty members were mostly students. The association was headquartered at the Dangriga Kitchen restaurant, though British authorities had deported its owner, African American Joseph Leon Coppage, under claims that he was a "breeder of discontent." Coppage had been in Honduras for about a year and was a supporter of Mischek Mawema, a schoolteacher from southern Rhodesia. While in Rhodesia, Coppage had been the secretary of the Mazazi Union of Students and a leading member of the United General Workers Union. In 1963, he had been a student at Kansas State University. While in Honduras, he expressed "Marxist ideas" through the militant newspaper *Corazel*.[72]

Mischek was the brother of Michael Andrew Mawema of the Zimbabwe African National Union (ZANU). In 1965, Mawema was ZANU's coordinating secretary in the southwestern United States. The British were quite concerned with his presence in Honduras, his contacts with Cuba and his politicization of students. Yet authorities felt that if he were forced out of the colony, he might "cause trouble" elsewhere. As he had married into a Honduran family, they implied that it might be better if he remained there.[73]

While organizing the 1969 Bermuda conference, Kamarakafego spent time in the Dutch colony of Curaçao. On May 30, 1969, labor uprisings of about five-thousand workers broke out in the capital of Willemstad. These were referred to as *Trinta di Mei* in the Afro-Curaçao creole language of Papiamento. Jamaica's *Abeng* felt that the disturbances were evidence of the white violence and power, reporting that the oil workers had caused $20 million worth of damage in Willemstad. The workers had commandeered an island radio station and forced it to broadcast their demands that the government resign or face violence. Telephone operators joined the strike in support of increased pay. During the demonstrations, police shot one worker in the chest. This prompted arson, looting, and shootouts between armed demonstrators and police officers. Fifty buildings were destroyed. Three hundred Dutch marines, trained in riot control, where sent from Holland after the weekend of violence that saw two killed and a hundred injured. Two American warships were also sent to the island. Meanwhile, Curaçao's prime minister falsely claimed that foreign-trained Communists were behind the uprising.[74]

The uprising prompted Stanley Brown, Amador Nita, and Wilson "Papa" Godett to form the radical socialist Frente Obrero Liberashon (FOL). The CIA claimed that the FOL was a well-organized black militant group with "some training in terrorist tactics." Godett was a leader of the dockworkers' union. Brown, a schoolteacher, was "the apparent leader of the black radicals." He was arrested and charged with arson. His newspaper, *Vitó*, allegedly used racist and inflammatory material to stir up resentment against the "white establishment." Published in Papiamento, *Vitó* became a rallying point for black activism in Curaçao, which was marked by Black Power symbolism and rhetoric. The CIA claimed that these activists created the Antillean Black Power Organization in the aftermath of the uprisings.[75]

Canada's Caracas-based embassy was quite concerned by the uprising and the potential for Black Power to spread across the region. As read a 1970 Canadian report, "Anyone who would prefer to close his eyes to the storm clouds on the horizon might be advised to recall the disastrous aftermath of last summer's violence in Curaçao." For "understandable reasons," claimed Canada, the Netherlands Antilles, in an effort to downplay the movement's impact, described the uprising as labor discontent as opposed to a Black Power protest. However, the vast majority of the rebels were black, the FOL candidly referred to their movement as Black Power, and Dutch officials admitted privately that the uprising had strong racial undertones."[76]

According to a 1969 article by *Race Today*, the journal of the London-based Institute of Racial Relations, Kamarakafego spent several days in Havana as a guest of Fidel Castro before the Bermuda conference. Indeed, the Cuban Revolution served as a tangible example of Black Power's potential. Cuba's granting of refuge to African American activists such as Robert F. Williams and Black Panthers Eldridge Cleaver, Angela Davis, Huey P. Newton, and Assata Shakur is well documented. In June 1967, Cuba's *Granma* supported "SNCC's militant stand in favor of the peoples of Asia, Africa, and Latin America who were struggling for liberation." Nine SNCC members attended Havana's 1966 Tricontinental Conference. The next year, Ture participated in Cuba's Organization of Latin American Solidarity conference. There he informed attendees that Black Power was linked with the global struggles of oppressed peoples against imperialism and capitalism. Some sixty thousand Cubans attended the conference's Cuban Day of Solidarity with the African American People on August 18, 1967. Ture recalled seeing the effects of racism and poverty in Cuba but no signs of present racism. His unwavering admiration for Cuba was matched by Castro's own appreciation of Ture. Castro pledged his support and protection to Black Power's international icon, suggesting that Cuba was Ture's spiritual home. Clive Nunez of NJAC also attended the conference and expressed support for a Castro-type revolution in Trinidad and Tobago.[77]

Puerto Rico's connection to Black Power was most visibly seen through the activism of the Young Lords. Their work centered on self-determination for Puerto Rico and the Global South and the empowerment of barrios across the United States. Emerging under the leadership of Chicago's José Cha Cha Jiménez, the group forged alliances with the Black Panther Party and produced a brilliant newspaper, *Palante*. The Young Lords were

brutally repressed by the FBI's COINTELPRO, as was the Puerto Rican In-
dependence movement in general. In 1967, Ture traveled to Puerto Rico and
established an alliance between SNCC and Puerto Rico's Movimiento Pro
Independencia (MPI). Also linked to Black Power in the United States, the
MPI eventually became the Puerto Rican Socialist Party. Guyana's Cheddi
Jagan also had close contacts with the MPI.[78]

Puerto Rico's Ana Livia Cordero was also involved with the MPI. A physician by trade, Livia Cordero married Julian Mayfield and moved to Nkrumah's Ghana. While there, she served as W. E. B. Du Bois's personal physician. She returned to Puerto Rico in 1966 after the coup. In 1968, Puerto
Rican police arrested her and twelve other members of the pro-indepen-
dence group *Liberacion* in Barrio Tortugo. Accused of fomenting a revolution, Correro was arrested on the orders of a former aide of J. Edgar Hoover.
Livia Cordero felt that it was primarily the Black Power movement in the
United States that supported Puerto Rico's struggle against imperialism and
police repression.[79]

In March 1970, Venezuela claimed to enjoy harmonious race relations.
Canada's Caracas-based embassy felt that this was because the country
had not yet been affected by the black consciousness sweeping the region.
This was only about a decade after the rule of dictator Marcos Pérez Jiménez, whose official Plan of the Nation included "whitening" the population through selective immigration. According to Jesus "Chucho" Garcia,
in 1968, African-Venezuelan Luis Beltran Prieto Figueroa, of the Acción
Democrática Party, was not allowed to run as its presidential candidate because he was black. Afro-Venezuelans organized around issues of race and
political culture. In 1969, Afro-Venezuelan activists in Curiepe sought to
prevent its San Juan festival, which honored a black saint, from becoming a
tourist commodity. Interestingly, in 1975, the Mexican film *El Poder Negro*
(Black Power) was filmed in Venezuela. The film starred Afro-Cuban body-
building champion Sergio ("the myth") Oliva.[80]

The CIA claimed that "rebel priests" initiated a Black Power movement in
Buenaventura, Colombia, in 1970 and that it was receiving foreign aid. This
included African American crewmembers and passengers who participated
in a "program of indoctrination" and provided guidance and propaganda.
Allegedly, members of this group joined a spree of uprisings and looting in
June 1970.[81]

This was the complicated world of Black Power in which Kamarakafego
lived and loved. The movement scorched through the Caribbean largely in response to the unfulfilled socioeconomic promises of political independence

and continued colonialisms. It asked the political, economic, and cultural questions that political independence had not sufficiently answered. This was reflective of the movement's diversity across an uneven region in terms of politics, culture, memory, economics, ethnicity, languages, environment, and demographics. A critical assessment of Black Power would be in its ability to structurally transform societies that were demographically black. As the next chapter shows, Kamarakafego would certainly be tested in his efforts to organize a Black Power conference in Barbados.

6

Black Power in the Caribbean,
Signed Stokely Carmichael

Pauulu Kamarakafego's passport spoke many languages. It was May 1970, and over the past eight months, it had been opened, stamped, rejected, and photocopied by immigration officials across the globe. A tireless ally, it documented Kamarakafego's efforts to organize both the first and second International Black Power conferences in Bermuda and Barbados on behalf of the National Black Power conference. It now found itself in the anxious hands of immigration officers stationed at Barbados's national airport. Kamarakafego was being expelled from the Caribbean country in response to his Black Power activities.

Barbadian prime minister Errol Barrow had initially agreed to host the Black Power conference that July. But now, with the conference a mere two months away, he rescinded this offer in a meeting in his office. Watching Kamarakafego masterfully unleash a barrage of expletives at Barrow and his deputy, Cameron Tudor, was New York's Sonny Carson, who was there to "keep things calm." Instead, the police were now escorting both of these men to the airport. But where there is smoke, there is usually fire. Resting somewhere in between the conservative demeanor of Trinidad and Tobago's Eric Williams and the political shrewdness of Guyana's Forbes Burnham, the infallible Barrow did have his reasons to reverse his decision.[1]

Only days before, Kamarakafego and Carson had picked up Kwame Ture from the same airport where they now stood. Ture had been invited to Barbados to speak at a People's Progressive Movement (PPM) rally. He had just flown in from Guyana, where his speeches on Black Power called for revolutionary violence, bloodshed, and guerilla struggle. His trip to Barbados was thus in question. Weeks earlier, Trinidad and Tobago's Black Power leaders Mackandal Daaga and Clive Nunez were denied entry into so-called Little

England, joining Ture and Kamarakafego on the prohibited-persons list of Black Power activists that was being circulated among immigration officials across the West Indies.[2]

But Barrow had overturned these bans; his cabinet had passed the order in his absence. His ministers included those, like Tudor, who claimed that "Black Power was as irrelevant to the Caribbean as White power was to Sweden."[3] Barrow had to fight for a compromise, which included the passing of a Public Order Bill that would allow Ture entry if he agreed to not make any public appearances or speeches.

Upon his arrival at the airport, Ture was asked to sign a document stating that he would not speak publicly. He signed it, "'In order to free OUR land, we will have to *KILL*,'" Stokely Carmichael." Soon after, he was met by Kamarakafego and Carson, and they approached an ostensibly white-owned taxi. This prompted a group of black cabbies to hail, "Why are you, who stand up for the colored mass, traveling in a white-owned car?" Duly admonished, Kamarakafego, Carson and Ture changed taxis. Black Power could not have asked for a better way to start a Sunday night.[4]

This small shift in plans triggered alarms among the Special Branch officers who were closely monitoring the group. British police commissioner Wilfred Parmer lurked close by with three riot squads on hand, prepared to swarm the PPM's rally at Independence Square and arrest Ture on stage. The group instead went to the home of Lucius Cools. Cools was the father of Anne Cools, one of the students charged in Montreal's Black Power sit-ins. He was also related to Bobby Clarke, the local coordinator of the second international conference. Clarke was also very influential among Bridgetown's "young and unemployed."[5]

The group had their own meeting and was eventually joined by about seventy people who had attended the PPM rally. Palmer had placed the house under close surveillance. His officers tried to record all who entered the house by photograph and name. His informants allegedly heard Ture state that Barbados was lethargic and that blood had to run. The first target was to be Palmer, followed by any others who hindered Black Power. This included "white-hearted" Barrow, who also needed to be murdered. Action was needed to draw the police out in Bridgetown, leaving Clarke to lead an attack on the police station. The Caribbean Broadcasting Corporation, Cable and Wireless, and the telephone company were to be taken over. The lessons of Trinidad and Tobago needed to be learned—Barbados stood in the way of the Caribbean Black Power revolution.[6]

Ture's "vitriolic" speech was passed to Barrow. Coupled with the fact that

Trinidad and Tobago was still smoldering from its massive Black Power uprising, Ture's alleged calls for violence against him were likely part of Barrow's decision to ban the conference. Days later, he presented Kamarakafego and Carson with a long list of demands for the conference, claiming that this was due to external foreign pressures that would negatively impact the tourist industry.[7]

Kamarakafego promptly informed the *Bermuda Recorder* that the government of Barbados had issued demands to the Black Power Conference that "in preservation of its autonomy" were impossible to agree to. This included stating that they could not exclude anyone from attending (namely, white persons could participate), that conference participants could not attend or speak at any meetings or assemblies, could not address educational institutions, and could not make any video or tape recordings.[8] He found it "a matter of grave concern" that no black government in the Caribbean had "the freedom or power to open its facilities to our Conference." He understood that the foreign American, British, French, and Dutch colonial interests were fearful of even the least expression of Black Power. They had joined forces with white Caribbean bankers, hotel owners, sugar planters, bauxite company executives, and black bourgeois governments in the region to block the conference. This collective claimed that acts of protests in the Caribbean had escalated since Bermuda's Black Power conference. Kamarakafego linked this agitation to decades of anticolonial resistance, including the 1920s and 30s activism of Marcus Garvey and George Padmore. For these reasons, it was clear that that conference could not be held in the Caribbean.[9]

At the time, Chuck Stone was chair of the National Conference on Black Power. He and the Executive Committee of the national conference remained committed to holding a meeting that year. Hence, in September 1970, with the critical support of Amiri Baraka, the conference took place in Atlanta, Georgia, as the Congress of African Peoples (CAP). This chapter details Kamarakafego's global efforts to organize the Barbados conference, and describes how the road to CAP passed through Africa, Oceania, Europe, and the Caribbean.

Black Power and Pan-Africanism

The initial idea for the Barbados meeting had emerged at Bermuda's 1969 Black Power Conference. Here, according to the CIA, considerable attention was given to "long-range plans for international coordination of the

Black Power movement." Such enthusiasm led to plans not only for the 1970 Barbados conference, but also for a Sixth Pan-African Congress (6PAC).[10]

Cyril Lionel Robert James, a longtime mentor to Kamarakafego, was central to these discussions. While best remembered for his classic work on the Haitian Revolution, *Black Jacobins*, James's critical relationship with the Black Power movement deserves much more scholarly attention. James remained in Bermuda for about a week after the conference. During that time, he and Kamarakafego had a "long and fruitful" discussion about the global status of black people. Kamarakafego raised the idea of a subsequent conference, 6PAC, and the need for participation from black people who had historically not been represented at such meetings. This included black communities of Oceania and the South and Central Americas. James instructed Kamarakafego to use his contacts to find out what black communities in those areas thought about Black Power and a 6PAC. This launched a five-year process of organizing and collaboration with activists from around the world.[11]

In late July 1969, Kamarakafego left Bermuda on a global tour to organize both meetings (his activities surrounding 6PAC will be discussed in the next chapter). He traveled through London and Paris, where he met with Aimé Cesaire. At James's suggestion, Kamarakafego then traveled to Guinea to seek the consul of Nkrumah, who he had not seen since 1962.[12]

Nkrumah had lived in Conakry since Ghana's military coup of 1966. There is much warranted visibility surrounding the relationship between Nkrumah and Kwame Ture. But Nkrumah influenced, was visited by, and corresponded with scores of Black Power activists and groups during his time in Guinea. This dynamic of Nkrumah's, as well as his writings about Black Power, have not been sufficiently unpacked by Black Power literature. Nkrumah's contacts ranged from little-known groups and personalities, such as Washington, DC's, Blackman's Volunteer Army of Liberation, Pharaoh Alymphaa Nkongo, and Los Angeles's James 34 X, who warned Nkrumah to "be on the lookout for the CIA."[13] Nkrumah's correspondents also included known personalities such as Shirley Graham Du Bois and James and Grace Lee Boggs.

In May 1968, London-based Nigerian Obi Egbuna introduced himself to Nkrumah by letter. Egbuna urgently requested a personal audience with Osagyefo, describing himself as a "true Africanist" and an "invincibly strong believer in Nkrumah." He asked to spend two weeks in Guinea to work on a play that he was writing, *The Trials of Kwame Nkrumah*. Egbuna also sought counsel about his revolutionary activities; he was the president of the Universal Colored People's Association (UCPA), the new organ of Black Power in Britain. He stressed that he understood what it meant to be a "philosopher in chains" and misunderstood by the people that he was fighting for.[14]

Egbuna and the UCPA were central players in Black Power's spread in Britain. In 1966, Egbuna toured the United States while visiting SNCC. In London, Black Power "came to dinner" in 1967, when Egbuna, Ture, and James were keynote speakers at the Dialectics Liberation conference. It never left. The movement rooted itself within urban black communities such as Brixton and Notting Hill—the backyard of Trinidadian Communist and founder of West Indian Carnival Claudia Jones. Spearheaded by West Indian and African migrant communities, Black Power refused to bow to police brutality, white violence, and Britain's racist education system. Placed under constant pressure by British police officers, Black Power rallied around Caribbean restaurants, Rocksteady dancehalls, Rasta, and the historic hub of black radical speech making, Hyde Park. As it had been elsewhere in the world, the movement was an emphatic response to racism, police brutality, the criminalization of black youth, white xenophobia toward black immigration and culture, racist housing practices and social discrimination, an education system that denied West Indian and African heritage, and Britain's support of apartheid and neocolonialism in Africa.

After leaving the UCPA, Egbuna formed London's Black Panther Party in June 1968. According to Scotland Yard, the London Black Panthers swiftly grew to about eight hundred members, most of whom were Nigerian. According to the police, the militant party used extreme violence against people who disagreed with its views. It produced a booklet, *Black Power Speaks*, and met every Sunday at Hyde Park, where it "baited and subsequently assaulted the police and members of the public." In response to these activities, on June 9, 1968, a Black Panther Party member, Maxwell Warren, was arrested and charged with wounding a police officer. Egbuna allegedly ordered the party to the police station in an effort to break Warren out.[15]

Displeased by the arrest, Egbuna handwrote a document, "What to do when cops lay their hands on black men at the Speakers Corner." The Nigerian playwright found it a disgrace that "eight cats in police uniforms" were able to kidnap, club, and dump in a Black Maria van three black men, and then take them to their "police Klan Headquarters" while hundreds of black men stood watching. Egbuna felt that the police were able to do it not because these men were cowards, but because they did not know what to do in response. His pamphlet thus gave a plan of action for the next time it happened. This included having all black men present to surge forward like a "black steamroller" and beating the cops until the men were freed. For Egbuna, it made no sense to beat up a cop unless you wanted to "beat him unconsciousness or dead." Hence, at the end of any such rescue mission, no single cop could be left standing on his feet and therefore able to identify anyone.[16]

Allegedly, Egbuna sought to place the document in *Black Power Speaks*. Two other Black Panthers, Nigerian Peter Martin and Fijian Gideon Keteuni Turagalevu Dolo, accompanied him to the printer, where Dolo asked for two thousand copies. Instead, the printer informed the police, claiming that he heard Egbuna tell them that the party was going to be "armed to the teeth" and planned to learn judo, karate, and how to use shotguns. He also claimed that Egbuna said that Nkrumah was going to give him funds for the party when they met in Guinea. In July, Dolo, Egbuna, and Martin were all arrested and tried and spent several months in prison. This was days after Egbuna returned from Guinea.[17]

While in Guinea, he recorded on a cassette what would become Nkrumah's historic "Message to the Black People of Britain." Egbuna introduced the message: "[This] recording is the first of its kind, it is a message to the black peoples of Britain from Conakry by Osagyefo, by president Kwame Nkrumah. We are recording it from his villa. Any noise you might here it is the sea, singing like a whispering, as it pays its respect to the overland."[18]

Nkrumah greeted "members of the Black Panther Movement, and all [his] black brothers and sisters, comrades and friends from the Caribbean, Africa, Asia, Latin America and all corners of the Third World." He stated that Black Power was the power of the four-fifths of the world population that had been "systematically damned" into a state of underdevelopment by capitalism, colonialism, and neocolonialism. Black Power was the sum total of the economic, cultural, and political power in which the black world needed to have in order to achieve survival in a highly developed technical society, and in a world ravaged by imperialism, colonialism, neocolonialism, and fascism. Black Power was the "struggle for the possession of the economic, cultural, social and political power which . . . in common with the oppressed and the exploited of the earth," black people needed to have in order to "stampede and overthrow the oppressor."[19]

Black people were in Britain not by chance or by choice; they were there because of British colonialism and the strangling of their home countries by British neocolonialism. They lived in the "citadel of British imperialism" and thus had a significant role to play in the international black revolutionary movement. Just as how in Nkrumah's days in London, the black community organized the Colored Men's Association, today, Black Power produced groups like Michael X's Racial Adjustment Action Society and Egbuna's Black Panther movement. These two organizations needed to "mobilize, educate, and re-awaken the black people of Britain to the full realization of their revolutionary potential." The discrimination, prejudice, and racial hostility that blacks experiences in Britain went on in the United States, apartheid South Africa, Latin America, Australia, Rhodesia, Angola, Mozambique, and Portuguese Guinea. Nkrumah argued that what was "important is not where you are but what you do"—black people needed to fight wherever they found themselves, whether home in Africa or in the Diaspora. Finally, he stated that he was not in exile but at home in Conakry, for he would be at home "in any part of the black world." Nkrumah accepted a request to be a patron of Black Power, and he stood behind Black Power's "revolutionary endeavors." In return, he asked that the black people of Britain answer his "call when the clarion sounded."[20]

Egbuna carried the cassette back to Britain. He transcribed and edited this statement, which was later published in Nkrumah's *The Struggle Continues*. In August 1970, he sent Nkrumah a review copy of his heartfelt *Destroy This Temple: Black Power Speaks in Britain*, which he wrote while incarcerated. However, Nkrumah felt that his discussion of race and sexuality would harm the African revolution, the Black Power movement, and his personal reputation.[21]

By this time, Black Power in Britain had spread across London, Manchester, and Birmingham via groups like the South East London Parents Organization. Panthers like Darcus Howe, Jamaica's Olive Morris, Trinidad and Tobago's Althea Jones-Lecointe, and poet Linton Kwesi Johnson rose to the occasion. In March 1970, sixteen Panthers were arrested during a demonstration at the US embassy in support of Bobby Seale. In August 1970, they led a protest against racism and the aggressive policing of the West Indian Mangrove restaurant. When a clash with the police broke out, the "Mangrove Nine" were charged with assault, possession of an offensive weapon, and incitement to riot. Also in August, Panthers fought off police during a raid of one of its social events at the Oval House, leading to the arrest of Jones-Lecointe and others.[22]

Nkrumah discussed Black Power extensively with James and Grace Lee Boggs. In 1968, the couple informed him that the Black Panther Party was the organization that had come closest to having a program that black youth could identify with, but they felt that the size of its membership was increasing more rapidly than its "politically educated and disciplined cadres." While there was a growing militancy in African American youth, the Boggses felt that the weaknesses in the movement were emerging as a result of a "worship of success," illusions about overnight revolution, a tendency to envision "revolutionary war only in terms of Western-style shoot outs," and an "unconscious racism which found it hard to accept serious theoretical-political leadership from Africans or Afro-Americans." The Boggses felt that some members of the movement needed to comprehend that its military wing needed to be politically minded—the best guerilla fighter was a "politically educated one." They hoped that Nkrumah's writings could help in these efforts.[23] They felt that the Panthers needed to come to grips with these fundamental questions—the cult of personality, the inseparable relationship between political theory and militancy, and illusions about overnight success. They also argued that fratricidal conflict had broken out at the New Jersey and Philadelphia Black Power conferences. The Boggses called for Nkrumah to publish pamphlets relating the African revolution to the Black revolution in the United States.[24]

Nkrumah was also critical of the Black Power movement in the United States. He felt that the movement was adopting tactic after tactic without an overall strategy and thus could not ultimately succeed in seizing political control of the white power structure in the United States. According to Nkrumah, Black Power needed to organize scientifically through a vanguard party, and African Americans had to improve the conditions of blacks in the United States, embarrass the US power structure, and volunteer to participate "in the armed phase of the African revolution on African soil." He also asserted that the African revolution was "indissolubly linked" to the black revolution in the United States."[25] Nkrumah felt that the impact of Black Power did have imperialist and neocolonial structures trembling. His contemporary Amy Jacques Garvey certainly agreed, asserting that Black Power struck fear in the hearts of whites. Nkrumah argued that the only way to achieve African liberation was through armed struggle and believed that Black Power's emergence had made the African American freedom struggle "militant and armed."[26]

Nkrumah saw Black Power as a "daughter" of pan-Africanism. His 1968 pamphlet, *The Specter of Black Power*, stated that the movement had descended on the world like a "thunder cloud flashing its lighting." Black Power had emerged from the "ghettoes, swamps, and cotton-fields of America" to now haunt its streets and legislative councils. After historicizing Black Power in the struggles of the black world since the Atlantic slave trade, he centered it in the 1965 urban uprising of Watts. For Nkrumah, Black Power was "part of the vanguard of world revolution against capitalism, imperialism and neo-colonialism that had enslaved and exploited oppressed peoples." Black Power was part of the world rebellion of the oppressed against the oppressor. It operated across Africa, North and South America, the Caribbean, and the entire African Diaspora. It was linked with the pan-African struggle in Africa.[27]

It was this level of political discourse that led Kamarakafego to visit Nkrumah in Guinea, and he immensely enjoyed these fruitful talks. Kamarakafego left Nkrumah for East Africa to continue organizing 6PAC and the Barbados conference. He traveled through Zaire, Uganda, Kenya, Mauritius, Kenya, and Tanzania. From East Africa, he continued on to Australia and Oceania.[28]

Kamarakafego returned to Bermuda in October 1969. He was aware that the Progressive Labor Party (PLP) had invited Barrow to speak at its annual banquet. The spirit of Black Power was in the air. Barrow spoke in front of PLP members such as party leader Lois Browne-Evans, who had just been Bermuda's lone delegate to the Commonwealth Parliamentary Association Conference in Trinidad and Tobago. While there, Browne-Evans informed the *Trinidad Express* that the time was "fast approaching when oppressed Black people all over the world" would get what was theirs. Wearing a dashiki, wooden earrings, and an Afro, she told the press that Black Power's challenge to the established system meant that every effort was being made to suppress it.[29]

Kamarakafego spoke with Barrow while he was in Bermuda. While here, the prime minister agreed that the conference could be held in Barbados. After subsequently meeting with his cabinet, Barrow gave Kamarakafego the green light to inform the Black Power Committee about the confirmation. After doing so, Kamarakafego continued to organize for the talks.[30]

It was not a given that Barbados would be the conference location. Howard University president James Cheek turned down a request by Chuck Stone, chair of the National Conference on Black Power, to hold the conference on its campus in April 1970, claiming that the school was planning to use spring recess to conduct rehabilitation work on several buildings after the intensive use of its facilities during the regular academic year.[31]

By March 1970, plans for the Barbados conference had gained much traction. The *Bermuda Recorder* noted with much anticipation that the conference was going to be held in July. It contextualized the previous five Black Power conferences in the histories of Marcus Garvey's "Back to Africa

Movement," W. E. B Du Bois's NAACP, and George Padmore's Pan-African Movement. Barbados was a "tolerant and small society" that welcomed "all brothers and sisters." White colonial oppression was a daily nightmare, and there was a "growing trend towards black genocide." Hence, the conference sought to establish techniques, methods, and alternative strategies to help black people achieve political, economic, educational, and cultural power. Applications for the conference were available at the PLP headquarters. Bermuda's Donald Smith Travel Agency, which was organizing trips to the conference, advertised in the *Recorder* that roundtrip tickets were set at $175.[32]

Advertisements for the talks also appeared in African American media such as the *African-American Teachers Forum*, the newsletter of the New York–based African-American Teachers Association. Its March-April 1970 edition noted that with the Black Power conferences becoming more successful, the Bridgetown conference was about "Black survival and Black consciousness through Black operation harmony." With a registration fee of $10, preregistration was to be directed to Kamarakafego in Bermuda.[33]

Kamarakafego communicated with activists from across Africa, the Americas, and Oceania about the conference. In March 1970, Nkrumah wrote to Kamarakafego, thanking him for a recent letter. He noted with interest that there would be "a meeting of Black people from Africa, Asia, the Americas, the Caribbean, Australia and other parts of the world. . . . I shall be glad to be an official patron."[34]

However, by April 1970, two major events had taken place that influenced Barrow to change his mind about the talks. One was the Black Power revolution in Trinidad and Tobago. The second was Kwame Ture's electrifying Caribbean tour.

Black Power in Trinidad and Tobago was driven by student radicalism, militant trade unionism, and a 15 percent urban unemployment rate. It was also greatly moved by the Montreal protests at Sir George Williams University. Daaga, a student at the University of the West Indies (UWI), St. Augustine, traveled to Canada to meet with the Montreal defense committee. While in route in New York, he met with the local branch of the Black Panther Party. Reportedly, the party turned down his request for financial assistance to "help bring about a revolution in Trinidad."[35]

Daaga was former president of the Students Guild of UWI. In solidarity with Montreal's students, in February 1969, he helped to form UWI's NJAC, a "pressure group" that emphasized Black people's rights. One of the committee's strengths lay in Daaga's ability to forge relationships with labor organizations like the Oilfields Workers Trade Union and its president-general

George Weekes. In April 1969, NJAC held demonstrations in support of a strike by Nunez and the Transport and Industrial Workers Union.[36]

In August 1969, CIA officials claimed that Black Power in Trinidad had lost "a unique opportunity to fill the vacuum . . . of political opposition" to Prime Minister Eric Williams's government. Strikingly, the agency saw this failure as being a result of "poor leadership, lack of organization and concentration on purposeless demonstrations that" did not "capture the imagination of the people," noting that the movement had failed to "transfer nebulous theories of Black power into issues with which the populace is genuinely concerned." With "little popular appeal," the movement's political influence, according to the CIA, was "nil." As such, while Black Power had probably initially been "considered a serious threat" to Williams, the CIA felt that this was no longer the case.[37]

In 1970, the CIA's assessment was decisively proven to be wrong. Black Power messages and iconography were seen and heard during Carnival via Calypso artists and other participants. In February, Daaga, NJAC, and the UWI Students Guild launched demonstrations in protest of the trial of the Montreal students. George Weekes and the Oilfield Workers' Trade Union soon joined in. Weekes had just spent a month in the United States and Canada, where he reportedly made Black Power contacts. Amid government indecision, NJAC mobilized over ten thousand people and established a "people's parliament." During a march that included several hundred people, Canadian banks and a Roman Catholic cathedral were damaged. Nine protestors were arrested, rallying several thousand more demonstrators in support. At the March trial of these "ringleaders," clashes broke out with police, who injured many with batons. However, NJAC's attempts to organize a mass march to the cane fields in solidarity with East Indian sugar workers failed to convince them to join wholeheartedly.[38]

The acquittal of the Trinidadian students in Montreal of the most serious charges and the government's decision to pay the fines that had been imposed temporarily reduced tensions. During a radio and television address, Williams admitted a "failure of communication and promised immediate reforms." This was a classic case of too little, too late. Nunez warned that the payment of the fines was not the end. The struggle "had only just begun and would only end when NJAC controlled the economy of the country." Nunez expressed support for a Castro-type revolution in Trinidad. He and Daaga "were not interested in participating in a national government, but in spearheading a revolutionary movement throughout the Caribbean."[39]

In early April, one protestor was shot and killed after allegedly threatening a policeman with an ice pick. Amid his calls for the nationalization of the oil and sugar industries, Weekes threatened to lead a general strike. This prompted Williams to declare a state of emergency on April 21. Weekes, Nunez, and Daaga were all arrested, prompting the mutiny of eighty soldiers at the Teteron Bay barracks. Investigations alluded to a conspiracy to overthrow the government.[40] Williams requested military support from the United States to put it down. Three leaders were charged with treason and a number of others with sedition. Two of these men, Raffique Shah and Kumar Mahabir, had reportedly received three weeks of guerilla training in Cuba in 1968.[41]

The fifty-six-day uprising pushed the CIA to change its position. By June 1970, the agency was forced to admit that NJAC had emerged from "relative obscurity . . . to challenging the stability of the Government." This reflected a "deep underlying resentment" of Williams's "slow-moving efforts to promote socio-economic change." It had been a long fourteen years of economic "sufferation" and the rising of urban unemployment. In a sense, Black Power was helping to "vocalize and accelerate a trend already in existence." Lloyd Best, UWI lecturer in economics, argued that the "February revolution" had proved the government to be irrelevant.[42]

In February 1970, John Marson and Jitu Weusi (Les Campbell) of the New York–based Afro-American Students Cultural Association visited the demonstrators. While there, they called for "global revolutionary struggle and action" against "black men with white minds." A history teacher by profession who worked closely with Sonny Carson, Weusi would later form Uhuru Sasa Shule (the Freedom Now School) and the EAST organization.[43]

Other Black Power groups in Trinidad and Tobago included Aldwyn Primus's Black Panther Organization, the Young Power Group, and the National Union of Freedom Fighters (NUFF). Years later, NUFF lost members such as Beverly Jones while engaging in armed struggle against the state. Jones's sister was Althea Jones, who would head London's Black Panther Party. In 1969, Best and the New World Group formed Tapia House and its radical journal, *Tapia*. Black Power publications in the country included the United National Independence Party's *Moko*, *Pivot*, and *East Dry River Speaks*.[44]

Never Honored: Kwame Ture in the Caribbean

Bob Marley's 1978 song "Black Survival" lamented that "a good man is never honored in his country." The song could have written about Kwame Ture.

During Ture's Caribbean tour in the spring of 1970, he was not permitted to pass through the land of his birth, Trinidad and Tobago. He was also prevented from entering Montserrat, St. Vincent, Bermuda, and Jamaica.[45] However, he did reach Guyana, where his trip came to a head.

Black Power in Guyana public was driven by two main organizations: the Ratoon group and the state-endorsed African Society for Cultural Relations with Independent Africa (ASCRIA), which had been formed in 1964 by Eusi Kwayana (Sydney King) to develop "educational programs related to African history, culture, and language to emphasize the African heritage of Black Guyanese." Kwayana was born on April 4, 1925, in Demerara, the site of the massive 1823 anti-slavery rebellion. Raised in a "poor African family," he was a longtime African-centered organizer. A schoolteacher by trade, Kwayana started a private school in the village of Buxton in 1956. In 1961, he formed the African Society for Racial Equality. Appropriately defined by Nigel Westmass as an "organic pan-Africanist," Kwayana's grassroots support came from primarily non-urban village communities.[46]

In contrast, US embassy officials in Guyana described the charismatic Kwayana as being a "fanatic" who was a highly ascetic and disciplined person. A vegetarian, he did not smoke or drink alcohol and lived and dressed in simplicity. The embassy claimed that Kwayana shunned social occasions, abjured romantic relationships with women, appeared incorruptible, and though soft-spoken, was "intense and deadly serious." Indeed, the embassy felt that he was "capable of deception and violence." In 1968, at a government-sponsored memorial service for Martin Luther King, Kwayana allegedly called "for the lives of two white persons for every black American killed" in Vietnam. The embassy felt that Guyana's prime minister Burnham needed to watch him closely.[47] Burnham did not need to be told that.

Kwayana called for a black Guyanese economic system developed along the lines of African socialism. During a visit to Israel, he was impressed by the communal Kibbutz settlements. In 1968, he launched a "cultural revolution." His pamphlet, *The Teachings of the Cultural Revolution*, was comprised of popular Guyanese cultural proverbs. It urged blacks to adopt African names and to revive African culture by studying models such as the "philosophy of creation of the Akan peoples, in which Nyame" made man, nature, knowledge, order, and death. He also referenced Central Africa's Kimbundu and called for the education of children to follow that of East Africa's Kikuyu. Members of ASCRIA also studied Kiswahili.[48]

Britain's Foreign and Commonwealth Office (FCO) claimed that ASCRIA emerged from the "tough Negro village of Buxton" and Georgetown. From its formation, ASCRIA expressed solidarity with international black movements. In 1966, it protested human rights violations in the United States and supported a solidarity day for black prisoners. By 1969, it had grown to about two hundred members and thousands of sympathizers.[49]

In March 1969, ASCRIA held its third annual convention at the Buxton high school, of which Kwayana was principal. One hundred delegates representing some twenty of thirty-seven chapters attended. Kwayana called for ASCRIA to reject all things white, and to seek the "material, cultural, political, spiritual salvation for the black people of Guyana, the Caribbean and the Western Hemisphere." This included Global South solidarity with African communities in the Caribbean, Cuba, Brazil, Surinam, and Africa.[50]

Kwayana told his audience, "We have not in ASCRIA seen fit to use the slogan of Black Power as our mode of struggle. But we want it to be understood that so long as Black Power means the overthrow of white power by non-whites, by black men and brown men and yellow men on a world scale, we identify ourselves with it completely and without reserve." According to the CIA, this reflected Kwayana's reorientation of ASCRIA to an "aggressive racist position with the avowed goal of destroying white influence in the country." Kwayana continued, asserting that "we could never be true soldiers of Bandung" unless we first accept "our African heritage as Black people." He also attacked "certain professed Black Power movements" in London for contradicting themselves "by falling under the power of militant white international movements that [did] not share the aspirations of the revolutionary black people of the world."[51]

While organizing the Bermuda conference, Kamarakafego met with Janet Jagan and Kwayana in Guyana. As a result, at the ASCRIA convention, it was decided to "campaign hard" with Bermuda's "regional Black Power Conference for a Caribbean General Certification of Education" instead of one from London. The talks also called for: a drama festival of African plays; invitations of Afro-American folk singers; the establishment of cooperatives in savings, forestry, mining, and small industry; the spreading of Guyanese history through lectures and literature; and bringing international black athletes to the country. Ndugu Merwyn Salaam, an African American member of the Nation of Islam, discussed black resistance in the United Sates, arguing that revolts against slavery originated the Black Power slogan, "Burn, baby, burn."[52]

Black Power in Guyana was part of a political chess game played between Kwayana and Prime Minister Burnham. Burnham appointed Kwayana chairman of the Guyana Marketing Corporation. During the convention,

Kwayana thanked Burnham for declaring at a 1968 Youth Power Now rally that Black Power was the consolidation of black men and brown men over their resources and destiny. This was strikingly similar to ASCRIA's own definition of Black Power. Kwayana also congratulated the Guyanese government for "steering clear of the anti-Black hysteria" of Jamaica, Trinidad, and Surinam, and he demanded that it provide sanctuary to black liberators. For its part, ASCRIA did not regard the ideas of Malcolm X, Ture, Elijah Muhammad, Walter Rodney, or Muhammad Ali as being subversive. On this note, ASCRIA welcomed a group of black "Muslim brothers and sisters" who had recently moved to Guyana. The meeting ended with the singing of the Guyanese National anthem.[53]

The politically shrewd Burnham used Black Power for his own purposes. He handled Kwayana "gingerly." Kwayana's positions within the government seemingly gave him influence within Burnham's Peoples National Congress (PNC). Yet Burnham benefited by having Kwayana kept under close watch. The CIA felt that Burnham's Westernism prevented him from totally supporting Kwayana. For example, Burnham disavowed PNC members from publicly participating Black Power activities.[54]

On February 23, 1970, Guyana became a republic. This was the 207th anniversary of the revolt of Coffy (Kofi) in Berbice. Burnham referred to Coffy as Guyana's first national hero. He later informed his PNC Congress:

> We have carried out the political revolution. We are independent, we are a republic, we have our national hero—Cuffy . . . The economic revolution can no longer be delayed . . . I have been referring to the social and economic revolution, the national ownership and control of Guyana's resources, and their development by and for Guyanese. That is what Black Power is about.[55]

In conjunction with the Republic celebrations, Guyana hosted a three-day Pan-African and Black Revolutionary National Seminar. During the meeting, Burnham expressed solidarity with Black Power. He used Guyana as an example of how "political power [did] not give economic power" to blacks. In contrast, he argued, *his* cooperative economic scheme—led by Kwayana—included the development of black economic power. Seemingly in response to ASCRIA's calls of the last year, he stated that "exiled freedom fighters" could find refuge in Guyana.[56]

This occurred during the growing Black Power dissidence in Trinidad and Tobago. The CIA felt that Burnham was "trying to disarm Black Power militants by acceding to their demands and adjusting his policies in their direction." At an April Caribbean heads of state meeting, Burnham had unsuccessfully tried to convince other West Indian leaders that "violent agitators should be controlled after they arrive in a country but should not be banned." He felt that Black Power in the Caribbean was a "force to be reckoned with," and if its dissidents were not controlled, "the Movement could be turned against all authority."[57]

Burnham's true feelings on Black Power were perhaps best described in his statement that Caribbean heads of state were "all sitting on a volcano." The developments in Trinidad were a "threat to the entire establishment." He argued that he had been able to control Black Power by giving it some ground. Still, his ministers took steps all the time to preempt those who might cause trouble. This included ASCRIA, which Burnham's minister, Sonny Ramphal, felt had been given too that many concessions—as had "those gentlemen at the University," the Ratoon group.[58]

Ratoon was much smaller than ASCRIA. Comprised primarily of radical university students and faculty, its monthly newsletter *Ratoon* stressed Black Power, New World, and Leftist themes. University of Guyana professor Walter Green Omowale, who was also the junior vice president of ASCRIA, led the organization.[59] Clive Thomas was also a member.

Ture had been invited to Guyana by Ratoon. He arrived there with his wife, Mariam Makeba. Always one to make an impression, his short time in the country was full of controversial public statements. He was placed under tight surveillance. At a May 5 press conference, Ture stated that he had been "banned from Trinidad & Tobago because of American and British pressure" that had been placed on Williams. America controlled the island, and Williams had "sold out to the imperialists." Yet he would eventually "return to the island because the people would eventually run it." Ture defined Black Power as "a movement of liberation to encourage Black people to come together and organize themselves for freedom, using any means necessary." This meant political and economic control of resources. Black Power "did not connote black visibility" but instead the "ability to perform functions as human beings in a society which dehumanized us." Blacks did not own or control land but "were victims of capitalism and racialism." The "African struggle was going to be long and fierce," and blacks needed to organize. He applauded the Guyanese government's support of "free speech" and intelligence in allowing him to visit.[60]

According to one FCO official, Carmichael's visit was Guyana's most significant week since its 1968 elections. He claimed that Ture had "abused Guyanese hospitality by preaching murder and violence." This "virtually

destroyed" the Ratoon group, undermined Cheddi Jagan's East Indian over-
tures toward Black Power, and identified Black Power with "unremitting
study and an end to jollity." Ture's first public talks took place at secondary schools. He told students that they needed to "be prepared for violence
since there could be no remission of sins without the shedding of blood."
Yet the "cat among the pigeons" was when he defined "Black Power as African Power and specifically excluded Chinese and Indians from the Movement." After arguing that the highest expression of Black Power was pan-
Africanism, a number of non-African students left the talks. This left some
confusion on the platform, as the Ratoon group had gained popularity via
its multiracial composition.[61]

The day's next drama came when Carmichael spoke at an ASCRIA "Con-
key Reception." When members of the crowd refused to be silent, Carmichael threatened to leave. Kwayana convinced him to stay, and calm was
eventually restored. This time when he began to speak, the lights in the hall
went out. He continued to speak about "kill or be killed." The following
day was the University of Guyana's turn. Standing firm in a jacket and tie,
Carmichael was the keynote speaker at an "Ideology and the Black Revolution" symposium. He received a "boisterous reception" while expressing his
pleasure at being in Guyana despite the "rudeness" shown to him. After giving thanks, he returned to his pleas for violence, remarking that in Guyana,
there would have to be "bloodshed and guerillas." He would not have the
last word of the night.[62]

Representing Ratoon, Thomas took to the rostrum to read a paper on
Black Power that expressed the group's disagreement with Ture. It argued
that pan-Africanism was an African ideology that had revolutionary potential everywhere except in three societies: Surinam, Trinidad, and Guyana. In
contrast, Ratoon's ideology was correctly based on "Afro-Indian solidarity
at all and every stage in the struggle against imperialism and white racism."
This divergence of views headlined Guyana's and the broader Caribbean's
newspapers.[63]

Allegedly, Burnham had pressured Ratoon to ensure that Ture did not
use Guyana as a launching pad from which to attack Williams and other
Caribbean leaders. Burnham himself was pressed to make a statement sepa-
rating himself from Ture. For example, Jamaican prime minister Shearer
telephoned Burnham in protest against Ture's attacks on other West Indian
governments.[64]

After the university talk, Ture went to a meeting in Tiger Bay with the
"roughs" of Georgetown. Ratoon was apparently not aware of this meeting.

He held a public rally at Guyana's National Park, reiterating the need for bloodshed. Critically, he attacked his denunciation by a local paper, the *Evening Post*, but accepted its idea that he should not attack Williams from Guyana. He also conceded that Ratoon had a democratic right to disagree with his position on Black Power, which ASCRIA, in contrast, agreed with.[65]

Radio Demerara's Robert Williams denounced Ture. Williams claimed that when Ture, the "High Priest" of Black Power reached Guyana, he found that the movement had been adulterated to fit various shapes and forms. At every public appearance, he reiterated that Black Power "embraced only Black people, people of African descent." He also allegedly stated that other non-white races were natural allies of black people, with common enemies of white imperialism and capitalism. Still, they needed to organize themselves separately. He also referenced constantly the "necessity to kill." Biblically speaking, "there could be no remission of sins" except by the "shedding of blood." He also referred to ASCRIA as the only ideologically pure Black Power movement in Guyana and that other institutions, including the government, were only giving "lip service" to Black Power.[66]

Carmichael left Guyana on May 10. His time in Guyana was publicly criticized and condemned. The president of the Maha Sabha, Guyana's largest Hindu organization, attacked Carmichael's definition of "Black Power as African Power" and chastised Ture for undoing the efforts of the government and other organizations to rebuild the "fabric of national unity." He also blamed the groups that had sponsored Carmichael's visit for the troubles. Cheddi Jagan found himself at a loss, for he could not associate himself with either ASCRIA or Ratoon because he shared Carmichael's anti-imperialism. Yet even he conceded that Ture's Black Power thesis "made a mockery of the Guyanese national motto of One People, One Nation, One Destiny."[67]

Former mayor of Georgetown Archie Codrington publicly alleged that Carmichael's "campaign of murder, arson and confiscation" aroused "feelings of disgust and derision." Furthermore, it "reminded his listeners that Nkrumah . . . was a man discredited and repudiated by" the masses of Ghana. The government-sponsored *Sunday Chronicle* took the opportunity to criticize Ture. In the *Sunday Graphic*, renowned journalist Carl Blackman asked, "Oh my God, Stokely, what have you done?"[68]

Carmichael found that ASCRIA was being most closely associated with his views on Black Power. Yet Kwayana may have been concerned with the public image of ASCRIA, which had not been associated with violence. The FCO gleefully reckoned that Ratoon needed a "period of convalescence" before it could "venture again into the public eye."[69]

The PNC attacked Ratoon in its newspaper, *New Nation*. The article, titled "Ratoon Men Earn 4-Figure Salaries," attacked the group as a "confused bunch of kids." It asserted that while Ratoon claimed to be an anti-elite champion of the people, it was comprised mostly of members of the University of Guyana. Yet they did not march with the people during one Labor Day, and were perhaps too busy "enjoying the luxuries of life." It argued that Omowale, Rickey Singh, Miles Fitzpatrick, Thomas, Josh Ramsammy, and Compton Bourne were "not poor boys" and were doing quite well. As a professor of social sciences, Thomas earned $1,010 per month. Furthermore, they put in less hours of work than did Burnham.[70]

Ture had not spent much time in Guyana, but the FCO felt that it would be "weeks or months" before his full impact was felt. Jagan's political momentum had been slowed, as he had been arguing for weeks about the East Indian identification with Black Power. The FCO problematically asserted that this was the "first real confrontation between the real Black Power fanatic and the cheerful and easy-going Caribbean population." According to one FCO official, at one speech, Ture was "obviously dismayed by the local capacity for alcoholic consumption by a great many Guyanese Africans." Condescendingly, he remarked that this was a "considerable compliment to the Guyanese attitude and outlook." This was no compliment.[71]

The FCO felt that Burnham had correctly handled his trip. In contrast, the prime minister felt that Williams had been slow to address Black Power in Trinidad and Tobago. British high commissioner Kenneth Ritchie "knocked on wood" after remarking that events in Trinidad and Tobago had not sparked any similar issues in Guyana. This, he thought, was a tribute to Burnham's handling of the movement. Ritchie was forced to agree with Burnham's tactics, even as he suspected that Burnham adeptly exaggerated pressures "to achieve a particular objective in London or in Washington."[72]

Burnham closely communicated with the FCO throughout the entire process. In one meeting, Ritchie commented that the pressure from Black Power had waned since Ture's visit and that it had been a "very good week for Burnham." Burnham agreed—Ratoon "had been hit very hard and Jagan knocked even harder." Ritchie suggested that Burnham could "carefully exploit all this." Burnham felt that Ture "had misjudged the people of [Guyana], who knew more about violence then he did."[73]

In the same conversation, Burnham questioned Ritchie's concern about his plans to speak with two bauxite companies, Reynolds and Demerara Bauxite Company (DEMBA) about securing equity participation for the government. According to Ritchie, the two companies were "worried stiff" about Burnham's plans. The prime minister's response was that he was determined to be retired at fifty-five and not before then, and if he did not quickly "get on with radical policies," then the latter would happen. The forty-six-year-old prime minister questioned Ritchie's concern about DEMBA, a subsidiary of Aluminum Canada. Ritchie retorted that he was there to "watch the interests of British companies," and what happened to other companies could happen to those under his sphere as well. After pressing Burnham for his plans for the sugar industry, Burnham, "with his most angelic expression," remarked that the sugar companies were locally owned, and if he felt that something needed to be done with them, there would be "a full and friendly conversation first." Ritchie told Burnham that he was making it "bloody difficult" to sympathize with him and that he needed to do "something urgently to reassure" his "US colleague," as he knew that certain people in Washington were "pretty restive." This brought a lecture from Burnham on the "difficulties of talking to dull men."[74] Put another way, Burnham was prepared to maintain political power by any means necessary, and if this meant entertaining Black Power, then he was all for it. But he also reserved the right to use violence against his detractors if he felt the need to do so.

Barbados

Ture was on his way to Barbados. Burnham was not Barrow, and Guyana was not Barbados. In the latter, Black Power was driven by the PPM and the University Student Front (USF). Formed in 1966, the PPM had a membership about fifty people. Driven by Cuban- and Chinese-oriented Marxism, it occasionally contacted Jagan. Its *Black Star* paper was heavily focused on Black Power themes but had ceased publication in May 1969. Still, the Black Star Bookshop remained a hub for Marxist and radical literature.[75]

The USF was based out of the Barbados campus of UWI. The CIA claimed that the group had "alienated the majority of the population" by "rowdy and disruptive behavior" during rallies. In a public radio confrontation with USF, Barrow caustically derided "Black Power slogans calling for the overthrow of West Indian society." He labeled Black Power as being "highly subversive" and advised the students to "tend to their studies rather than destroying society."[76]

Barrow decided to "ban" the Black Power conference. Unlike Burnham, Barrow publicly denounced Black Power's supposedly "racist tactics and revolutionary declarations." His position had only hardened as a result of

Trinidad and Tobago's revolution. Black Power "militants" were banned from the island, and all non-Barbadians were prohibited from speaking at public rallies. All speakers and topics had to be vetted by the government before permits would be issued for public meetings. The government's new Public Law and Order Act made it a "crime to preach racial hatred or violence."[77]

But Barrow was also not Williams. He was actively involved in the social life of the island, whereas Williams may have "isolated himself from the people." This enabled Barrow to curtail the Black Power movement, which lacked a clear leader. The FCO felt that this was not because Barbadians were not interested in Black Power, but because of "third-rate opportunists."[78]

Intimately involved with Nina Simone, Barrow was seen everywhere across the country. So said the FCO:

> One day he is aqua lunging with the underwater boys, and then attending their annual dinner. Next morning we can be "buzzed" by the Prime Minister flying himself on a tour of inspection of Barbados. Sometime during the week he may be either buying or selling a cow; and he will certainly be driving himself around in a Vauxhall Viva or an 1100, shunning chauffeurs and ceremony. At 5:30 in the morning he can . . . be seen riding down Broad Street on his bay mare—incidentally, the wrong way on a one-way street, or shooting duck. He will perhaps lunch at the American Businessmen's Club. . . . No one can say that he is cut off or aloof. He is well informed of every new thought and new movement in this island.[79]

Ritchie had informed John Bennett, an FCO official assigned to Barbados, about Ture's visit in Guyana. He was told to warn Deputy Prime Minister Tudor that Ture "had expressed revolutionary views in Guyana and was quite unpredictable in his utterances." The visit had been carefully handled internally to prevent any problems. After thanking him, Tudor responded that as the Barbados Workers' Union had come out in support of the Public Orders Act, the government decided to ban Carmichael from Barbados. However, Barrow disagreed with the decision, arguing that Carmichael should be allowed to land but not to attend any political meeting or make any public speech. If he accepted these conditions, he would be allowed to spend one or two nights in Barbados.[80]

On May 14, 1970, Ritchie had a confidential lunch with the British police commissioner Palmer and his wife. The police commissioner called the meeting, as he wanted "a frank and full discussion of the problems of unrest in Barbados." He asked the high commissioner to drive himself to his house and to not use a chauffeur; for security reasons, Palmer arranged for his domestic staff to take the day off. The main course at lunch was a discussion on Black Power and Ture's impending visit. According to the commissioner, all members of the cabinet except Barrow called for a ban against Ture's visit. They had reached a compromise was reached whereby Carmichael would be allowed to land but would not be allowed to speak or attend a public meeting.[81]

From Bridgetown to Atlanta

This was the context in which the Barbados Black Power conference was banned. Kamarakafego's efforts to organize for the talks were being thwarted across the region. Along with PLP leaders Freddy Wade and Arthur Hodgson, Kamarakafego was now on the stop lists of St. Lucia, Antigua, St. Vincent, Anguilla, and the Cayman islands.[82]

In April 1970, Barrow asked Kamarakafego to come to Barbados to discuss the talks. As described earlier, it was then that Barrow informed him that he had rescinded his initial support due to "international pressures." In a May 4, 1970, letter to Kamarakafego, Barrow stated that recent events in the south Caribbean had prompted a number of questions about the Black Power conference. Barrow's government wanted assurances that the occasion would not be used by "dissident elements in Barbados" and neighboring territories to initiate "violent demonstrations." He wanted guarantees that no one attending the conference would advocate the overthrow by violence of Barbados or any other friendly democratic government in the region or incite racial hatred or discrimination against any groups, that no one would be excluded based upon race or color, and that adequate staff would be there to handle logistics, control participants, and cooperate with the government.[83]

In April, Stone had questioned the National Conference on Black Power's Executive Committee about the need for a national Black Power conference in the United States, given that Kamarakafego had planned the Barbados meeting. On May 4, Kamarakafego wrote to Stone, asking him to give remarks at the Barbados conference. Signed "Revolution and Peace," he now had other things to ask the chair of the Black Power Conference Continuation Committee.[84]

As a result of Kamarakafego's announcement to the committee that Barbados was a "no go," in a Washington, DC, meeting later that month, the

Executive Committee made a few critical decisions. According to Hayward Henry Jr., it was decided that a World Congress of African Peoples would be held in Atlanta, Georgia, in September 1970. The meeting would be international in scope and focus on the theme "From Black Power to Pan-Africanism." Secondly, it would aim to create a national structure that could provide a basis for operational harmony within the larger black freedom struggle. At the meeting, they hoped to develop a possible structure for the World Congress Assembly. Furthermore, the National Conference of Black Power and its Continuations Committee were to be abolished and replaced by Planning and Structure Committees.[85]

Haywood Jr. was chair of the Planning Committee. He informed the group that he was securing a meeting space at Paschal's Motor Hotel in Atlanta, Georgia, for a June planning meeting. The hotel was a historic meeting place for organizers of Atlanta's civil rights movement. Kamarakafego was also on the Planning Committee, and Amiri Baraka was selected to be on Structure Committee. According to Jimmy Garrett, Baraka was invited into a leadership role because he had the organizational apparatus that could hold such a conference at late notice.[86] All of this is the subject of the next chapter.

7

Aborigine—Not Puerto Rican!

Bruce McGuinness was a 5'5½" stoutly built Koori activist from Australia with straight hair and a pale complexion. At thirty-one years old, he was secretary of Melbourne's Aborigines Advancement League (AAL). But on the streets of Atlanta in 1970, he pretty much looked just like another American white liberal interested enough in Black Power to brave the Congress of African Peoples (CAP).[1] Kamarakafego was the program director of CAP. It was he who had invited McGuinness to the congress, along with indigenous Australian activists Patricia Korowa, Bob Maza, Jack Davis, and Sol Bellear.

At CAP, McGuinness learned much about race and Black Power in the Americas. But he had also fielded a lion's share of questions about his racial background, and, quite frankly, it was getting to be a bit much. One incident had escalated to a physical clash with a Black Panther, who incorrectly assumed that he was white. But now, in a closed workshop session, he had the perfect opportunity to settle the issue of his ethnicity. McGuinness took pains to explain his ancestry within the context of colonial violence in Australia. After hearing his lament about genocide, complexion and heritage, a workshop participant sought to console him: "But brother Bruce, you could always pass off as a Puerto Rican." McGuinness blew a gasket. Lacing his response with expletives, he retorted, "I'm not a . . . Puerto Rican! I'm a . . . Aborigine from Australia and the sooner you get to . . . know that the better!" He then stormed out the room.[2]

Profanity aside, this moment captures the essence of this chapter, which is centered on the international dynamics of the congress. One of Black Power's most critical meetings, CAP convened September 3–6, 1970, at Morris Brown College, a historically black institution. A four-day political whirlwind, it was as politically hot as the 90° weather that scorched the concrete sidewalks of Atlanta. The congress called for four ends of Black

Power—self-determination, self-sufficiency, self-respect, and self-defense for the black world.[3] In an intense space of protest and contestation, leading activists, scholars, scientists, students, and artists from across the black world rallied around Black Power and pan-Africanism.

The congress's official speakers were primarily black men, and included Hayward Henry, Jesse Jackson, Louis Farrakhan, Yosef Ben-Jochannan, Larry Neal, Haki Madhubuti, Kenneth Gibson, Ralph Abernathy, Acklyn Lynch, Howard Fuller, Julian Bond, Amiri Baraka, Surinam's Cyriel Karg, Guinea's ambassador Hajj Abdulaye Touré, and Dominica's Rosie Douglas. Its eleven workshops spanned black technology, economics, communication, education, history, creativity, history, law and justice, religious systems, social organization, and political liberation. According to Baraka, the congress was a contemporary manifestation of African men such as Blyden, Garvey, Du Bois, Hayford, Nyerere, Nkrumah, Touré, Elijah Muhammad, and Malcolm X. Yet as this chapter shows, black women from across the world were central to the talks.[4]

The Congress represented an impressive ideological collage of black political thinkers. Baraka defined CAP as being in the tradition of international pan-African gatherings, such as the previous five pan-African congresses, and the Black Power conferences of Washington, DC, Newark, Philadelphia, and Bermuda. These efforts for international African liberation served to help African people across the world understand that they were brothers and sisters.[5]

Still, McGuinness's experience reminds us how centuries of white hegemony, surveillance, colonialism, and miseducation had dislocated black communities physically and conceptually from one another. As such, the road to global black solidarity was not always smoothly paved with asphalt and flanked by sidewalks of black gold. It was a rocky one, logistically littered with dead ends, stop lights armed with surveillance cameras, political pot holes, and side tracks of ideological contestation, Olympics of suffering, and misplaced racial expectations of global blackness. Furthermore, the drivers of Black Power also had to cope with an intelligence network of sleeping policemen that included the FBI, the CIA, Australia's Security Intelligence Organization (ASIO), Britain's Foreign and Commonwealth Office, and France's Direction Générale de la Sécurité Extérieure. Still, activists stepped over these speed bumps, hills, and valleys to use the lessons learned at the talks to further their political struggles at home and abroad.

The congress reflected both the necessity and complications of black internationalism. As did other Black Power conferences, it served as a critical berth where black activists could be politically reeducated about the geo-graphical scope of the black radical tradition. Still, scholarship has not given enough detail to CAP's global scope and significance. This chapter aims to do so by unpacking Kamarakafego's specific involvement in the con-gress and the experiences of international participants such as the black Australian delegation. It also highlights Black Power in Australia. While the movement there was driven by organizations such as Australia's Black Panther Party (1970) and the Aboriginal Tent Embassy (1972), this chapter shows how the AAL became a critical international conduit of Black Power in Oceania through its engagement with Kamarakafego and CAP.

From Back-of-Town to the Block

During Bermuda's 1969 Black Power conference, Kamarakafego received a phone call from Gerald John Frape, a journalist from Melbourne's radio sta-tion 3AW. During the live interview, Frape asked him about the meaning of Black Power. In response, Kamarakafego stated that blacks in the Americas were concerned about the human and land rights of their indigenous black brothers and sisters in Australia.[6]

A month earlier, Frape had interviewed Maza for a *Broadside* magazine article, "Black power in Australia?" Perhaps flamboyant, dark complex-ioned, and bearded, Maza expressed affinity toward African Americans and continental Africans who lived in white minority–ruled societies. Maza was vexed that white Australian society had violently divided Aboriginals into different groups—those in the Northern Territory outback, those on church missions, fringe survivors on the outskirts of the urban cities, and an assimilated group that was trying to become white. He also found it con-ceivable that Aboriginal peoples could resort to violence in their fight for freedom—they had nothing to lose by embracing militancy. Black Austra-lians would risk annihilation for their cause, and Maza was willing to "take up arms" if necessary. "We'll just go underground," he declared, "and then it will be on."[7]

The twenty-nine-year-old greatly admired Malcolm X, whom he felt had given black people an identity and ancestral pride. The minister's legacy, he argued, was evidenced by the emergence of black lecturers in US colleges, courses on black history and culture, and soul food. Malcolm X "let every white man within reach know" that he was black, and Maza hoped that upon his own death, he would still be able to say that it was beautiful to be black.[8]

Frape described Maza as representing an emerging generation of Aboriginal organizers who were studying Malcolm X, watching African American uprisings on television, and growing tired of waiting for what was rightfully theirs—sovereignty and land. He gave a recording of his interview with Kamarakafego to Korowa, Maza, and McGuinness, suggesting that they "had to hear" it. At the time, all three were leaders in the AAL.[9]

Victoria's AAL was formed in 1957. An inner-city organization, its initial charge included assisting people of Aboriginal descent to acquire full citizenship rights, promoting integration in Australian society, and informing federal policy for the advancement of Aboriginal peoples.[10] In 1969, its director was veteran Aboriginal activist Pastor Doug Nicholls, a rugby player who was very popular among Australia's Aboriginal community.[11]

Korowa, Maza, and McGuinness were re-radicalizing the AAL in the direction of Black Power. They listened to the tape with interest. Korowa recalled hearing Kamarakafego discuss how delegates to the Bermuda conference had been harassed by the United States, British, and Bermudian governments. The three activists were particularly moved by his call for black people from across the world to attend the Barbados conference. They looked at one another in excitement. "A Black Power Conference in Barbados!" they exclaimed, "We should go!" The next day they cabled Kamarakafego in Bermuda and expressed interest in the talks.[12]

Once he received the cable, Kamarakafego spoke to the Central Black Power Committee about going to Australia. He reasoned that because he had to travel to Africa to organize for the Barbados conference and then return via California, it made sense to go to Australia before reaching the United States. The committee was supportive. Given that the AAL had reached out to him, it suggested that Aboriginals in Australia were already organized. It was decided that he would head to Australia from East Africa.[13]

Weeks later, Kamarakafego arrived in Tanzania. While there, he met with Prime Minister Julius Nyerere, who agreed to host the Sixth Pan-African Congress (6PAC). Kamarakafego sent a cable to the AAL: "Arriving Melbourne from Nairobi on a Qantas flight." Though the telegram was signed as Browne, Korowa, Bob, and Bruce were confused as to its origins because it came from Kenya. "Where's Nairobi, Kenya? Where's Kenya, Africa? Who do we know in Africa? Is this a joke? Who is Browne?"[14]

Korowa recalled that moment:

All of a sudden, there was this eye-to-eye contact between Bruce and Bob. . . . They said, *Roosevelt* Browne. One of them said, Black Power.

> [We] began to whisper "Black Power, Black Power" to one another, as if to say, "What have we done! He's coming! He was the embodiment of Black Power, and we were the ones causing it!"[15]

Kamarakafego passed through Mauritius, where he met with its prime minister, Seewoosagur Ramgoolam, about 6PAC. Concerned about Australia's immigration restrictions, from Port Louis he sent a wire to Australia's prime minister requesting that a visa be arranged for him. He announced himself as a Bermudian MP and asked to be met in Sydney. However, the prime minister's office received the telegram a day late. While Sydney's chief traffic officer supervisor of Qantas confirmed his arrival on August 26, 1969, from Johannesburg, South Africa, they were unaware of his whereabouts.[16]

When Kamarakafego arrived in Perth, Western Australia, he listed the 3AW radio station as his address. When asked by immigration officers if he was an entertainer, he said yes. Eventually arriving in Melbourne, ASIO agents placed on the AAL were awaiting him at Victoria's Essendon Airport. Photographs taken by ASIO show Kamarakafego dressed in a suit and carrying a small piece of luggage, flanked by Maza and McGuinness. The trio was closely followed and photographed along its travels through the suburbs of Melbourne via Old Bulla Road, a stop at the Koori Club in Fitzroy, and a departure from Maza's house, where Kamarakafego resided.[17]

Since the previous week, ASIO agents had been on standby for Kamarakafego's arrival. They had anticipated a meeting at Maza's home to coincide with his landing, where "something political" would be discussed that would "put the black man" on the front page of newspapers. Such a gathering did not occur until a week later.[18]

On Kamarakafego's first evening in Australia, he met with AAL and Aboriginal activists at Maza's home. Australian security claimed that participants had been told that he was "Stokely Carmichael's first lieutenant" and that the meeting was to launch an Australian Black Panther Party. Kamarakafego showed attendees his bullet wound from Cuba, as well as scars from the rope burns he sustained after the Klan attack in South Carolina. The ASIO was told that Kamarakafego claimed that black students rescued him and killed his attackers. Its agents deduced that his philosophy was "retaliatory violence—get him before he gets you." Bruce Silverwood, AAL director, who happened to be white, had been told that views expressed at the meeting were so sinister they were frightening.[19]

Korowa, Maza, and McGuinness bonded immediately with Kamarakafego. He "looked like an ordinary black man" and not like the "violent

FIGURE 7. Bruce McGuinness, Bob Maza, and Roosevelt Browne, Essendon Airport, Melbourne, Australia, 1969. Courtesy of the National Archives of Australia.

Panther" that they had perhaps expected. They had hoped to make face-to-face contact with him and to continue organizing to attend the Barbados conference. He only spent a few days in Australia, but they made sure to take him to spaces critical to Koori struggle and suffering in Melbourne. At one settlement, Kamarakafego met a fifteen-year-old Aboriginal girl who had become pregnant after being raped by a white man. He also spent more time at the Koori Club, which McGuinness launched in January 1969.[20]

A few days later, Maza suggested that Kamarakafego conduct a press conference on Black Power. Initially not open to the idea, he conceded after Maza reasoned that Aboriginal peoples needed to know that the black world stood in solidarity with them. The AAL leader also felt that the conference could inspire other indigenous movements in Oceania. Kamarakafego agreed, but insisted that the conference be held on the day of his departure and that he be referenced as the chairman of Bermuda's international Black Power conference.[21]

Kamarakafego's press conference has become enshrined in the lore of Black Power in Australia. Held at the AAL's headquarters, it was attended by AAL members and several Australian journalists. Seated next to Maza, Kamarakafego fielded several questions: Why had he come to Australia and why was his trip shrouded in secrecy? What was the difference between the political situations of West Indians and Australian Aborigines? Why was he in Australia to talk to black people, and what did he plan to do with that information? What was Black Power? How did he plan to help Aboriginals? Were any Australians invited to the next Black Power conference? As violence was the only way to get justice in South Africa and America, how did this apply to Australia or the Caribbean? Why did he want Black Power or supremacy as opposed to black equality? And had he himself been a victim of violence?[22]

Kamarakafego retorted that he entered Australia covertly because he was concerned about Australia's racist immigration policies. Furthermore, he felt that white Australians would denounce him because he was a Black Power advocate. The difference between West Indians and Aborigines was that the former were brought to the Americas as enslaved persons, while Aborigines had been in Australia before Europeans arrived. He identified land rights as the central problem facing Aboriginal peoples. Black Power was the empowerment of black people, but the movement also had white supporters. Kamarakafego had come to Australia because while Black Power advocates in the Americas discussed Aboriginal peoples at conferences, they did not have any concrete information about their situation. It was unwise to rely only on books written by (white) anthropologists, and it was important to speak directly to Aboriginals. Kamarakafego affirmatively stated that indigenous persons would be invited to the next Black Power talks.[23]

In response to the question of violence and the Caribbean, Kamarakafego stressed that Black Power was diversely applicable to different countries. He referenced Malcolm X's phrase about the ballot or the bullet, asserting that the Caribbean's majority black populations could use the vote to achieve political power. However, in Australia, where Aborigines did not have the numbers, Australia had a chance to do something about the political situation before things got out of hand. Kamarakafego saw himself as a simple advocate of Black Power as opposed to a leader. He emphasized that black people had as much right as any other group to seek power over their own destiny. Although he had been the recipient of white violence, he did not seek to do the same to whites. However, he was not naïve. The pattern was that whenever anyone, white or black, sought to bring about justice for black people, they would be "rubbed out." This included Marcus Garvey, Patrice Lumumba, Medgar Evers, John F. Kennedy, Martin Luther King Jr., and Malcolm X.[24]

It was at this point that AAL codirector Nicholls directly challenged Kamarakafego, demanding to know who had invited him to Australia. Kamarakafego refused to tell him who did so, which only made Nicholls more irate. Nicholls pressed further, claiming that Kamarakafego had not talked to the Aboriginal people or veteran leaders to know enough about their situation. Kamarakafego retorted that he had not implied as such, but that it was impossible to talk to everybody. He had only been there a few days, but apologized to Nicholls if had indeed offended him.[25]

Interestingly enough, Nicholls was aware that Maza, Korowa, and McGuinness had invited Kamarakafego to Australia. He had overhead the three activists discussing him, and out of respect, they informed him of the details. As expected, he was totally against the trip. According to Korowa, in contrast, some white AAL members were excited by the "buzz" of Black Power, whose advocates were portrayed in the Australian media as guntoting Black Panthers, a fiery Malcolm X, and racial violence.[26]

Australia's government was also intrigued by Kamarakafego's time in Australia. As was his entry, Kamarakafego's exit was closely monitored by the ASIO. Agents took photographs of and notes on Korowa, Maza, Frape, Myra Atkinson, and Kamarakafego at the airport. On his way back to the United States, Kamarakafego passed through Fiji and Hawaii, where he visited the East West Center in Honolulu. During these travels, he continued to meet activists from Oceania. This included Chief Tabuke Rotan of Kiribati's Banaba Island, whom he met in Fiji's airport. Rotan challenged British phosphate mining on Banaba. This environmental injustice led to the forced migration of Banabans to Fiji's Rabi Island.[27]

These experiences would greatly affect Kamarakafego's work in Oceania in the years to come. Within a week, he wrote to Kwame Nkrumah, informing him that the "Black people of Australia" would "be more than happy" to

FIGURE 8. Patricia Korowa, Bob Maza, and Roosevelt Browne, Essendon Airport, Melbourne, Australia, 1969. Courtesy of the National Archives of Australia.

receive any of his books. Passing on the addresses of Maza and McGuinness, Kamarakafego continued to work with the AAL in their efforts to attend CAP.[28]

Black Power in Australia

According to Australian Black Power activist and scholar Gary Foley, Kamarakafego's visit propelled Black Power into the popular vernacular of Australia. For Korowa, Black Power in Australia was essentially about sovereignty, self-determination, and "the necessity for black people to define the world in their own terms." It was a response to genocide, environmental injustice, and the ongoing quest for land rights. Marked by the 1972 Aboriginal Tent Embassy and Brisbane's Black Panther Party, Black Power's most striking impact was arguably in Sydney's black neighborhood of Redfern. Led by Paul Coe, Sydney's young group of activists read literature such as the *Autobiography of Malcolm X*, *Black Power*, and Cleaver's *Soul on Ice* just as much as *Bury My Heart At Wounded Knee*. They established police patrols, an Aboriginal legal aid center, a medical service, and a wide canon of print media.[29]

However, Australia's indigenous radical tradition against white violence was as historic as European colonialism on the continent. Aboriginal peoples experienced genocide, invisibility, insults, trauma, and torture at the hands, bayonets, chains, nuclear bombs, poisons, and firearms of British invaders. Furthermore, Australia's constitution was based on the doctrinal racist myth of *terra nullius*—that the land was unhabituated by humans until Europeans arrived.[30]

As such, Black Power in Australia could call on the names of indigenous freedom fighters like Yagan of the South Western Noongar, Truganni of Tasmania, and Pemulwuy of the Bidjigal. Indigenous historian John Maynard details black resistance in Australia in the twentieth century through the Sydney branch of the Universal Negro Improvement Association (UNIA) and the Australian Aborigines Progress Association. Yet the emergence of Black Power did reflect a shift in black Australian protest from the civil rights struggles of the 1950s and 1960s. For Foley, Australia's UNIA and Black Power movements were both critical moments of Aboriginal radical black internationalism.[31]

In between these two movements lay decades of civil rights and human rights activism. In the post-WWII era, this included the massive organizing efforts of black women like South Sea Islander Faith Bandler and Aboriginal poet Oodgeroo Noonuccal (Kath Walker). Both women were leaders in the Aboriginal-Australian Fellowship and the Federal Council for the Advancement of Aborigines and Torres Strait Islanders (FCAATSI) and members of the Communist Party of Australia. Noonuccal's son, Denis Walker, founded Australia's Black Panther Party in 1971.[32]

Formed in 1957, FCAATSI's charge included assisting people of Aboriginal descent to acquire full citizenship rights, working toward the complete advancement and integration of Aboriginal peoples into Australian society, and coordinating various groups in Victoria who worked on behalf of Aboriginal peoples. In 1967, it launched a successful campaign for a national referendum to have Aborigines counted in the country's census.[33]

Typical of the era, FCAATSI was controlled, formed, and heavily supported by white liberals. In April 1969, at FCAATSI's annual conference, Aboriginal delegates called for Aboriginal leadership of the institution and its representative organizations. Walker's speech there galvanized black attendees such as McGuinness and Korowa. "When you leave this conference," Walker asserted, "and go back to . . . the rat holes you call homes, that you have inherited from the Australian society, unite your people, and bring them out fighting!" This speech, "Political Rights of Aborigines," was widely reprinted in Aboriginal print media, including in the AAL's newsletter, *Smoke Signals*. Korowa had first met Walker through her father in 1962, and joined FCAATSI and later the AAL through her instigation.[34]

Kamarakafego's time in Melbourne was a short but transformative political spark that electrified Australia's emerging Black Power movement.

Denounced in the media, his conference and exchange with Nicholls made national headlines. Victoria's minister for Aboriginal affairs stated that he would be "perfectly happy if he never heard from Black Power leader Browne." Allegedly on behalf of Victoria's Aboriginals, he stated that they were "happy to forget" Browne, who had come to stir up trouble. He claimed that a Black Power movement would not be tolerated in Australia, and called for trust and patience from Aboriginal peoples to achieve equality.[35]

While Kamarakafego's speech about black self-determination was "fairly harmless," Foley suggests that it received a tremendous backlash because Australia had always been a white supremacist nation. Thus, Australia's collective psyche was simultaneously violent toward and paranoid about black agency. White Australians claimed Aborigines were being infected by foreign ideas. Ironically, this "overreaction" only hastened the spread of Black Power in Australia, as younger Aboriginal activists quickly embraced Browne's proposition of self-determination.[36]

This included the AAL. The day after Kamarakafego's departure, McGuinness informed Victoria's *Herald* that he agreed with Kamarakafego's definition of Black Power as black empowerment. He also argued that Black Power had been in Australia long before Kamarakafego's visit. For example, he asserted that Victoria's Aboriginal Tribal Council *was* a Black Power movement and whites could not enter their meetings or influence their decisions. The AAL also published its own monthly newspaper, the *Koorier*.[37]

Galvanized by Kamarakafego's visit, Maza, McGuinness, and Korowa sought to radicalize the AAL into a voice of Black Power. White liberals— or "do-gooders"—dominated the leadership of the league. Aware that they would face resistance from Nicholls, they proceeded to remove white leadership from the organization.[38]

In the September issue of *Smoke Signals*, the AAL released its definitive statement on Black Power. This began with an excerpt from Jean-Paul Sartre's foreword to Fanon's *Wretched of the Earth*—"Not so very long ago, the earth numbered 2,000 million inhabitants: 500 million men, and 1,500 million natives." This, the AAL argued, was the essence of *white power*. In contrast, Black Power was the post-WWII movements for self-determination by black and brown communities against white domination.[39]

For the AAL, Black Power did not entail one single form of action. It was not inherently violent or an expression of black supremacy, but it could be if necessary. The statement drew on a 1968 essay by Barrie Pittock on Black Power, which indicated that Black people were likely to achieve freedom if they worked together as one group. According to the AAL, Aboriginal communities had already adopted Black Power in idea if not in name. Expressions of black Power included the Aboriginal delegation's push at the 1968 FCAATSI's Easter conference and the United Council of Aboriginal Women. Most importantly, the AAL felt that it needed to provide a forum from which Aboriginal peoples could discuss Black Power. Its non-Aboriginal members needed to take a step back while its Aboriginal leaders made decisions for the group.[40]

Immediately following the statement, *Smoke Signals* printed a full transcript of Kamarakafego's press conference, "Roosevelt Brown Meets the Press." The AAL's October newsletter stated that the small gathering with Kamarakafego had caused alarm and fear of Black Power, on one hand, and excitement and hope on the other. Yet the newsletter declared that three other international visitors had also stimulated their thoughts on Black Power. These were Papua New Guinea's Leo Hannett and Albert Maori Kiki and four Indian nuns who had come to Australia to work with Aboriginal communities. Hannett had made a "world wind visit" to Australia on behalf of Bougainville's (a province in Papua New Guinea) struggle against ecological injustices. Kiki was a secretary of the Pangu Pati, which was driving decolonization in Papua New Guinea.[41]

On October 6, 1969, Maza conducted an interview for Australia's *Newsday*. The AAL's executive committee had just been reconstituted to include only Aborigines. According to the paper, Black Power had "woven its embryo" and "won its first victory." The article described Maza as the "face of Black Power, a prophet to a lost tribe—a whole race—which had grown tired of waiting." He was part of a growing legion of activists who preached the same religion—"black is beautiful, proud, and equal," positions only to be proved by power. If their message had indeed originated from America's Negro rebellion, Indigenous activists in Australia had stamped it with their unique brand. Maza stated that there would be "no violence, no clenched fist salutes, no black armies," as these were not necessary. Aboriginal power would be "black representation" and "power for the Koories to make their own decisions." Aborigines were the world's greatest socialists. They shared everything—and now they wanted their share. When offered a cigarette by the interviewer, Maza retorted that he wanted "none of those white men evils." Instead, he called for reparations for Aboriginal peoples.[42]

Kamarakafego's trip prompted ASIO to open a file on Maza. It was pressed to take Black Power more seriously. It proceeded to inquire through the Social Services Department about Maza's family status and his two young daughters. The organization also asserted that Kamarakafego's visit had spurned a split in the AAL. Nicholls was concerned with the branch's connection with Black Power under the leadership of Maza and McGuinness. At a November AAL meeting of about three hundred people, Silverwood resigned.[43]

In a November 1969 report titled "Black Power and the AAL," ASIO claimed that McGuinness and Maza had become inactive in establishing a Black Power movement in Australia. The report claimed that McGuinness's views on Black Power had changed—he now spoke against the movement and was against multiracial groups and black internationalism. However, ASIO believed that he was only "covering" himself after Kamarakafego's visit, as his actions suggested otherwise. For example, it was reported that he had intended to travel to Northern Australia to establish a National Aboriginal Liberation Front.[44]

As for Maza, the report continued, he was the only AAL member who openly stated that he could not rule out violence as a tactic of liberation. This all depended on the Aboriginal community's negotiations with Australia. Opposed to white control of Aboriginal organizations, ASIO found him to be "violent with words," but a dedicated family man who was "kind at heart." One Hilas Maris had been receiving a monthly booklet from the World Black Power movement. However, it claimed that other branches of the AAL expressed disproval at Kamarakafego's visit.[45] Despite all this, Maza, McGuinness, and Korowa continued to communicate with Kamarakafego regarding the Barbados conference. When they found out that the talks would be held in Atlanta, there was little disappointment. The chance to come to the Americas to be part of a worldwide black freedom struggle was more than enough.

Surveillance

The promotional materials for CAP described the talks as being the successor to the national and international Black Power conferences. Its proposal for funding defined it as the logical outgrowth of the four Black Power conferences held between 1966 and 1969. Bermuda's First Regional International Black Power Conference had added an important global dimension to the talks, as it sought to address the global problems of black self-determination. The theme of CAP was "Black Nationalism and Pan-Africanism," and the congress was to provide an ideological framework for the Black Power movement, create an organization structure for black liberation, and create concrete plans to build black institutions at the local, national, and international level.[46]

Featuring leading activists from across the black world, it aimed to be a working rather than a merely talking session. It sought to create and implement models for black institution building at the local, national, and international levels. The congress's initial schedule included Julius Nyerere, Eusi Kwayana, Kwame Ture, Miriam Makeba, and Kamarakafego's cousin, leader of Bermuda's Progressive Labor Party (PLP), Lois Browne-Evans. Entertainers were to include Rodolfo "Corky" Gonzales, Don Lee, Baraka, Spirit House Movers, Stevie Wonder, and Pharaoh Saunders. This initial schedule was likely finalized by Kamarakafego, who was the delegated head of the program. However, a July 31 report of the Program Committee—apparently under the stewardship of Baraka—claimed to have stabilized the program and schedule.[47] Browne-Evans was no longer on the schedule; yet her presence as a featured speaker would have made a significant impact at CAP, which was otherwise dominated by black men at the lecture level.

Writing in December 1970, *Ebony* editor Alexander Poisnett poetically covered the meeting. Given the colorful collage of dashikis and *bubas*, he felt that Atlanta's airport could have been that of Nairobi—"*except* for the white faces and flies." The sidewalks of Morris Brown could have been the streets of Mombasa. He recalled how CAP was originally slated to take place in Barbados. Abruptly canceled, with less than three months of planning, CAP welcomed some 2,700 delegates, including 250 attendees from Africa and the Global South.[48]

By June 1970, the FBI had become aware that CAP was going to be held in Atlanta. The national office launched a concerted effort to notify its Atlanta office of potential attendees. It called for its "racial informants" (read, black, or brown) to attend the Black Power conference, and call the local office with secure discretion when they reached the city.[49]

Kamarakafego arrived in Atlanta in late June for a CAP planning meeting at Paschal's Motor Motel. FBI agents observed him there, along with about thirty other black activists. They reported that as a member of Bermuda's "Negro" political activist PLP, he was making arrangements for an expected five thousand at CAP. During a social event, agents spotted him seated on a floor. They claimed that he told people there that he would not be able to stay in Atlanta very long because he had not brought sufficient clothes. Allegedly, he remarked that he was unhappy with Atlanta because he had not met any suitable women.[50]

In anticipation of the Barbados conference, in April 1970, the FBI furnished all of its offices with a report of Kamarakafego's "extremist" views. As this document circulated, it conducted background checks on those persons whom he had met with at Paschal's. It hoped to use those details for "informant development" at CAP via the organizations that they represented.[51]

In July, a "reliable informant" provided the FBI with the minutes of a preliminary meeting between CAP's host committee and presidents of historically black colleges and universities in the area. The congress garnered some support from that academic community; Morehouse College tentatively granted the use of its Atlanta University Center and gymnasium, Morris Browne College provided its athletic field and stadium, Spelman's chapel was made available, and Clark granted other facilities.[52]

In early August, the FBI, still unsatisfied with the operations of its Atlanta's office and feeling that CAP was not receiving the investigative action that it warranted, intensified its efforts. Since CAP was open to "All brothers," an FBI phone call to its Atlanta office confirmed that the bureau wanted its Jackson, New Orleans, Miami, Tampa, and Memphis offices to have their "racial informants" cover the conference. These informants were to make wide contacts with conference attendees and were encouraged to use cameras and tape recorders to minimize security risks. The bureau hoped to obtain the registration cards of the 2,200 persons who officially attended CAP and create lists of those persons present.[53]

Informants were given specific targets and made special efforts to note the names, physical descriptions, and black "extremist" affiliations of all participants. Officials instructed them to obtain information about the character, personality, and weaknesses of participants, as well as their degree of dedication to revolution. They were to gather copies of all revolutionary publications, tapes, and films and to attend events that they deemed to be the most revolutionary or potentially violent. Agents were not to make statements calling for violence or to engage in illegal activities; however, if they needed to do such things, the Atlanta office was to be contacted immediately. The FBI found CAP to be a great opportunity to fully utilize its "ghetto informants." These individuals were to be visibly present at CAP in case they needed to be called upon in any prosecutive actions. This would have allowed the bureau to maintain the secrecy of informants of "continuing value" by using "ghetto informants" in court as opposed to informants who actually gathered the information. Speeches of extremists were to be recording according to May 1969 FBI memo, captioned "Use of Concealed

Recording Devices in Covering Public Appearances by Black and New Left Extremists."[54]

The FBI pressed for information that could lead to the capture of Angela Davis, H. Rap Brown, and "other missing black extremist fugitives." If necessary, informants were instructed to look at pictures in the field office's photograph album of black nationalists. It was also aware of CAP's international dimensions. Its agents sought to establish contacts with foreign attendees to gather data about their connection with "black extremists" in the United States. They hoped to establish "social and political rapport with foreign black extremists" at CAP and to create permanent relationships for additional exploitation. It noted that international participants included ten persons from Bermuda (including Kamarakafego) and others from Angola, Ghana, Nigeria, Jamaica, Puerto Rico, South Africa, Australia, Tanzania, Southwest Africa, Guinea, Ethiopia, Canada, Trinidad and Tobago, and Kenya.[55]

The Australian delegation's activities at Atlanta's "full-scale Black Power get together" were closely documented by ASIO. Maza's ASIO file included an August 1970 interview about the upcoming trip. He refused to divulge any details about the other Aboriginal participants. When asked why he would not reveal their names, he said that they needed protection. His secrecy was also in response to threats that he had received during the black takeover of the AAL. Maza described how CAP was going to hold workshops on economic autonomy, political liberation, creativity, religion, education, history, law and justice, black technology, communications and system analysis, and social and community organizations. When asked if "violent extremists" would attend the conference, Maza responded brilliantly, pointing out that he would hardly call the Reverend Jesse Jackson a man of violence. Furthermore, nonviolent entertainers like Miriam Makeba, Nina Simone, and Ray Charles would also be there. When pressed again about extremists, Maza asserted that CAP was about black people getting together to solve their problems by working along with white people.[56]

On August 21, 1970, Kamarakafego, as program director of CAP, formally invited McGuinness and the Australian delegation to the congress. In a written letter, he stated that the congress would reimburse the group upon their arrival at the talks. The congress also agreed to pay for their accommodations while in the United States.[57]

At this time, ASIO believed that K. Walker and journalist John Newfong were part of the delegation. Its officials noted the financial challenges that the group was having in raising funds for the trip. Their contacts at Qantas airline were poised to notify the agency as soon as their travel arrangements were made. The airline did its part; ASIO was informed that a check for $5,796 had been paid to Qantas for airfare. Most of the funds had come from an Aboriginal Scholarship Fund, while Korowa took out a loan. The organization noted the passport applications of Maza and Korowa and documented their departure to Atlanta. With a team of three agents, ASIO undertook surveillance of the group and friends in the departure lounge of Tullamarine airport.[58]

Australian and US officials corresponded about the delegation's trip. The US consul in Perth, Western Australia, informed its Australian counterparts that it had received several complaints from Australians that Davis had been given a visa to the United States. Australian officials asked its Washington, DC, office about the outcome of CAP and the part played in it by the Australian delegation. Australia's director of Aboriginal affairs, Barrie Dexter, was concerned with the contact between Aboriginals and Black Power organizations abroad. He felt that it would be distressful if the ideologies of global Black Power were "imported" into Australia. He noted that the Aboriginal delegation had visited the Panther office and Nation of Islam (NOI) headquarters in New York. Dexter, who believed the McGuinness was not accepted at CAP as an "authentic aborigine," passed on Davis's notes about the trip to ASIO.[59]

The delegation compiled a report of the trip, published by Abschol as "Aborigines visit the US." The report included a breakdown of CAP workshops—"Political Liberation," "Economic Autonomy," "Creativity and Arts," "Religious Systems," and sessions on education, history, law, technology, communications, social organization, and community organization. Most of these sessions were framed as being pan-African and referenced global black struggle.[60]

McGuinness's detailed account was written with political wit. He detailed the delegation's journey to the United States, which included his dismay at not seeing indigenous Fijians in positions of authority in Fiji's airport, anxiety of getting their boomerangs through the airport in San Francisco, and choosing between approaching a black or white customs officer. Kamarakafego met the group at Atlanta's airport and arrived with three other persons armed with pistols for their protection. This challenged the misperceptions of America held by Australia—the delegation had been subjected to American news reports of "race riots, killing, burning, looting, plane crashes, assassinations, and sabotage." They expected to see armed black people "snarling" at armed whites, and other black people huffing around with their eyes facing the ground muttering idioms—"yassah and nosah, dis and dat." Hence, he was surprised when Kamarakafego introduced him to CAP's welcoming committee, whose members were articulate academics and professionals. In one incident, McGuinness approached a policeman for directions; the latter grabbed for his gun and told him to take his hands out of his pockets. The lesson he learned was that on alien soil, take a cab and "never ask a cop anything."[61]

During the opening ceremony, the Aboriginal delegation was introduced to the conference. According to McGuinness, the reception was fantastic and the applause deafening. On one evening, Queen Mother Audley Moore introduced the women participants from overseas and delegates from Bermuda and Ethiopia. This included Korowa, whose assurance and confidence as a veteran organizer made her someone whom "everyone loved." According to Korowa, the Aboriginal delegation was enamored with Moore, who had also been a notable force at the Bermuda conference. In a 1978 interview, Moore claimed that it was she who had given CAP its name. Having served on the organizing committee of CAP, she insisted that "the brothers" use African in the title as this implied a nationality. Otherwise, she asserted, they would have given the talks a name such as "black something," but black did not refer to a national identity.[62]

The Australian delegation interacted with the NOI, Black Panthers, Republic of New Afrika, and black reformist groups. This allowed them to directly engage firsthand a spectrum of black activism in the Americas; this was a unique opportunity. For example, McGuinness noted that the Australian press did not publicize the Panther's Breakfast Program, which, in Harlem alone, was supplying five hundred free breakfasts to black children.[63]

At CAP, the Australian delegation split up to attend separate workshops—Davis, community organization; Korowa, communications; McGuinness, literature; Maza, creativity; and Bellear, education. The congress *moved* them. McGuinness recalled meeting Baraka, who kept him spellbound during their conversation. Escorted by his personal bodyguard of six well-armed Karate experts, he felt that Baraka was treated "like a god."[64]

Featured in the media, Maza, Davis, and McGuinness did a three-hour radio interview with Waymon Wright on Atlanta's WRNG radio station. According to McGuinness, they fielded questions from racists, "Negroes, militant blacks, kindly old ladies, and antagonistic young ones." Maza also conducted an interview for Poisnett's *Ebony* article. Gracing a photograph in the piece, he stated that a white person in Atlanta had informed him that whites were afraid of black people. He retorted that Australia was no different. Out of 140,000 Aborigines, only nine had university degrees. Not one of the former, Maza was nevertheless schooled in the writings of Malcolm X, Julius Lester, and Cleaver. For Maza, black Australia's biggest problem was isolation; blacks in Australia were not thought of when people considered the black world. Maza attended the "Economic Autonomy" workshop to gain information on how to establish Aborigine-owned communications enterprises. He informed the congress that blacks in Australia were measuring their work by the yardstick of African Americans. It was "nation time!"[65]

Indexed in the FBI's reports, Maza was a visible presence at CAP. During the Saturday luncheon session, Maza spoke on behalf of the AAL. He discussed the history of Australia and the origins of Aboriginal peoples. Maza was reported to have stated that Aboriginal struggle was a long way behind African American political movements. His main aim at CAP was to gather ideas for programs of action that could be implemented in Australia. One idea was to make contact with African American soldiers on R & R leave from Vietnam and get them involved in the Aboriginal movement.[66]

At the time of the trip, Korowa was president of Victoria's AAL. Married with two daughters, the *Australian* asserted that she was on her way to CAP to learn how to start a thought revolution. Amina Baraka directed her session on social organization. Here, the gendered politics of the Black Power movement were on full display. Baraka's paper was centered on Maulana Karenga's ideas of black womanhood—"What makes a woman appealing is femininity and she cannot be feminine without being submissive." For Baraka, this required being submissive to woman's "natural roles"—inspiration, education, and social development of the nation. Mother Moore was also a part of this workshop; there, she called for women to form an underground movement to help "brothers" escape from the police.[67]

Broken into two groups—one focused on the black family and the other on cooperative work—Canada's Brenda Dash directed the latter session. Dash would later cofound Toronto's National Black Liberation Action Committee at its Black People's Conference in 1971. Along with Douglas, the Committee aimed to build a revolutionary pan-African movement in Canada.[68]

Bellear was totally inspired by the intensity of CAP's opening ceremonies. At nineteen years old, he was chair of the newly formed Aboriginal

Legal Service, but the congress was his first international experience. In preparation for the trip, he read about Marcus Garvey and the UNIA. He consumed Malcolm's *Autobiography* during his stay in the United States. At CAP, he brought dashikis and Nehru-style garments and threw his Australian clothes away. By his second week in the United States, he realized CAP's importance for the Global South and Oceania.[69]

Standing outside the "Political Liberation" workshop, McGuinness told Charlayne Hunter-Gault of the *New York Times* that he had come to CAP because Aborigines needed to make alliances with other people engaged in liberation struggles or face extinction. He compared the situation of Aborigines in Australia to that of American Indians, both of whom had been "placed on reservations, mission stations and settlements" and denied the right to think. McGuinness felt that CAP could help to apply pressure on the Australian government that could be used to help Aborigines develop economic independence. Otherwise, the Aboriginal race would either be exterminated or they would revolt and be killed.[70]

Amira Baraka directed the "Political Liberation" workshop, a critical session that represented CAP's international promises and transnational tensions—both personal and political. The workshop resolved to establish a World African Party—a local-international nationalist party capable of dealing with local and international African problems. It also called for the establishment of CAP centers across the United States and an international infrastructure that included Africa, the Americas, and Australasia. Baraka also argued that the local success of activists in Newark through voting mobilization should be studied and used as an example for political model across the United States.[71] However, many international delegates felt that the workshop lacked the expected global pan-African focus and instead focused primarily on African American issues. Among the workshop's critics were Surinam's Karg and Dominica's Douglas, who vocalized their concerns. Karg was president of an alleged three-thousand-member Black Power movement of Surinam, which had been formed that past July. He argued that black nations needed to build a Black United Nations, an economic plan for global black freedom, and a global communications network. In Surinam, he asserted, the Dutch had used every trick in the book to keep people of color divided. The congress was "the best thing that could happen to black people." He also called for CAP to hold its next meeting in Surinam, remarking that if the government there gave them difficulties, they would "burn down their Goddamn capitol." According to the CIA,

Karg's group was patterned after the Republic of New Africa. Apparently he had been active in New York's branch of the NAACP.[72]

Douglas was considered by FBI agents to be the "most powerful individual" in the "Political Liberation" session. The FBI also found that he gave the most spirited talk during the Sunday sessions. Douglas had concerns about the immediacy of CAP's agenda. He talked about the Black Power uprising in Trinidad and Tobago, where brothers were being shot, and sought funds for equipment (as in weapons) and legal assistance for the 108 brothers in prison facing the firing squad for treason. He passed out cups for donations.[73]

Douglas felt that the contributions of Caribbean pan-Africanists such as Garvey and Henry Sylvester Williams, "an African born in Trinidad," had been dismissed at CAP. This he felt was unfortunate because it was important to understand the roles that Africans in the Caribbean had played in the development of pan-Africanist thought and in the liberation of African people wherever they lived:

> Today there are 130 million African people in the Americas. Let us understand that there are only 35 million Africans in America. Therefore, we have to move to unite 130 million African people in the United States, in Latin America, and the Caribbean and this can only be done if we are serious about realizing that we can only depend on ourselves; we cannot depend on liberals; . . . we cannot depend on Marxists.[74]

He also stated that blacks were fighting not only against the United States but also against Europe, NATO, and, "when the time comes," the Soviet Union.[75]

For its part, the CIA felt that Douglas's paper was one of CAP's most significant presentations. It took his comments to mean that the success of revolution in the United States would depend on the success of West Indian revolutions for liberation. Douglas felt that this would not likely take place in Trinidad and Tobago, and he suggested that effort needed to be spent on the political takeover of another island.[76]

According to the CIA, Kamarakafego complained that the conference was more "Afro-American than Pan-African" and that delegates had concentrated more on US domestic issues to the exclusion of foreign matters. Along similar lines, Kamarakafego proposed to this workshop that a permanent black political party be established in the Caribbean. Baraka rejected this idea, advocating that a single political party should be established and operated in all countries where black people resided.[77]

Douglas and other international participants relayed to Kamarakafego that they were disappointed with the conference. They were particularly concerned with the "Politics" workshop and what they believed to be its exclusive focus on the problems of "Newark and New Jersey." This prompted him to ask for all non-US delegates to meet with him; a handwritten note kept by Larry Neal suggests that they met at the Paschal's Matador Room for a side meeting. International delegates collectively passed on a number of resolutions to the congress at its closure.[78]

Kamarakafego had been quite busy. He moderated the opening session at the Morris Brown gymnasium, which was attended by about 1,700. There, he gave a short talk that introduced the Caribbean delegates. In one workshop session, Kamarakafego suggested that all those in attendance furnish their names and addresses so that he could stay in contact with them. He informed the group that he would be calling another Black Power conference and that other CAP conferences would continue.[79] He hoped that these future talks would be decidedly international in practice, to avoid some of the issues of marginalization.

Kamarakafego was particularly concerned that CAP did not reimburse the Australian delegation for their expenses in traveling to the United States. He impressed Bellear with his knowledge about black political struggle in Australia, and he consistently checked on them to make sure they were okay. These issues bothered Kamarakafego tremendously. In addition, a serious rift developed between himself, Baraka, and what he would call the "Newark, New Jersey group." This was part of the reason why he resigned from CAP later that year.[80]

The black Australian delegation was also bitter about the issue. Bellear was clear that CAP was *always* supposed to be international. He felt that CAP's international dynamics were marginalized because "people abuse history." The Australian delegation found that most conference delegates knew very little about their experiences and raised unnecessary questions about their African identity. He witnessed internal jealousies at CAP and felt that a number of interviews by its participants gave the impression that it was just a localized affair. Their published report about CAP, "Aborigines Visit the US," stated that they had been confronted with a "shattering new world of belligerent black solidarity." It also reported—with some bitterness—that CAP had not honored its written promise to pay the delegation's airfare.[81] Still, their trip to the United States was not over.

What Is Harlem?

After CAP, the Aboriginal delegation traveled the eight-hundred-mile journey by bus to New York. Their trip was memorable. They swapped stories with black people all the way through Georgia, the Carolinas, Philadelphia, Delaware, Maryland, Virginia, New Jersey, and New York. Harlem captivated them—it was a place where blacks were regarded as "all Black." For McGuinness, it was a site of black oppression and resistance—depressing, exciting, dirty, and beautiful. Harlem was a place where junkies rubbed shoulders with tourists, where "cops beat up kids and kids beat up cops," where muggers and prostitutes were common, where Panthers fed kids and Muslims gave religious guidance, where "kids dodged dope pushers" among abandoned cars, bars, brothels, and pawnshops, where he could stand on the same corner at Lennox and 125th St. that King, Malcolm X, Carmichael, H. Rap Brown, and Queen Mother Moore had once stood. They ate soul food at Sylvia's restaurant, devoured bean pies, an engrossed themselves in black culture.[82]

"What then was Harlem?" asked McGuinness. Harlem was "Black and beautiful." But the term's main value laid in its ability to "pull Black people out of the depths and lift them into a once again proud and dignified race." However, to really understand it one needed to "sit in an auditorium with 3,000 Blacks" and listen to Nina Simone singing "To Be Young, Gifted and Black."[83]

Ken and Betty Jenkins hosted the delegation across the state of New York. Hofstra professor of law David Kadane helped them present a petition at the United Nations. This statement called for relief from genocide, $6 billion of reparations for Aboriginal persons, and Aboriginal ownership of all lands that these communities occupied. The delegation traveled all across Long Island visiting educational institutions. They visited institutions such as the African-centered school Uhuru Sasa, Barbara Ann Teer's National Black Theatre company, Moore's Universal Association of Ethiopian Women, the Shinnecock Indian Reservation (whose nation included African Americans), and a birthday celebration for Richard B. Moore, veteran organizer of the African Blood Brotherhood.[84]

The delegation's Jack Davis enjoyed his time in "Africa-America." The indigenous poet experienced Atlanta as a world of both black poverty and wealth. He felt that the colors, costumes, and jewelry of the "Back-to-Africa" movement were apparent in the dress of Atlanta's black women. Davis felt that Australia's "black scene" for self-determination could benefit from the African American freedom struggle by pushing for an Aboriginal cultural renaissance, developing news media for propaganda, and increasing national solidarity through organizations such as the recently formed Tribal Council of Australia.[85]

Davis enjoyed the good smells of food and sights of a half million well-dressed black folks amid the worn streets of Harlem and Spanish Harlem. The delegation visited Harlem's tenements, an all-black church, and Roosevelt and Hempstead High School on Long Island, where they did boomerang exhibitions. Davis recalled meeting a number of popular African American poets and playwrights. From New York they flew to New Hampshire's Dartmouth College, where they spoke before its students. They visited an automobile factory in Detroit and met with black and Native American students at the University of Michigan, Ann Arbor. They had a fascinating time with the latter, because, Davis argued, Native Americans had the same problems as Aboriginals in Australia. Davis felt that they needed to continue their cultural exchanges with black and indigenous Americans. He was told that a group of Native Americans and African Americans were going to stage a protest at the Australian consulate in protest of the White Australia policy and the denial of Aboriginal land rights.[86]

Davis read poetry at a number of schools, and his work was well received. African Americans loved poetry, he wrote, and he felt that he could sell millions of his books in the United States. In New York, he played the didgeridoo at an urban education program. At the United Nations, the delegation sought support from delegates from Tanzania, Zambia, Guinea, Guyana, Chile, Fiji, New Zealand, and Papua New Guinea. The group met with Angola nationals, whom Davis felt compelled to help.[87]

The veteran organizer felt that Black Power in Australia could gain international sympathy for Aboriginals by bringing attention to the fact that Australia had not signed the charter of human rights. Aboriginals were suffering in a land that had one of highest standards of living in the world. White Australian sacred places—such as statues and monuments—needed to be desecrated with red paint to signify the blood of murdered Aboriginals. All Australians needed to be educated about the crimes perpetuated against its indigenous peoples. Davis retold of these atrocities throughout his report.[88]

Davis claimed that in Australia, Kamarakafego stated that Aboriginals were not ready for Black Power in the American sense. Because Aboriginals could not bring sufficient economic pressure to bear on the system, boycotts and marches could not work. Davis agreed—Black Power in Australia would require force. Aboriginals needed to be prepared to go to jail for breaking the law and be willing to be injured or be killed. Since the 1967 referendum, there had been a "return to Aboriginality," so much so that even Aboriginals who could pass for being Europeans were claiming Aboriginal heritage. This significant change would bring intellectual growth to the Black Power movement, which needed to attack pseudo Australian pride—white Australians had no heritage of their own, and their claims for heritage were imagined narratives.[89]

Returning to Oceania

After the Australian delegation returned from CAP, ASIO intensified its surveillance of the group. It noted that Maza arrived back in Australia in late November 1970. Before his departure to CAP, Davis was reported to have said, "People who think four aboriginals are going away to bring black power back to Australia are stupid." Still, his time in the United States emboldened his concern for Aboriginal land rights.[90]

The organization opened a file on Bellear, who later chaired Redfern's Aboriginal Medical Service and served as minister of defense for the Australian Black Panther Party. In 1972, Maza formed the National Black Theatre and participated in the Aboriginal Tent Embassy protests that same year. Perhaps in relation to the incident with the alleged Panther, McGuinness reported that he initially felt out of place at CAP because of his skin complexion. However, the "brothers and sisters" soon showed him that he was like them, and now, "in the Black Bag," he was accepted. Still, McGuinness left the trip early. The agency referenced this, reporting that his complexion prevented his becoming a confidant of the congress. It further claimed that upon his return, McGuinness expressed "trepidation" over the lengths that black militants in other countries were prepared to go for freedom. However, Maza and Korowa were completely embraced by the talks and were expected to become more militant as a result.[91]

Yet McGuinness's subsequent reflections suggest that he did appreciate the talks. Nine months after CAP, he noted that the ability to study the African American experience in America was an indescribable experience. He was thoroughly convinced that culture was the key to Aboriginal advancement. He argued that if Australia's white power structure was not threatened by Australia's 140,000 black citizens, then they needed to look to New Guinea and the Pacific islands for support.[92]

Korowa shared the same perception. She was elated to have met black people and organizations from across the Americas, Africa, and Asia. These included Vertamae Smart-Grosvenor, Louis Farrakhan, Queen Mother Moore, members of the National Black Theater, the Barakas, and the National Council of Negro Women. She also recalled Julius Nyerere's arrival at New York's JFK airport for a meeting at the United Nations.[93]

In the United States, Korowa was seen as Aboriginal. But although she had been born in Australia, Korowa was actually a proud South Sea Islander—a descendant of over sixty thousand Melanesians forcibly taken from Vanuatu to work on Australia's sugar and cotton plantations in the mid-nineteenth century. After CAP, Korowa traveled to Vanuatu to visit her ancestral island home, "Tanna the Earth." Arriving in October 1970, she stayed there for about two weeks. Korowa was ecstatic to be among Vanuatu's black communities. While there, she happily fielded questions about Black Power, South Sea Islanders, and her meetings with African Americans.[94]

This was Korowa's first trip to Vanuatu, a political condominium of France and Britain then known as the New Hebrides. Along with ASIO, British and French colonial administrators monitored her activities there with trepidation. Indeed, they were more than concerned about the concrete relationships between Black Power, pan-Africanism, and Melanesian nationalism in Vanuatu and Oceania. The French referred to Korowa as an associate of Kamarakafego who had attended CAP "*pour l'émancipation de la race noire*"; their British counterparts were informed that she discussed Black Power with Vanuatu's English-speaking community, with Fijians, and with Tongans. In Tanna, she distributed some twenty red, black, and green Black Power badges, all items that she obtained during her trip to the United States. British officials could only conclude that, given Korowa's "Afro-style" dress, her "bitterly anti-European" remarks, and comments that all black people originated from Africa (and that Jesus Christ was black), she was strongly influenced by Black Power. The British government deemed her to be "undesirable" to New Hebrides, and prevented her from reentering the archipelago in 1971 and 1977.[95]

Kamarakafego soon followed Kowora's footsteps to Vanuatu, with dramatic consequences. The French were aware that during the month of Korowa's visit, Jimmy Stephens and Susan Moses of the Na Griamel movement had corresponded with Kamarakafego about land struggle in Vanuatu.

Stephens informed Kamarakafego that Na Griamel was 22,000 members strong. Yet French and British merchants had stolen their land, and, since 1955, their complaints to the colonial officials had gone unheeded. They were in desperate need of overseas help to get the land of their "mother's home" back. They needed highly educated teachers, Peace Corps members, and help for the "naked" children of New Hebrides. As farmers, they did not want for food, but they sought connections with overseas liners to export their crops of taro, pumpkin, lettuce, sandalwood, peanuts, pineapples, and paw paw. Stephens was ready to travel and meet Kamarakafego. In return, Kamarakafego expressed his sympathy for Na Griamel and sought further political contacts in Fiji.[96] As a result of his visibility through Bermuda's Black Power conference and CAP, Kamarakafego's black political connections were fast expanding over Oceania. These concrete relationships would intensify as he proceeded to organize for 6PAC.

8

Minecrafting a Black World

The Sixth Pan-African Congress

Black freedom struggles have held intriguing relationships with the ideas of technology. On the one hand, black movements have historically viewed science as being an avatar of oppression linked to enslavement, surveillance and environmental injustice. Yet they have also perceived technology to be a lever of liberation essential to racial uplift and self-determination. Black Power's legitimate anxiety surrounding technology was perhaps best bench-marked through the era's black poetry, music, and literature. For example, Gil Scott-Heron chided "whitey's" presence on the moon in the midst of his sister's impoverishment, and Marvin Gaye denounced the ecological devastation of the earth's blue skies. For Bob Marley and the I Threes, Baby-lon's spaceships were sailing a million miles away from the troubled world's reality of concrete jungles. The *Black Scholar's* 1974 special edition, "Black Science," lamented racism's exclusion of African Americans from the world of science and technology, which it claimed had generated an "attitude of anti-science" among blacks. Activists in Oceania decried nuclear testing in the region as an offshoot of colonialism.

But this chapter shows that black political movements did not totally disavow science. Decades before the release of Marvel's *Black Panther*, black activists, scholars, and artists also saw technology as a "crucial ally." The Black Panther Party's ten-point program called for "community control of modern technology." The Melanesian island of Bougainville used green technology to win an environmental revolution against the multinational corporate exploitation of its copper resources. With radical imagination, Black Power activists engaged technology to globally forge Diaspora.[1]

These women and men sought to create a new world in an unpredictable era of social upheaval, political misadventure, and capricious nights and days, much like the protagonists in the iconic video game *Minecraft*. Their inventory was full of tools innovatively forged from the deep bedrock of global black freedom struggles. Black Power activists lived, dreamed, and loved in survival mode. Their antagonists were not *Minecraft*'s hostile mobs of zombies, creepers, and ender dragons, but state machinery, interpersonal glitches, and shape-shifting agent provocateurs. *What were these freedom dreams of obsidian if not distorted memories of the nightmares of technological captivity?*

The Genesis of 6PAC

Black Power's fixation on technology traversed through and beyond the domain of radical imagination. The Black Power conferences of the 1960s and '70s all held sessions on "Black technology." This theme of science was critical to Tanzania's monumental Sixth Pan-African Congress (6PAC), which was held June 19–27, 1974. It hosted approximately 600 official delegates, 300 observers, and 129 journalists from across Africa, the Americas, Britain, and Oceania. Dominant themes that emerged from 6PAC included a commitment to defeat neocolonialism, racism, and imperialism across the African Diaspora, support of the struggles of the Global South, and strengthen the relationships between science, technology, and black liberation.[2]

The congress represented the political, generational, and cultural crossroads of the 1970s African Diaspora. A massive logistical undertaking, it involved organizers from across the black world. Kamarakafego worked closely with its North American Steering Committee, which was led by organizers such as Sylvia Hill, Courtland Cox, Charlie Cobb, Jimmy Garrett, C. L. R. James, Sonia Sanchez, James Turner, Geri Augusto, and others associated with the DC-based Center for Black Education (CBE) and the Drum and Spear Bookstore. This included Eddie Wilson, Mary Jane Patterson, South African poet Keorapetse Kgositsile, Liz Gant, and Judy Claude, who was studying economics at Temple University.[3]

The organizing meetings of the congress occurred across Bermuda, Jamaica, the United States, Guyana, Tanzania, and Canada, in cities such as Toronto, London, Birmingham, and Paris, and at institutions such as Temple University, Oakland University, and Atlanta University. These ranged from small committee sessions to larger events that were multi-day conferences in and of themselves. Bermuda was the initial hub for these discussions. Garrett argues 6PAC's genesis was the reading of a letter by Kwame Nkrumah letter at Bermuda's 1969 Black Power conference, which called for a meeting to be held in Africa. Kamarakafego stated that he asked James about the need for 6PAC in the days immediately following the conference. Encouraged by Nkrumah and James, he proceeded to organize it; Hill, secretary-general for 6PAC's North American delegation, echoes this sentiment.[4]

According to Cox, 6PAC would never have occurred without Kamarakafego, who had both originated and promoted the idea of the congress. With an uncanny ability to "appear and disappear at will," Kamarakafego was not the kind of activist who stayed in one space to organize, write, or make speeches. Rather, states Cox, he was the kind of conduit who traveled frequently and seemingly knew everybody in the black political world. Kamarakafego's "incredible Rolodex" included black leaders from across Africa, Asia, Oceania, the Caribbean, and the United States.[5]

According to Cox, one of Kamarakafego's most critical contributions to 6PAC was in getting Nyerere to host the congress in Tanzania. He was able to do this through James and Nkrumah. Nyerere's progressive pan-Africanist politics, his support of Africana liberation struggles, and Tanzania's hosting of repatriates from the Africana world, made Tanzania an ideal venue for the congress. In the fall of 1969, while on his way to Australia, Kamarakafego visited both Nyerere and Nkrumah in Africa. They discussed the congress and corresponded over the course of the year. In October 1970, Nkrumah wrote Kamarakafego, stating that he was happy that the congress was being planned for Tanzania in 1971. Promising to help from Africa, Osagyefo also suggested that Kamarakafego write directly to Nyerere to ask him for permission to hold the congress there. In February 1971, Tanzania's secretary of foreign affairs, D. N. M. Mloka, wrote to Kamarakafego in Bermuda, informing him that Nyerere agreed to host the Congress in Tanzania but asked that it be postponed until 1972.[6]

Both James and Nkrumah were veteran pan-Africanists who had attended the 1945 Fifth Pan-African Congress in Manchester, England. In most circles, their support gave the talks legitimacy by placing the congress within the historical tradition of the Pan-African movement.[7] This garnered support from other black political icons—6PAC's official sponsors included Amy Jacques Garvey, Lerone Bennett, Eusi Kwayana, Norman Girven, and Shirley Graham Du Bois. In a political world full of personal relationships, "ideological Olympics," and tensions of gender and generations, this was immensely important. For example, in January 1973, Graham Du Bois received a letter from Guyana's Brindly Benn of the Afro-Asian American Association. After a 6PAC representative acted "queerly" in a Guyana meeting, Benn doubted if 6PAC was truly a successor to the 1945 congress. Graham Du Bois initially shared similar concerns but allayed his fears. Writing from

Cairo, Egypt, she stated that although the 6PAC Steering Committee had asked for her sponsorship, she did not respond to the request—she was "extremely cautious" about attaching her husband's name to anything, particularly to a project that she did not recognize. But months later, she received a call from James. After learning that Nyerere was behind the congress, she agreed to be an official sponsor.[8]

Du Bois found that anything originating from Washington, DC, was "suspect." Yet she was convinced that the meeting could be worthwhile, and she made plans to be in Tanzania. In March 1973, she wrote to Cox, regretting that she could not attend an organizing meeting at Kent State University, although she wanted to come to Washington, DC, to discuss with James and the Steering Committee how the congress needed to be "deeply grounded in Africa." She happily received materials about Jamaica's organizing, which affirmed for her that the ideas of pan-Africanism were being embodied earnestly.[9]

Kamarakafego called 6PAC's first organizing meeting in Bermuda. James suggested that Easter weekend of April 1971 was best for him. Attendees included Abbas Sykes (Tanzanian ambassador to the United States), Courtland and Frankie Cox, Fay and Jimmy Garrett, Calvin Hicks, Sanchez, Acklyn Lynch, and Bermuda's Joann Darrell and Suzanne Cann. James was denied entry into Bermuda. According to the CIA, the Black Beret Cadre's John Hilton Bassett was also part of these discussions, and he met with Hicks to discuss the congress.[10]

This collective conceptually divided the black world into East, West, North, and southern Africa, North and South America, the Caribbean, Europe, Asia, Australia, and Oceania. Given his UN experience and global contacts, Kamarakafego volunteered to help organize for the talks across Central and South America, Europe, Asia, and Oceania. James was responsible for writing the official call to congress—"The Call"—and for organizing in Africa and the Caribbean.[11]

Kamarakafego stressed that the congress should focus on areas like technology, science, education, and economics in addition to politics. He also felt that it needed to support sustainable development in independent black states. Writing from Bermuda, he called a second planning meeting for May 1971. This took place at Vermont's Goddard College, where Hicks directed a short-term, residency-based Third World Studies Department. Cox, Sykes, Haiti's Anselm Remy, Winston Wiltshire, Garrett, and Kamarakafego attended this meeting.[12]

Formed in 1970, Goddard's program saw itself as being distinct from "the last dying gasp of anti-poverty program syndrome known as Black Studies." It called for administrators to produce, and for faculty to teach and take their craft, missions, history, and responsibilities seriously. The program did not aim to "coddle trifling students." Its journal, *Gumbo*, was a mix of "poems of love, rebellion, hate, and life." It stressed both academic excellence and the implementation of intellectual skills in social and political action. By 1972, it had built relationships with community organizations across Cuba, Tanzania, the Soviet Union, Uganda, and, through Kamarakafego, Bermuda and Vanuatu. Among its sixty students from the Global South were those from Africa, Mexico, Bermuda, and Puerto Rico.[13]

Kamarakafego himself was part of Goddard's program. In the spring trimester of 1971, he taught biology. His teaching evaluations reveal that his students found him to be very good and that they requested other faculty members like him. Those who took his classes admired his ability to explain complex medical, biological, and technical terms via everyday experiences. In addition to relating biological science to survival skills, students learned politics and African history. Another student saw him as a "cultural symbol" and an "educational stimulant with practical and theoretical experience."[14]

In addition to referring students from Bermuda to its program, in 1972, Kamarakafego helped Goddard to establish a graduate program in Third World Studies. He wrote to Philip Littlejohn of the Inter-Religion Foundation for Community Organization, hoping to receive funds for a program at the Goddard-Cambridge Graduate Program in Massachusetts. Kamarakafego regarded the Third World Program as the best program of its kind that he had experienced.[15]

By 1972, the CBE had become the central hub for the 6PAC Steering Committee. Directed by Garrett, CBE was also affiliated with Cox's Drum and Spear bookstore. Wiltshire had served as secretary-general of 6PAC, but this arrangement did not work out. Kamarakafego convinced Cox to take on the role of secretary-general. An experienced organizer, Cox had been a member of Howard's Non-Violent Action Group and SNCC.[16]

Along with this core of organizers, Kamarakafego traveled the world canvassing for the congress. They were continually challenged by subsequent organizers about the origins of 6PAC. Kamarakafego felt that these attacks usually came from Baraka, which was not entirely accurate. Apparently, the two had "been going at each other" since the Congress of African Peoples in 1970. Kamarakafego's response was typically that 6PAC was supported by James, Ras Mokennen, and Nkrumah, all of whom had organized the Fifth Pan-African Congress.[17]

On July 20, 1971, the Guyanese government granted permission for James, Garrett, Remy, Wiltshire, Sykes, Cox, Hicks, Sanchez, Josef Ben-Jochannan, Sharon Burke, and SNCC activist Stanley Wise to have a meeting there. This meeting never occurred, as Eusi Kwayana, who was expected to organize the meeting locally, had come under intense pressure from Burnham. With some drama, Kamarakafego still made to Guyana with Sanchez. While on route he was prohibited entry in Trinidad and Tobago. Both he and Sanchez were placed under house arrest. Kamarakafego managed to secretly meet with Daaga at night.[18]

In January 1972, Garrett, Kamarakafego, Gant, James, and Sykes traveled to Europe to organize for 6PAC. In Paris, they sat down with the Federation of Black Students (FEANF) and the General Association of Guadeloupian Students, and, in Marseille, Martinique's Workers Federation. The mention of Sekou Touré's involvement often brought challenges from anti-Touré groups based in France. However, Gant, who spoke French, had helpful talks with Alioune Diop of *Presence Africaine*. Diop put them in touch with Carlos Moore. However, the Afro-Cuban did not support the term "pan-African" and was adamant that not all blacks were African.[19]

Through James and his nephew Darcus Howe, in England they met with several groups across London, Manchester, and Birmingham. In London, they spoke with Andrew Salkey and met with John Anthony La Rose at his home. La Rose was founder of New Beacon Books. He was concerned about how ethnicity posed a challenged to nationalism in Africa. They also spoke to the Black Panther movement, the Black People's Liberation Party, and Afro-Caribbean Self-Help. In Birmingham, they met with one group that had already established connections to develop land in Tanzania.[20]

According to Garrett, most of those involved in the talks were working-class black males, with a few black women who were college students or graduates. These discussions were rarely productive. The organizing cohort of 6PAC had assumed that these groups would welcome 6PAC. However, in England, they received pushback regarding the term "pan-African," as the political vocabulary of black activists in the region was centered around Black Power, not pan-Africanism. According to Garrett, they tended to associate pan-Africanism with Garveyism, ideas of back-to-Africa and "reactionary nationalism." The cohort was pressed with a plethora of critical questions that they were not yet ready to address, particularly around 6PAC's positions on neocolonialism and imperialism. This was before the Call was written. In addition, in London, 6PAC's proposal to organize around science and technology was seen by some as being middle class and reactionary. This was not the last time that the unfair charge of "bourgeois science" would be launched at the organizers.[21]

Science, Technology, and Pan-Africanism

According to Cox, C. L. R. James was the central intellectual architect behind the Call for 6PAC. Augusto also extensively contributed to the drafting, political thought, and production of the document. The Call began, "The twentieth century is the century of Black Power." A document of its time, it linked Black Power to Third World liberation struggles against colonialism and saw the congress as being part of one of the greatest global movements toward human freedom. The Call aligned 6PAC with the prior Pan-African congresses. It called for black self-reliance, the support of armed struggles in Africa, and a fight against the global capitalist "mega-machine." The machine, technology, and the scientific method were *causes as well as effects* of racism, colonialism, slavery, exploitation, oppression, and genocide. The document called for a pan-Africanist emphasis on science and technology and warned against the African people being automatons of Western civilization. As such, it urged that 6PAC establish a pan-African science and technology center. It also drew on the political ideas of Negritude, George Padmore, George Jackson, Malcolm X, and Frantz Fanon. It linked the political incarcerations of Malcolm X, George Jackson, Angela Davis, and H. Rap Brown with those of Nkrumah, Jomo Kenyatta, and Patrice Lumumba. Unfortunately betraying a tradition of pan-Africanist women, the only black woman mentioned in the call was Angela Davis.[22]

The call's focus on science and technology was consistent with the 6PAC Steering Committee's six areas of focus: agriculture, political cooperation, health and nutrition, communications, support of liberation movements in Africa, and science and technology. Its five broad objectives included increasing unity between Africa and its Diaspora, furthering self-reliance for the black world, supporting the liberation struggles of southern Africa and Guinea-Bissau, creating global black independent mechanisms of communication, and establishing a permanent 6PAC secretariat. Its two stated goals were to create a pan-African science and technology center and an African information center of a global scope.[23]

In an interview with Augusto, James said the African science and technology center would be supported and run by African people. Geared toward political self-determination, it would fight against the dominance that scientists and technologists of Western countries exerted over black development. The center was to be headquartered at an African university and have satellite branches across the world. It was to engage in research projects aimed at solving the African world's technological issues. In doing so, it would serve as a clearinghouse for technological questions about geography, mineral resources, health, epidemiology, agricultural, and economics.[24]

The center was to include a global Society of Scientists and Technologists for African Development (SSTAD). The society would encourage a "new attitude" among black people in regard to using science and technology for the benefit of the Diaspora. The Steering Committee's "Working Paper for an Association of African Scientists and Technologists" argued that it was indisputable that science and technology were powerful weapons in the arsenal of development and self-reliance. However, a much longer list of "indisputable facts" charged that black technologists worked in isolation from one another; that African skilled talent and natural resources were exploited for the development of other peoples; that scientific techniques being used in black communities were often alien or inadequate; that black youth were discouraged from studying science; and that America and Europe monopolized the mechanisms for legitimizing scientific practices. Yet, the paper argued, progressive scientists from across the Diaspora were determined to change these issues.[25]

The SSTAD wanted to promote the study, design, and use of science and technology by African people for the benefit of the African world. It was to encourage the interchange of scientific information and best practices between the "African Diaspora in the best scientific and African tradition." The society was to be locally, nationally, regionally, and internationally structured across 6PAC's established regions of the black world. The SSTAD aimed to launch a few projects over its first two years and send contact letters to one hundred individuals in North America, one hundred fifty in Africa, fifty in Europe, and twenty-five in Oceania.[26]

The society proposed establishing adult and youth local chapters. These would organize field trips, set up apprenticeship systems, and organize other projects to develop future technologists among African children. It was hoped that this next generation would understand its crucial role as "partners with the people" to achieve black self-determination. The North American Steering Committee aimed to obtain tax-exempt incorporation for SSTAD in the United States and in at least one African country. It aimed to solicit and develop papers on health and nutrition, agriculture and water supply, transportation, mineral resources, the center, energy sources in developing countries, communication technology, and a five-year plan for SSTAD. These papers were to be presented at the congress. The proposal also called for the production of a technological journal with articles for both popular and specialist audiences. Its five-year plan spanned publishing, research, information gathering and dissemination, and fundraising.[27]

The tentative agenda for 6PAC's science and technology workshops was to include a keynote speech on the economic importance of science and workshops on increasing human resources in technology for African development, a twenty-five-year plan for food security in Africa (addressing transportation, drought, and animal husbandry), and industrial development in Africa.[28]

Cox surmised these ideas in a 1973 article, "Black Technology." Published in *African Affairs*, it stated that congress papers were being developed to accelerate a "political framework for African scientists" that would "make technology a tool for the people's liberation." The Sixth Pan-African Congress aimed to turn technology from being a master of African peoples to being their servant. Science, Cox argued, needed to be evaluated by its political implications. In an effort to help black communities control their material circumstances, scientific resources needed to be utilized for their benefit. In addressing the question "Where do we go from here," African people needed to carefully consider the role that technology would play in achieving their goals. Cox argued that the achievement of pan-African goals heavily depended on the mobilization of African scientists. There were obstacles preventing scientists and technologists from living up to their destiny as partners in the liberation of African people. This included powerlessness and black people's suspicion of science. Calling for reliance on indigenous resources, the SSTAD would seek support from African and Caribbean governments in these efforts.[29]

Such questions were being debated constantly across 6PAC's preparatory meetings. For example, in February 1974, a Southern Forum was held at Atlanta University. Its science and technology panel asked how science could assist the struggles of oppressed people. Presided over by organizers such as Hill and Turner, the panel discussed a proposed pan-African science academy. The contact person for the Committee on Science and Technology was Don Coleman of Howard University's Engineering Department. Other key members included Howard University assistant professor of engineering Neville Parker and dermatologist Fletcher Robinson. According to Garrett, the science group brought the most complete presentation before 6PAC. Ironically, the center did not get enough support to be included in the final resolution of the science workshop.[30]

Kamarakafego attended a number of these meetings on technology. This included a March 1974 talk at the CBE with Edie Wilson, Hill, Coleman, Parker, and Robinson. They discussed logistical needs, the structure of the science and technology meetings, and necessary equipment. The group also asked for invitations to be sent Luka Abe, a Ugandan agriculturalist, and Sarah Lee, who had moved to Ghana to form its first dental clinic.[31]

Surveillance of 6PAC

The real or imagined potential ramifications of 6PAC—black activists from across the world logistically organized under the banner of pan-Africanism—had literal relevance for the Global South across the Atlantic, Indian, and Pacific Oceans. This possibility was not lost on Western governments across the world that benefited from the socioeconomic oppression of black communities. Across the Americas, Europe, and Oceania, state officials monitored its organizers.

American embassy officials in Tanzania saw 6PAC as a potential forum for criticism of the US naval presence in the Indian Ocean. Tanzania's government had been "implacably critical" of the construction of a US military base on Diego Garcia. As such, the embassy recommended that journalists from Tanzania not be allowed to enter the island for the duration of 6PAC. Amid dubious agreements between the British and US governments, by 1971, the black inhabitants of Diego Garcia had been forcibly displaced to places such as Mauritius and the Seychelles.[32]

Surveillance by the FBI covering four years of 6PAC meetings produced thousands of documents. Claiming that "black extremists" were actively among its organizers, the FBI legitimized its concerns about the congress via statements made by Kwame Ture. This included his 1973 speech on pan-Africanism at the University of Iowa, where he called for the utter and complete destruction of "racist American imperialism." Ture felt that Africans in America had a vital role to play in that destruction. "Revolutionaries got to pick up the gun. . . . It follows scientific principles that the gun must be picked up," Ture posited. Ture may no longer have been Black Power's "Nubian God," but by 1973, he was certainly not a "political zero."[33] The FBI referred to Ture as a self-styled leading proponent of revolutionary

Pan-Africanism. The bureau expressed concern about the domestic and international relationships of black political organizers. It considered Garrett to be a "key black extremist" and was aware that he and Kamarakafego were actively using the CBE to organize 6PAC.[34]

The bureau investigated 6PAC's organizers at the district, regional, and international levels. It had the Kent State University chief of police provide a list of names of all attendees at a 1973 meeting of the North American Planning Conference at the Ohio-based school. It also documented a September 1972 6PAC meeting in New York City that included Canada's Rosie Douglas, agent Warren Hart, Malcolm X Liberation University's Owusu Sadaukai, Jamaica's Marcus Garvey Jr., Kwayana, James, and Nyerere. The bureau reported that Kwayana had been contacted by Douglas in 1971 during the latter's visit to Guyana; he reportedly traveled to Bermuda to meet with "black extremist" Kamarakafego. The FBI noted that Kamarakafego had left Bermuda in September with New York's Mitzie Kenner. Kamarakafego gave his address as 410 Central Park West, but Bermuda's police did not believe that he had any intentions of residing there. The bureau instructed all its offices to furnish any details about the meeting; the "growth of the Pan African ideology was growing among extremists," but this opportunity to monitor the New York meeting needed to be fully exploited.[35]

Kamarakafego was one of the bureau's DC-based international targets. This list included Howard University student Anthony Ferguson, James, Coleman, Robinson, and Cox. On March 23, 1974, at least two FBI informants attended a CBE forum where he was the speaker. The meeting included Robert Taylor, Eric Stark, Phillip Goodman, Tony Kadiri, Sam Awobamise, Veta Connor, and Kenya's Rachier Mbeche. Introduced by Loretta Hobbs, Kamarakafego discussed the struggles of black people in Australia and Oceania. One FBI report described him as a Caribbean-born, 5'11" to 6-foot medium-built Negro male. It falsely claimed that he had attended Australia's Sydney University and that he was a Tanzanian citizen. He reportedly stated that he would be in the Washington, DC, area for a few weeks preparing for 6PAC.[36]

One FBI agent claimed that Kamarakafego was "no orator," commenting that his talk was largely based on a written fact sheet that he passed around. He discussed white minority rule in Australia, the sufferings of Aboriginal peoples, and Koorie political struggles. While discussing Australia's physical, ecological, and sexual abuse of the Koories, he remarked that some indigenous persons had "African traits" while others looked "whiter."

However, he asserted, the Western world pointed out the physical differences of black people in Oceania to cause disunity.[37]

Kamarakafego's document was entitled "The Struggle of Black People in Australia and the South Pacific Islands." It described Britain's colonization of Australia through violence, the poisoning of water holes, the distribution of diseased garments, and racist laws. Yet the Koorie continued to fight against European and American imperialism. He described the annihilation of Tasmanians and the Aboriginal quest for land rights. "Aborigines know that they were always there," he remarked. White anthropologists had referred to them as being "dark-skinned people with Negroid features" who had descended to the region from South Asia. He also discussed how Australia's new 1971 government gave Aboriginal communities conditional land rights while asserting state control of any mineral resources. Kamarakafego discussed the AAL and the National Aboriginal Tribal Council. He also detailed his travels across Oceania, decolonization in Papua New Guinea, and Vanuatu's struggle against British and French colonialism.[38]

Kamarakafego's discussion was consistent with 6PAC's inclusion of Oceania. In February 1973, a planning conference was held in Jamaica. It was directed by 6PAC's Caribbean secretariat, Roderick Francis and held at Jamaica's Sheraton-Kingston hotel. The meeting was titled Domiabra—a Twi word meaning, "If you love me, join me." Its purpose was to hear the issues facing black people in the Caribbean and South America and to measure the region's scientific capabilities.[39] Australian Black Power activist Roberta (Bobbi) Sykes also attended the meeting.

Captured in an iconic photograph taken by the *Daily Gleaner*, the opening forum was addressed by Jamaican senator Dudley Thompson, Amy Jacques Garvey, Tanzania's ambassador to the United States Paul Bomani, Ken Hill, Cox, and Sykes. Thompson, Garvey, and Hill had all attended the 1945 Pan-African Congress. Meanwhile, Count Ossie and the Mystic Revelation of Rastafari provided "mood music."[40]

Jamaica's meeting called for 6PAC to declare all black people in the Diaspora as being African and stressed that all Africans had the right to repatriate to Africa. Thompson opened the talks, calling for black people to experience Africa for themselves. Jacques Garvey spoke about black exploitation in Jamaica. Citing Marcus Garvey, she argued that the island's white alien elite and "white-minded" black people were stumbling blocks to black liberation. In the spirit of the UNIA, she set the tone for the talks. She informed the opening rally of 250 delegates that black economic independence was needed to match political sovereignty.[41]

Given Rastafari's living legacy on the island, the meeting's focus on repatriation was fitting. Generally dismissive of the congress, American ambassador to Jamaica Vincent de Roulet reported a dispute between Julius Garvey and a Rasta participant about what kinds of black people would be eligible for repatriation. De Roulet alleged that Garvey argued that color counted most and claimed that one needed to have "all black features" to qualify. In contrast, the Rasta delegate claimed that psychic orientation was more important than complexion.[42]

The next day's sessions were centered on science and technology, repatriation to Africa and reparations from Europe, liberation of southern Africa, black people in Oceania, and a structure for 6PAC. The committee on southern Africa called for 6PAC to provide material support to African liberation movements. The talks declared North Africa, West Africa, East Africa, southern Africa, the Caribbean and South America, the Pacific, and North America as the regions for 6PAC. This committee was chaired by Brazil's Abdias do Nascimento, whose involvement brought him to the attention of the FBI. Months later, informants reported that Nascimento was a black-studies professor at the State University of New York at Buffalo and that he was active with a faction of Puerto Ricans who sought to connect themselves with the "Third World." The FBI reported that his close friend, African American Evelyn Scott, spoke "Puerto Rican fluently" and was his liaison between "the blacks and the Puerto Rican" Third Worldists.[43]

Possessing its own concerns with black Australia's connections with the Global South, the ASIO was troubled by Sykes's presence in Jamaica. Agents connected with the Australian embassy in Washington, DC, informed ASIO official "SCORPION" of her activities there. They obtained reports of the Jamaica meetings and writings that Sykes distributed in the island about racism in Australia.[44]

Sykes was an international icon of Black Power in Australia. The daughter of an African American WWII veteran and a white Australian mother, she was involved in the Aboriginal Tent Embassy protests. In 1972 she had traveled to Papua New Guinea and New Zealand to galvanize support for Australia's black movement. In the fall of that year, she visited London through the advocacy organization ABJAB. While there, she made contacts with black groups from across the city and suggested ways in which they could support Aboriginal peoples. During a December 1972 protest, the Black Unity & Freedom Party, the Black Liberation Front, London's Black Panthers, the Croydon's Collective, and the Fasimbas took up these ideas.[45]

Sykes made her way to Jamaica from Britain. She informed the meeting's opening audience that the scope of black liberation included Australia, Papua New Guinea, and New Zealand. The next day, she chaired the Committee on Black People in the Pacific, which declared that the black world needed to be informed of the struggles of the Black Pacific and to place their cases before the UN and the Organization of African Unity (OAU).[46]

Weeks before, Sykes had penned an open letter to 6PAC. She wrote that she wanted to add another dimension to Barbadian novelist George Lamming's definition of black as referring to persons of the Caribbean, Africa, and the United States who had originated in Africa. Sykes stressed that there were people in the world who "had not been in the position to previously refute or challenge this definition, but who were definitely black." These were the black people of Oceania who may not have known of any clear "African origins in their past, yet who wished to be recognized as part of the struggle."[47]

Sykes defined Australia as historically being a black man's country. However, two hundred years prior, European colonists triggered the genocide of indigenous peoples and significantly reduced their numbers to about half a million. Black people had not been counted in Australia's census until 1967. Significantly outnumbered by a white population that was close to thirteen million, black Australians had little reason to hope that a revolution could be successful. Furthermore, she supported 6PAC's idea of bringing together Africana scientists, and she regretted that she would likely not be able to attend the talks for financial reasons.[48]

Sykes's letter argued that the existence of Aboriginal peoples would perhaps rely on assistance from outside Australia. Marked by slum occupation, police victimization, and unemployment, conditions for urban black Australians paralleled those of urban African Americans. However, reflected in the lack of black Australian doctors, lawyers, and engineers, their educational opportunities there were vastly different than black communities in the United States. Aboriginals on reserves lived in conditions similar to those of American Indians. Australia was theoretically a system of apartheid, and the government's policies to place communities on reserves were similar to South Africa's racist policies. Barriers such as the "white Australia policy" prevented black travelers from coming to Australia to bear witness to their existence. This allowed the government to "murder, starve, rape, and to strip every vestige of worldly possessions" from Australia's black community. The congress, then, would be a significant opportunity for activists from Oceania to join in "international black brotherhood."[49]

Sykes was right. In her memoir, *Snake Dancing*, she recalls meeting Rastafari participants at the Jamaica meeting. She willingly answered their questions about black struggle in Australia. She also gave them copies of her 6PAC report, "The Condition of the Black People of Australia." The document stated that while Australia had been a black man's country for thirty thousand years, it was now been dominated by "western-Europeans" who had murdered, rounded up, and confined to reservations its indigenous persons. This had led to a situation in which the infant mortality for Australia's blacks was the "highest in the world." While rape of black women and children was rampant, black people made up 47 percent of the prison population despite constituting 1 percent of the total population.[50]

The document asked, "How can a Jamaican help?" It then described specific ways that Jamaicans could assist Aboriginal communities. This included protesting their conditions to the Australian government and to white Australians who traveled to Jamaica or America for study or sport. Sykes asserted that black communities could not afford to play international hosts to whites who supported racism back in their home countries. In addition, black countries needed to not support black athletes who had turned their backs on the suffering of their peoples; such public figures needed to be made aware that "it would be better to go against the oppressor than to go kicking or batting a ball" for the economic benefit or entertainment of oppressors in other countries. Signed a "Black Australian," the document read "AUSTRALIAN WHITES PLAY CRICKET, AUSTRALIAN BLACKS STARVE, DOWN WITH AUSTRALIAN RACISM."[51]

Sykes's reference to sport was actually an indictment of a Cricket test match between the West Indies and Australia that was being held in Jamaica from February 16 to 21. Her Rasta visitors had told her that Australia's predominately white players had historically sexually exploited and impregnated Jamaican girls during these matches. Overlooked by the Blue Mountains of Nanny Town, members of this Rasta collective handed out copies of her statement at the match at Kingston's Sabina Park. Jamaica's Special Branch made note of this remarkable moment of transoceanic black solidarity and promptly interrogated Sykes at her hotel about the flyer.[52]

Versions of the document were distributed and published across various black media outlets. Jacques Garvey forwarded Sykes's report to *Black World*, which printed it in June 1973. For Jacques Garvey, Sykes had intelligently exposed black genocide that aimed to "keep Australia white." Of course, Jacques Garvey was well aware of black Australia's struggles. In the

1920s, she corresponded with members of Australia's branch of the UNIA. In April 1973, Sykes's piece had been printed in Brooklyn's *Black News*. This time, the question was asked more broadly: How can the *African*—and not Jamaican—help?[53]

Interestingly, a few pages across from Sykes's statement was an article titled, "Black Bermuda." Written by Kasisi Adeyemi Al-Muqaddim, the essay discussed colonialism, Black Power, and the dramatic assassinations of British commissioner George Duckett (September 1972) and Bermuda's British governor Richard Sharples and his aide-de-camp (March 1973). Many black groups came under immediate suspicion, including the Nation of Islam. It was alleged that "a group of anti-social Bermudian youths known as Rastafarians" had been mounting racial placards in front of City Hall. Dreadfully growing in numbers and influence, the police had been keeping the group of about fifty black and five white youths under surveillance since 1972. But most pressing, US State Department officials listed "Black Power, anti-colonialism, and terrorism" as primary motives for the murders. They remarked that the Black Beret Cadre—an anti-colonial, terrorist organization that was "Che Guevara at his most militant"—was a prime suspect.[54] In 1977, Beret associate Erskine "Buck" Burrows was hung for assassinations, prompting an island-wide revolt.

This is critical because Kamarakafego remained an advisor to the Berets, several of whom were detained for the killings. He was well aware that he was also held under suspicion for the incidents. He believed that it was only that he was abroad at the time that he was not held by colonial officials. For instance, London's *Guardian* referred to Kamarakafego as a Marxist, frequent visitor to Cuba, and the PLP's resident extremist. Describing Kamarakafego as being self-styled as his "adored [Che] Guevara," the paper mused that Bermuda was ill prepared for "all his talk of mid-Atlantic Revolution." But Kamarakafego had not been seen in Hamilton's "ghettos" for a while, and though most linked the assassinations to the Cadre, a few wondered where Kamarakafego had been during that Saturday night. Bermuda was swarming with Britain's detectives, but like T. S. Eliot's Macavity, "when the Yard's around, Browne's not there."[55]

In April 1974, Bermuda's commissioner of police informed the FBI that Kamarakafego was observed at New York's Penn Station. Carrying luggage, he was apparently at the station to meet a "tall black male." Former Beret Beverly Lottimore accompanied him. The turban-wearing Lottimore was known to have visited the Nation of Islam's Mosque No. 7 in Harlem. The commissioner also asked for the FBI's assistance in locating Berets John Hilton Bassett and Ottiwell Simmons Jr. The commissioner was aware that Kamarakafego was a coordinator of 6PAC and knew that efforts were being made to have young Bermudians attend. Still, Kamarakafego had not been in Bermuda for over a year; he was in Africa and Tanzania.[56]

Where Do We Go from Here?

Over the years, Cox received a number of critiques from black activists about the direction of 6PAC. Some were legitimate, and some were not. Cox was quite disturbed by one letter that he received from SNCC activist and long-time friend Bob Brown. Brown had apparently heard that charges of elitism had been launched at Cox and other 6PAC organizers.[57]

In July 1973, twenty-four-year-old Augusto expressed concern about a lack of an 6PAC international steering committee, whose delegates needed to be elected region by region. She also called for extensive participation at the decision-making level by "Africans from the continent." This matter of political necessity needed to occur before the spring of 1974, which would save the congress "unnecessary grief." Furthermore, she called for clarity on a number of 6PAC's political positions, particularly around the issue of science and technology. Augusto traveled to Tanzania as part of the secretariat; while she expressed that she was not willing to head the international office there, she was instrumental in organizing the congress as its information officer.[58]

Another critique came from the Malcolm X Liberation University's Sadaukai. In October 1973, he returned from a trip to Africa on behalf of the African Liberation Support Committee (ALSC). Sadaukai privately wrote to Cox, legitimately questioning how neocolonialist heads of states were using their relationship to 6PAC to appear to be progressive. He was concerned that if Caribbean delegations to 6PAC were not representative of their communities, the political position of the congress (in terms of racism, imperialism, and non-capitalist development in Africa), the actual structure of the congress, and the makeup of the North American representatives would be compromised. This very important letter was made public, and Cox sought to address these concerns head on.[59]

Augustine Ingutia and the Pan-African Canadian Group echoed Sadaukai's questions. At a Washington, DC, meeting, Ingutia presented the views of the ALSC, which had met in Toronto that October. The ALSC felt that black governments needed to provide funds for grassroots organizations to attend the conference, that Tanzania should provide for their living expenses, that half of the delegates to 6PAC needed to be from the grassroots level, that the grassroots firmly supported Sadaukai's letter to Cox, that the congress did not really address the issues of all black people, and that black West Indians in North America needed greater representation in 6PAC.[60]

Weeks later, Sadaukai voiced these concerns directly to Cox during an extended weekend meeting of the North American Steering Committee in Washington, DC. Partly held at the historic All Souls Unitarian Church, the meeting included the likes of Charles Cobb, Garrett, Queen Mother Moore, Claude, Jane Patterson, Turner, Cox, Awobamise, and Canada's Ingutia and Brenda Paris. An intense debate followed. Moore questioned Cox about his political background. After detailing his work with SNCC and Drum and Spear, he stated that he expected many problems to emerge at 6PAC because of the diversity of black approaches to liberation, but that he was more concerned with bringing people into the struggle than with keeping them out.[61]

Cox found Sadaukai's concerns to be "valid and frank." He sent his detailed response to the North American Committee, to international sponsors, and to those who attended the November meeting. In terms of the political position of 6PAC, he directed Sadaukai to examine the official call of the congress. He expected the ideology of 6PAC to be as broad as its delegates. Clear that capitalism was responsible for the Atlantic slave trade and the colonization of Africa, he argued that self-reliance was a key element in black liberation. However, he said, this focus on self-reliance needed to not be construed as a lack of position against the evils of imperialism and capitalism. Cox stressed that while Caribbean patrons included Jamaica's Michael Manley, Guyana's Forbes Burnham, and Barrow of Barbados, the organizing of the Caribbean-South American region of 6PAC was the responsibility of nongovernment contacts such as Tim Hector, Francis, and Kwayana. He argued that these organizers would solicit the support of the grassroots community whether or not they disagreed with the black governments. They had the responsibility of electing their own delegates, and an upcoming regional conference in Guyana was going to iron out these details.[62]

James gave the keynote address at the Guyana meeting in December 1973. Paul Bomani, Tanzanian ambassador to the United States, also attended. Focused on the "Caribbean Reality," the meeting's representatives included Bermuda's Jerome Perinchief (Black Beret Cadre), Barbados's Bobby Clarke (People's Democratic Movement), Antigua's Hector (Afro-Caribbean Liberation Movement), Jamaica's Francis, St. Vincent's Kenneth Maloney (Organization for Black Cultural Awareness), Trinidad and Tobago's Daaga (NJAC), and Kwayana (African Society for Cultural Relations with Independent Africa). It was decided that this steering committee would select the Caribbean delegates to 6PAC. The committee also represented Grenada's New Jewel movement and Jamaica's Pan-African Union.[63]

However, the same Caribbean leaders that suppressed Black Power sought to thwart 6PAC. Burnham, once again, showed them the way. Not only did he offer to give opening remarks to the Guyana meeting, but he also pledged material support of $10,000 as an official sponsor of the talks. But with this kind of political and financial clout, he and other leaders, rather than the aforementioned non-governmental committee, significantly influenced Caribbean delegates to 6PAC.[64]

The Guyanese government claimed that it was attacked during the Caribbean Reality meeting. Ambassador Bomani was also displeased. This caught the ear of the US State Department, which acknowledged Burnham's angst at the Black Power group's meeting. Guyanese minister of state Kit Nascimento claimed that the committee was not interested in relations with Africa but were only trying to find a podium for protest. Burnham then pressured Nyerere, stressing that 6PAC should not be allowed as a platform for dissidents to attack their governments.[65]

Meanwhile, Cox had traveled to Tanzania to attend a 6PAC Steering Committee meeting at the Tanganyika African National Union's (TANU) headquarters. Here it was decided that delegations could only be those sponsored by governments, those from ruling parties, liberation movements approved by the OAU (even Puerto Rico's nationalist movements "did not meet the criteria for participation"), and parties not objectionable to the governments of states they came from. From Europe, black delegates from France did not plan to attend, those from Britain wanted nine persons, and African embassies in the Netherlands were to solicit interest from persons of African descent there. According to Garrett, this dramatically changed 6PAC's initial framework. It went from being an NGO congress with government participation to a governmental congress with "open participation for blacks from nonblack states and qualified participation by progressive leaders from black states."[66]

Cox was also informed that the Guyanese and Tanzanian governments did not think favorably of the Guyanese meeting. Yet, Nyerere still informed Burnham that the Caribbean government and non-governmental representatives should attend 6PAC. Cox's attempts to work out the situation were unsuccessful. In the end, Nyerere informed Burnham that Tanzania's guidelines for attendees to the congress would be government delegations, ruling parties, liberation movements, and groups approved by the government. Cox objected to these conditions and asked for a Tanzanian delegation to assume full responsibility for this decision by directly informing the Caribbean organizers themselves. They did not do this, but government spokespersons from Guyana, Trinidad and Tobago, French Guiana, and other states made public the decision to exclude NGOs from the Caribbean.[67]

The Caribbean Steering Committee accused Cox of betraying the West Indian delegates. In June, Daaga informed Trinidad and Tobago's *Express* that this betrayal was "unforgivable and unforgettable." The NJAC leader unfairly held that Cox had collaborated with conspirators of Caribbean governments to block black militants from going to Dar es Salaam.[68]

Strikingly, Cox's detractors included aforementioned Howard University student Ferguson, whom the FBI had "interviewed" repeatedly since 1972. Ferguson was also a leader of Howard's Caribbean Student Association, the Caribbean Unity Conference, the 6PAC Steering Committee, and was a member of the university's football team. He attended the Guyanese and Jamaican regional 6PAC meetings and traveled to Tanzania. Ferguson furnished the FBI with critical information and documents regarding 6PAC, African Liberation Day, ALSC, and visits to Howard by Grenada's Maurice Bishop, C. L. R. James, and Guyana's Walter Rodney. Special agents of the FBI initially interviewed him at his DC-based residence, pressuring him with a possible violation of the Foreign Agents Registration Act.[69]

On June 9, James officially resigned as a sponsor of 6PAC. He had heard of the decision to restrict Caribbean delegates and found this to be in direct violation of months of work building a broad delegate base from the region. He told Cox that he could not lend his name to such a situation. He was left with the "overwhelming task" of explaining to the thousands of people that he had misled. Yet to avoid encouraging any publicity that would harm 6PAC, he confirmed that he would not express his disappointment publicly. In a letter to Tanzania's foreign minister, J. S. Malecela, James reiterated his position, stating that the congress had become vastly different from what was initially envisioned.[70]

Cox wrote back to James, expressing regret about his absence. Cox knew that James had worked harder than anyone else to make it happen, and though he explained the situation, it was to no avail; James's decision was final. Yet Cox was adamant that 6PAC needed to occur; otherwise, the forces of imperialism would have won.[71]

In the end, fifty-one delegations attended the congress. The talks were facilitated by three main committees: Economics (vice-chaired by the Mozambique Liberation Front's representative and poet Marcelino Dos Santos and reported by Canada's Paris); Science, Technology, Culture, and Education (vice-chaired by Neville Parker); and Politics (vice-chaired by Jamaica's Patricia Cooper).[72]

Cooper was a part of Jamaica's delegation, which included Rex Nettleford and Tony Phillips. The Jamaican delegation's letter to 6PAC on behalf of the government and the people of Jamaica called for men and women of the African Diaspora to draw spiritual strength and courage from Africa, otherwise they would remain empty shells of their metropolitan masters. Noting the Caribbean's involvement in the Fifth Pan-African Congress through activists such as Ashwood Garvey, Padmore, and Thompson, the delegation stated that several elders of that generation resided in the afterlife, where Nyankopon (the almighty) and ancestors still participated in their liberation struggles.[73]

Over one hundred papers, speeches, and messages were presented, among which were messages from the American Indian movement and the Afro-Asian People's Solidarity Organization. Audiotapes were made of the lectures, which were translated into Arabic, English, French, and Spanish. The congress's general declaration called for an end to neocolonialism, racism, and imperialism across Africa, Oceania, the Caribbean, and South America and for the harnessing of science and technology for liberation. It adopted nine resolutions on economics, science, culture, Mozambique, black women, Palestine, the Caribbean, French colonialism, and southern Africa. Its resolution on black women considered the key role that black women had played in revolutionary struggles against imperialism and racism, recognized that women had been subjected to racial, class, and sexual oppression, and pledged total support for the political struggles of black women. Delegates also donated 111 pints of blood to African liberation struggles. The Pan-African Students Organization of the Americas noted that the congress held that scientific socialism was the only viable way forward for the progress of African peoples.[74]

Parker's address on the "Pan-African Imperative for Increased Emphasis on Science and Technology" spanned the political implications of science. He stated that it was virtually impossible for black scientists in America to make a living without being employed by the very system that oppressed black people. He also called for the creation of the Pan-African Center of Science and Technology and the Association of Scientists and Technologists for Pan-African Development. His report also suggested the implementation of certain projects, such as one focused on combating the effects of desertification and the progression of the Sahara desert.[75]

The Science Committee called for technology and science to be used for black liberation and to overthrow (neo)colonialism and imperialism. It called for the assessment of pan-African skills, technology for the development of natural resources, and a focus on black health and nutrition. As such, the congress resolved that through self-reliance, technical skill development among the masses of black people needed to be mobilized and that pan-African scientists needed to exchange scientific information and techniques for the benefit of all African societies and the pan-African working class. It recommended that African scientists develop ways to harness solar and nuclear energy peacefully in consideration of the environment, and condemn the use of nuclear testing for warfare.[76]

Pan-Africanism and the Pacific

Sometime in 1973, Kamarakafego had backed away from 6PAC as a result of internal conflicts and other issues, but, like Cox, he felt that the congress had to happen. In the spring of 1974, Kamarakafego returned to help organize delegates from Oceania. Carrying an official letter of permission from Cox to speak on behalf of 6PAC, he canvassed the region in the months leading up to the talks.[77]

He also made sure to be in Tanzania. At the time, he was lecturing part time in biological science and ecology at the University of Nairobi. Arriving in Tanzania about three months before the congress, Kamarakafego offered his services in organizing the venue at the University of Dar es Salaam. The secretariat did need assistance. Kamarakafego designed the plans for the talks, which were submitted to Gesiler Mapunda, political education secretary of TANU.[78]

Kamarakafego drafted and oversaw the menu for 6PAC. He had the food purchased from local farmers, as the organizers did not want to import anything. For two weeks, he worked with the university chefs in cooking samples of food. Given his penchant for the kitchen, this was unsurprising.[79]

The congress shared the university with a World Council of Churches (WCC) Familia 74 meeting, also known as Ujamaa Safari. According to Kamarakafego, the kitchen separated two dining rooms. After attendees to Familia 74—who were largely white—observed that the food was better in the dining room dedicated to 6PAC, they attempted to eat there. Kamarakafego asked them to leave. A scuffle broke out when one of the WCC participants poked him in the chest.[80]

From the perspective of Ujamaa Safari's Rex Daniels, organizing the meeting was a "nightmare" because 6PAC had completely taken over the campus. The talks featured sessions by Paulo Freire and the Mozambique's Liberation Front's (Frelimo) Daniel Mbwenze and Janet Mondlane. Sponsored by TANU, participants visited and worked in the Ujamaa villages. Participants to Familia 74 included a married couple from Vanuatu, Peter and Helen Taurakoto.[81] The Taurakotos were members of the indigenous New Hebrides National Party (NHNP). Formed in 1971, the party promoted the advancement of the ni-Vanuatu socially, educationally, economically, and politically. It sought to develop Vanuatu into one nation. The Taurakotos had hoped to use their participation in Familia 74 as a means to covertly attend 6PAC, which was being attended by the party's secretary-general John Bani, its deputy chairman Barak Sope, and Sope's wife and party member, poet Mildred M. Sope. The NHNP saw 6PAC as an opportunity to boost its international network in its bitter liberation struggle against French and British colonialism.[82]

Kamarakafego had invited the group to 6PAC. He had met them in Vanuatu in April 1974. From Suva, Fiji, he telegrammed NHNP leader Walter Lini. Referring to himself as a friend of Fijian activist K. C. Ramrakha, Kamarakafego gave his arrival to Vanuatu the next day along with a flight number. To the consternation of the British colonial officials, Kamarakafego was hosted by the party and while there displayed a "bitter anti-white racialistic outlook." They knew that he was there to attract its leaders to attend Tanzania's "World Gathering of Black Power adherents."[83]

The Sopes and Bani arrived in Dar es Salaam in early June. They were most pleased that Kamarakafego had greeted them at the airport. Still, their arrival was not without hiccups. Bani lost his luggage and travel funds. Barak telegrammed the party, asking if more money could be sent with Taurakoto in care of Mildred Sope. They had expected 6PAC to have started earlier, and were surprised by its postponement to June 19.[84]

Sope gave a critical address at 6PAC. He began by thanking the Cuban delegation for introducing them to the congress. He presented a paper attributed to himself and Bani, "The Struggle Against Anglo-French Colonialism in the New Hebrides." Having listened to several speeches, he wondered if the audience knew of the 4.5 million exploited people in the Pacific. He denounced nuclear testing, asking the Algerian delegation where they had told the French to take their nuclear bombs. Indeed, he stated, France's nuclear tests in Oceania were poisoning their fish and waters in colonized places like Tahiti's (French Polynesia) Mururoa Atoll. Referencing the Kenyan delegation, he remarked that British colonialists in Vanuatu were openly using the same laws that they used to suppress the Mau Mau. He also denounced America's historic use of Guam to fly B-52 bombers into Vietnam.[85]

Noted by the US State Department, Sope called for 6PAC to recognize the political struggles of the black and brown peoples of Oceania. Discussing the relationship between imperialism in Africa and in the Pacific, he urged 6PAC to pass resolutions denouncing colonialism and nuclear testing. Stressing Oceania's connections to Africa, he asserted that the people of New Hebrides were proud of their color and "had sailed from Africa to the Pacific with canoes and sails." Better sailors than James Cook or Magellan, they had navigated the globe before Europeans knew that the world was round. Sope listed the abuses of colonialism and blackbirding, arguing that Vanuatu's fight was the same as the liberation struggles of Angola, Mozambique, Guinea-Bissau, Zimbabwe, Namibia, and South Africa. Sope described how the party had the support of the island's masses and had raised funds from across its rural, urban, Western-educated, and traditionally educated supporters. The congress was a critical moment for the NHNP to gain international support. It was the first time that Sope felt that people in America, the Caribbean, and Africa were ready to help them in their common struggle. He added, Africa had to look to the struggle of the Black Pacific.[86]

Australia's High Commission office in Dar es Salaam compiled a file on 6PAC. It pointed out that 6PAC's general declaration called for the support of "the struggling people" of Australia, New Zealand, and the Pacific Islands and noted its reference to the New Hebrides and to French colonialism. The British Foreign and Commonwealth Office also shared a very substantive report about 6PAC written by the British High Commission in Tanzania. It passed these on to Australia's secretary of foreign affairs.[87]

The High Commission was highly dismissive of the congress. It argued that it had made little impact, that its hateful and unrealistic resolutions to end colonialism and imperialism showed "every lamentable sign of confusion and bigotry" and were disagreeably intemperate. It also called Nyerere's push to attach the congress to the OAU to be a token appeasement to the "bearded fuzzywuzzies from California" and perhaps "Queen Mother Moore herself, the most spectacular of participants, a majestic old negress of Royal African lineage from New York." In a world of racial strife, the commission found it surprising that this "considerable jamboree" made little stir in the global press. However, this was not to be regretted, because this talk in the "Dark Continent" was "not a constructive event." He wrote that 6PAC "will not be recorded as a memorable occasion. It leaves nothing behind it; not even a secretariat to promote . . . its frenzied resolutions." But as it had marked "the discontent of radical Third World opinion," "the well-nourished folk in Brussels and Washington" needed to take account.[88]

To be sure, the architects of 6PAC felt differently. In his closing remarks to 6PAC, Cox stated that the major weakness of the congress was in the composition of its delegates, asserting that it needed more representatives from people's movements, from women, and from younger people; he was sure that history would take the congress to task for that omission. Still, he felt that a positive contribution of 6PAC was its call for the political use of modern science and technology in the struggle to defeat Africa's enemies and to build a black world. He stressed that he knew of no other forum that had brought together freedom fighters from southern Africa, African islands, brothers and sister from North and South America, Britain, the Caribbean and Oceania. This alone had made it worthwhile.[89]

Understanding the historical significance of the moment, Cox argued that 6PAC's organizers had a responsibility to document the congress for future students of African political history. This included putting the documents of 6PAC in "the obscure libraries and museums of the imperialists." The secretariat produced a book, recorded a videotape (recorded by Howard University's School of Communications), proposed a film, submitted documents to TANU and the Afro-Shirazi Party, and passed written materials to the libraries of the University of Dar es Salaam and Howard's Moorland Spingarn Research Center. Interestingly, delegates from Guyana and Jamaica agreed to sponsor a Seventh Pan-African Congress. Cox noted that the congress received financial contributions from Tanzania (over $37,500), Jamaica ($11,500), Guyana ($10,000), Libya ($5,000), Trinidad & Tobago ($2,500), Liberia ($2,000), and Somalia ($2,000).[90]

Like Cox, Kamarakafego found that 6PAC had more positive than negative results. One example of that success was that Hill had successfully organized the distribution of medical supplies to the revolutionary groups of Mozambique, Angola, South Africa, and Namibia. Another was that political relationships were formed between black freedom struggles of the Atlantic, Indian and Pacific Ocean worlds. Kamarakafego was a central factor in this process.

Kamarakafego was partly responsible for closing the office in the aftermath of the congress. Cox wrote to him, asking to have some documents sent to him via East Africa Airways. His letter reiterated that if it were not for Kamarakafego's raising of the idea for the congress and his yeoman's work during the talks, the event would never have occurred. In a photograph of Kamarakafego in Tanzania, Cox captioned that he was the one who suggested 6PAC to James and himself. "No doubt Allah will bestow his blessings on you," he wrote in August 1974.[91]

9

Les Nouvelles-Hébrides
sont le pays des noirs

The New Hebrides National Party's (NHNP) delegation to 6PAC returned to Port Vila, Vanuatu, full of political ideas for its struggle against British and French colonialism. In Tanzania, delegation members met leaders such as Julius Nyerere and representatives of the African National Congress, South West African People's Organization, the Cuban government, and Algeria's National Liberation Front. Before leaving East Africa, the party invited Kamarakafego and other members of 6PAC's science committee to come to Vanuatu and help train activists with skills that could be of use to their movement.[1] In 1974 and 1975, both Kamarakafego and Jimmy Garrett traveled to the condominium to assist in the party's rural political education programs.[2] To the chagrin of the British and French administrations, Kamarakafego's time in Vanuatu solidified the deepening linkages between Africana liberation struggles and decolonization in Oceania. This chapter shows how this process also transformed his life and personal relationships.

The NHNP sought to incorporate Tanzania's lessons of self-reliance and African socialism within its political movement. During 6PAC, party leader Walter Lini traveled to New York to speak before the United Nations Committee of Twenty-Four, initiated by the efforts of the Tanzanian and Jamaican governments. After doing so, Lini traveled to Tanzania. There he was introduced to the grassroots organizational structure of TANU. John Bani, the Sopes, and the Taurakotos also had this opportunity while there. Subsequently, the party endorsed Tanzania's model of development around self-reliance—Ujamaa—and organized itself via village party cells.[3]

This troubled Vanuatu's French and British colonial administrations. In May 1974, French resident Robert Jules Amédée Langlois alleged that Lini and the Pati were engaged in a *"liaison dangereuse"* with Tanzania. He claimed that this "dangerous connection" was certain to set back France's efforts to thwart political independence in Vanuatu. Langlois felt that there was a risk that the National Party would mobilize the condominium's indigenous population and found Lini's abilities to link with pan-African organizations and countries like Tanzania to be problematic. He was concerned by Sope's and Bani's attendance at 6PAC, Kamarakafego's invitation, and the "Black Power organization" in general. He was also aware that the Tarautokos had been invited to Ujamaa Safari by the World Council of Churches (WCC) as a cover for their participation in 6PAC. Langlois was certain that Kamarakafego had advised the party to take its movement underground. While the resident believed that the party's older leaders would be reluctant to do so, he felt that its younger organizers such as Sope and Kalkot Mataskelekele would be open to such subversive action. This was partly because they were students at Fiji's University of the South Pacific (USP) and the University of Papua New Guinea (UPNG), respectively, and could also be radically influenced by leftist professors who taught at these institutions.[4]

Vanuatu's police force knew Mataskelekele quite well. In February 1975, he and a friend had entered Port Vila's British Ex-serviceman's Club (BESA) and ordered drinks. They were refused service by a patron and challenged by the police superintendent. Mataskelekele responded by grabbing a picture of the queen of England that was hanging in the club and, according to one witness, he "wrapped it around the superintendent's neck." Mataskelekele was imprisoned for two weeks.[5]

French officials were also concerned about the party's success in asserting itself as the only political representative of Vanuatu's Melanesian population. With its focus on issues of political independence and land rights (including its calls that land taken by European settlers be returned to their Indigenous communities), and buttressed by its international affiliations with the WCC, the Black Power movement, and the Organization of African Unity (OAU), the French felt that the party's chances of success could not be overestimated. With an inadequate police force, the joint administration believed itself to be an uncomfortable and dangerous position—that the indigenous black population of Vanuatu could actually achieve political power—*Black Power*. The French were unsettled by the "incessant" activity of Lini, Bani, and Sope, who devoted all their time to the NHNP; this allowed the party to flourish not only in Vila but also in other islands, such as Santo. This gave it a significant advantage over other indigenous political groups such as Nagriamal that were localized or that collaborated with the British and French administrations, European planters, or American capital interests.[6]

The trip to Tanzania had given the party new audiences and embold-ened audacity. The French administration feared direct and subversive in-tervention by the Black Power movement or the OAU. It heard rumors that New Hebridean "boys" would be selected for political training in Tanza-nia. Under such conditions, Langlois believed that Vanuatu could become a foreign *"point d'impact d'actions subversives"* across France's colonies in Oceania, namely New Caledonia and Tahiti. It was a real possibility that the party would make connections with "subversive" Kanaky political groups from New Caledonia, such as Groupe 1878 and the Foulards Rouges (Red scarves).[7]

Vanuatu was geographically, politically, and linguistically hinged on the Melanesian, British, and French worlds. This made the archipelago an ideal relay for black internationalism. Langlois felt that, given the British gov-ernment's apparent passivity toward the party, this would be easy to do, as his colonial colleague did not intend to intervene against this "danger." He informed Paris that this issue needed to be taken on unilaterally by the French, and he called for "means of action" adapted "á la menace" to be made available to him as soon as possible. Given an increase of land dis-putes between indigenous peoples and European landowners, the French resident felt that the burden of social maintenance and restoration of order rested on his shoulders. Halting the momentum of the party would prove to be an insurmountable task, as Langlois admitted that he could not find a way to slow the National Party's "parade of activities," which had managed to paralyze other political movements in the condominium.[8]

In July 1974, the party held a public meeting at the Anglican Mission of Tagabe bay. Chaired by Lini and Sope, it was attended by about four hundred people. Sope and Bani spoke about their trips to Tanzania. They constructed a notice board of photographs and materials from 6PAC, and sold mimeo-graphed copies of their speech at the congress for 20¢. Langlois believed that Courtland Cox had "fine-tuned" the speech in Tanzania, who allegedly gave Sope a copy to bring back home. The Party added a page to the document, titled *Niu Hebrides Emi Ples Blong Black Man—Les Nouvelles-Hébrides Sont le Pays Des Noirs.*[9] Originally written in Bislama and translated in French, in English this read as, "New Hebrides is the Land of the Blacks." It continued:

> Today everything changes quickly. New Hebrideans must be aware of this change. The National Party is fighting resolutely for the Blacks to take control of the New Hebrides and that is why we demand inde-pendence. But independence is not something Whites, from France

or England, are willing to give us. . . . We must demand it. And if both refuse to leave, we must fight to get it. Whites only came to the New Hebrides to make money. They did not come for the progress of the country. White people use Blacks of the New Hebrides for their sole benefit. They pay them inadequate wages for food and clothing. They took the land and they killed Blacks to create their plantations. The two Governments help the French and the English, but what do they do for the Blacks? . . . England and France must leave the New Hebrides immediately. The majority of New Hebrideans no longer want whites to stay here. . . . The New Hebrides is the land of the Blacks. Any White man or foreigner who wants to stay there must follow what the true New Hebrideans say. Black Power.[10]

Sope urged all true New Hebrideans to unite and work for independence. He held that the best way to economically develop Vanuatu for the benefit of the indigenous community necessitated the study of the countries that had already done so. Referencing Tanzania, he argued that 6PAC had brought more than two hundred delegates together from across the black world. There, he had learned how European colonialism continued to oppress Africa. This included Portugal's atrocities in Mozambique and Britain and France's sale of arms to apartheid South Africa. He and Bani had visited a guerilla training base in Tanzania, and they saw how these "*combattants de la liberté*" (freedom fighters) were training to "help their black brothers in South Africa." They also visited a hospital and donated blood for these soldiers. He expressed that one day, he would see Vanuatu's name placed on the map of these black freedom struggles.[11]

While in Africa, Sope realized that many people wanted to help New Hebrides gain independence. Black people of various trades were ready to come to the island as skilled volunteers. This was in contrast, he argued, to whites who administered the archipelago for profit with little social contact with blacks. He listed white clubs such as the BESA and golf and Kiwanis clubs as examples of racial discrimination in Vila. Furthermore, while whites did not occupy menial jobs in Vanuatu, this did not mean that they belonged to a superior race. New Hebrideans needed to be proud of their color and, if they wanted freedom, they had to be ready to fight for it.[12]

Bani stressed that freedom was not just characters printed on a sheet of paper, but "a way of thinking." He denounced white society's poisoning of the spirit of blacks in Vanuatu. This persuaded them to believe that they were second-class citizens and that they needed to be content with being domestics in a society that was based on master-servant relations. He called on his audience to consider independence in the context of their indigenous political history. New Hebridean people would choose their own system of government that would not necessarily be based on a European model. Before whites had arrived, he argued, they had their own customary laws that would have to be incorporated in any new form of government. Finally, Bani announced that the party had organized a scholarship scheme that would allow New Hebridean students to study in Tanzania and the United States. Bani noted that in Tanzania, black people held all positions of responsibility, and he saw no reason why this should not be the case in Vanuatu. He urged his listeners to be racially self-reliant and to work for independence so that the "black people of the New Hebrides" could run their own country.[13]

French officials considered Sope's speech to be ripe with "racist theories" and felt it unsurprising that he had come back from Tanzania "brimming with anti-white and anti-colonial propaganda." Yet they hoped that far from the "overheated mood" of 6PAC, Sope would become a "peaceful inhabitant" of Vanuatu. Without question, both colonial administrations equated the party's calls for political independence and land rights with Black Power. This public meeting was the first time that the French had been able to document the party's formal reference to Black Power. Langlois felt that this reflected a critical element of the NHNP's political evolution, conceding that it would be difficult to stop it from achieving Black Power.[14]

In November 1974, the Pati held a governing council meeting. During these talks, Taurakoto spoke about the need for adult education and education for self-reliance. He referenced his and his wife's travels across Tanzania's Ujaama villages, stating that there was not much difference between what the East African nation was doing with education with self-reliance and what could be done in Vanuatu.[15]

The Party understood the value of technology and science in their liberation movement. It invited Garrett to investigate the possibility of training their members via technical skills and political education. Garrett arrived in August 1974. Greeted at the airport by Lini, the group went to the party's office located at Tagabe's Anglican Church. He spent most of his trip with the NHNP's executive. He was referred to as a leader of the Black Power movement and a professor who specialized in education.[16]

Garrett informed a closed Party meeting that he had met Sope and Bani at 6PAC and that they had invited him to Vanuatu to assist in the party's training of students. Addressing his enthralled audience of about two hundred, Garrett talked at length about the African American freedom struggle since the era of slavery to black oppression in ghettos and contemporary urban uprisings. He described how white violence killed and incarcerated black leaders. To gain freedom, he explained, black people in United States had to fight for it. They had learned how to make their own weapons and were now ready to teach these techniques to other freedom struggles.[17]

Garrett called for black people to take up technical subjects and to give up beliefs that they were incapable of harnessing technology. This included, for example, flying aircraft, which black people were doing all across the world. He announced that the Center for Black Education (CBE) was teaching various kinds of technology to black youth and that New Hebrideans could study there if they wanted to.[18]

Garrett expressed criticism of missionaries who preached love and charity to black people but did not live by those principles themselves. Across the world, he declared, black communities needed to be able to live without being bothered by white racism. He expressed sympathy for the people of Vanuatu in its liberation struggle and offered the assistance of the Black Power movement. He warned his audience to be wary of black people who thought white, as these persons "posed a threat to black nationalism."[19]

Garrett's short trip was full of similar events. He was a guest of honor at the barbecue organized at Tagabe. Hosted by Taurakoto, he visited and spoke at Léleppa island during its "Feast of the Assumption." Organized by NHNP member George Kalkoa, he talked again to a crowd of about two hundred persons at Mélé village, the largest community on Efate island.[20]

The party decided to send Daniel Nato and Peter Salemalo to Los Angeles to work with Garrett and the CBE. Born in the island of Malekula, Nato headed the party's Youth Wing. He had met Kamarakafego the prior year in Vanuatu. Nato respected Kamarakafego as "a father figure" and Garrett as a brother. The pair arrived in the United States in April 1975. To their dismay, Garrett was unable to meet them in the airport. Having also lost his address, they were not able to contact him. They telegrammed Lini and Mataskelekele from the airport for help.[21]

About three days later, Kamarakafego called Nato and Salemalo, who were staying at the nearby Sands Motel. Nato cried with joy when he heard Kamarakafego's voice. Kamarakafego picked them up the next day and drove them to Garrett's home, which was about an hour away. Garrett provided them with warmer clothing, and they flew to San Francisco, where they stayed with Oba T'Shaka and the Pan-Afrikan People's Organization. They spent about six months there at T'Shaka's Malcolm X Unity House. The engaged in all kinds of lessons—African American history, politics, martial arts, and break dancing. They also met activists from Southern Africa and attended a rally in support of Angela Davis. At Oakland's African Liberation Day, they spoke about Vanuatu's liberation struggle.[22]

Appropriate Technology in Longana

The National Party's strategic plans aimed to encourage economic self-reliance, appropriate technology, and national consciousness at the grassroots/village level. This had long been the idea of Lini. For eight years, he had studied in the Solomon Islands and New Zealand at an Anglican theological college. In New Zealand, he cofounded the Western Pacific Students' Association and, along with Bani, edited its journal *one talk*. Featuring essays, correspondence, poetry, *kastom* stories, political satire, literature, photographs, visual art, and comic strips, *one talk* was a cultural and political expression of Melanesian identity. Upon his return to Vanuatu in 1970, Lini became a parish priest at Longana, Ambae island. Along with Bani and Donald Kalpokas, Lini formed the magazine *New Hebrides Viewpoints* and subsequently the New Hebrides Cultural Association. On August 17, 1971, they transformed the association into the NHNP.[23]

In 1971, Lini founded the Longana Peoples Center on Ambae island, some 270 kilometers from the British colonial administration on Efate. This was essentially a project of Vanuatu nationalism and black internationalism. Lini's vision was to use the center to "encourage a community spirit" of self-reliance beyond the village level. By 1974, it had become a critical base for the party. It aimed to create community development programs and link them with other satellite centers. Each center was to organize social, educational, cultural, and political activities. These included sports events, courses, seminars, and conferences. Organized by chairpersons, committee members, and village residents, each center would be administered by appointees chosen by each village. All centers were to be wholly New Hebridean–controlled and independent of religious missions and colonial administrations. Upon independence, these would be transformed into educational institutions.[24]

The WCC supported this initiative and the party in general. In 1976, it granted the NHNP US$10,000 in support of the struggle of the country's black majority over its white minority. Working through the network of the WCC, Lini sent community leaders to other countries to receive training.

This included Edison Mala, who had been at the center since 1970. Between 1973 and 1974, Mala traveled to Papua New Guinea's Port Moresby community development group for rural community training.[25]

This was part of the party's efforts to build relationships with the broader black world. In March 1975, it invited Kamarakafego to Vanuatu to conduct political education among its "rural indigenous masses" and advise the party in adult education and youth activities. Lini had informed the British commissioner that after a stay of about four weeks, they intended to retain Kamarakafego's services for at least a year.[26]

The British and French residencies had concerns about the "leading Black Power figure" since his 1974 trip to the condominium. British resident commissioner Roger du Boulay had intended to proclaim him as an "undesirable immigrant." Through covert surveillance, he knew Kamarakafego's whereabouts (Warwick, Bermuda—May 1970; Dar es Salaam, Tanzania—April 1972; Claremont, California—February 1975). However, he sought advice from the Immigration and Visa Department of the Foreign and Commonwealth Department (FCO) as to how his office could inform Kamarakafego of this prohibition without "prejudicing the sources" of their information and how Kamarakafego's address could be obtained through normal channels. Routine investigations discovered that although Kamarakafego was on the United Kingdom's "watch list," he was not a prohibited immigrant anywhere. Still, the Immigration and Visa Department asked both Bermuda's chief immigration officer and the US State Department to help determine his address so that he could be notified that he was an undesirable immigrant.[27]

All this was perhaps too much, but it was definitely too late. Kamarakafego arrived in Vanuatu in early May 1975 on a one-month visa. While traveling with Peter Taurakoto, he gave a speech to about one hundred attendees on Lelepa Island. According to the head of Special Branch, Taurakoto introduced him as an "African who had come to talk" about what was going on in Vanuatu and the world between blacks and whites. Kamarakafego discussed how whites were covertly selling the land of New Hebrideans to foreign investors. He talked about the impact of blackbirding on Vanuatu (British agents agreed that his account was correct). Kamarakafego also detailed how Europeans had inflicted diseases on indigenous communities that decimated their populations. He described how Korowa had been prevented from returning to Vanuatu. Similar to Korowa's own talks in Vanuatu, Kamarakafego told his audience that religion started in Africa and not Europe. Proof of this was that there was no mention of France or Britain in the Bible.

Furthermore, Europeans distorted history to keep oppressing black people. But America had been discovered by African sailors—not Christopher Columbus. Speaking at length about atomic testing by Europeans, he explained that it would poison fish and kill off the population. The only answer was to "chase the Europeans out of the country" and then "prepare to defend it against their enemies." A "long diatribe against the white man" supposedly followed, including an attack against family planning.[28]

Several questions followed his talk, and he was asked if Ni-van communities would get their land back after independence. To this Kamarakafego responded, yes, if they voted for the party. Participants also asked him to address the British secondary schools, but he replied that he could not do so as long as "the whites" were in power.[29]

The British attorney general studied Kamarakafego's lecture but could not find anything seditious about his speech. It was true that Europeans were selling land in the New Hebrides for profit and were blackbirding, that European diseases did indeed shatter the population, and that the effects of nuclear testing described by Kamarakafego were legitimate. He felt that Kamarakafego was a person of considerable experience who knew how far he could go to keep within the bounds of the law.[30]

Lini told Kamarakafego that the party wanted to train the masses of young people who had completed elementary school but had little opportunities to continue their education. Kamarakafego suggested that he tell the colonial authorities that they were going to "take the children off the streets and train them." The concept of training "drop-outs" seemed to be well-received by merchants and colonial administrators, who supplied them with all the tools that they requested. They loaded a boat with equipment and sailed to Ambae.[31]

The British and French were aware of the pair's efforts to remain covert. They noted Kamarakafego's "rather feeble attempt" to conceal his movements as Lini had purchased six boat tickets in his own name. Three days later, on May 23, Kamarakafego addressed a public meeting in Longona attended by two hundred people. Introduced by Lini, Kamarakafego said that he had come from Africa especially to set up a young people's center at Longana. He was happily there at the invitation of the party, which had paid all of his expenses. Along the lines of his comments at Léleppa, he warned New Hebrideans to become educated about the covert activities of whites in the country. After discussing blackbirding, he chastised missionaries for not teaching that "true religion began in Africa and that Jesus Christ was black." He argued that Ni-Vans needed to retain their culture, ignore family planning, produce local food, and avoid unhealthy European diets. He added that as a scientist, he had studied such matters. He encouraged his audience not to sell any more land to whites.[32]

Kamarakafego also spoke about his plans for the youth center, which included teaching technical subjects. As a qualified sports coach, he would instruct young men in activities such as football, singing, dancing, and dialog. Kamarakafego announced that Salemalo and Nato would lecture at Longana and that six other individuals from Africa would come to continue the work that he had started.[33]

The implemented program was called the School Leavers for Longana People Center. Training was based on self-reliance and praxis and included making coconut oil, producing sugar from sugar cane, making mattresses from coconut fiber, building things with local materials, domesticating animals, building homes, maintaining tools, tending to gardens, and practicing self-care. Courses were free and would last for two years. Students would live in the neighboring villages so that they could become part of their communities, for whom they would provide services and assist in the construction of homes, *nakamals* (traditional meeting halls), schools, and churches.[34]

"Come and learn to work with the knowledge you have!" read a party communication about the program. It invited all interested school leavers to make their way to Longana. They were asked to bring their own mats, bedding, knives, football boots, cups, plates, and utensils. Sample courses proposed for Longana included basic woodwork and metalwork, technical drawing, building low-cost housing, making salt, sugar, oil, and mentholated spirits, brick making, machine maintenance, using a pit saw, techniques of ferro cement and firing clay and lime to form cement, techniques of building cheap water supplies (such as ferro-cement tanks and solar evaporators of saltwater), boat building, building cheap wind mills and solar energy machines, basic mechanics and electronics, canning and food preservation, and processing of food.[35] These projects, which Kamarakafego worked on intensively for six weeks, were designed to build local self-reliance by enabling rural residents to produce key commodities and provide key services, thereby empowering their communities to reduce their dependence on Australian and New Zealand firms.[36]

Longana's community fondly remembered his work. Children flocked to him for his chocolate sweets. Adults laughed at how he caught chickens to prepare meals. In a night full of pouring rain and kava, the aforementioned Mala recalled Kamarakafego's time at Longana and how he also showed the community how to use coconut shells in building fences. Kamarakafego built great relationships with the humble community, and all was going well. As far as the British and French officials were concerned, it was going *too* well.[37]

According to Special Branch, Kamarakafego's presence had "given rise to alarm" among French expatriates and opponents of the NHNP. Paris regarded "all Black Power propagandists as a threat to security." Langlois called for Kamarakafego's immediate expulsion, while du Boulay preferred just to not extend his visa. The British resident also had been informed that Kamarakafego was encouraging the party to recruit Kanak youth leaders from their Melanesian neighbor, New Caledonia.[38]

But what was perhaps most disturbing to the British resident was the impact of Kamarakafego's "gospel" on his audiences. While FCO officials claimed to not have underrated the "insidiousness" of his message, they hoped that his approach would be "so novel and sophisticated as to be somewhat above the heads" of Vanuatu's rural communities. However, they felt that he had been "well-briefed" and was adapt at "matching his style for the occasion." For these officers, this situation had become a "difficult and potentially dangerous problem."[39] One could only assume that they would have disagreed with the FBI's earlier assessment that Kamarakafego was "no orator."

The colonial administration had long since pressed Lini about his activities at Longana. For example, in 1971, the British information officer thanked Lini for informing him that the center had been formed. However, he preferred such news to come quickly, otherwise, he wrote, it was not news but history. But now, the British police commandant had other concerns—Kamarakafego had made "quite an impact on the people" and he was considered to be "very well educated and intelligent."[40]

On May 15, newly arrived French resident commissioner Robert Gauger wrote to du Boulay lamenting that his worries about Kamarakafego's presence in the archipelago "refused to leave him." He imagined that du Boulay felt the same. From Gauger's perspective, the British resident's reports about the "subversive" Black Power agent's speech in Vila reflected intense propaganda and xenophobia. If the party adopted such ideas, it would "incite racial hatred and public order disorder." Gauger felt that it was up to the NHNP to decide how it presented itself. However, he asserted that the "public power" that he and the British resident collectively represented could not remain indifferent to the risk that awakened political passions could result in "violent animosities" in the condominium's upcoming elections. He felt it obvious that Kamarakafego's presence would not remain unnoticed for long by the French community. He asked, "Did the Joint Administration intend to respond or would it allow the country's politics to lead towards violence?" He warned du Boulay that if they did not "stop it quickly," they would "incur a serious responsibility towards the populations" that they had a duty to protect. As Kamarakafego was a British subject, he wanted to know what plans the British resident had to remove him from Vanuatu.[41]

Du Boulay's response was unsurprising. He agreed with Gauger about the "perniciousness" and potential "damage" of Kamarakafego's Black Power doctrines in Vanuatu. His collaboration with the French residency about how to counteract the spread of black consciousness in Vanuatu included a public speech that he himself gave about Black Power. Both the British and French residencies had considered long and carefully about declaring the "two agents of the Black Power Movement"—Garrett and Kamarakafego—as prohibited immigrants, but they concluded that this would do more damage than allowing them into the archipelago under supervision. Furthermore, they doubted if their speeches would draw any persecutions in court. Now, with Kamarakafego back in the condominium, the British preferred to not extend his four-week stay.[42]

On May 16, du Boulay summoned Lini to his office. He claimed that Kamarakafego was doing harm to Lini's, the party's, and Vanuatu's future. He told Lini that he would have to be convinced that Kamarakafego would "really behave himself" before he would prolong his stay. In response, Lini said that he would be personally responsible for ensuring that Kamarakafego "ceased propagating Black Power doctrines." Lini asserted that the NHNP was still mulling over the need to extend Kamarakafego's permit, particularly if other persons would be able to continue the programs that he had established. Kamarakafego had been invited to launch the party's social programs, which the British residency claimed were "unexceptional" but "beneficial."[43]

While Lini had informed du Boulay that Kamarakafego had been "warned" not to intervene publicly in local politics, British officials believed that Kamarakafego would "run rings" around him. Still, du Boulay felt it best to wait a week to see if Lini could "make good his promise to put an end to Black Power propaganda," if Kamarakafego would leave Vanuatu, and, if so, who would continue the social programs of the party (possibly as a Black Power cell). He doubted Lini's understanding of, or ability to control, these undesirable manifestations. Yet he was hopeful that New Hebrideans, who would not forget the injuries done to them by the initial white settlers and traders, would largely "recoil from these repugnant Blank Power doctrines . . . if suitably encouraged to do so by" the colonial administrations. The British preferred to encourage indigenous leaders to embrace the "right" kind of leadership and not to harm to the situation by overreacting, handling the matter clumsily, or ignoring it totally.[44]

The British clearly underestimated the ideological unity that existed between Lini and Kamarakafego, and the NHNP's leader's shrewdness. Kamarakafego's presence in the country was a manifestation of his long-term political vision. According to Lini's sister Hilda, her brother saw in Kamarakafego someone who shared his views and understood his vision.[45]

The French and British officials unsuccessfully tried to convince the party that it should not associate with a Socialist, Communist, and Black Power activist like Kamarakafego. But for the NHNP, this was *exactly why* they embraced him. According to Sope, they had already been advocating for Black Power. For example, Sope wore an Afro as both an expression of his Black Power politics and traditional indigenous aesthetic; he also named his daughter Angela after Angela Davis.[46]

On June 5, British officials served Kamarakafego notice that his permit had expired and that he had become an "unlawful immigrant." He was ordered to leave Vanuatu by June 27. The British hoped he would do so voluntarily so that they could avoid the fracas of a forced deportation. From their perspective, the "undesirable" Kamarakafego intended to stay. He had the support of the party and village extremists. Du Boulay pressed the NHNP to not make an issue of this move, with an upcoming election and Kamarakafego's "extreme racist propaganda." He felt that Kamarakafego should not have been allowed to pass through immigration at the airport as he did not have a return ticket.[47]

Lini wrote to du Boulay from Longana. He informed the British resident that the Pati had decided to employ Kamarakafego for three years to help run the School Leavers program. He reminded the resident that although there had been talk from the joint administration about developing the agricultural standards of the community, little had been done. Instead, the party aimed to use school leavers to serve that function, and it was prepared to pay Kamarakafego and provide him housing as part of this effort.[48]

Lini wrote to both the British and French residents. He challenged a number of public statements made by du Boulay that referred to the NHNP as being a Communist Black Power movement. He wanted to know the resident's definition of power. The presence of the French and British administrations proved that there was "White Power in the New Hebrides." For Lini, du Boulay suggested that the party preached Black Power simply because they were black New Hebrideans focused on political independence. But the party had neither confiscated anyone's land nor divided anyone's land to sell to others—these acts were expressions of *white power*. By those standards, neither Kamarakafego nor the NHNP were Black Power. There was nothing wrong with what they were doing or with Kamarakafego's presence in Vanuatu.[49]

Du Boulay's response was unsurprising. He reiterated that he did not think that Kamarakafego's presence was in the interest of the party or the people of Vanuatu. Black Power did not accept peaceful democracies or universal suffrage, and it believed that changes could only come about by racial violence. He argued that Kamarakafego was determined to propagate Black Power in Vanuatu. It was not in the interest of the archipelago to allow the continued "presence of a person whose approach was to dwell on the past." Kamarakafego had to leave. Du Boulay claimed that Lini should not be surprised if the NHNP's association with a well-known Black Power leader and "apparent acceptance of his attitudes" was regarded as evidence that it also believed in racial violence as the only solution to the problems of Vanuatu.[50]

Days later, the British resident informed the FCO that Kamarakafego and extremists in the NHNP had prevailed. They had "decided to provoke a confrontation," but he could not confirm any intention by them to resist by force. Yet he sought to have a British police officer, corporal, and district agent visit Longana to arrest Kamarakafego. If they met resistance, they were to assess the strength of the opposition and withdraw. In the meantime, they continued to put pressure on local leaders. It was out of the question that he would rescind his removal order, which would not only undermine British authority in Vanuatu but also be unacceptable to the French. "British prestige" was at stake.[51]

Du Boulay felt that a combined British and French local force could extract Kamarakafego from Longana, but it had to be a "clean and effective" operation. This contingency plan would reinforce the local police and require the total strength available to handle a "hostile crowd of five hundred of more persons" that could be materialized by the party. Yet this would leave Vila open to "local party adherents supported by unruly elements."[52]

Also of concern was the strong French antipathy toward the NHNP, which could have led to violent clashes with French forces and possibly sabotage Britain's constitutional program for neocolonialism. Du Boulay stressed this to the FCO: "It would be most, repeat, most undesirable either to invite French participation in possible raid on Longana or to seek gendarmerie reinforcements" from Noumea, New Caledonia, some 336 miles south of Port Vila. He preferred only British reinforcements.[53]

The FCO disagreed. It preferred that a special operation to extract Kamarakafego should be undertaken by a joint Anglo-French police force. Furthermore, officials called for French gendarmeries from New Caledonia to be placed on standby in Vila. To complement these troops, they considered the possibility of flying in British soldiers from Singapore or Fiji, or importing Gurkhas from Hong Kong. This was politically, practically, and logistically preferred to using troops located in the United Kingdom.[54]

The FCO painstakingly thought through Kamarakafego's arrest. The commander of the British Forces lent his advice. A company of the First New Hampshire Regiment was in Fiji on a training exercise, but the plane that they were utilizing was too heavy to land in New Hebrides. A "poor bet" was to bring troops from Hong Kong, some forty-eight hours away. A Royal Air Force Britannia aircraft on its way back to Britain could be turned around to pick up Gordon Highlanders from Singapore and take them to Vanuatu. All things considered, it was felt that First New Hampshire Regiment flown in from Fiji on a civil airlines flight would make the most sense in terms of speed and political concerns.[55]

According to Ben Lowings of Radio New Zealand International, London's Ministry of Defense constructed "detailed plans to dispatch a warship, a landing party, transport planes and soldiers from Hong Kong." However, they had concerns about whether Indonesia and the Philippines would allow them to utilize their airspace. Furthermore, they were afraid that the equipment used by French forces in Vanuatu would be incompatible with that of the British military.[56]

Du Boulay remained skeptical about using French participation in Ambae, a Party stronghold and the center of Lini's community-development activities. He felt that given the historic hostility of the French toward the Pati, this community would be particularly resentful of this intervention. Furthermore, he felt that the "French police would include several European gendarmes" who, sharing colonial mentalities and attitudes, would be tempted to use the notorious riot-control methods of the Compagnies Républicaines de Sécurité. Violent demonstrations or counter demonstrations that necessitated further French reinforcements could also result in the postponement of the upcoming elections and would diminish British ability to "influence events."[57]

Despite all these preparations, Kamarakafego was arrested in Longana

with little incident; being practically unarmed, with only three people owing
muskets that they used for hunting (any other firearms had been taken by
the police years before), the community was hardly in a position to offer any
real resistance. Members of the community remember the morning of his
arrest. The police plane landed right in the immediate vicinity of the village,
and people were shocked when the officers arrived. Kamarakafego did not
resist, and they took him away. Father Lini was there. When they asked him
why Kamarakafego had been taken, Lini told them not to worry; Kamarakafego would see them again. They were left with rumors. One morning,
Kamarakafego had told one youth in Longana that the community had all
the natural materials they needed to make a bomb, prompting the child to
run away. Through "coconut news," they assumed this was why he had been
arrested.[58]

As described in the introduction, Kamarakafego's arrest was timed to
surprise the party. It was delayed by three days to coincide with an out-
going commercial flight from Vila. Kamarakafego was taken to a deserted
American airstrip in North Efate, where he spent the whole day berating his
accompanying British police commissioner, the Australian pilot, and five
Ni-Vanuatu officers.[59]

Several hours later, Kamarakafego was flown to Vila's main airport to
match the arrival of the Pacific Air flight headed to Fiji. This time, twenty-
six NHNP members caught "the police on their wrong foot." Through their
own intelligence networks, they had received word of the British resident's
plans. At the party's Tagabe headquarters, organizer John Naupa informed
Mataskelekele that there "was a person who was working with Father Walter
and the police have gone to arrest him. They are now flying a special plane
to bring him to Vila to deport him today." The group sprang into action.[60]

Taurakoto picked up Mataskelekele in his brown car, fashionably spray
painted with a black-and-white ring. Their plans for action ranged from
the spectacular to the splendorous. They initially considered "blowing up"
the airport. Another idea was to steal bags of money from airline counters,
but it was decided that this would not make "big enough of a splash." They
settled on rushing the airport's tarmac.[61]

Sope arrived first. They found him standing there in front of the airport's apron. The British police commissioner asked the group if they had
a right to be there. Taurakoto asked the commissioner if *he* had the right
to be there. As Kamarakafego's plane was taxiing to the back of the Pacific
Air plane, Mataskelekele shouted, "Let's go!" He jumped into the commissioner's car and tried to start it. The commissioner shouted, "Kalkot, what

are you doing?" Mataskelekele could not get the stick shift into gear, and he left the car. Led by Mataskelekele, Taurakoto, Sope, and William Edgell, four cars were driven in front of the plane. Shouting "Black Power!" they reached through the roofs of the vehicles they were in, pumping both fists to the sky. Sope stood on the roof of his car and raised his fist to the pilot. Mataskelekele could see the stunned pilot put on the brakes of the moving plane and noticed it rock forward and halt. They parked and locked their cars in front of the aircraft and threw away their keys. Mataskelekele instructed them to sit on the tarmac. Eventually joined by other supporters, they refused to move.[62]

They handed the British district agent a letter that included a list of demands. Written by Mataskelekele, it referenced a July 12 meeting between himself, George Kalkoa, and du Boulay when they expressed their displeasure with the latter's unreasonable position. It stated that Kamarakafego was employed by the NHNP, just as other institutions in Vanuatu had done with other foreign employees. Mataskelekele felt it a foregone conclusion that the French and British would reject any advisors of their liberation movement. As such, his letter included a description of seven white American, French, New Zealander, and Australian nationals and "yachties" who were allowed to reside in Vanuatu but who were working against the freedom of its indigenous peoples. This included the notorious American Eugene Peacock, who financed the Nagriamel movement. The letter demanded that Kamarakafego should not be deported before these persons were removed.[63]

According to the French, NHNP leaders also inscribed on the airport, "Boulay get out and stay out," and "Colonialism is white power." As party members argued with the district agents, the French resident placed his police at the disposal of the British commandant. At one end of the runway were Kamarakafego and his escorts. On the other was the plane, its disembarked passengers, the police, and NHNP members. Three hours later, the police moved in at nightfall and arrested the demonstrators so that the crowd could not clearly see what was happening. With the British prisons overcrowded and insecure, the French resident agreed to take all of their current incarcerated persons to make room for the protestors. He refused to take any of the party members, because of charges of police brutality that were launched against the French forces during an incident the prior year. Meanwhile, Kamarakafego was sent to Fiji.[64]

All of those arrested were fined 1,000 FNH or two weeks imprisonment. Godfrey Toa, Sope, Naupa, and Taurakoto were all fined 2,000 FNH or one month's imprisonment. When Taurakoto arrived home later that evening, his wife questioned him as to his whereabouts. He told her that he had used his car to chase cattle off of the airport. When she heard about the incident on the radio, she cussed him out.[65]

The incident was spread across media in Vanuatu and beyond, including in a brief report in Fiji's *Pacific Islands Monthly*. The NHNP discussed the "Brown affair" in its newsletter, *New Hebridean Viewpoints*. In its August 1975 issue, Taurakoto wrote that du Boulay's claims that Kamarakafego was racist were surprising. He found it "heartbreaking to see the few persons who wielded power . . . ruthlessly insist on the exploitation of other human beings." His letter stated that Kamarakafego had been a lecturer at the University College of Tanzania when he had heard about their struggle. They sought him out because he was once a petitioner to the UN Committee of Twenty-Four. Those in the rural areas who had heard him speak agreed that he was intelligent. Kamarakafego's speeches there addressed racism, reminding the British commissioner that he had done the same just a year before. Kamarakafego's discussion of the slave trades between Africa and America and the Pacific Islands and Australia were also well known. The British government's failure to address their request to keep Kamarakafego there led him to believe that Vanuatu was "another South Africa," with one immigration law for whites and another for blacks.[66]

Viewpoints detailed the peaceful demonstration and twenty arrests at the Bauerfield Air terminal against du Boulay's "unscrupulous and inconsiderate supremacist" deportation of Kamarakafego. It denounced the British resident for disregarding the importance of someone as skilled as Kamarakafego, for accusing him of "preaching Black Power," and secretly expelling him. The demonstration was primarily a show against the immigration laws and the "racist attitude" imposed upon the party. Finally, the writer hoped that the colonialists would get it into their "fatty brains" that they would continue to break laws that stood in the way of their freedom struggle. [67]

The June 1975 edition of *Viewpoints* addressed Black Power specifically, arguing, "The people who accuse the party as being a Black Power movement do not know what Black Power means." It challenged the following quote made by du Boulay in a public speech against Black Power: "If a white man has wronged a Black man, it is no remedy for a black man to wrong a white man now. White supremacy movements are as misguided and mischievous as Black Power movements."[68]

The NHNP felt that if the colonial administrations called them Black Power, then the French and British must have been White Power. According to Sope, there could be no justice for the black masses under colonialism and the morally and politically unjust exploitation of Vanuatu. For Taurakoto, Black Power meant self-determination, self-rule, and decolonization.[69]

The party held its fourth congress in January 1976 at Lelepa Island. It resolved that as Kamarakafego's arrest was racist and not legal, those charged would refuse to pay their fines or go to jail. If they were arrested, the police would have to arrest all the NHNP's supporters. This was partly in response to court notices that called for the immediate imprisonment of those involved if they did not pay the fines. At the time of this writing, Taurakoto had yet to pay his fine.[70]

Concerned about negative local and international publicity, both British and French administrations addressed the incident through their own publications. The British Information Office's *New Hebrides News* simply stated that Kamarakafego was removed because his visa had expired. It made no mention of Black Power or the NHNP, simply mentioning that a group of protestors were detained after they drove their cars onto the airport. Du Boulay suggested that if questioned, British ministers should falsely state that Kamarakafego was allowed to enter temporarily *despite* his Black Power association. Then they would claim that it was only when he publicly attempted to "stir up racial hatred" and "promised assistance with revolutionary methods" for the "overthrow of white supremacy" that it became impossible to tolerate his stay.[71]

The British then considered banning both Kamarakafego and Garrett indefinitely, but preferred not to make a declaration until after Vanuatu's upcoming elections. Officials of the FCO stressed that the French and British administrations should make a joint regulation surrounding race relations. This they hoped would strengthen their ability to deal with any visitors or residents who attempted to "propagate the Black Power doctrines."[72]

The French administration's paper *Nabanga* used a Léopold Sédar Senghor quote that "*les grandes civilisations sont métisses*" (the great civilizations are mestizo) to challenge racist ideologists in Africa or Vanuatu as being xenophobic and "nasty shepherds" of the myth of "herrenvolk." It followed this front page statement with a story about the airport incident. Unlike the British administration's *New Hebrides News*, *Nabanga* referred to the West Indian Kamarakafego as a Black Power advocate and friend of the NHNP. It also stated that crowds stood outside the roadblock and that at least two women joined the demonstration. The paper's photographer took pictures of the passengers standing outside of the plane but claimed that the party prevented him from taking pictures of themselves. Curiously, the article referenced the Student Non-Violent Coordinating Committee as launching Black Power as a slogan and advocating urban guerilla warfare.[73]

Kamarakafego's popularity among Ni-Vans was clear to all observers. The French felt that his autarkic subsistence activities at Longana's "so-called center of community activity" had given him an "undeniable ascendancy" among the party and that he "indoctrinated" populations. In the aftermath of his deportation, Lini wrote to Mataskelekele, stating that it was good to hear of the heroic act at the airport. He admitted that the party did not do much to stop his arrest in Ambae, because he thought that they had agreed to go along with it. This guesswork by both him and Kamarakafego was because they had not heard otherwise. At the time, they had ten students who were making a number of useful things, ranging from cooking oil, candies, mattresses, sugar, pig's food, cocoa pruning, and leather from cattle.[74]

Return to Oceania

Kamarakafego's flight from Vanuatu stopped in Fiji. He was detained by immigration authorities there and put on a Pan-American flight for Honolulu and Los Angeles. Shortly afterward, however, British authorities remained unaware of Kamarakafego's whereabouts. United States officials expected that he would go to New York before returning to Bermuda.[75]

But Kamarakafego was determined not to go back to the island. Though it had been about two years, he remained concerned that he would be questioned about the assassinations of Bermuda's governor and police commissioner. While in Fiji, he had called and arranged for a friend, Thais Aubry, to meet him outside Los Angeles Airport. It is likely that Kamarakafego first met Aubry during his time in California in 1958–59. During the flight, he befriended and convinced an African American passenger to pick up his luggage for him. He memorized her phone number so that he could call her later to pick up his bag. All that was left for him to do was to evade his lanky security escort in the crowded airport. In this, his height came in handy. After stooping down to tie his shoelaces, he did this successfully. Aubry met him as arranged and they drove to her place. He later got his baggage.[76]

While in California, Kamarakafego stayed with Aubry, whom history has been proverbially unkind to. Scholarship remembers the Spanish- and Portuguese-speaking linguist as "the friend of David Baldwin," who attended the 1963 meeting between his brother James Baldwin, Lorraine Hansberry,

Attorney General Robert Kennedy, Kenneth Clark, Lena Horne, and Harry Belafonte. However, the brilliant Aubry, who earned a BA in international relations from UCLA in 1959, was a "staunch advocate for black power well before it became fashionable."[77] Months later, in October 1975, she attended Fiji's Pacific Women's Conference (PWC), which was organized by Fijian activists Vanessa Griffen, Claire Slatter, and Amelia Rokotuivuna. Rokotui-vuna radicalized Suva's Young Women's Christian Association as its director and mentored both Griffen and Slatter. Rose Catchings, the executive secretary of the United Methodist Church's Ministry of Women, facilitated funding for the trip. While at the PWC, Aubry meticulously presented on Africana freedom struggles. In January 1976, she visited Vanuatu. Hosted by H. Lini, she worked at Longana's Community Center for about a week.[78]

In contrast, Kamarakafego could not return to Vanuatu, as he had been marked as prohibited immigrant for six months. Faced with the nagging question of resources, he reached out to his network of activists and artists for support. One of his contacts at an African embassy was able to secure a new passport for him. He received help from some unexpected sources as well.[79]

Kamarakafego's Rolodex included visual artist and chairperson of Howard University's Art Department, Jeff Donaldson. A major figure in the Black Arts movement and cofounder of Chicago's AfriCOBRA, Donaldson had also attended 6PAC. He was now asked to assist Kamarakafego in his return to Oceania. In February 1976, Donaldson penned a somewhat cryptic letter to his contacts, including Toni Cade Bambara:

Some of us well recall the dramatic speech delivered by Brother Sope, Secretary-General of the New Hebrides Nationalist Party at [6PAC]. . . . Before hearing Sope's address I had only vague knowledge of the existence of Black people in New Hebrides and other Pacific Islands. Indeed, this was my first exposure to the already protracted Liberation struggle.

He continued:

According to exceedingly reliable sources 10–20 million Blacks of African descent have been engaged in survival/liberation warfare for over 10 years on several of these Pacific Islands. Some of these military conflicts are with synthetic countries such as the Philippines, Indonesia, and Australia who have been their mortal enemies prior to WWII.

As in other parts of the world, these synthetic nations are mere robots for the Grand Manipulators of the West pursuing their self-righteous imperialistic and genocidal actions against these Pacific Africans. But our Pacific Sisters and Brothers are confident these forces can be re-pelled—they have time, terrain and, they hope, us on their side.[80]

Donaldson had been informed that these "Survival/Liberation forces" in Oceania viewed the struggles of black people in the United States "in quite a different light from many of our own misguided rightist Brothers and other assorted enemies." Photographs and documents demonstrated how they had derived inspiration and direction from the black symbols and na-tionalist heroes of the era. Now, wrote Donaldson, "these Pacific Africans" had asked for material support from the black world. Their greatest needs were "weapons and ammunition, medical supplies, technicians, and other technical necessities for the continuation and escalation of the war." While they had time, they needed help. Donaldson had been asked to solicit airfare of approximately $1,200 dollars for a technician to go to one of the islands under siege. This technician, wrote Donaldson, was "known to all of us, but for obvious reasons" could not be referred to by name. The person was "a medical specialist with expertise in organizing, ecology, drafting, carpentry, botany, and other useful skills." For twenty-five years, the letter continued, "this technician had worked for our common good on four continents," as well as the island in question. Once there, the "Brothers and Sisters in the Pacific" would provide his accommodations and subsistence.[81] This covert reference to both Kamarakafego and Vanuatu acknowledged broader con-cerns about the surveillance of the Oceania's black freedom struggle.

Donaldson himself contributed and implored others to provide at least $20 each. Of course, this was "not a tax-deductible contribution," but the rebate could help the freedom struggle of a "little known and acknowledged part of the African world." He promised that the person would keep them abreast of developments in Oceania, that he would personally be involved in purchasing the ticket, and that he would give each person an accounting of the funds received. He also attached a copy of Sope's 6PAC speech to the letter.[82]

Donaldson successfully secured funds from at least sixteen visual art-ists, writers, poets, and activists—Gwendolyn Brooks Blakely, Arthur Monroe, Val Gray Ward, Lerone Bennett Jr., Joan Brown, Bobby E. Wright, Mari Evans, Leslie Richards, Don Coleman, Florencia Arnold, Eric Stark,

Samella Lewis, Harold Bradshaw, Elizabeth Catlett, C. L. R. James, Ademola Olugebefola, and Jacqueline Cole. James and Evans contributed $100 each. Arnold, an art teacher at Illinois Teachers College, mailed Donaldson a twenty-dollar check "toward liberation." Based in El Garambullo, Mexico, Catlett received Donaldson's letter over a month after he sent it. She mailed back $20 the next day, hoping it was not too late and wanting to know about any other concerns. In addition to her contribution, Brooks filled Donaldson in on the health of both Dudley Randall and Broadside Press.[83]

Kamarakafego had become a conduit for how the black Diaspora was engaging Oceania as a "Black Pacific." In March 1976, Gayleatha Cobb interviewed him in *Black World* about the liberation struggles of Oceania. He discussed how he had first met Pacific Islanders as a petitioner to the United Nation's Committee of Twenty-Four. He talked about his appropriate technology projects in Vanuatu. Cobb's informed questions led him to discuss colonialism, imperialism, and racism across the region, including in New Caledonia, Tahiti, Guam, Hawaii, and Samoa. Kamarakafego also referenced blackbirding. The interview included Kamarakafego's personal photographs of himself, Korowa, and Bob Maza, and a member of the Australian Aboriginal Legal Service. He described Melanesian people as being "very much like African people" in terms of pigmentation and physical features (such as hair and nose structure). He talked about the Revolutionary Front for an Independent East Timor (Fretilin), which, inspired by Mozambique's FRELIMO, was fighting against Indonesian imperialism in the former Portuguese colony. He also discussed the Vanua'aku Nasional Pati, Black Power in Australia, and Maza and the National Black Theatre.[84]

A contextual article written by *Black World*'s managing editor, Carole A. Parks, followed his interview. According to Parks, blacks in Africa, the Americas, and the Caribbean who despaired of Europe's racially geographic classification system would be appalled by its impact in Oceania. The mass media and allegedly scholarly literature had obscured the fact that the majority of people in the region were "negroid," even by the standards of European racial terminology.[85]

Kamarakafego described "full-blooded" Melanesians as having "dark skin, broad features, and generally wool-like hair." In this light, Parks denounced reference works, such as the 1964 edition of the Encyclopedia Britannica, that referred to Polynesians as being more advanced than Melanesians, Micronesians as having once had "superior intellect," and Melanesians as showing "little instinct" for social order, lacking seafaring skills, and being addicted to magic and totem worship. Such books claimed that European colonialism curbed Melanesia's affinity for cannibalism and tribalism. For Parks, this is why Kamarakafego's account was important. While reference texts also asserted that Oceania "needed" colonialism, his work demonstrated how the Pacific Islands no longer wanted to be "impoverished pawns" in the superpowers' quests for "military security, natural resources, and captive consumer markets." Parks finished her piece with small briefs of "mainly black islands"—American Samoa, Australia, Gilbert and Ellice Islands, the Moluccas, Nauru, New Caledonia, Papua New Guinea, Portuguese Timor, Vanuatu, and the Solomon Islands.[86]

By February 1976, Kamarakafego was ready to return to Vanuatu. His six-month ban from the condominium should have expired by then. He wrote to Griffen and Slatter, stating that he was coming to Suva in March or April. He also asked Slatter to contact Lini and Sope. Griffen relayed all this by telephone to Slatter, who was in Papua New Guinea at the time. Concerned that any letters to the Pati would be intercepted by the colonial state, Slatter preferred to contact the party directly through intermediaries or through "cryptic cables." She wrote to Lini and Sope from the office of Papua New Guinea's prime minister, Michael Somare. Signed "Seli Hoo," she also hoped to see Mataskelekele back at the University of Papua New Guinea.[87]

"*Seli Hoo*" was the call and response cry of the NHNP. A popular phrase in Vanuatu, it was often used when persons were collectively performing physical labor together. It loosely meant "uniting together, working together." Sometimes called while raising a fist, it was naturally reminiscent of a Black Power salute.[88]

Griffen and Slatter were former students at Suva's USP. In 1973, they attended the South Pacific Action for Development Strategy conference; this conference in Vila was called for by Lini and sponsored by the WCC. Central figures in the Nuclear Free and Independent Pacific movement, they formed the Pacific People's Action Front in the aftermath of its 1975 conference in Fiji. Griffen edited the Front's newsletter, *Povai*, a "Pacific people's struggle paper."[89] Given all of this, they had extensive contacts with the freedom struggles of Oceania. This is why Kamarakafego reached out to them.

Slatter and Griffen hosted Kamarakafego in Fiji when he arrived in April. They were somewhat skeptical about doing so; only weeks before, they had hosted a rather "unfriendly" Carlos Moore. The Afro-Cuban journalist was traveling from West Papua, where he was investigating the guerilla struggle of the Revolutionary Provisional Government of West Papua against Indonesian imperialism. He had been dispatched there from Dakar, Senegal, where the Revolutionary Provisional Government's Ben Tangghama had established a base with the support of Léopold Senghor.[90]

But to their delight, Kamarakafego was different. In Fiji, he awaited a response from the NHNP. Through Slatter, he wrote Donaldson, stating that he still had to "be cool as ever" but expected to reach Vanuatu in late May. Attached to the letter was information about Oceania's liberation struggles, including an essay about the party's political battles, and a March/April 1976 copy of *Povai*. This issue contained reports of political struggles across West Papua, Australia, New Zealand, Timor, New Caledonia, Vanuatu, Hawaii, Micronesia, and Fiji. It also included information about the Nuclear Free and Independent Pacific Movement and the PWC. Kamarakafego followed this with a Fijian post card, asking if Donaldson had received the information.[91]

Donaldson wrote back to the group of sixteen contributors, whom he thanked for having "a sense of the larger dimensions of the world-wide struggle for the independence of Afrikan peoples." He also confidentially attached a copy of Kamarakafego's résumé, which he felt was testimony to his longstanding work for the development of the Africana world. Kamarakafego expressed his appreciation for their support.[92]

However, Donaldson had incorrectly remarked that Kamarakafego had made it to Vanuatu. The latter eventually did heard from Sope in early May. Wishing him revolutionary greetings, Sope apologized for not having contacted him earlier. Party member and poet Grace Mera Molisa had told Sope directly that Kamarakafego was desperately waiting for a letter. The NHNP had repeatedly pushed the British residency to allow him back in the island. Yet British officials—despite the fact that his ban of six months had expired—refused to not let him in. As such, Party members felt it would be "a waste of time and money" if he was stopped at the airport.[93]

The Executive Committee of the party had decided that the time was not ripe for Kamarakafego to come. It stressed that he should wait until called upon. The struggle had become increasingly more difficult and was possibly going to require underground work in the future. Yet the longer they could freely move around "to mobilize the masses, the better for the struggle." The committee felt that Kamarakafego's presence would inflame the suspicions of the colonial administrations and make the secret police even more watchful for the party's growing "militant plans." This included participation in a representative assembly in the hopes that peaceful pathways to self-determination could be achieved. If this did not work, then force would have to be used against the colonialists—this possibility the Executive Committee had never ruled out, despite publicly proclaiming that independence needed to be achieved by peaceful means. It saw Kamarakafego as being a part of these plans.[94]

As such, Sope did not want Kamarakafego to think that the NHNP was rejecting him. They did not want to become "a white puppet government" like those in Africa or the Caribbean that had denounced organizers like him. It was their tactical judgment of the present political situation that they had asked him not to come.[95] Yet as they themselves had clearly stated, it would have been a fight to even get him through immigration.

Still, Kamarakafego was disappointed. He had sacrificed much and worked hard to return. He certainly did not want to disappoint his material and ideological supporters. As disheartening as this was, all was not lost. Unbeknownst to him, he would soon be in Papua New Guinea, where his contributions to decolonization in the Oceania would flourish in perhaps some unexpected means.

10

Papua New Guinea

A House For Every Family

Kamarakafego would not return to Vanuatu until after it achieved political independence in 1980. However, Vanessa Griffen's and Claire Slatter's extensive sociopolitical networks included Papua New Guinea's (PNG's) civil service. Through their direction, Kamarakafego worked in PNG in the area of sustainable development and appropriate technology from 1976 to 1980. His experiences in Melanesia definitively marked his environmental and political work across the Global South for the rest of his career.

Melanesia's largest country by land space and population, PNG secured political independence from Australia in 1975 under the direction of Michael Somare and his Pangu Party. Through institutions such as the University of Papua New Guinea (UPNG) and the Papua New Guinea Institute of Technology (Lae), PNG served as a beacon of Melanesian political and cultural nationalism and black internationalism in Oceania the era of decolonization. Via organizations like the South Pacific Appropriate Technology Foundation (SPATF), it also was a hub for the sustainable development movement in Oceania. Across the region, self-determination in the mineral-rich island represented the tangible potential of black liberation. All these factors marked PNG as an ideal home for someone of Kamarakafego's political and technical pedigree.

Established in 1966, UPNG faculty and visiting scholars included scholars from African institutions such as Uganda's Makerere University. This included world-renowned historian of Africa, Ali Mazrui. Starting in 1967, UPNG's annual Waigani seminar debated and grappled with issues affecting Melanesia, such as economics, development, culture, decentralization, education, history, land tenure, environment, politics, gender, Pacific literature, and urbanization. While debate continues over the impact of the talks, scholars, students, and political leaders from across the Global South enthusiastically attended them.[1] Through the mid-1970s, this list included activists such as Vanuatu's New Hebrides National Party (NHNP) members George Kalkoa, Donald Kalpokas, Barak Sope, and Peter Taurakoto; Brazil's Paulo Freire; Trinidad and Tobago economist Lloyd Best; and Solomon Island educator Francis Bugotu.

Critical participants to the seminars included Leo Hannett and John Kasaipwalova, UPNG students who cofounded its Niugini Black Power Group (NBPG) in 1970. The NBPG was established in the morning hours of one of many "anti-colonialist hate sessions." Hannett described the NBPG as a "[Frantz] Fanon-inspired African Negritude" movement. It included an emerging group of nationalist organizers who studied Africana liberation struggles, political thought, and liberation theology. This collective engaged the ideas of Fanon, the Negritude movement, Melanesian nationalism, Black Power, pan-Africanism, and the liberation struggles of the Global South within the local concerns of PNG. It studied the masculinist political thought of the Black Diaspora, from the words of Martin Luther King to Malcolm X, James Baldwin, and Kwame Ture and Charles Hamilton's *Black Power*. Through art, literature, demonstrations, and debates, the NBPG pushed for black self-determination, environmental justice, political independence, and an end to colonialism in Oceania. More specifically, this reflected a fight against the exploitation of Bougainville's mineral resources by multinational companies, police repression, South African apartheid, Australian colonialism, and Indonesian imperialism in West Papua.[2]

Members of the NBPG took African literature courses taken with UPNG professors Prithvindra Chakravarti and Ulli Beier. Beier, of German-Jewish descent, had previously taught at Nigeria's University of Ibadan. He was hired in UPNG's English Department to teach creative writing. The NBPG read the works of Wole Soyinka, Chinua Achebe, Léopold Senghor, and the Negritude movement's *Presence Africaine*. They produced memoirs, novels, poetry, theatrical productions, and short stories in English, indigenous languages, and Tok Pisin. Through their publication of literary journals like *Kovave, Papua Pocket Series, Modern Poetry From Papua New Guinea*, and *Papua New Guinea Writing*, these artists became visible conduits of Melanesian transnationalism across Oceania.[3]

Kasaipwalova's 1971 poem "Reluctant Flame" called for the fires of Niugini nationalism to "take fuel from brother struggles" and for its linking pipe to connect with black uprisings in Johannesburg and New York. Dramatist and NBPG member Arthur Jawodimbari founded PNG's National Theatre Company after touring Japan, Ghana, Nigeria, and the United States in 1974.

During this trip, he visited Nigeria's Obi Egbuna, Ghana's playwright Efua Sutherland, and Barbara Ann Teer's National Black Theatre in Harlem, New York.[4]

This black internationalist body of Melanesian art, scholarship, and literature challenged what Epeli Hau'ofa, iconic Tongan anthropologist and former tutor at UPNG, called the over two-hundred-year-old "pedigree of literature on Oceania." Such writings were created by explorers, navigators, beachcombers, missionaries, colonial officials, and the like who had "romanticized Polynesians and denigrated Melanesians." Because of these discourses on black radicalism, UPNG attracted students, scholars, and activists from across Oceania.[5]

This included Griffen and Slatter, who knew the political, social, and physical cartography of PNG quite well. While students at Fiji's University of the South Pacific (USP), both women enthusiastically embraced the anticolonial literature, scholarship, poetry, and activism emanating out of UPNG. In 1974, they conducted graduate studies in PNG. Griffen studied drama at the PNG Creative Arts Center and toured with Jawodimbari's company. Both women thought that PNG would be an ideal place for Kamarakafego to conduct his rural development work. During their studies there, they had befriended Pedi Anis, provincial secretary for the province of New Ireland. At their suggestion, Anis hailed from Umbukul, a community located on the island of New Hanover; he arranged for Kamarakafego to work as a volunteer there.[6]

Interestingly, the director general of the Australian Security Intelligence Organisation (ASIO) detailed Kamarakafego's arrival in Port Moresby, PNG, on September 13, 1976. He noted that the "well-known Black Power organizer" had passed through the city in 1974 while organizing for "Ghana's Pan African Black Power Conference," obviously a reference to 6PAC. Aware of his deportation from Vanuatu, ASIO was also curious as to his relationship with Fiji's Pacific People's Action Front (read, his connection with Griffen and Slatter), which supported political independence in Vanuatu, New Caledonia, and Tahiti. The director general believed that a branch of the Action Front was established at UPNG in early 1976 and was responsible for the publication of a pamphlet (likely a reference to *Povai*) that defended West Papua's struggle against Indonesia. Still, ASIO did not yet know why Kamarakafego was in PNG.[7]

Thousands of miles away from home, Kamarakafego was "adopted" by Anis' community in Umbukul. They provided him with modest but crucial lodging in a half-constructed house and food from their gardens. The island had no electricity. His time there required long, eight-hour ocean rides by speed boat to the provincial capital of Kavieng for supplies such as batteries, flashlights, and lamps. In Umbukul, he established projects around coconut oil, rural water supplies and sanitation, and constructed a community center there. Griffen frequently visited Kamarakafego; in Fiji, the two had started a fruitful intimate and working relationship that lasted for several years.[8]

Kamarakafego's professional career as an ecological engineer blossomed in PNG. By October 1976, he was working with New Ireland's Motloung Development Association. He continued to correspond with C. L. R. James, who wrote to him and found his activities there to be beyond belief— modern, contemporary, and immensely pleasing; according to the veteran Trotskyite, even Lenin would have approved.[9] However, this belies the logistic, interpersonal, and professional challenges that both Kamarakafego and Griffen were having.

Kamarakafego was frustrated with the process of decolonization in PNG. According to Griffen, he wanted to do his rural work, but "no one could work at his pace" or at his strength. He oftentimes found himself with little to no material support. This was very trying for the couple, as they had to rely on other persons for shelter. Said Griffen, "We were running back and forth, and I did not know what he was waiting for." It felt like they were not "getting anywhere."[10]

Griffen also grew troubled by Kamarakafego's growing anger in response to the situation. His violent temper expressed itself at New Ireland's white expatriates, including a school principal who was particularly unsupportive of his projects. He had a few altercations on the streets of Kavieng, one in which he almost punched a white man. While she typically agreed with him in principle, Griffen was anxious that he was possibly jeopardizing a situation that she and Slatter had facilitated through their personal contacts. Griffen had intended to stay for a year, hoping to be joined by her lifelong Fijian comrade. But after six months, she headed to Australia in early 1977; she could not take the intense effort that it required to remain there.[11]

Kamarakafego soon left as well. He received invitations to give a talk on ecology at a university in Hong Kong, to assist in organizing a Commonwealth Rural Technology workshop in Arusha, Tanzania, and to participate in a UN desertification conference in Nairobi, Kenya, as a representative of 6PAC's Science and Technology Committee. He arrived in Hong Kong in early August 1977, only to find that he was a prohibited immigrant there. A British police officer ordered him to depart on a South African Airways flight. After Kamarakafego retorted that he "would not travel on any airline that kills black people," the officer hit him with his truncheon. In response, Kamarakafego punched, bloodied, and broke the officer's nose. Detained, he traveled to Kenya on a British Airways flight five days later.[12]

Questions of science, technology, and development continued to be held in Africa at the governmental and NGO levels. In 1979, the Organization for African Unity established an African center for the development, transfer, and adaption of technology. The regional Africa office for UNESCO's Science and Technology division was based in Nairobi. This reflected how East Africa was an important space for international conversations on appropriate technology, environmental justice, and development.[13]

Both Nairobi's conference on desertification and Arusha's conference on rural technology were held between August 29 and September 9, 1977. Over five hundred delegates from across ninety-four countries met in Nairobi to discuss the global problems of desertification, which appeared as "the deterioration of land, water and other natural resources under ecological stress." The talks spanned drought in the Sahel, the effects of weapons of mass destruction on the environment, and desertification as a result of colonial practices. They also generated a collective and diverse Plan of Action to Combat Desertification, aimed to prevent and halt the global advance of desertification and, where possible, to reclaim such lands for productive use.[14]

Kamarakafego prepared a detailed proposal aimed at halting the desertification of the Sahara across West and North Africa. Replete with diagrams, formulas, sketches, and housing designs, the project aimed to "reclaim the Sahel" through agriculture, population settlement, communalism, irrigation, power and water supply, construction, transportation, and economics. Specifically, this included building man-made pyramids, lakes, mountains, and new societies. The plan called for the creation of population settlements of 250–300 people over 100 × 50 mile sections that would include people from the African Diaspora. It included the planting of casuarina, coconut, palm, and date trees; houses designed for the environment; and schools, power plants, and hospitals. Based on ideas of African communalism, each community was to include tradespersons, teachers, engineers, and a comprehensive system of education. Kamarakafego estimated that $8 billion were needed for the establishment of six settlements. This included machinery, equipment, and resources such as a four-person airplane, helicopter, trucks, three electric turbines or generators, livestock, bulldozers, and tractors.[15]

Kamarakafego initially wrote the paper in 1972, which he presented at the NGO forum at the UN Conference on the Human Environment in Stockholm, Sweden. In 1975, he was invited by the OAU to work with a group of European scientists who were interested in desertification and the reclamation of the Sahara. He refused to do so, because he felt that this group had been aware of the issue for decades and refused to do anything about it. In 1976, he was informed by a colleague that some of his materials had been used in an article, "A Tragedy of the Commons in the Sahel," written by two professors at the Massachusetts Institute of Technology (MIT). Published in MIT's *Technology Review*, the article used data collected from the Sahel and "impressions which emerged from discussion with African leaders, aid organizations, and people at research institutes" to create a computer simulation model that tested the interactions between humans, livestock, and the ecosystem. The purpose was to test long-term plans for the recovery and restoration of the Sahel. While it is not clear if the authors used Kamarakafego's work, there are similarities between the article and his paper, particularly around the use of livestock and cultural transformation. Kamarakafego believed they had perhaps gotten it from OAU officials.[16]

The Commonwealth secretariat sponsored Arusha's Rural Technology meeting. It featured discussions and displays of projects on appropriate technology from countries across East, Central, and southern Africa. The secretariat considered the meeting in Tanzania to be a great success, as participants worked to create ways that technological devices and information about them could be shared between developing regions.[17]

This included Kamarakafego, who conducted rural technology workshops there. A week later, he received a letter from Simon Nkonoki, the associate director of the University of Dar es Salaam's Institute of Development Studies. Nkonoki thanked Kamarakafego for his wonderfully "stimulating and challenging ideas" in Arusha and asked him to forward any materials he had on appropriate technology. Nkonoki was particularly interested in materials about soapmaking, papermaking, soil studies, and ecology.[18]

While in Tanzania, Kamarakafego met with PNG's public service commissioner, who offered him a job as PNG's director of the Office of Village Development (OVD). As was Vanuatu's National Party, PNG's government was focused on Tanzania's Ujamaa model of rural development. But unlike Vanuatu, the country was politically independent. The government invested in appropriate technology as a means of village development for the 86 percent of its population—those who lived in the rural areas. The multilateral Commonwealth Fund for Technical Co-operation (CFTC) provided funding for Kamarakafego's position. Formed in 1971 by the Commonwealth secretariat, the program provided technical assistance to Global South and developing countries by providing Commonwealth countries with technical experts. In 1978, there were nearly three hundred CFTC experts in the field. A secretariat office in PNG was established in 1974 as the largest country program of its kind.[19]

Kamarakafego considered this post to be one of the best assignments of his career. Based in Boroko, the OVD was logistically located in the office of Prime Minister Somare. Kamarakafego was given a two-year contract. He sent James extensive literature describing his work with the office, detailing his excitement to be working with black people at the village level. Griffen joined him in Boroko. Their relationship had been sustained through long-distance collect phone calls from East Africa to Australia. She worked as a publications officer in PNG's Department of Health.[20]

The OVD position was dramatically different from the one in Umbukul. Appointed to the position by Somare and provided with a home, an office, and a team of people, Kamarakafego was able to do meaningful work across the country. The OVD's basic concern was rural development. As an extension of the government's national development strategy, it was specifically centered on self-reliance and appropriate technology. This included transferring appropriate technologies to rural communities via its staff of over two hundred. The office also represented village communities in negotiating deals surrounding mining, timber logging, and fishing, as well as for the projects undertaken by anthropologists and PNG's Cultural Institute.[21]

Kamarakafego found that villagers and government officials were often unaware of the scope of the government's rural programs. He directed the OVD in gathering and filing information relevant to "village activists." He compiled a register of names, addresses, and phone numbers of individuals who could provide information or services to villagers. Kamarakafego also collected information about village organizations and groups (such as youth, village, church, and women's associations) regarding their financial needs, activities, means of communication, and leadership. This was to allow development programmers to communicate effectively.[22]

Kamarakafego was intricately involved in the OVD's Development Fellowship Scheme, which provided funding to individuals for development projects in their villages. The program provided opportunities for public servants and students to return to their rural communities to focus on local development. All PNG nationals above the age of sixteen were eligible to apply. One successful project was that of Peter Piaeon, who established self-reliance projects with school leavers in the Enga province. This included the growing and selling of produce and maintaining a chicken farm.[23]

Information about the Fellowship Scheme was successfully spread through an Information Service. The OVD received 346 letters after releasing a radio announcement about the scheme. By October 1977, it had awarded twenty fellowships spanning boat building, electrification, agriculture, marketing and fishing, and poultry, pig, and cattle husbandry.[24]

In May 1979, traditional healer and doctor Luke Silih-Tau wrote to Kamarakafego, asking for support from the OVD fellowship program for his Plitty Aid Post. This health center treated patients entirely with indigenous herbs and medicines. Located on the southern coast of Manus Island, the Plitty Aid Post was created by Luke and his brother Sokolo in 1970. During a previous decade of epidemics, Luke and his wife, Augustu, lost three of their seven children. In 1969, the Silih-Taus lost their father to a respiratory infection; he died while they were on route to get medical attention at the nearest hospital some thirty kilometers away. These deaths reflected a "disillusionment with the white medicine introduced to the island by missionaries and colonial administrators." This was also a reminder that their traditional practices of healing were disappearing. In response, the Silih-Taus began interviewing their clan elders about the properties of roots, leaves, and barks, and they began to produce old medicines.[25]

Within a few years, the Plitty Aid Post established a reputation for successfully treating patients with traditional herbs secured from rainforests that overlooked the settlement. In 1975, the center was officially recognized by the Manus Health Department as specializing in indigenous herbal medicine. Some patients were referred to it by Lorengau's provincial hospital, which was some forty kilometers and five hours away by outboard-motor canoe. The center staff consisted of twelve nurses and Silih-Tau family members, who prepared medicines from the barks of trees that were sun dried, milled to powder, stored, and then applied. The center used at least twenty-two plants to create medicines addressing malaria, diarrhea, hookworm, asthma, backaches, pneumonia, mental illness, bruises, and ulcers. With six hospital wards, two outpatient wards, a storage building, a staff house, and a guesthouse, the center had a stellar reputation in the community. With Luke and Sokolo as its two main herbalists, it treated upwards of five hundred patients a year.[26]

Kamarakafego ecstatically responded to Silih-Tau's plans to transform three plots of one hundred hectares of land to use for growing medicinal crops. Kamarakafego visited the center, which was located in an area sparsely populated by the Pohowa, a community of about eight hundred. Set deeply inland, the challenging journey took him two days' travel through over land and sea across areas absent of roads and electricity. Kamarakafego regarded all this to be worth the trip. He became involved with the hospital and organized a traditional medicine conference there. He was also able to secure a two-year fellowship for the center amounting to $200 a month.[27]

In 1979, UPNG sponsored an expedition to survey traditional medicinal plants across PNG, including in Manus and New Ireland. This team included botanists from the PNG National Herbarium and UPNG students. They conducted research at Plitty and found the health center to be an "example of self-reliance." Noting the material contribution of the OVD, the team saw it as a model "project worthy of encouragement and financial support."[28]

The OVD's initiatives were publicized in its magazine *Yumi Kirapim* (Together making change). By December 1977, it had a circulation of five thousand copies. Prime Minister Somare himself contributed to the magazine and thanked Kamarakafego for his work. In its December edition, he referred to *Yumi Kirapim* as essentially a rural officer's newspaper. The role of the paper was to assist people in being creative in their own environments. Its readership included urban-based public servants as well as rural villagers.[29]

Written in basic language and illustrated with diagrams, pictures, and pictograms, the pages of *Yumi Kirapim* included pieces about nutrition, the solar salt industry, youth development, the Fellowship Scheme, rural credit facilities, basic mechanics, business development, culture, and village electrification. It also offered manuals on appropriate technology, lists of rural development handbooks for purchase, and inventories of tools and machinery that could be purchased through the OVD. It contained quotes from philosophers such as Khalil Gibran and Mahatma Gandhi and articles such as "What is Self-Reliance," by PNG philosopher Bernard Narokobi. Written in English and Tok Pisin, the magazine asked readers to submit photographs, projects, and comments to the director's office.[30]

Via *Yumi Kirapim*, the OVD stressed that PNG activists needed logistical support to improve the success of their rural projects. It created booklets, magazines, radio programs, and film and slide sets to do so. Its booklets spanned topics that included village blacksmithing, gravity-fed water, and food-operated threshers.[31]

The magazine also publicized the work of the SPATF. Directed by PNG's Andrew Jauleni, the foundation was formed in February 1977 as a project and technical arm of the OVD. It was designed to "actively promote and develop appropriate technology for self-help village development," defining appropriate technology as "ways of doing things that do not require a lot of money nor require dependence on foreign experts or imported equipment."[32]

According to the OVD, PNG was a "nation of small villages." Its "constitutionally enshrined" principles for development "called for self-help, self-reliance and the use of traditional ways." Thus, SPATF was charged with using appropriate technologies that could "foster individual, village, and national self-reliance" to minimize dependence on foreign exports and imported equipment, encourage environmentally and culturally compatible development initiatives, provide technological alternatives and complements to capital intensive strategies, stimulate self-employment, and improve the quality of rural life.[33]

The foundation maintained a library of films, pamphlets, books, and papers to supplement its workshops and centers. Via publicity and grassroots education, it sought to create awareness of the "relative advantages of appropriate technologies." This included facilitating seminars, conferences, and workshops to "train people to become teachers."[34] Aiming to operate on a local, regional, and international level, SPATF was to gather information from throughout Oceania and the wider world, act as a clearinghouse of cutting-edge appropriate technologies, and help to establish national appropriate technology institutions throughout the region. The initial proposal for SPATF was created with extensive input from Melanesian villages and from appropriate technology materials collected from across the world. One of its three-day conferences on appropriate technology included over one hundred delegates from PNG. It also held two and three-week national appropriate technology workshops for villagers and provincial trainers. This included observers from Fiji, Vanuatu, and the Solomon Islands, who were seeking to launch appropriate-technology programs in their respective countries.[35]

Somare addressed the launching of SPATF. Writing in *Yumi Kirapim*, he felt that the harnessing of appropriate technology would help individuals and governments toward self-reliance. The foundation aimed to gather information on tools, techniques, and ideas on appropriate technology, develop these in ways suitable to Oceania's environment, distribute this information for entities working toward self-reliance and demonstrate that appropriate technologies could foster individual, community, and national self-reliance.[36]

In 1978, the foundation cosponsored the three-week National Women's Network on Appropriate Technology. Held at Popondetta's Agricultural College, SPATF's contribution focused on tradition-linked technology through eight hands-on activities. Attended by about fifty-six women, these included the use of "kunai kitchen," the construction of a drum oven, village home technology, traditional technology, blacksmithing, sewing machine repair, and agriculture.[37]

Funded by the OVD, SPATF produced a range of manuals on appropriate technology. These included how to build an oil drum stove, hydrolytic ram pumps, and pelton wheel waterpower generators. It also published position papers on rural and decentralized national development systems. Its manuals were distributed through print media such as New Nation, which reached communities beyond PNG. For example, in an April 1979 article written by Canadian ex-patriot Sandy Kalmokoff, SPATF announced that its "how-to-do" booklets on appropriate technologies, libraries, and information exchange were available to all of Oceania.[38]

Kamarakafego helped to launch SPATF before he left for East Africa later in 1977. As director of the OVD, he worked closely with its technicians. He was particularly endeared to SPATF's flagship training program, which made up the majority of the foundation's work. The workshop program was geared toward rural communities, women, and younger individuals. The workshops had male and female participants and were aimed at disrupting gender codes about technology. The workshops spanned food security, water harnessing, housing, and rural electrification in health and community centers. In June 1978, Anis wrote to Kamarakafego, stressing that developments in New Ireland had gotten to the point that certain projects could not be done without his assistance. This was particularly the case with appropriate technology in the villages. He also asked Kamarakafego for his assistance in exploring aid for outboard mechanics, diesel engines, and car maintenance via German-based institutions.[39]

However, Kamarakafego's relationship with SPATF also appeared to be a tenuous one, reflecting broader challenges of racism, class, and colonization. Papua New Guinea's postcolonial state was marked by a large number of white Australian and British expatriate civil servants. These positions were extremely lucrative, with salaries set higher for expatriates than nationals. This included white women, who, often despite a lack of professional qualifications, dominated the administrative assistant sector. According to Griffen, one could walk into a government office and see "all white faces." This was very much a carryover from the colonial government.[40]

Kamarakafego clashed with some of these white technicians, who preferred to be a part of their own organization as opposed to being under the umbrella of the OVD. Griffen recalls that SPATF personnel "did not like [Kamarakafego]" and that he "did not like them." They practically waited for him to fail, as they did not like the positive work that he was able to do across the country. This created an unhealthy working relationship in which he did his work "over here," and they did "their thing over there."[41]

A 1983 Intermediate Technology Development Group review of SPATF perhaps hints at these dynamics. It notes that SPATF was located in the same office as the OVD. Laced with references that the office was ineffectual, that the OVD thought that SPATF was "its possession" and sought to run it as government organization, that SPATF called for a "different level of competence" from that of giving technical information to village volunteers under the OVD, and that its white expatriate technicians were excellent, it also concluded that as a result of OVD's directorship, SPATF was not as effective as it could be.

Interestingly, while the sixty-seven-page report lauded SPATF technicians specifically, it never once mentioned Kamarakafego by name. It challenged the charge that SPATF leaders were to report to the OVD as opposed to its own board. This, the author claimed, prevented the group from having direct contact with other governmental agencies and handicapped the group, as the OVD and its development scheme were not fully operational. Finally, it argued that while SPATF was to be fully integrated into the activities of the OVD and its two hundred village fellows, the scheme did not function well. It claimed that its fellows became disillusioned and lost motivation from a lack of feedback from the OVD. This, the report suggests, and the lack of reporting to Somare about its work "resulted in the eventual demise of the OVD" in 1981. Of course, none of this was attributed to the "hard working, well-meaning expatriates" from Australia who carried with them to PNG white paternalism, incompetence, racism, or sexism.[42] This "demise" also occurred around the time that Kamarakafego left PNG, a moment that we will return to later in this chapter.

Kamarakafego's own work in appropriate technology was also published through the OVD. This included his manuals on making soap from coconut oil and his widely sought-after *House for Every Family*. The twenty-eight-page manual was designed to address one of the critical problems facing the Global South—"adequate low-cost housing for the poorly housed masses." Kamarakafego argued that high costs of imported building materials and technology had pushed housing beyond the reach of most people. However,

PLANS OF THE HOUSE

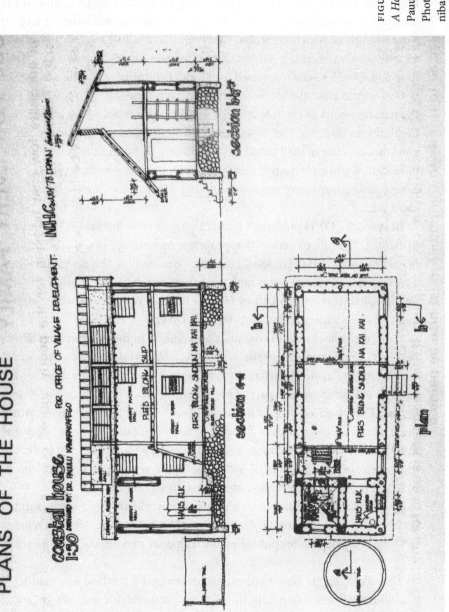

FIGURE 9. Plans from *A House for Every Family*, Paulu Kamarakafego. Photo courtesy of Rronniba Kamarakafego.

if the use of imported resources was excluded or greatly minimized, housing costs across the Global South could be reduced, and by self-help, this problem could be solved. The home was constructed with bamboo plastered with cement and the ceiling laced with woven mats.[43]

Kamarakafego argued that anyone with the proper supervision could build a house. His method included using materials that he found in the country, to lower costs. The frame of the home was made up of treated woven bamboo, which grew abundantly in PNG. While treated timber was expensive, Kamarakafego included treating the timber by soaking it with lime and divai—a local root used for killing fish for consumption. Another option was to treat the timber with juice from a cassava plant, which had the natural toxins of cyanide and arsenic. This also reduced the trunk's vulnerability to termites. He suggested varnishing the roof with lime coating aids; this element of traditional house building in Bermuda allowed for the purification and collection of rainwater. With these methods, he felt that the lowest-paid government employee would be able to own such a house over eight years.[44]

In 1980, the OVD published Kamarakafego's *How to Make a Water Tank* in *Point 5*, the office's series of appropriate technology manuals. With the plans drawn by PNG's National Housing Commission, the design included a two-thousand-gallon water tank made with bamboo and cement. In 1983, he published this in Vanuatu as *How to Build a Water Tank with Bamboo and Cement*. Griffen designed its striking cover.[45]

Griffen also included his manuals on bamboo homes and water tanks in her book, *Knowing and Knowing How: A Self-Help Manual on Technology for Women in the Pacific*. Published in 1981, the book was primarily designed for rural or village women as part of her Pacific Women's Resource Kit. *Knowing and Knowing How* helped to spread knowledge of Kamarakafego's work. For example, Niue's director of works, T. Tonatule, came across *A House For Every Family* in Griffen's book. Since the country was seeking to use more local materials in the housing sector, Tonatule wrote to Kamarakafego in 1983 seeking more information about this project.[46]

Kamarakafego's ideas traveled across the world through organizations such as the UN's Industrial Development Organization, whose October 1980 monthly newsletter published his recipe for making coconut-oil soap:

The OVD, Papua New Guinea, has developed a method for making coconut-oil soap. To obtain the oil from coconuts, the nuts are grated and as much milk as possible is squeezed from the pulp. The residue is heated over a low fire until it changes in color to between light brown and brown. After cooling, it is strained and the residue is squeezed, leaving a clear, golden oil. This oil can be used for cooking, as a fuel in kerosene lamps, for cosmetics, or for making soap. Soapmaking requires the use of lye, either purchased directly or obtained from wood ashes or the residue from the burning of high-alkaline plants. The lye is mixed with water in a non-aluminum container and heated until it dissolves; it is then allowed to cool to about 30°C. The oil is heated to about 44°C, and the lye solution is added slowly. The correct thickness is achieved in ten to twenty minutes. The soap is ready after twenty-four hours. It must then be cut into pieces and stored for ten to fourteen days and protected from drafts and cold. The soap must not be allowed to freeze. For further information contact: Dr. Pauulu Kamarakafego, Office of Village Development, P.O. Box 6937, Boroko, Papua New Guinea.[47]

Technology experts, government officials, NGOs, and individuals from across the Americas, Africa, Asia, Europe, and Oceania reached out to Kamarakafego to obtain his manuals. Between 1978 and 1983, requests for his coconut-oil soap manual came from countries such as Ecuador, Tanzania, Madagascar, Malawi, India, and Austria.[48]

Kamarakafego had other responsibilities as well. He secured international resources for rural development projects and served on the board of PNG's University of Technology. On the campus of UPNG, he built a model Melanesian house. In 1979, he coordinated with the DC-based engineering company CIFAC and Guy Francis Stark and Associates to secure loans for PNG's government. This was through African American engineer Eric Stark, whom Jeff Donaldson had reached out to assist Kamarakafego in his return to Oceania. Stark also was involved in 6PAC.[49]

In October 1979, Stark put African American engineer Knox Tull in touch with Kamarakafego. Tull informed Kamarakafego that they had both been active at the CBE. As a partner in the Jackson and Tull civil and structural engineering firm based in Washington, DC, he had designed major rural projects in water supply and sewage disposal in Guinea, Conakry, and Sana, Yemen. He hoped to be of service to PNG.[50]

Kamarakafego also served on an aid recipient committee that advised Prime Minister Somare on contracts with multinational companies, usually Australian. In contrast to Australian advisors who served in similar capacity, he often advised the PNG government against accepting exploitative

Right: FIGURE 10. *How to Build a Watertank with Bamboo and Cement*. Editor/ Book Designer—Vanessa Griffen; Graphic Art—Patrick Fong.

Below: FIGURE 11. How to build a water tank from bamboo, model. Photo courtesy of Rronniba Kamarakafego.

How to build a watertank with bamboo and cement

Overflow outlet.

deals that did not benefit PNG. This bothered some members of the national leadership, who may have stood to profit individually from these arrangements. True to form, Kamarakafego had a few physical altercations; his detractors used these incidents to encourage Somare to remove him from his post.[51]

Toward a Black Pacific

Kamarakafego and Griffen generously opened their home to friends, activists, and colleagues who visited them in PNG. Their networks included students and faculty at UPNG and diverse guests from Oceania, Africa, and the Americas. With food, music, dancing, and discourse, they generously placed these organizers in contact with one another.

Ever the political socialite, Kamarakafego loved to cook for his visitors. He repeatedly told his son Baizum Kamarakafego that "his kitchen was his chemistry lab." It was a place where he put to full use his recipes for Caribbean and West African dishes like peanut stew chicken, salt fish, brown rice, ginger beer, Bermuda's codfish and potatoes, and lemonade richly flavored with cloves.[52] Even in such festive atmospheres, however, Kamarakafego never suffered fools lightly. For example, in the summer of 1979, F. C. Kawonga, assistant director of the Commonwealth secretariat's youth program, organized workshops in PNG. Subsequently writing from London, Kawonga thanked Kamarakafego for holding a lively party for workshop participants. He recalled how the latter had "lifted a rascal shoulder high" to put some sense in him. Kamarakafego's hospitality had left "lingering memories" of himself and the PNG community. Impressed with the prototype Melanesian house that he had built at UPNG, Kawonga also asked for materials on the cost-effective homes that he had designed.[53]

Participants in the workshops included Trinidad and Tobago's Sam Roystone Neverson. Based in Guyana, he affectionately wrote to Kamarakafego about the pleasant experiences that he had with his UPNG colleagues, professors Kwasi Nyamekye (Department of Political and Administrative Studies) and Kenyan Henry Olela (philosophy). Nyamekye extensively studied the Free Papua movement's activities against Indonesian imperialism, publishing his book *Organisasi Papua Merdeka* in 1979.[54]

The day after the party, the group had lunch at Olela's home. Kawonga enjoyed seeing Kamarakafego there, as he was much more relaxed than he had been during the incident with the "rascal." Olela was a former assistant professor of Afro-American studies at Duke University. His courses on black studies and the philosophy of black liberation spanned the writings of Harold Cruse, Albert Memmi, Fanon, Nkrumah, Ture, and Cleaver. After three years at Duke, Olela abruptly resigned in July 1975 in response to the administration's lack of commitment to the department. He joined the faculty at UPNG that fall.[55]

Olela also edited *The Melanesian Way*, a critical book written by PNG lawyer, political leader, and philosopher Bernard Narokobi. Published in 1980, *The Melanesian Way* was a compilation of articles written by Narokobi for PNG's *Post-Courier* newspaper between 1976 and 1978. In 1981, Olela published his *From Ancient Africa to Ancient Greece: An Introduction to the History of Philosophy*. This placed Olela among a generation of writers who detailed ancient Egypt's contributions to science and philosophy, such as George James and Yosef Ben-Jochannan. In 1986, Ben-Jochannan presented a paper to the Association for the Study of Classical African Civilization meeting, where he referred to Olela as an African scholar who had taken it upon himself to become an African authority on Africa and Africans.[56] Ben-Jochannan certainly knew Olela—he had met him in PNG.

From July 15 to August 11, 1979, Ben-Jochannan visited Kamarakafego in Boroko. Stepping off an Air Niugini flight via Hawaii, he was greeted by his long-time friend at the airport. It had been a long four years since they had seen each other. The iconic Harlem-based Africana historian was currently an adjunct professor of history at Cornell University's African Studies and Research Center, which was directed by James Turner. Kamarakafego had organized a few lectures for Ben-Jochannan to present at UPNG on African classical civilizations; having just led a tour of Kemet with a group of forty persons, Ben-Jochannan had also written several books, pamphlets, and articles on the subject. At the time, his most popular books were perhaps *Black Man of the Nile*, *African Origins of the Major Western Religions*, and *Africa: Mother of Western Civilization*.[57]

Ben-Jochannan gave at least eight public lectures in PNG. This included two talks at UPNG, one on the African origins of Judaism, Christianity, and Islam, and the other on social justice. Students also requested that he lecture on Nile Valley civilizations. Speaking before hundreds of university and community persons, he attributed the intriguing reception of his talks to his focus on the commonalities between black people in Oceania and Africa. These lectures were advertised in PNG's daily *Post-Courier*, which referred to him as an "African expert and controversial Egyptologist."[58]

Ben-Jochannan had traveled all across the black Diaspora—Africa, the United States, the Caribbean, and Europe. Still, he was astonished to find

"Africa in PNG," and he "saw himself" everywhere he turned. He was captivated by how black people across the Diaspora "seemed to all look alike"—
Papua New Guineans, Africans, African Americans, and Afro-Caribbeans.
The faces of PNG were common throughout all the world's great black enclaves—Watts, Harlem, Giza, and Port of Spain. Ben-Jochannan remarked
that he had seen around thirty persons in PNG who had identical twins in
New York's Harlem, the South Bronx, or Bedford Stuyvesant. More so, several women competing in PNG's national beauty contest could have been
revelers in New York's West Indian parade.[59]

Ben-Jochannan was certain that these connections went beyond pheno-
type. This moved him to find racial, cultural, and prehistoric connections
between PNG and the African Diaspora. At the PNG National Museum,
he compared its extensive collections of Melanesian masks, artifacts, and
musical instruments to those he had studied in Africa. He also found similarities between PNG and Africa's traditional dancing, drums, and music
traditions.[60]

Treated with total hospitality, he felt just as home in PNG as he had felt in
Harlem, Southern Egypt, Trinidad and Tobago, and Guyana. In fact, in PNG
he had found his paradise. Its community of African American, Afro-Caribbean, and African expatriates cemented his reception there. But Kamarakafego—and certainly Griffen—he commended the most. Ben-Jochannan
lived as a guest in Kamarakafego's home, with accommodations, food, and
transportation provided without charge. As did Kamarakafego's last guest
from the Americas, dermatologist and 6PAC organizer Fletcher Robinson,
Ben-Jochannan met news reporters, activists, and students like Vanuatu's
Hilda Lini at their house.[61]

Of course, this did not mean that paradise was drama free. Ben-
Jochannan decried the impact of both neocolonialism and Christianity on
the country. Having witnessed several traditional dances and performances,
he was particularly disturbed by the wearing of "Western Missionary" pant-
ies and brassieres in contrast to "traditional clothes." This for him was an
"ugly spectacle of missionary colonialism." There was also an incident when
two boys hailed him, "Hey N-gger!" Challenged by Ben-Jochannan, the
boys retorted they meant no harm—they had heard the word in a Richard
Pryor movie.[62]

Ben-Jochannan extensively detailed his three-week trip in PNG in a report of over two hundred pages. Replete with maps, photographs, and images, he wrote it as a historical and socio-anthropological travelogue. Ben-
Jochannan turned Kamarakafego's kitchen into his office, where he first

began to transform the report into a manuscript. In 1980, he published it as half of his book *They All Look Alike: All of Them? From Egypt to Papua New Guinea*. The book contained pictures of black people from across the Diaspora, interspersed between photographs that he and Kamarakafego took in PNG. Ben-Jochannan argued that if anyone could look at these images and yet claim that there were no racial or historical connections between himself, Kamarakafego, and Melanesians, they needed "psychiatric care or extra powerful . . . glasses."[63]

They All Look Alike gives historical context to Kamarakafego's time in PNG. For example, Ben-Jochannan writes about an incident at an elaborate dinner at Griffen and Kamarakafego's home. While there, a Marxist Socialist guest associated with UPNG called Ben-Jochannan a "reactionary nationalist." This guest then insulted other visitors, chided the alcoholic beverages, and denounced the whole affair. This left Kamarakafego to "remind the dialectician"—in his "unique way"—that he was in his home.[64] This was likely our rascal from the earlier account.

Ben-Jochannan observed firsthand Kamarakafego's rural development work in various villages. He described his comrade as "someone who lived, worked and planned with the local people of the villages." The unique text also contains photographs of Kamarakafego and his OVD activities, such as his workshops on sustainable bamboo housing and furniture making in Mungi (Mangi), Pangia (Southern Highlands) and Popondetta (Northern Province), where crowds anxiously awaited the arrival of Somare to open the workshop.[65]

They All Look Alike contains photographs of a large-scale crocodile (*pukpuk*) commercial farming project that Kamarakafego administered. Lying just outside of Port Moresby, the farm sought to replace the haphazard and wasteful hunting of wild crocodiles for skins by harvesting young ones to be reared to commercial size. This aimed to ensure that village communities benefited from the industry but also that the sustainability of crocodiles in their natural environment was secured. The farms included "smaller village holding pens, medium-sized business farms, and large technically sophisticated farms able to withstand drought, produce their own food and deal with husbandry and disease problems." The program was partially aided by the UN Development Program and Environmental Wildlife Project.[66]

Ben-Jochannan's pan-African and First World nationalist philosophy led him to identify with his brothers and sisters in PNG. Taken in by the indigenous making of tapa cloth, the wearing of *lap laps*, and the chewing of betel nut mixed with white lime, he remarked that he had found the Black

Madonna in Africa and PNG. He thought about retiring there and "becoming a war counselor" to younger freedom fighters. He had learned a lot in PNG, where it was taught that "when the battlefield has become too hard and too fast for an old man's bow and arrows, his sight, coordination and strength are no longer one/unity; thus he must be strategically moved to the rear [village] to counsel the younger men."[67]

After forty years of giving lectures across the African Diaspora, Ben-Jochannan found UPNG to be a place where his lifetime's collection of original and unpublished manuscripts, books, maps, and papers could be donated before he "became an ancestor." This commitment was rooted in Ben-Jochannan's belief in the "thousands of wide-eyed Brothers and Sisters" of Oceania who would make each page "cry out for rest." Unfortunately, he lamented, he was not so sure about "Negroes and colored folks" in the Diaspora who "cursed slave masters for genocide but did want to let them go." He hoped to get an appointment at UPNG, whose faculty included black professors from across Kenya, Uganda, Jamaica, Ethiopia, Jamaica, Trinidad and Tobago, St. Lucia, and African America.[68]

With his revelations about the Black Pacific, Ben-Jochannan joined a tradition of Africana scholars who thought similarly. This list included Howard University professor of diplomatic history Merz Tate, who in 1943 argued that the "darker persons of the world lived in the Netherlands East Indies, India, Asia, the Malay Peninsula, Polynesia, Oceania, and Melanesia, which contained the Negroid inhabitants of the Central and Western Pacific." In 1976, black artists, journalists, activists, scholars, and scientists from across the African world, including C. L. R. James, Harold Cruse, and Shawna Maglanbayan, attended Wole Soyinka's Seminar for African World Alternatives in Dakar, Senegal. The seminar's "Declaration of Black Intellectuals and Scholars in Support of the People's Struggle of West Papua New Guinea and East Timor Against Indonesian Colonialism" expressed alarm over Indonesia's "campaign of extermination" against the "Melanesian (black) populations of West Papua New Guinea and East Timor." Since at least the 1990s, scholar Runoko Rashidi has actively discussed Oceania in his lectures and tours of the Global African Presence.[69]

According to Ben-Jochannan, it was Kamarakafego who first stimulated his interest in PNG. In 1969, Kamarakafego had given him a copy of the Australia's Black Power–inspired magazine *Koorier*, which he had obtained during his trip there. Ben-Jochannan passed the paper on to Australian Maev O'Collins, who at the time was a doctoral student in social welfare at New York's Columbia University. In a letter to the *Koorier*, O'Collins expressed her appreciation of the paper for doing its part in the international struggle against racism and pledged to return to Australia to do make her own contribution.[70] O'Collins served as a professor of anthropology and sociology at UPNG from 1972 to 1989 and was thus teaching in PNG during Ben-Jochannan's visit.

In PNG, Kamarakafego built lasting relationships with activists from across Oceania. This included Vanuatu NHNP organizers Hilda Lini and Hanson Mataskelekele. Hilda studied journalism at UPNG and the two sisters were leaders of the party's Women's Wing. Hanson was married to Kalkot Mataskelekele; New Caledonia's Australian Consulate described their relationship as the party's "dynastic marriage." The consulate considered Hanson, a secondary school teacher, to be fairly politically radical, even more so than her brother Walter Lini. Drawing on intelligence provided by the British residency in Vanuatu, it reported in detail the party's activities in PNG.[71]

The consulate also informed Australia's high commission in PNG about the activities of Kalkot, who studied law at UPNG. It referred to him as the key organizer in the NHNP's impressive 1975 election victory. Aged twenty-seven, Mataskelekele was considered by the commission to be the most impressive of Vanuatu's emerging leadership and likely its future leader. It placed him on the radical side of the NHNP along with Barak and Mildred Sope, Peter Taurokoto, Hanson, Shem Rarua, Fred Tau, and Egell. As such, the consulate felt that someone from the high commission needed to reach out to Mataskelekele "in a discreet and un-pushy way" to get an idea of his beliefs and "make a good impression on somebody who" seemed destined to become a leader of Vanuatu.[72]

Kalkot Mataskelekele also spent a lot of time in Vanuatu with Kamarakafego, who frequently visited them on campus and critically influenced him and other UPNG students in the process of "mental decolonization." Mataskelekele recalls Kamarakafego's building of a "model Melanesian home" at PNG's National Gardens next to campus. This house was designed based on Melanesian social customs. As a group, they went for drives around PNG to see his work with the OVD.[73]

This collective had extensive political dialogs. Kamarakafego shared with them stories about African history and talked about the African origins of science. When Kalkot would recite in detail the history of European "discoverers" in Oceania, Kamarakafego would press him about the region's indigenous histories. This encouraged students like him to look beyond the boundaries of colonial history; Kamarakafego was "wiping away something" and decolonizing them through conversation.[74]

Hilda Lini's activism in the NHNP began while she was a high school student. She was drawn to the political potential of journalism. She distributed the party's *New Hebridean Viewpoints* and became its editor in 1976. Lini forged a close relationship with Griffen through the Pacific Women's movement and Oceania freedom struggles. She first met Kamarakafego in Vanuatu in 1975 when he stayed at Walter Lini's home. She was upset by his deportation because of the good things that he was doing at Longana People's Center. Her brother Walter then dispatched her to Longana, which was the first rural center in the country. Eventually they established a radio, library, and savings bank there.[75]

Lini frequently visited Griffen and Kamarakafego in PNG. For her, "Pauulu was everything." She knew him as an advisor and hairdresser who cut hair, tailored garments, and meticulously managed his house. He was always dancing around their home and playing music. Self-reliant, he did not eat junk food, cooked well, and loved to knit. She saw Kamarakafego as being a strong man, but he was also very much an entertainer who used to take her and her niece dancing.[76]

Lini's conversations with Kamarakafego, like those of Mataskelekele's, usually centered on mental decolonization. As an educator, Lini talked in very common-sense ways about indigenous human rights for black people, Black Power, and decolonization. While they were also told these things from the party's older leaders, it was important to hear about black struggle from a global person like Kamarakafego. He helped them to link themselves to other black freedom movements, and he showed them photographs and material culture from Black Power meetings like the Congress of African Peoples and Bermuda's Black Power Conference.[77]

But Kamarakafego was "not a writer." Griffen was instrumental in his efforts to dictate, write, and record his story on tape cassettes—a project that he begun in 1974. Griffen planned to transcribe these tapes before someone inadvertently recorded over a cache of these cassettes with music. These efforts to complete his autobiography, *Me One*, were not completed until 2002.[78]

In PNG, Kamarakafego befriended the Black Brothers, a well-known West Papuan pop music group. Formed in 1974 by Andy Ayamiseba, the Black Brothers were internationally vocal advocates of West Papua's liberation struggle. Through a 1961 deal brokered by the Kennedy administration, the former Dutch colony was claimed by Indonesia, which violently suppressed West Papuan nationalism. In the 1960s, the John F. Kennedy administration looked at West Papua's seven hundred thousand indigenous people as being the farthest from ready for self-determination of any other group in the world. One of its policy papers labeled them as "stone-age peoples living in semi-nomadic groups speaking hundreds of mutually-unintelligible languages and dialects." They projected them as practitioners of witchcraft and headhunters unacquainted with "the arts of self-government."[79]

This racist framing of West Papua was perhaps matched by the vision of white nationalism expressed by Kennedy himself. In a 1963 meeting, the foreign minister of the Netherlands questioned the president about the United States' role in the conflict between Indonesia and the Dutch. Kennedy's retort was that he saw "the United States and Europe as having a common civilization, common forms of government, and common color-*white*," with Atlantic unity just on the horizon.[80]

Within this context, the cultural activism of the Black Brothers was immensely important for West Papua, which aligned itself with the freedom struggles of Melanesia and the Black Diaspora. Papua New Guinea was a critical site for making such linkages. At UPNG, the Black Brothers forged a long-lasting relationship with Kamarakafego, the Mataskelekeles, Lini, and the NHNP. Influenced by Reggae and Black Power, the Black Brothers shared much in common with Kamarakafego, who also admired their music. They had first heard about Black Power in West Papua. There they embraced African American political aesthetics, wore bell-bottoms, donned Afros, and were drawn to black movie stars such as Jim Kelly. This connection continued in PNG, where they frequently interacted with Kamarakafego. Ayamiseba regarded Kamarakafego as an engineer of Vanuatu's freedom struggle and felt that NHNP members looked up to him as a political elder. For example, both Sope and Mataskelekele stated that Kamarakafego was one of the key voices that encouraged the NHNP to change its name to the Vanua'aku Nasional Pati (National Party) in 1977.[81]

Back to Vanuatu

The Vanua'aku National Party secured independence for Vanuatu in 1980. The transition from British and French colonialism had been an intense, difficult, and violent one. Kamarakafego was invited to the new country's independence ceremonies, where he was given a liberation medal. He felt this to be a tremendous honor; the only other person outside of Vanuatu to have received such an award was Cuba's Fidel Castro.[82]

While there, the new government invited him to come back to Vanuatu in 1981 to serve as its rural development advisor. On a two-year contract, Kamarakafego's position was once again paid for by the CFTC. His salary was £12, 580, in addition to a housing allowance of 30,000 Vatus.[83]

As prime minister of Vanuatu, Walter Lini saw rural development as using already-standing community values and *kastom* (culture) as forces for development as opposed to hindrances to modernization. Vanuatu's majority rural population had a "perfectly satisfactory system" that just happened to be different from modern development theory. He argued that rural change could take place through human development (as opposed to the creation of more administrations) and social programs that could help unify the country's scattered communities. As Lini had done with Longana, the government wanted to create efficient community centers that could host events, films, sports activities, entertainment, recreation, and marketing programs. For Lini, such programs would complement Vanuatu's historic economic system of "Melanesian socialism" that was based on "egalitarian distribution" of income, employment opportunities, and wealth.[84]

Kamarakafego's responsibilities were to advise Vanuatu's Ministry of Social Affairs in developing rural development policy, to assist in the implementation of these community centers, to establish a welfare department with an emphasis on rural development, to create a manual of these programs that could ensure their continuity at the end of his contract, and to train a national counterpart. He was also charged with assisting ex-rural vocational-training participants in establishing their own community businesses, accessing progress of the community-center programs (four pilot projects had been established), assessing and establishing cane-furniture manufacturing centers in Vila, and running rural-development workshops in the areas of fishing, water supplies and storage (i.e., water tanks), village sanitation, nutrition, cash crops, and other forms of appropriate technology. In the government's first National Action Plan (1982–86), Lini thanked him for being an advisor to Vanuatu's Planning Commission. He also served as Vanuatu's first secretary for the Ministry of Health. In this capacity, he was recognized by World Health Organization for his "splendid cooperation and strong support" to the group.[85]

His work took him across the country. He organized bamboo and cement water-tank projects for women and youth across Melee, Efate, and

Malekula, where he worked closely with Nato. His relationship with the Linis and the National Party continued to grow. For example, he built the Linis a family home on Pentecost Island.[86] While no longer in livable conditions, it was still standing as of 2014. The importance of Kamarakafego's work in Vanuatu is evidenced by the remaining presence of water tanks and homes that he built across the country, including in Melee, the largest village on the island of Efate.

Kamarakafego arrived in Vanuatu with the ability to speak Tok Pisin, PNG's primary creolized language. This helped him learn Bislama, which he was familiar with from his earlier visits in the country. In Vanuatu, he started an intimate relationship with Melee's Rose Cuong. The two first met at a restaurant near to Lelippa, where Kamarakafego had made his first Black Power speech. Raised in France's colonial education system, Cuong primarily spoke French. Her grandfather was a descendent of one of over six thousand Vietnamese laborers brought to work on French plantations in Vanuatu. In 1931, six Tonkinese were publicly guillotined for the killing of a French settler. This marked tensions between French colons and Vietnamese laborers, who were largely repatriated in 1963. Cuong's father was one of the three hundred people who remained in Vanuatu; the chief of Melee village adopted him as a young child.[87]

Rose and Kamarakafego conceived a son, Baizum. Kamarakafego crocheted baby clothing for Baizum, and shawls for Rose and her mother. As an adult, Baizum described his father as a very loving mentor and a fighter who taught him, among other things, how to make Bermuda's iconic dish, codfish and potatoes.[88]

According to Cuong, Kamarakafego often wore a neck brace while he slept. He claimed to have chronic neck pain from the injuries he sustained during his clash with the KKK in South Carolina in the 1950s. Although he shared this story with Cuong, he was reluctant to do so with others. His politics were clear—he often become irate when "white people treated black people like slaves." However, Cuong knew little about his global activism. Kamarakafego was secretive and possessed several passports. When Cuong inquired about it, he responded that he needed to use different passports because he was being watched by the Establishment.[89]

An extra passport can have many uses. As a case in point, Kamarakafego was in Vanuatu when France staged an unsuccessful military coup to sabotage the country in the dawn of its independence. Aware of this plan, the National Party invited the PNG military to ostensibly to take part in its independence ceremonies. However, they were prepared to put down the revolt, which took place in the island of Espiritu Santo via Jimmy Stevens. According to Sope, in response, the party proceeded to deport French co- lons—Kamarakafego had suggested that they all be removed. As the condo- minium's administrations had not created passports for Ni-Vans, the party did not know what size to make the deportation stamp. In an ironic twist of fate—as Kamarakafego's passport carried such a stamp—they used one of *his* passports to mark its dimensions. Sope humorously recalls that they deported so many persons that they ran out of ink and wore out the stamp.[90]

In Vanuatu, Kamarakafego was known for cooking, crocheting, and ha- bitually listening to music. He played artists from across the African Dias- pora, such as West African highlife musicians and Reggae artists such as Bob Marley. According to Sope, Kamarakafego wired speakers throughout his home—including in the bathroom. He never had political conversations unless music was playing, as he felt that the music would interrupt any wire- taps.[91] Ayamiseba recalls this as well. The Black Brothers went into self-exile in Vanuatu in 1979 and performed at its independence ceremonies. Mean- while, they continued to build relationships with Kamarakafego.

In 1983, Kamarakafego's contract in Vanuatu expired. The personal, pro- fessional, and political relationships that he embraced in Oceania signifi- cantly impacted on the rest of his life. The next and final chapter spans his return to the Americas, where his activism in the areas of sustainable development, renewable energy, and pan-Africanism continued over the next two decades.

11

Environmental Justice

A Global Agenda for Pan-Africanism

On June 16, 1989, the *Bermuda Sun* ran an article titled "Pan-Africans Mourn CLR James." Two weeks before, the elder pan-Africanist organizer had passed away in London at the age of eighty-eight. In the post, veteran journalist Meredith Ebbin interviewed Kamarakafego about his thirty-year-plus friendship with James. Playing on James's astute use of cricket as a political metaphor, Kamarakafego described him as a "good batsman" who had "an extremely good innings" and was not bowled out but retired.[1]

James had arguably more political significance on Kamarakafego's life than any other figure. As a physical presence, as words handwritten on letters sent from across the world, in the books that he mailed to him, as a harsh or comforting voice over a long-distance telephone call—James had *always* been there for Kamarakafego through his adult life. And the feeling was mutual—in 1970, James asked Kamarakafego to travel with him to Trinidad and Tobago as his bodyguard. Theirs was far more than a political relationship. In fact, Kamarakafego often disagreed with Trotskyite James politically. For example, Kamarakafego was not a Marxist. He often shared a story from Tanzania as shorthand for explaining his position on Marx. After a Western professor attempted to explain to a farmer that the latter's practice of distributing equally to his neighbors his excess harvests was "an excellent Marxist principle," the farmer asked, "Who was Marx?" When the professor pressed that Karl Marx was German, the farmer retorted that his father's father had taught him that the Germans had been their colonial enemies—as such, what did this make Marx? Finally, the farmer asserted in Kiswahili, with arms extended, that this thing called Marxism was an extension of traditional "African socialism."[2]

Still, Kamarakafego did share James's commitment to the liberation of all oppressed peoples. Their relationship spoke to a form of masculine friendship of physical security, while Kamarakafego's preparation of Caribbean foods for James often obscured the intensity of their political movements. Over the years, Kamarakafego had listened to James and his father decry racism, visited him in London, cooked James ackee and saltfish, invited him to Bermuda to speak at the 1969 Black Power Conference, traveled to see him, and called on him to sponsor 6PAC. But for the twenty years after his transition, James was not there to physically witness, critique, or assist in Kamarakafego's life as the former continued to make an impact across the Global South in the areas of environmental justice.

Loss is a part of life. But despite losing James, Kamarakafego was far from being politically alone. He lived by a mantra: "Two together, one never lonely." According to Garrett, this referred to the idea that activists who had at least one ally working against oppression somewhere in the world was not working alone.[3]

Upon his return to the Americas, Kamarakafego worked extensively as an environmental activist, broadly in the area of renewable energy within the framework of the UN's Commission on Sustainable Development (CSD). His networks across the Global South expanded through his advocacy of Small Island and Developing States (SIDS) and NGOs focused on sustainable development. From Bermuda, he served as the coordinator for the International Network of Small Island Developing States, NGOs, and Indigenous Peoples (INSNI). By 1994 he had helped to officially establish the pan-African movement as an NGO in the CSD. His dual advocacy in the areas of pan-Africanism and environmental justice demonstrate an oft-overlooked relationship between black political and environmental freedom struggles across the Global South. Still, he found time to mentor generations of activists, students, and political organizers in Bermuda.

At the time of the *Sun* article, Kamarakafego was the publicity and participation secretary for the international coordinating committee of the Seventh Pan-African Conference (7PAC). James had agreed to serve as a patron for the congress. In 1990, the Executive Council of 7PAC included Nigeria's chairperson Naiwu Osahon, Papua New Guinea's (PNG) Bernard Narokobi, Guam's Laura Torres, Vanuatu's Grace Mera Molisa, and Acklyn Lynch. Fiji's Griffen also communicated extensively with Osahon regarding delegates from Oceania. The demographics of the committee reflected Kamarakafego's decades of building pan-Africanist relationships with organizers based across the Atlantic, Indian, and Pacific Ocean worlds. In February 1992, Kamarakafego discussed goals for 7PAC in the pan-African movement's journal, *Third World First*. Osahon edited the journal, which was published through his Heritage Books (formally Di Negro Press). He self-published several books, such as *Black Power: The African Predicament* (1976).[4]

If the journey toward organizing the Sixth Pan-African Congress (6PAC) was a long, tenuous, and complicated one that has been largely ignored by scholarship, the road to 7PAC was an even more quietly cantankerous and drawn-out affair. Correspondence between Osahon and Kamarakafego reveal the latter's intricate involvement in the talks. In October 1988, Osahon wrote to Kamarakafego suggesting that by virtue of his experience in convening 6PAC, he was an invaluable asset to 7PAC's international Steering Committee. He agreed with Kamarakafego's apparent suggestion that he needed to be on 7PAC's Planning and Coordinating Committee. Osahon invited to the talks all of the persons that Kamarakafego had suggested and agreed with his proposal to divide the world into West, East, North, South, and Central Africa, North and South America, the Caribbean, Europe, Asia, and the South Pacific. Working with scholars such as Chinweizu, he hoped that it would take place in Nigeria, since that country had the black population, market, and intellectual and technological capacity to launch the black "race strongly into the twentieth century."[5]

Kamarakafego submitted to the 7PAC secretariat a globally relative discussion paper with recommendations for the talks. He argued that the goal of 7PAC should be to establish a working relationship of cooperation between people from the Global South to work toward independence, self-determination, self-defense, dignity, prosperity, and empowerment. The congress would collectively pool human and natural resources and skills for the liberation of "our people—the African citizens . . . of Africa, the Polynesians, Melanesians, and Micronesians . . . of the South Pacific, the Aborigines of Australia, the Maoris of New Zealand, the South Americans, the citizens of the Caribbean, and the blacks and minorities in Europe and America."[6]

For Kamarakafego, the common denominator that linked these groups was their economic conditions, as the multinational companies and industrialized countries raped their natural and human resources. These communities needed to collectively combat these commercial interests that inhibited their efforts for self-determination under the guise of private enterprise and with the backing of industrialized military might and state power. As such, it was important to politically "organize the largest mass of people possible" across the world. Furthermore, 7PAC needed to be an open forum where people from all countries could have a voice.[7]

Kamarakafego saw 7PAC as a continuation of Garvey's "Back to Africa" movement, Du Bois's NAACP, George Padmore's Pan-African movement, the Maasina Ruru self-determination movement of the Solomon Islands, the efforts of Malcolm X and Mahatma Gandhi, and the fights against British colonialism by Pemulwuy's guerillas in Australia, the Maoris in New Zealand, and the indigenous warriors of Fiji.[8]

He called for the congress to function as a unified body to put pressure against colonial and multinational company exploitation in places such as New Caledonia, Tahiti, Maori communities of New Zealand, East Timor, the Moluccans, South Africa, Aboriginal communities in Australia, the Carolina Islands, Hawaii, Guam, Guadeloupe, Martinique, Saba, Eustatia, Anguilla, Turks and Caicos Islands, Puerto Rico, the Netherland Antilles, French Guiana, and Bermuda. The members of these semi-stateless communities, Kamarakafego argued, were "on the bottom rung of the economic ladder."[9]

Southern Africa needed to be a central theme of the congress. Kamarakafego stressed that the bulk of the Western world's finances—thus its power over the Global South—came from its mining, through the exploitation of African labor, of South Africa's gold, diamonds, and other precious metals. "Eighty-five percent of the gold in the possession of Europe and America," he argued, came from South Africa. "Once a month gold [was] transported from South Africa to Switzerland in boxcar carriers escorted by six fighter jets." This hard currency of diamonds and gold kept the Western world's dollars, pounds, yen, lira, and francs afloat. Hence, southern Africa's liberation would help significantly to free the oppressed world.[10]

He thus called for 7PAC to develop a formal method for gathering and codifying intelligence about the production and distribution of precious metals and ores from across Africa, Oceania, South America, and the Caribbean. This included raw industrial materials and energy sources like uranium, iron ore, platinum, and uranium oxide, which were cultivated in South Africa, Australia, and Namibia but drove factories in the West. The bulk of the world's copper came from Chile, Zambia, Zaire, and PNG; most bauxite was extracted in Jamaica, Australia, Guyana, and Guinea; and the mass of phosphates for fertilizers was culled from Mauritania, Morocco, Spanish Sahara, Nauru, and Banaba.[11]

Kamarakafego's paper also addressed food security, rising populations, sustainable housing, the creation of a technologically advanced research center, education, culture, history, identity, diet, and the nuclear-free zone in Oceania. He argued that while the Global South produced the world's supply of food and raw materials, it still carried the burden of issues of starvation and inadequate housing. He attached his proposals on reclaiming the Sahara desert, *A House for Every Family*, and an appropriate-technology policy paper produced by 6PAC's Society of Scientists and Technologists for African Development.[12]

Kamarakafego's paper also called for the expansion of cultural centers to "reinforce the true nature" of the heritage of the Global South. He cited a 1987 UN General Assembly resolution that called for the return of all works of art to the countries of their origin. He remarked that France held artifacts from New Caledonia, Tahiti, Wallis and Futuna, and Vanuatu, and that Britain held pieces from Africa, the South Pacific, the Caribbean, and Asia. He asserted, "We must get back from all the museums and universities our cultural artifacts and fossils, even if we have to organize vigilante groups to take them back."[13]

Amid much controversy—and the absence of Osahon—7PAC eventually took place in 1994 in Kampala, Uganda. It passed twenty-nine resolutions. A full analysis of these is out of the scope of this project, but mention must be made of them. The congress called for a representative pan-African parliament and a pan-African secretariat to further institutionalize the congress; an African country to be placed on the UN Security Council; the congress to have observer status at the Organization of African Unity (OAU); the recognition of Malcolm X as a pan-Africanist (noting that his Organization of Afro-American Unity had established chapters in Ghana, Trinidad and Tobago, France, London, and Manchester); Africana governments ensure the protection of rights and development of black children, with an emphasis on girls and street children; the formation of a pan-African medical association to address health issues in the Diaspora (like the AIDS epidemic) and that would respect African traditional medical practices; the protection of the pan-African movement from state repression; the OAU to ask the United States to release all its political prisoners; an end to colonialism in the Caribbean, including in Puerto Rico, Martinique, Guadalupe, Curaçao, Aruba, the British Caribbean, and the Virgin Islands; emancipation from mental slavery and the marginalization of black people living in Brazil and Latin America; and reparations for the African holocaust.[14]

Specifically referring to the United Kingdom, 7PAC demanded support for asylum seekers there; an end to police harassment and surveillance of black, migrant, and refugee communities under the pretext of immigration control; halting the criminalization of illegal entry and over staying of migrants; the removal of police, security forces, and private security firms in detentions and deportation enforcement; and the immediate release of detainees in prison and detention centers in violation of their human rights. Recalling the Chinese, Vietnamese, and Cuban revolutions and the words of Marcus Garvey, 7PAC stressed that "Africans at home and abroad" should control their means of production and ensure financial independence of the congress.[15]

The Seventh Pan-African Congress adopted the calls by women participants that a women's section be constituted within the 7PAC secretariat and that a pan-African women's movement be established to ensure the equal partnership of African women in the struggle. It called for the formation of a pan-African youth congress to facilitate networking between youth movements in Africa and the Diaspora, educational programs for the technological transfer and science, and respect for youth movements, in particular the Rastafari community and student groups.[16]

The congress called for the Diaspora to make concerted efforts to connect with Brazil to globally participate in its day of African consciousness (November 20) in recognition of the seventeenth-century quilombo leader Zumbi. It recognized the syncretic African religions of the Diaspora (such as Lucumi, Vodun, and Candomblé), and urged the Brazilian government to end black cultural genocide, the systematic killing of impoverished Afro-Brazilian children, and human rights violations against Afro-Brazilian prisoners and activists. The congress noted Cheikh Anta Diop's observation that Africans shared a common soul with Aborigines, the peoples of PNG, and other black indigenous peoples. It called for global attention to be placed on the crises in Rwanda, Somalia, Sudan, Haiti, and Angola and for the support of Cuba, Palestine, South Africa, Libya, and North Korea. Finally, it decided that an eighth PAC should be held in Tripoli, Libya.[17] The focus of 7PAC on questions of immigration, xenophobia, South Africa, and the Global South not only spoke to the political moment of black politics in the 1990s, but also have contemporary relevance.

In July 1989, Kamarakafego attended the 13th World Festival of Youth and Students in Pyongyang, North Korea. Organized by the anti-imperialist World Federation of Democratic Youth, the North Korea festival was the largest of its kind. Hosting some twenty-two thousand people from 177 countries, it was notably held previously in Cuba (1978 and 1979), the Soviet Union (1985), Algeria (2001), and Venezuela (2005). These festivals are underappreciated sites of black internationalism. For example, Angela Davis attended its 1962 festival in Helsinki, Finland.[18]

In this same year, Kamarakafego began serving on the UN's international task force for its 1992 Conference on Environment and Development. Held in Rio de Janeiro, Brazil, this historic meeting is now popularly known as the Earth Summit. As a member of the NGO steering committee, he worked on three pre-circulated documents for the talks—biodiversity, human settlements, and poverty, affluence, and consumption. He cochaired the NGO forum at preparatory talks for Rio in March-April 1992. He served as secretary on a plenary session that included Yolanda Kakabadse and the secretary-general of the summit, Maurice Strong. Kamarakafego also contributed to sessions on the transfer of environmentally sound technologies for sustainable development.[19]

More than 2,400 NGO representatives attended the two-week talks in Brazil. Kamarakafego helped to organize a parallel NGO forum at Rio's historic Hotel Gloria in which over seventeen thousand people participated. The summit produced a program of action for global sustainable development known as *Agenda 21*. This document argued that human beings were entitled to "a healthy and productive life in harmony with nature" and that the eradication of poverty, the worldwide reduction of disparities in standards of living, and the full participation of women, children, and indigenous communities were indispensable for achieving sustainable development. This included increasing the proportion of women as decision makers in the fields of environment and development. Sustainable development also entailed empowering indigenous communities and protecting their lands from "environmentally unsound" or "socially or culturally inappropriate activities."[20]

Rio was a fitting place to raise such questions. It held over 550 *favelas*, the largest of which, Rocinha, was located about thirteen kilometers from Hotel Garcia. The most populous of Brazil's *favelas*, Rocinha reflected the tensions of racism, capitalism, sexism, youth exploitation, and state violence in the country with the largest black population outside of Africa. With its "ramshackle and partly illegal electricity supplies and intermittent water supply but no closed sewers," Rocinha had only three schools and two small health clinics servicing its 250,000 inhabitants. According to journalist Andrew Garton, between seven and eight million children lived on Brazil's streets.[21]

The Earth Summit was thus set to be a prime moment for Brazil's social movements to place such concerns on the international stage. However, just the opposite occurred. In preparation for the summit, Brazil's police forcibly removed hundreds of street children from the wealthier parts of Rio and "dumped" them across favelas like Rocinha. During the summit, a heavy police and army presence of over twenty-five thousand troops marked the streets of Rio.[22]

Severina Euega, president of the Women's Association of Rocinha, decried these acts. In response, she organized walking tours for the summit's delegates and journalists to see these children and the challenging conditions of the favela. Kamarakafego likely participated on this tour. Two uncaptioned photographs in Me One depict him in Rio surrounded by about ten children—one young enough to have a pacifier in his mouth.[23]

The hotel was transformed into a site of protest, as a group of over fifty thousand trade unionists, welfare groups, religious groups, and their supporters protested the Brazilian government's logistical and financial support for the summit. Organized by Sonia Pimiento and the residents' associations of the State of Rio de Janeiro, marchers walked to the rhythms of Antenor de Assis's Samba "The Eco-Oppressed People" and chanted slogans such as "What is the use of all this ecology if our people are oppressed and massacred?"[24]

These voices of dissent were not heard inside the summit. Indeed, the talks were not inherently progressive, radical, or departures from the perspectives of the Global North. For example, Bermuda's official representative was the United Bermuda Party's Gerald Simons. However, a number of heads of state did speak for the Global South and influenced Agenda 21. Fidel Castro's statement asserted that consumer societies created by "old colonial metropolises and imperial policies" were mostly to blame for the environment's destruction. These societies accounted for only 20 percent of the world's population but consumed three fourths of the energy generated across the globe. They had "poisoned the seas and rivers," perforated the ozone layer, and created climatic changes whose catastrophic consequences were clearly evident in disappearing forests, desertification, and rapidly rising sea levels. Castro found it impossible to blame this on the formerly colonized Global South, as it was plundered by an "unjust international economic order" and had taken extreme and environmentally unfriendly measures just to survive. The answers to underdevelopment and poverty were linked to questions of ecology, and he called for a better global distribution of resources and technologies.[25]

Comprised of "brothers and sisters from the Caribbean, the Indian Ocean, the Mediterranean, and the Pacific Ocean," the Alliance of Small Island States (AOSIS) played a critical role at the summit. Its representatives pushed Agenda 21 to recognize their concerns, as sustainable development in SIDS was "complicated by small size, limited resources, geographic dispersion, isolation, and ecological fragility." Yet global warming and subsequent rises in sea level would render such states more vulnerable to storms and could lead to the loss of arable land.[26] This reflected AOSIS's efforts to collectively organize around issues of environmental justice. In 1987, the Maldives experienced record-setting tides that flooded its capital city of Malé. While the "science of climate change was still in its infancy," emerging evidence suggested a causal relationship between greenhouse gas emissions, burning fossil fuels, and rising global temperatures and sea levels. This prompted Maldives president Maumoon Abdul Gayoom to invite representatives from fourteen island states to the 1989 Small States Conference on Sea Level Rise. Its "Malé Declaration" on global warming and sea level rise was a pioneering global call for climate action that stated an intention "to work, collaborate and seek international cooperation to protect the low-lying small coastal and island states of the world from the dangers posed by climate change, global warming and sea level rise."[27]

These talks gave birth to AOSIS at Geneva, Switzerland's, 1990 Second World Conference on Climate Change. In Geneva, Vanuatu chaired the meeting through its permanent representative to the United Nations, Ambassador Robert Van Lierop. Originally from Surinam, Van Lierop was a veteran civil rights activist and lawyer in the United States. His documentary *Aluta Continua* focused on Mozambique's freedom struggle against Portuguese colonialism. In 1994, Ambassador Annette des Iles of Trinidad and Tobago became the second chair of AOSIS when the position rotated to the Caribbean.[28]

Now at Rio, Gayoom informed the summit that he was there as a "representative of an endangered people." As a result of rising sea levels, there were concerns that the islands might disappear from the face of the earth during the next century. He feared that the conference was the last opportunity to initiate global action to save these states from "becoming environmental victims." Gayoom projected an internationalist vision of SIDS that extended across the Atlantic, Pacific, and Indian Oceans. He argued that fifty thousand years ago, humans crossed the sea from Southeast Asia to establish Melanesia and Australia. Indian Ocean peoples founded the Maldives some 3,500 years ago, and the farther islands of the central Pacific followed 2,000 years prior. And when Columbus crossed the Atlantic a "mere" five hundred years ago, he found "prosperous and healthy people" already living in the Caribbean. These longstanding legacies on these islands established a tremendous cultural, religious, and linguistic diversity based on harmony with nature. Despite these varied patterns, such societies shared much in common—environmental dynamism, nautical knowledge, fishing, boat-building, sailing, and rope making. Now they had a common basis for unity through dependence on the sea and marine resources.[29]

While these societies had traditionally learned to adapt to such changes, their longstanding balance with the environment had been irrevocably changed by the over exploitation of natural resources and unprecedented population growth. Their severe local environmental problems included solid-waste disposal, marine pollution, coastal zone management, short-falls in supplies of construction materials, food and drinking water, and depletion of marine resources. The typical scientific and technical solutions for environmental issues had been devised for larger countries and did not work in SIDS where issues of scale, small and fragile economies, and "limited indigenous scientific and technical expertise" made such methods seemingly impossible. But, shared Gayoom, the Maldives had not "sat still" to wait for external solutions.[30]

Representatives of AOSIS, including the president of the Marshall Islands, Amata Kabua, echoed Gayoom's speech. Vanuatu's prime minister, Maxime Carlot, was pleased by *Agenda 21*'s island program. Denouncing nuclear testing in Oceania, Kiribati's Teatao Teannaki felt that *Agenda 21* should have given more consideration to radioactive pollution from nuclear weapons and other toxic substances. He also noted that Kiribati was party to the South Pacific Nuclear-Weapon-Free Zone Treaty.[31]

Bailey Olter, president of Micronesia and chairman of the South Pacific Forum, made his remarks on behalf of Australia, the Cook Islands, the Federated States of Micronesia, Fiji, Kiribati, the Marshall Islands, Nauru, New Zealand, Niue, PNG, the Solomon Islands, Tuvalu, Tonga, Vanuatu, and Western Samoa. He stated that many forum members sought stronger conventions on climate change and clear commitments to reducing carbon dioxide emissions. Climate change and rising sea levels were the most serious environmental threats to the islands of Oceania. Yet these islands had not created these problems, and the solution lay with those who purchased their "development with polluted currency." The region was also made vulnerable by the "attitude of many developed countries" that the Pacific was "a great, unpopulated void" that offered "opportunities to the rest of the world for convenient disposal of toxic, radioactive or otherwise harmful wastes, and for the conduct of any dangerous or obnoxious activity that could not safely be done in their own homes."[32]

While atomic hydrogen bomb testing had been suspended in the Marshall Islands for years, Olter stressed that inhabitants of the Marshall Islands still suffered from disease and disfigurement. There were also other threats. For example, the United States was carrying out a program on Johnston Island to incinerate stockpiles of chemical weapons. However, forum countries declared that Oceania should not be an area for "the development, storage, dumping or disposal of hazardous materials" and chemical weapons. Furthermore, while France had recently conducted nuclear testing in the Pacific, the Forum urged that this be turned into a permanent ban.[33]

Bikenibeu Paeniu, prime minister of Tuvalu, spoke about AOSIS's formation at Geneva, where "the world learned for the first time about the fate of the inhabitants of the small low-lying atoll nations" of the earth. It was there that he realized that as the only SIDS head of government from the Global South, he was on a mission to tell the world of the negative realities of climate change for SIDS, as opposed to scientific uncertainty. Now at Rio, he felt that their fight was just beginning.[34]

Erskine Sandiford, prime minster of Barbados, was somewhat disappointed with the summit, which he felt had not effectively dealt with the real impact of climate change. He urged for the stabilization and reduction of carbon dioxide and other greenhouse gas emissions, which were direct threats to SIDS. Noting that it had been agreed that a special conference on sustainable development and SIDS should be held in the next year, he offered Barbados as the venue for that conference.[35]

Kamarakafego returned to Bermuda after the summit. In 2012, Felix Dodds, Michael Strauss, and Maurice Strong recognized him as being one of the individuals who, since the original Earth Summit at Rio, "had provided invaluable dedication and wisdom to making multi-stakeholder cooperation work on the international stage." In July 1992, Kamarakafego informed Bermuda's *Worker's Voice* that the best thing about Rio was that it served as a networking space in which NGOs brought a grassroots focus into the UN. They had produced a host of alternative treaties on food security, sustainable agriculture, communication, and networks, such as the Treaty of the People of the Americas and the Treaty on Consumption and Lifestyle. These were living treaties that could be expanded on.[36]

Kamarakafego continued his involvement with SIDS through the CSD, which was formed to monitor the implementation of the Earth Summit's recommendations and *Agenda 21*. Kamarakafego attended the Preparatory Committee (PrepCom) meeting for the Barbados Global Conference on the Sustainable Development of SIDS in New York. Critical NGO voices included Jocelyn Dow of the Guyana Working People's Alliance. In August

1993, Dow informed PrepCom that SIDS were fighting for the right of self-determination and that others were determining their very survival.[37]

At PrepCom, Kamarakafego was selected to coordinate the Barbados NGO Forum, a series of workshops centered on alternative action models of sustainable development for SIDS. Parties interested in the forum contacted him at the NGO Liaison Secretariat in Garrison, Barbados. These efforts occupied his time through 1993.[38]

Pressed to do "a year's work in six months," his commitments did not go unnoticed. In November 1993, Tonga's Lopeti Senituli wrote to him in Barbados. The longtime Nuclear Free and Independent Pacific Movement activist and director of the Fiji-based Pacific Concerns Resource Center sent him greetings from Suva: "I hope you are well prepared for the 'unenvious' task ahead of you. Come to think of it," he continued, "it seems that organizing the 'unorganizable' seems to be a passion of yours! Rio! New York!" Senituli wished him well in his preparatory work. As he was working with other Fijian NGOs to prepare for Barbados, Senituli asked Kamarakafego to keep him abreast of new information about the talks.[39]

The Barbados talks were the UN's first Global Conference for the Sustainable Development of SIDS. Held from April 25 to May 6, 1994, it featured delegates from over 130 countries. Kamarakafego represented the pan-African movement at the NGO Forum. During its plenary session, he argued that sustainable development needed to be rooted in sustainable livelihoods, human development, and respect for the rights of indigenous peoples. Other pan-African movement representatives there were Panama's Waldaba Stewart and Cuba's Damodar Peña Penton, who called for the end of the economic blockade of Cuba and debt forgiveness for SIDS.[40]

According to *Earth Negotiations*, the newsletter of the International Institute for Sustainable Development, the NGO Forum was a "source of great energy and unity" in Barbados. It stimulated future international collaborations between NGOs, which were critical of AOSIS for not adequately addressing their concerns. Without these NGOs, the conference would have been solely an exercise in diplomatic rhetoric rather than an experience that could truly benefit the people of SIDS. *Earth Negotiations* expressed disappointment over the Barbados Declaration, which, while intended to be a program of action, was little more than the "Barbados Whimper"—a "glorified UN resolution." Yet without NGO input, it would have been "less people-centered." The impact of NGOS was clearly seen in the program's language around partnerships with women, local communities, youth, and indigenous people.[41]

The NGO action plan called for a resolution to establish INSNI. In Barbados, elected NGO representatives from across the Atlantic, Indian, and Pacific oceans formed the network. It also included members of these groups who were part of Diasporas living across Europe, America, and Australia but who wanted to contribute to the development of their island homes. Headquartered in New York City, INSNI was based on a database of names and contact addresses established in Barbados.[42]

Kamarakafego served as INSNI's international coordinator, which lobbied governments around issues of renewable energy, clean air, and the phasing out of fossil and nuclear fuels because of their environmental hazards. Over the years, it worked with NGOs such as the Caribbean Policy Development Center, the Caribbean Community and Common Market (CARICOM), and the Fiji-based Pacific Resources Center.[43]

By 1995, INSNI was headquartered in Bermuda. In the spring of 1997, it proposed a Caribbean Regional Public Awareness Project to CARICOM's Caribbean Ministerial Meeting. According to Hazel Brown (executive officer, Network of NGOs of Trinidad and Tobago for the Advancement of Women), the five-year anniversary of the Rio summit was a good moment to review sustainable development in the Caribbean, the experiences of Caribbean SIDS and NGOs, and the implementation of *Agenda 21* in the region. The network was linked with networks of NGOS centered on sustainable development in the Caribbean and beyond. Its regional and international structure made it an influential vehicle for maintaining linkages with other NGO and governmental networks. It had the capacity to serve as a clearinghouse of outreach and public relations materials around sustainable development and could provide current information of relevance to the Caribbean. Through its "participatory, democratic and inclusive structure," it could ensure that other Caribbean countries—particularly non-independent ones—could be become fully involved in the globally integrated activities of SIDS. Given its broad technical expertise, INSNI could provide input for the sustainable economic and environmental conservation programs across the region. It sought to offer these services to Caribbean states as an independent contractor, including the capacity-building resources of the Southern Diaspora Research and Development Center, which was an outgrowth of the body.[44]

In April 1997, Kamarakafego participated in a two-week INSNI sustainable-community residency at Italy's world-renowned Bellagio conference center. He described this experience in the CSD/NGO Steering Committee newsletter *Outreach/Eco*. Hailing from across the Caribbean, Oceania, and the United States, the team of seven successfully demonstrated the feasibility of building a sustainable community. Samoan poet and president of the Pacific-Asia Institute for the Arts and Human Sciences, Caroline Sinavaiana-Gabbard, led the group.[45]

Through dialog, performance workshops, story, song, theater, dance, and video, this collective exchanged their cultural values by drawing on their respective Oceanic, Caribbean, African American, and Western cultural traditions. Out of this work they acquired a sense of mutual trust to "take the kind of personal risks that go with the creative process." This included creating a script "for an interdisciplinary performance piece shaped around themes of environmental and social justice . . . key elements in the goal of sustainable development." In doing so, they devised an intercultural model for producing community-based media by performance art and video.[46]

These efforts were part of preparations for Earth Summit II, which took place in 1997. Held at the UN's New York headquarters, Earth Summit II was charged with reviewing the progress made since Rio. According to *Outreach/Eco*, Kamarakafego was responsible for organizing NGO caucus speakers at the talks. In May 1996, the CSD held a two-day, high-level session in preparation for the summit. It was the first to follow up the implementation of *Agenda 21* in regard to oceans, seas, and SIDs. On May 3, 1996, Kamarakafego spoke before the high-level nineteenth session as a member of the pan-African movement on behalf of southern hemispheric NGOS, INSNI, and indigenous peoples across the world.[47]

Kamarakafego began his talk with the language of the Barbados declaration:

> We, the people of [SIDS] and low-lying coastal states of the Pacific, Caribbean, Atlantic, Indian, and Mediterranean Oceans, following in the footsteps of our ancestors, commit ourselves to safeguarding, promoting, and protecting the natural resources of the earth on behalf of our children for posterity.[48]

He called for the commission to recognize the importance of the International Decade of the World's Indigenous Peoples and to organize a day to highlight their concerns regarding the implementation of *Agenda 21*. As the issues affecting SIDS were already spelled out in the agenda, he drew special attention to climate change, the socioeconomic dislocation of SIDs by unfettered free international trade as opposed to fair, two-way trade systems, the destruction of coral reefs and accompanying ecosystems, and the unchecked negative environmental impacts of ships and tankers on SIDs.

He also stressed that *Agenda 21* was being inhibited because the promises of financial assistance for implementation had not materialized. He also called on the UN to deal with the problems of colonialism.[49]

While in New York for the summit, Kamarakafego was interviewed by Amy Goodwin on Pacifica Radio's *Democracy Now* about the impact of climate change on SIDS. In the interview, which occurred on Earth Day (April 22, 1977), Kamarakafego described how global warming affected small islands and atolls because it triggered an unnaturally rapid rise of sea levels. He spoke specifically about the Maldives, whose high elevation was thirty-five feet (ten meters). He warned that global warming could negatively impact island economies, causing increased hurricanes, typhoons, and similar storms, leading to poverty and degradation.[50]

Kamarakafego argued that one helpful solution was for SIDS to use renewable energy sources instead of fossil fuels. This would allow them to contribute to the lowering CO_2 emissions and also put pressure on larger industrialized nations to do the same. He described how AOSIS had taken the lead to push for renewable energy vis-à-vis nuclear and fossil fuels. It was also lobbying for a clean-air act and trying to decrease the price that small islands paid for oil, which was set by fixed global prices. Economically, SIDs could use other energy systems like wind, solar, and biomass that could benefit their economies.[51]

During Earth Summit II, Kamarakafego served as an alternate for the commission's southern-based multi-regional NGOs, representing both the pan-African movement and INSNI. His UN commission colleagues included New York–based Panamanians Esmeralda Brown and the aforementioned Stewart. Brown was the founder and chairperson of the Southern Caucus of NGOs for Sustainable Development. She also represented the Servicio de Paz y Justicia en America Latina and the Commission for Human Rights in Central America. Stewart, a New York State senator from 1968 to 1972, represented both the pan-African movement and the Southern Diaspora Region Network. He and Kamarakafego presented a background paper on technological cooperation, science, and polices at the CSD's sixth session in 1998. Kamarakafego invited Brown and Stewart to Bermuda in 2004, where they gave public lectures at the Bermuda College. Officially sponsored by the Foundation for Bermuda Studies, Brown spoke on protecting the rights of indigenous peoples, while Stewart focused on colonialism in the Caribbean.[52]

Two years later, in September 1999, Kamarakafego participated in the

Forum for Energy and Development's (FED) Global Conference on Renewable Energy, held on the Danish island of Ærø. Thomas Lynge Jensen, island project coordinator for FED, thanked Kamarakafego and INSNI for coordinating the event. The talk brought together thirty-four AOSIS member states and was the first time since the Barbados talks that it was possible to collectively share experiences and discuss strategies for renewable energy development in SIDS.[53]

René Karottki, chair of the conference, stated that the motivation for SIDS to highly prioritize renewable sources of energy was double-sided. The reality of long distances and small markets meant that small islands paid comparatively high costs for energy sources such as diesel oil. To provide relief for end users, governments of these spaces often spent a significant portion of their limited public resources to subsidize energy costs. Not enough attention was being placed on more sustainable solutions, which included both indigenous renewable energy sources and modern technologies. In addition, many small islands across the Global South were immediate victims of climate change and instability, reflected by rising sea levels and the increased number and intensity of tropical storms. The main cause for these climate problems, Karottki argued, was the emission of greenhouse gases, such as CO_2, from industrialized countries. It was important for the small islands to convince industrialized countries to reduce their consumption of fossil fuels by demonstrating in practice how modern economies could be driven by renewable sources of energy.[54]

As a member of the conference's International Advisory Committee, Kamarakafego gave an opening speech. Based in Bermuda at the time, this was one of the most critical papers that he had presented in his political career. It also reflected his life-long growth into a global activist for environmental and social justice.

For Kamarakafego, the approaching new millennium called for the charting of a better future than the past through sober reflection of global issues such as the distribution of wealth, the pursuit of international political progress, the dominance of the Global North over the Global South, and the unchecked usurpation of resources from developing states. He referenced the 1994 UN conference in Barbados, and declarations made there served as the basis for his comments.[55]

Kamarakafego asserted that the avarice of the last century had left two billion people—almost half the world's population—without access to energy. Energy, he argued, was "the most fundamental necessity" for human progress. Without it, he continued, we would not "even begin to reverse the imbalance" that existed "between the prosperity of the developed, and the poverty of the developing states. . . . We must find a better way."[56]

He cited a report published by the CSD's secretary-general that highlighted the benefits of renewable energy as opposed to "traditional" sources of fuel. The report found that the infrastructures of SIDS were typically inadequate for their populations and rural inhabitants who suffered the most from the lack of energy sources. One reason was that transportation systems were not designed to deliver the large kinds machinery that traditional fueling methods needed to efficiently distribute electricity in these areas. As such, the secretary-general called for the use of renewable forms of energy to solve these two inherent problems of distribution and appropriateness. It was clear that SIDS could not continue to import fuels in the next millennium. This forced significant trade imbalances, created dependence, was inefficient due to transportation and distribution issues, and was also environmentally harmful.[57]

In contrast, Kamarakafego argued, renewable energy based solely on natural resources like wind, water, and solar could help create independence for SIDS. He commended Barbados for having success with a sound infrastructure and good distribution of energy; at the time the country utilized solar for 23 percent of its energy production. This, he felt, was based on a positive "marriage between political will, commercial ingenuity, and sustainable development." Encouraged by these successes in Barbados with alternative and renewable energy sources, INSNI recommended that SIDS should create regionally based talent banks, where technologies best suited for these areas could be studied and educational information about these projects shared. Furthermore, the cultural diversities that impacted energy consumption in various countries were not insurmountable hurdles to collective action.[58]

Just as AOSIS was established as unified international front, he felt that SIDS could create regional bases of influence by sharing technology. Such countries could significantly decrease their research and development costs by collaboratively finding the efficient technologies for their regions. By creating larger technological markets, commercial entities could broaden their economic resources, allowing them to be more creative in funding, supplying equipment, and maintenance programs.[59]

Kamarakafego also referenced Bermuda, arguing that it was the "will of the Government" as opposed to funding that was the "major barrier to the proliferation of renewable energy sources." However, he was hopeful, as the island's first change of government since the introduction of party politics occurred in 1995, with the black- and working class–supported Progressive Labor Party (PLP) winning a landslide election. The government had taken a step toward embracing solar power when it removed customs duty costs from solar equipment imports. He then called for a subsequent conference in Bermuda, as Bermuda's minister of the environment was "a great proponent of renewable energy."[60]

The INSNI conference was supposed to take place in Bermuda in June 2000 to follow up on the Barbados plan of actions and recommendations from Denmark. In 2001, Kamarakafego participated in an AOSIS meeting in Nicosia, Cyprus. Here, he reiterated his position from 1994, that SIDS should use their renewable energy sources, and focus on diversified forms of energy like biomass and fuel cells while facing out fossil fuels.[61]

In 1995, Kamarakafego developed a rural water supply project in Jamaica, and in 1997 and 1998, he attended expert meetings on sustainable development in Vienna, Austria. He also conducted appropriate-technology workshops in Madras, India (1975), and Bulawayo, Zimbabwe (1981) and rural development projects with the European Economic Community focused on the Global South. In 1996, he submitted a best practice case study to the 1996 UN Conference on Human Settlements conference in Istanbul, Turkey, also known as Habitat II. On behalf of INSNI, he exhibited his nominated plans for building a water tank and a house with bamboo, "Building of Water Tank and House using Indigenous Materials." He referenced his work in Kavieng, PNG, and listed his partners Daniel Nato and Pedi Anis. Between 1977 and 1983, he built over forty-three tanks and fifteen houses in Oceania. These included models in Fiji and the Solomon Islands that he constructed through the sponsorship of the CFTC. "Building of a Watertank" was awarded as an example of a "Good Practice" among the 100 Best Practice's exhibit.[62]

Upon his return from Istanbul, he presented the Bermuda National Library with his books *A House for Every Family* and *How to Build a Watertank from Bamboo and Cement.* During a press conference, he talked about his presentation at Habitat II. He stressed that the submissions were what the UN considered to be workable and practical solutions for dealing with issues in urban and rural environments.[63]

In 1997, Kamarakafego traveled to Livingston, Guatemala, where he participated in the second annual assembly of the Organización Negra Centroamericana (ONECA). Known in English as the Central American Black Organization (CABO), ONECA was formed in Belize in 1995 as a network of sixteen Afro-descendant organizations across Central America. Its president was the late Honduran Celeo Alvarez Casildo, who also founded the Organization for Ethnic Community Development (ODECO).[64]

The conference in Guatemala was held in the Garifuna community of Labuga and coincided with the two-hundredth anniversary of the forced removal of the Garifuna from St. Vincent to Honduras. Located on the Caribbean coast, ONECA's members included La Organización Negra Guatemalteca and the Asociación de Mujeres Garifunas Guatemaltecas. This was an important moment for the Garifuna community across the Americas. Here they worked on the National Garifuna Council's draft language for a policy statement and preservation plan for the Garifuna nation. Translated into Spanish by ODECO and later discussed and ratified by ONECA, the statement made reference to the UN Draft Declaration of the Rights of Indigenous People. Considered a critical step in the revitalization of the Garifuna language, it claimed the right of the community to educate their children in Garifuna. Kamarakafego fully participated in the meeting. He drummed, listened to speeches, took photographs, dined, and danced. It is likely that he also attended ONECA's 1999 assembly in Bluefields, Nicaragua, in 1999.[65]

In September 2001, Kamarakafego participated in the UN World Conference Against Racism, Racial Discrimination, Xenophobia, and Related Intolerance (WCAR). He also attended the final preparatory meeting for WCAR, which took place in Geneva, Switzerland, in the spring of 2001. At WCAR, which was held in Durban, South Africa, Kamarakafego represented the pan-African movement, whose delegation also included Stewart and Bermuda's Eva Hodgson, Patricia Pogson, Rolfe Commissiong, and Graham Nesbitt.[66]

Kamarakafego joined the African and African Descendants Caucus, which represented NGOs from across Africa, Europe, Canada, the United States, Central and South America, and the Caribbean. The caucus's proposals to WCAR were produced via contentious debates around questions of reparations for the victims of slavery, the Atlantic slave trade, and colonialism. Kamarakafego's views on reparations were intriguing. He argued that reparations should be given to communities of African descent in the form of programs and projects for sustainable self-reliance as opposed to hard currency. Examples of such programs included the complete eradication of debt for developing countries, a continental satellite-driven communications network for Africa, infrastructure of roads and mass transit systems, development of health and education programs, implementation of housing systems, an efficient renewable energy system based on solar, wind, biomass, mini-hydro, and thermo wave energies, water and sanitation projects, and an African-wide development bank. He also suggested that reparations could be used to deal with natural disasters such as hurricanes, typhoons, earthquakes, flooding, and droughts and the creation and/or development of universities and technology banks. He felt that these programs needed to last as long as the amount of time that African-descended persons had been enslaved and colonized. Furthermore, compensation for these African communities needed to come from all European countries who participated in the Atlantic slave trade, all member states and institutions that participated in the Berlin conference of 1884–85, all religious institutions that "aided and abetted the enslavement and colonization" of the African world, all financial institutions that funded slavery and the trade, the Australian government and settlement companies that engaged in blackbirding and the genocide of indigenous persons in Oceania, and all present states, institutions, and individuals that benefited from the enslavement and (neo)colonialism of Africans and African-descended persons. According to Kamarakafego, the caucus adopted some of these proposals.[67]

Generally speaking, the caucus called for the recognition that the slave trade, slavery, and colonialism were crimes against humanity; that reparations for Africans and African descendants were essential to ending the inequality that had been derived from the slave trade, slavery, and colonialism; and that the contemporary economic basis of racism was a continuation of the economic basis of these three scourges. It also called for the adoption of specific public policies that corrected institutionalized racism with emphasis on education, health care, and environmental racism; addressed African and African-descendant women; and recognized the intersection of race, gender, and sexual orientation.[68]

Despite resistance from European representatives about the inclusion of the word "reparations" and debates among black delegates surrounding the nature of compensation, WCAR officially declared that slavery and the Atlantic slave trade were crimes against humanity and "among the major sources and manifestations of racism, racial discrimination, xenophobia and related intolerance." Its program of action called for the creation of special reconciliatory projects and programs in collaboration with Africana communities, the facilitation of technical exchanges, and investments in health care systems, education, public health, electricity, drinking water, and environmental control—these recommendations reflect the kinds of ideas that Kamarakafego put to the caucus.[69]

In March 2002, Kamarakafego participated in the NGO Southern Caucus of the CSD Summit in Algiers, Algeria. This was in preparation for the Global Peoples Forum at the World Summit on Sustainable Development (WSSD), which would be held later that year in Johannesburg, South Africa. According to Brown, in Algeria, Kamarakafego presented a paper on "The Future of Sustainable Development." Here he was also given an award as an Eminent Person in recognition of his longstanding commitment to sustainable development.[70]

The Network for Environment and Sustainable Development in Africa felt that the Algeria meeting was a milestone in the WSSD process in that it allowed southern NGOs to specifically address their concerns around sustainable development. Its key priorities included poverty eradication, sustainable development in SIDS and Africa, and the protection of natural resources, along with health, economic, and social development.[71]

Indeed, the summit's Algiers Declaration declared that racism and discrimination were serious obstacles to sustainable development. It called for the WSSD to address the impact of environmental racism on the peoples of the Global South, "particularly African, African descendant, and Indigenous Peoples" who were disproportionately impacted by environmental racism. Environmental racism included "the trans-boundary shipment of toxic waste from the north to the south" to sites near these populations. It also referred to double standards used in the extraction of natural resources leading "to detrimental health, environmental, socio-cultural, and economic problems, and irreversible damage to land, air, water, and all living organisms and people" of the Global South. The declaration also called for reparations for colonialism and slavery.[72]

Months later, Kamarakafego represented INSNI at South Africa's WSSD. Along with Brown, he was a member of the summit's International Steering Group. In addition to facilitating daily feedback sessions, the steering group organized a solidarity march of over ten thousand persons through the poverty-stricken township of Alexandria. While there, he rubbed shoulders with African National Congress leaders such as Zola Skweyiya.[73]

Held at Nasrec's Expo Center, Global Peoples Forum delegates represented the major social groups named in Rio's *Agenda 21*—"women, youth, labor, indigenous peoples, farmers, NGOs, and others including, disabled people, the elderly, faith-based organizations, peoples of African descent, social movements, people under foreign occupation, and other underrepresented groups." As key agents of social change and sustainable development, they sought to advance their causes through networks of people's groups and "in solidarity with impoverished, marginalized, and subjugated people the world over." At Rio, it was agreed that the protection of the environment and the promotion of socioeconomic development were "crucial pillars of sustainable development." However, they were disappointed that ten years later, there was a "visible lack of progress in the implementation" of programs to address such concerns. This was evidenced by an increasing gap between the Global North and the Global South, socioeconomic disparities between the rich and the poor—particularly in regard to the African Diaspora—and the continued degradation of natural resources.[74]

Bermuda

In this era, Kamarakafego continued to politically educate young blacks in Bermuda. The PLP's accession to government encouraged him to remain on the island. Kamarakafego consistently involved younger Bermudians in his work and social life. He hosted people of all generations at his home, told stories about Tanzania and African socialism, showed photographs of indigenous persons of the Andaman islands, convinced younger people to campaign for the PLP, pointed at maps, knitted sweaters, and served ginger lemonade. He captivated his guests and comrades with his intellect, global experiences, tales of his enigmatic escapades, cuss words, personal mistakes, wit, and vicious sense of humor. He left behind an impressive catalog of appropriate and inappropriate phrases like "backside," "kick them like a Belgium prince," and "mash them up."

Delight Vickers accompanied him to the CSD's sixth session of 1998. While there, she was officially titled as youth delegate of the pan-African movement. Nesbitt, a key member of both Bermuda's Industrial Union and Rastafari community, also attended this session. Vejay Steede, a poet, and Vickers, a graphic designer by profession, both played key roles in the production of Kamarakafego's autobiography, *Me One*. Steede edited the massive 424-page book, which he referred to as "a testament to the power of the human spirit." Vickers designed the book's fitting jacket cover, a photograph of Kamarakafego juxtaposed over a map of the world. This image captured his political orientation as a citizen of the Global South.[75] With much anticipation and fanfare, the book was published in 2002.

In 1999, Kamarakafego visited poetry ciphers like Neno Letu at Hubey's Bar. In 2000, he spoke at the Bermuda College's commencement, where his talk centered on sustainability and education. In 2002, he talked to high school students at Cedarbridge Academy about black Bermuda's freedom struggle through desegregation, Black Power, and universal adult suffrage.

In 2003, on the request of the author, he gave a lecture at Howard University's History Department titled "Pan-Africanism Lives!" Here he spoke about the political potential of science. Later that evening, he enthralled a graduate US history class about Black Power before whisking off to meet Sylvia Hill and friends for dinner. In 2004, he gave a community lecture on laws and regulations in Bermuda. This was part of the Historical Heart Beats lecture series organized by Dale Butler, minister of community affairs and sports.[76]

In March 1998, Kamarakafego served on a panel organized by Bermuda's Commission for Unity and Racial Equality about universal adult suffrage. He began with a reference to Bermuda's talk shows, which by then had become a key medium for public discussions of race, politics, and economics in Bermuda. He had heard people on the radio comment that they did not want to discuss Bermuda's historic racial problems, but he felt that the future depended on understanding the past and the present. In his talk, he drew on the UN's creation of the Decade to Combat Racism from 1994 to 2003.[77]

He also raised the issue of reparations, highlighting Bermuda's 1834 act "For the Abolition of Slavery in These islands, in Consideration of Compensation." This he considered to be one of the colony's "best kept secrets." It demonstrated that whites slave owners "prior to emancipation made sure that they took care of themselves financially." He detailed the act, which called for the appropriation of the "the Sum of Twenty Million Pounds Sterling" for persons "entitled to the services" of the manumitted. This "head-start" for whites since emancipation meant that Bermuda's racial, economic, and political playing field in had never been even. "What did enslaved persons get with their freedom?" he asked. "Manipulation, exploitation, domination, humiliation, taxation, and no representation, and racism which dehumanized them."[78]

Kamarakafego also described the relationship between racism, segregation, and Bermuda's education system. He argued that slavery had "clouded the contributions . . . that Africans and their descendants in the diaspora" had "made to world history, science, and the arts." He found it unjust that the funds of taxpayers had been used to perpetuate segregation in Bermuda. This system operated to the educational disadvantage of black people, promoted the concept of white supremacy, and prevented the possibilities of mutual respect between both groups. He recalled not being able to go to the library to read because blacks were not allowed to use it. At the post office, only whites were clerks, but black postmen lifted the heavy mailbags. At Miles Meat Market, the clerks were all white, and black customers were hurried out of their stores. At the docks on Front Street, black men unloaded all the heavy cargoes while white men gave them orders. He witnessed only black people going to jail while whites "got off" in the courts. Furthermore, Bermuda's governor was always a white man. Kamarakafego also recalled how conversations with James about Nkrumah—"Seek ye first the political kingdom and everything else comes"—his experience in Cuba, and independent Africa urged him to push for universal adult suffrage in Bermuda.[79]

Kamarakafego was a firm believer in political independence for Bermuda. In 1998, he wrote a recommendation for decolonization. In 2004, he resubmitted this proposal to the Bermuda Independence Commission. Kamarakafego saw independence as the first step toward self-determination and the best remedy for the island's social, economic, and political ills. His ideas included transforming Bermuda into a high-tech information center, which would not require much land space. The island's geographic location meant that it could headquarter an array of global institutions. He suggested that the island could host space-friendly international events like chess tournaments. Bermuda could also harness its natural resources, such as the ocean, in ways that would generate income globally.[80]

Health

Beginning in the mid-1990s, Kamarakafego experienced serious health challenges. In 1995, while in Washington, DC, he suffered a heart attack. He survived after undergoing triple bypass heart surgery at Howard University hospital. Kamarakafego was blessed to have the support of his close friends and family. While recuperating, he stayed with his longtime comrade, Acklyn Lynch. Griffen flew to see him during this time as well. In September of that year, he affectionately wrote to Baizum from Jamaica, informing him that he would not be able to work until the end of 1996. This impacted his plans to arrange for Baizum to come live with him; he did make good on that promise to Cuong and his son a few years later.[81] Baizum came to Bermuda to live, and while there fostered close relationships with his siblings across the Americas, such as Suzanne Darrell, Rronniba, Carla, and Catherine Kamarakafego. Through the Caribbean Friends of Cuba society, Kamarakafego arranged for Baizum to study in Cuba. In fact, he did the same for a number of Bermudians.

In June 2003, Lazaro Fleita Rodriquez, president of the Friends of Cuba society, visited Bermuda. Speaking before the Bermuda Industrial Union, he spoke about health care, education, and student scholarships in Cuba. In 2005, Kamarakafego helped to arrange scholarships for eight Bermudian students—Iman Gibbons, Zahra Muhammad, Kevin Darrell, Keishen Bean, Misheal Paynter, Malachi Muhammad, Jason Iris, and Shuaib "Shuki" Worrell.[82]

In April 2007, Kamarakafego succumbed to prostate cancer. While hospitalized at Lahey Hospital in Burlington, Massachusetts, he lamented to his daughters Rronniba and Suzanne that his children were not with him. It is left to another project to truly unpack the complications of Kamarakafego's politic work in the context of family, sacrifice, contradictions, and personal relationships. During his painful fight with cancer, caretakers Sofia Mohammad and Lucinda Worrell miraculously tended to him.[83]

Strong enough to return to Bermuda, he passed away soon after his arrival. His family, friends, and allies from across the world mourned and simultaneously honored "Roose" at a celebration of his life, held at Bermuda's National Stadium on April 20, 2007. Its twelve-page program speaks volumes about his global life. The selection was James Weldon Johnson's "Lift Every Voice and Sing." His sister Irene Maybury presented his ashes, his nephew Eugene Maybury read poetry, and niece Karen Paynter read the tributes. His niece Donna Williams read his obituary, which referenced his children and retold his numerous escapades in Bermuda and beyond. Ewart Brown, Bermuda premier and leader of the PLP, gave remarks, as did Bermuda's current premier, David Burt, as the PLP Party chairman. Kamarakafego's daughter, Rronniba Kamarakafego, gave a tribute.[84]

Kamarakafego's longtime comrade, Jimmy Garrett, had much to share. In addition to working together around 6PAC and the Center for Black Education, the two had collaborated on UN sponsored NGO environmental projects across Papua New Guinea, Tanzania, Vanuatu, Cuba, and Barbados. They had developed sustainable development projects to promote solar, wind, and biomass energy in SIDS across the Caribbean, the Indian Ocean, and the Pacific Ocean.[85]

Esmeralda Brown gave a tribute on behalf of the Southern Caucus of NGOs for Sustainable Development and referenced his UN ecological work. Guyana's Eusi Kwayana mentioned his design for new levies in the aftermath of hurricane Katrina and contextualized him within the tradition of Caribbean pan-Africanists. Hilda Lini noted that the prime minister of Vanuatu held a memorial service in his honor at the Anglican Church. This was where Kamarakafego had first met Walter Lini.[86]

In that same month, Lynch called for a moment of silence in recognition of Kamarakafego at the Kwame Ture Society Conference at Howard University. In 2008, Premier Brown eulogized him as the Father of Universal Adult Suffrage in Bermuda and "a champion of unity across the world, and one who's spirit beckoned us to continue to right wrongs." In 2011, under Brown's leadership, Kamarakafego was deservedly made a Bermuda National Hero, in the first class of such awards.[87] Still, Kamarakafego was a citizen of the black world who committed his life to self-determination and environmental justice across the Global South. He should also be remembered as such. *Me One.*

NOTES

Introduction

1. The National Archives of the UK (TNA): FCO 32/1231, Roosevelt Oris Nelson Brown.

2. TNA: FCO 32/1231, May 22, 1975 RWH du Boulay to Monsieur Gauger.

3. Kamarakafego, *Me One*, 241.

4. TNA: FCO 32/1231, June 26, 1975 Du Boulay to FCO; June 27, 1975 Callaghan to Flash Vila.

5. Kamarakafego, *Me One*, 245–46.

6. TNA: FCO 32/1231, July 1, 1975, du Boulay to AEW Bullock.

7. Kamarakafego, 245–46; Smithsonian Institution Archives of American Art, Jeff Donaldson to Toni Cade Bambara, February 11, 1976, Fundraiser for New Hebrides Islands, 1976, Box 11, Jeff Donaldson Papers.

8. C. L. R. James to Roosevelt Brown, October 5, 1976, Kamarakafego, *Me One*, 283.

9. Ibid., 17.

10. Ibid., 103.

11. Ibid., 132–33.

12. See Abschol, *Aborigines Visit the US*, Print Collection, Australian Institute of Aboriginal and Torres Strait Islander Studies, Canberra, Australia (AIATSIS).

13. See, for example, Baraka, *African Congress*; Johnson, *Revolutionaries to Race Leaders*; Esedebe, *Pan-Africanism*; Samanga, *Amiri Baraka and the Congress of African Peoples*; Slate, *Black Power Beyond Borders*; and Woodard, *A Nation Within a Nation*.

14. See Adi, *A History of Pan-Africanism*; Farmer, *Remaking Black Power*; Markle, *A Motorcycle on Hell Run*; Rickford, *We Are An African People*; Walters, *Pan Africanism in the African Diaspora*; and Williams, *Concrete Demands*. See also La TaSha Levy, "Remembering Sixth-PAC: Interviews with Sylvia Hill and Judy Claude, Organizers of the Sixth Pan-African Congress," *Black Scholar* 37, no. 4 (Winter, 2007): 39–47; and Wilkins, "A Line of Steel."

15. See Banivanua Mar, *Decolonisation and the Pacific*; Broome, *Fighting Hard*; Foley, "Black Power in Redfern, 1968–1972"; James Garrett, "The Sixth Pan-African Congress," *Black World/Negro Digest* 26, no. 5 (March 1975): 4–20; Swan, *Black Power in Bermuda*; and Swan, "Black Power in the African Diaspora."

16. See Butler, *Freedoms Given, Freedoms Won*; Gomez, *Reversing Sails*; Davies, *Caribbean Spaces*; Guridy, *Forging Diaspora*; Harris, *Global Dimensions of the African Diaspora*;

Lemelle and Kelley, *Imagining Home*; Mullings, *New Social Movements in the African Diaspora*; and Tolbert, *Perspectives on the African Diaspora*.

17. Lea Kinikini Kauvaka, "Berths and Anchorages: Pacific Cultural Studies from Oceania," *The Contemporary Pacific*, 28, No. 1 (2016): 134.

18. See Blain, *Set the World on Fire*; Blain and Gill, *To Turn the World Over*; Edwards, *Practice of Diaspora*; Merz Tate, "The War Aims of World War I and World War II," *The Journal of Negro Education*, 12, no. 3 (Summer 1943): 521; Nardal, "Internationalism Noir"; Putnam, *Radical Moves*; Robinson, *Black Marxism*; Sharpley-Whiting, *Negritude Women*; and West, Martin, and Wilkins, *The Black International*.

19. See Chambers, *Race, Nation and West Indian Migration to Honduras*; James, *Holding Aloft the Banner of Ethiopia*; James and Harris, *Inside Babylon*; and Putnam, *Radical Moves*.

20. See Adi, *Pan-Africanism and Communism* and Esedebe, *Pan-Africanism*.

21. See Bedasse, *Jah Kingdom*; Campbell, *Rasta and Resistance*; Gaines, *American Africans in Ghana*; and Horne, *Mau-Mau in Harlem?*

22. Gomez, *Reversing Sails*.

23. Amiri Baraka, "Some Questions about the Sixth Pan African Congress," *The Black Scholar* 6, no. 2 (1974): 42–46.

24. Adi, *Pan-Africanism*; Bedasse, *Rastafarians*; Farmer, *Remaking Black Power*; Fenderson, *Building the Black Arts Movement*; Markle, *A Motorcycle on Hell Run*; and Plummer, *In Search of Power*.

25. See Davies, *Left of Karl Marx*; Hill, Interview, "From the Sixth Pan-African Congress to the Free South Africa Movement"; Maloba, *African Women in Revolution*; McDuffie, *Sojourning for Freedom*; Gore, *Radicalism at the Crossroads*; Higashada, *Black Internationalist Feminism*; Horne, *Race Woman*; Johnson-Odim and Mba, *For Women and Nation*; Sherwood, 2000; Ransby, *Eslanda*; Taylor, *The Veiled Garvey*; Terborg-Penn and Harley, *Women in Africa and the African Diaspora*; Theoharis and Woodard, *Want to Start a Revolution?*; and Williams, *Lois: Bermuda's Grand Dame of Politics*.

26. The term "Black Pacifics" emerged out of a 2019 Harvard University Radcliffe Institute Exploratory Seminar *Towards a Black Pacific,* convened by Quito Swan and Glenn Chambers. See Adi, *Pan-Africanism*; Anderson, *Bourgeois Radicals*; Bedasse, *Rastafarians*; Blain, *Set the World On Fire*; Broome, *Fighting Hard*; Daulatzai, *Black Star, Crescent Moon*; Davies; Edwards, *The Practice of Diaspora*; Farmer, *Remaking Black Power*; Fenderson. *Building the Black Arts Movement*; Frazer, *The East Is Black*; Ho and Mullen, *Afro Asia*; Horne, *End of Empires*; Horne, *Race Woman*; Horne, *The End of Empire*; Horne, *The White Pacific*; Makalani, *In the Cause of Freedom*; Matera, *Black London*; Maynard, *Fight For Liberty and Freedom*; Meriwether, *Proudly We Can Be Africans*; Onishi, *Transpacific Antiracism*; Perry, *London is the Place for Me*; Prashad, *Everybody Was Kung Fu Fighting*; Shilliam, *The Black Pacific*; Taketani, *The Black Pacific Narrative*; Von Eschen, *Race against Empire*; and West, Martin, and Wilkins, *From Toussaint to Tupac*.

27. Agarwal, and Narain, *Global Warming in an Unequal World*; Asher, *Black and Green*; Caldwell, *Health Equity in Brazil*; Glave, *Rooted in the Earth*; Kamarakafego, *A House For Every Family*; Leach and Mears, *The Lie of the Land*; Maathai, *The Greenbelt Movement*; Mackenzie, *Land, Ecology and Resistance in Kenya*; Mortimore, *Adapting to Drought*; Mullings, *New Social Movements in the African Diaspora*; Nelson, *Body and Soul*; Reij, Scoones,

and Toulmin, *Sustaining the Soil*; Smith, *African American Environmental Thought Foundations*; and Suliman, *What Does it Mean to be Green in Africa?*

28. Maathai, *The Greenbelt Movement*; Major P. Okuntimo, Chairman Rivers State Internal Security (RSIS), to His Excellency, the Military Administrator Rivers State, May 12, 1994, Correspondence, PEN Records, 10–11, Harry Ransom Center for Humanities, University of Austin-Texas. Austin, Texas.

29. Ture and Hamilton, *Black Power*, 195.

30. Rodney, *Groundings With My Brothers*, 28.

31. Blyden, "The Call of Providence to the Descendants of Africa in America."

32. Drake, "Diaspora Studies and Pan-Africanism," 451–515.

33. Abu-Jamal, *We Want Freedom*; Ahmad, *We Will Return in the Whirlwind*; Allen, *Black Awakening in Capitalist America*; Austin, *Fear of a Black Nation*; Ball and Burroughs, *A Lie of Reinvention*; Benson, *Fighting For Our Place in the Sun*; Biondi, *The Black Revolution on Campus*; Bloom and Martin, *Black Against Empire*; Bradley, *Harlem vs. Columbia University*; Bradley, *Upending the Ivory Tower*; Brown, *Fighting for Us*; Carmichael, *Stokely Speaks*; Cleaver and Katsiaficas, *Liberation, Imagination, and the Black Panther Party*; Daulatzai, *Black Star, Crescent Moon*; Diouf, Woodard, and Gibran, *Black Power 50*; Farmer, *Remaking Black Power*; Fisbach, *Black Power and Palestine*; Ford, *Liberated Threads*; Glaude, *Is It Nation Time?*; Horne, *Fire This Time*; Jackson, *Blood in My Eye*; Jeffries, *Bloody Lowndes*; Jeffries, *Comrades*; Jeffries, *On the Ground*; Jones, *The Muse is Music*; Joseph, *Neighborhood Rebels*; Joseph, *Stokely: A Life*; Jones, *The Black Panther Party Reconsidered*; Joseph, *Waiting 'Til the Midnight Hour*; Kamarakafego, *Me One*; Kendi, *The Black Campus Movement*; Lewis, *Walter Rodney's Intellectual and Political Thought*; Marable, *Malcolm X: A Life of Reinvention*; Meeks, *Narratives of Resistance*; Muntaqim, *We Are Our Own Liberators*; Murch, *Living for the City*; Nelson, *Body and Soul*; Ogbar, *Black Power*; Plummer, *In Search of Power*; Quinn, *Black Power in the Caribbean*; Rickford, *We Are An African People*; Rodney, *The Groundings with My Brothers*; Rojas, *From Black Power to Black Studies*; Ryan and Stewart, *The Black Power Revolution 1970*; Self, *American Babylon*; Shakur, *Assata*; Shilliam, *The Black Pacific*; Shoatz, *Maroon the Implacable*; Slate, *Black Power Beyond Borders*; Spencer, *The Revolution Has Come*; Springer, *Living for the Revolution*; Swan, *Black Power in Bermuda*; Taylor, *The Promise of Patriarchy*; Tinson, *Radical Intellect*; Tyson, *Radio Free Dixie*; Umoja, *We Will Shoot Back*; West, Martin, and Wilkins, *From Toussaint to Tupac*; White, *The Challenge of Blackness*; Williams, *Black Politics White Power*; Williams, *Concrete Demands*; Williams, *From the Bullet to the Ballot*; Williams and Lazerow, *Liberated Territory*; Wilson, *Blueprint for Black Power*; Van Deburg, *New Day in Babylon*; and Young, *Soul Power*.

34. Plummer, *In Search of Power*, 17.

35. Peniel Joseph, "Black Power Studies: A New Scholarship," *The Black Scholar* 31, no. 3–4 (2001): 1; Peniel Joseph, "The Black Power Movement: A State of the Field," *Journal of American History* 96, no. 3 (December 2009): 751–76.

36. In addition to titles listed in note 32, this includes, Anne-Marie Angelo, "The Black Panthers in London, 1967–1972: A Diasporic Struggle Navigates the Black Atlantic," *Radical History Review* 2009, no. 103 (Winter 2009): 17–35; Association for the Study of the World Wide African Diaspora, "African Liberation and Black Power: The Challenges of Diasporic

Encounters Across Time, Space, and Imagination," *African Diaspora Archaeology Newsletter* 13, no. 2 (June 2010): 1–2; Biko, *I Write What I Like*; Anthony Bogues, "Black Power, Decolonization, and Caribbean Politics: Walter Rodney and the Politics of *The Groundings with My Brothers*," *boundary 2* 36, no. 1 (Spring 2009): 127–47; Robin Bunce and Paul Field, "Obi B. Egbuna, C. L. R. James and the Birth of Black Power in Britain: Black Radicalism in Britain 1967–72," *Twentieth Century British History* 22, no. 3 (September 2011): 391–415; Campbell, *Rasta and Resistance*; Carmichael and Thelwell, *Ready for Revolution*; Clemons and Jones, "Global Solidarity"; Coombes, *Is Massa Day Dead*; Egbuna, *The ABCs of Black Power Thought*; Foley, "Black Power in Redfern, 1968–1972"; V. P. Franklin, "Introduction: New Black Power Studies," *Journal of African American History* 92, no. 4 (Fall 2007): 463–66; Chris W. Johnson, "Guerrilla Ganja Gun Girls: Policing Black Revolutionaries from Notting Hill to Laventille," *Gender & History* 26, no. 3 (November 2014): 661–787; William Lux, "Black Power in the Caribbean," *Journal of Black Studies* 3, no. 2 (1972): 207–25; Hanchard, *Orpheus and Power*; Joseph, *Stokely*; Kathy Lothian, "Seizing the Time: Australian Aborigines and the Influence of the Black Panther Party, 1969–1972," *Journal of Black Studies* 35, no. 4 (March 2005), 179–200; Nkrumah, *The Struggle Continues*; Palmer, "Identity, Race and Black Power in Independent Jamaica"; PKGC, "Black Power Conference"; Victoria Pasley, "The Black Power Movement in Trinidad: An Exploration of Gender and Cultural Changes and the Development of a Feminist Consciousness," *Journal of International Women's Studies* 3, no. 1 (2001): 2; Ryan and Stewart, *The Black Power Revolution 1970*; Thomas, *Black Power in the Caribbean*; Bert Thomas, "Caribbean Black Power: From Slogan to Practical Politics," *Journal of Black Studies* 22, no. 3 (1992): 392–410; Trew, *Black For a Cause*; Sawyer, *Racial Politics in Post-Revolutionary Cuba*; Singh, *Black Is a Country*; and Sykes, *Snake Dreaming*.

37. Garvey, *Black Power in America*; Nkrumah, "Message to the Black People in Britain"; Rodney, *The Groundings With My Brothers*, 28. Ture and Hamilton, 46;

38. Joseph, *Dark Days*, 9–10. For more extensive critiques of this perspective, see Ball, "Defining Black Power"; Jonathan Fenderson, "Towards the Gentrification of Black Power (?)" *Race & Class* 55, no. 1 (2013): 1–22; Quito Swan, "Caveat of an Obnoxious Slave: Decolonizing Black Power Studies From the Intellectual Governors of White Supremacy," *Journal of Pan-African Studies* 6, no.13 (2013): 56–71; and Malcolm X, "Message to the Grassroots."

39. See, for example, Austin, *Up Against the Wall*; Bukhari, *The War Before*; Churchill, *The COINTELPRO Papers*; Churchill and Vander Wall, *Agents of Repression*; Conway and Stevenson, *Marshall Law*; Davenport, *Media Bias, Perspective, and State Repression*; Hass, *The Assassination of Fred Hampton*; James, *Imprisoned Intellectuals*; James, *Warfare in the American Homeland*; Penn, *Case for Pardon*; Bin-Wahad, "Assata Shakur"; and West, "Seeing Darkly."

40. Cha-jua, Sundiata Keita, and Clarence Lang, "The 'Long Movement' As Vampire: Temporal and Spatial Fallacies in Recent Black Freedom Studies," *Journal of African American History* 92, no. 2 (2007): 265–88; Gore, *Radicalism at the Crossroads*; Hill, *Deacons for Defense*; Jeffries, *Bloody Lowndes*; McDuffie, *Sojourning for Freedom*; Murch, *Living for the City*; Perry, *London is the Place for Me*; Plummer, *In Search of Power*; Umoja, "Repression Breeds Resistance"; and Von Eschen, *Race Against Empire*.

41. See Bedasse, *Rastafarians*; Cabral, *Unity and Struggle*; Chinweizu, *The West and the Rest of Us*; Daulatzai, *Black Star, Crescent Moon*; Fela and Afrika 70, *Sorrow Tears and Blood*;

Levy-Hinte, *Soul Power*; Markle; *A Motorcycle on Hell Run*; Mokthefi, *Algiers, Third World Capital*; and Tyson, *Radio Free Dixie*.

42. "Interrelationship of Black Power Organizations in the Western Hemisphere," Intelligence Evaluation Committee (IEC), US Department of Justice, January 4, 1972, *U.S. Declassified Documents Online*, accessed September 11, 2018, Woodrow Wilson International Center for Scholars, Washington, DC.

43. Gerald Horne, "Toward a Transnational Research Agenda for African American History in the 21st Century," *Journal of African American History* 91, no. 3 (Summer 2006): 288–303.

Chapter 1. Corner Stones: Hamilton, Harlem, and Havana

1. Brownlow Place, interview by author.

2. *Negro World*, December 1, 1928.

3. Swan, "Bermuda Looks to the East: Marcus Garvey, the UNIA, and Bermuda"; *Wadabegei: A Journal of the Caribbean and Its Diaspora* 13, no. 1 (2010), 30–33.

4. Kamarakafego, *Me One*, 25.

5. Ibid.

6. F. Goodwin Gosling, "A Housing Scheme for Bermuda," June 30, 1930, CO 37, Bermuda Archives, Bermuda.

7. Kamarakafego, *Me One*, 25–31.

8. M'Baye, *The Trickster Comes West*.

9. Kamarakafego, *Me One*, 17, 25.

10. Ibid., 32.

11. Ibid., 27.

12. Ibid., 28.

13. Ibid., 25–32, 36.

14. Parsons, "Bermuda Folklore," *The Journal of American Folklore* 38, no. 148 (April-June 1925): 239.

15. Kamarakafego, *Me One*, 32.

16. "More Vexing Problems," *Bermuda Recorder*, October 12, 1935, 2, 7.

17. Kamarakafego, *Me One*, 30–31.

18. Ibid.

19. Ibid., 38.

20. William Drysdale, "Civilization in Bermuda," *New York Times*, July 6, 1890.

21. "A Celebration of the Life of Dr. Pauulu Roosevelt Osiris Nelson Brown Kamarakafego," Obituary, April 20, 2007.

22. Kamarakafego, *Me One*, 36.

23. Ibid.

24. Kamarakafego, *Me One*, 25–26, 84. For further discussion on Gordon, see Philip, *Freedom Fighters*.

25. Kamarakafego, *Me One*, 75.

26. Ibid.

27. Ibid.

28. "Cuba, Chaparra Sugar Factory," *International Sugar Journal* 3, no. 29 (May 1901):

229; "News From Our Havana Office," *The Louisiana Planter and Sugar Manufacturer* 53, no. 5 (August 1914): 73; McGillivray, *Blazing Cane*, xvi, 77.

29. Gott, *Cuba*, 127.

30. Howard, *Black Labor*, 125.

31. See Putnam, *Radical Moves*, 6–16.

32. Kamarakafego, *Me One*, 74.

33. Ibid.

34. Ibid.

35. Ibid.

36. Ibid.

37. Ibid.; "Names and Descriptions of British Passengers Embarked at the Port of Liverpool," September 8, 1953," Ancestry.com, *UK, Outward Passenger Lists, 1890–1960*.

38. "US Explorers go to Caribbean Jamboree," *Scout World* 42, no. 5 (May 1952): 1.

39. Kamarakafego, *Me One*, 75.

40. Ibid.

41. Ibid., 73–77.

42. Ibid.

43. Ibid.

44. Ibid.

45. Shayne, *The Revolution Question*.

46. Kamarakafego, *Me One*, 34, 75.

47. Ibid., 84.

48. Elton Beane, "So this is New York," *Bermuda Recorder*, September 4, 1954, 2; October 27, 1954, 2; August 28, 1954, 1; "Local Youths Return From Extensive United States Tour," September 17, 1955, 1; Kamarakafego, *Me One*, 84.

49. Scott, "Islander," 178–79.

50. "Letter from New York University Student Council School of Education to W. E. B. Du Bois," January 25, 1951; "Letter from W. E. B. Du Bois to New York University Student Council School of Education," January 31, 1951; W. E. B. Du Bois Papers (MS 312), Special Collections and University Archives, University of Massachusetts Amherst Libraries, Amherst, MA.

51. Kamarakafego, *Me One*, 84.

52. Ibid.

53. Ibid.

54. "Paul Robeson, Plaintiff-Appellant against Jean Foster Dulles, Defendant-Appellee, Document United States court of appeals, District of Columbia," 1956; Correspondence with Eslanda Robeson, Box 131-14, E. Franklin Frazier Papers, Moorland-Spingarn Research Center (MSRC), Howard University, Washington, DC.

55. Kamarakafego, *Me One*, 84.

56. See Horne, *Red Seas*; Jones, "An End to the Neglect of the Problems of the Negro Woman," 262; Claudia Jones, "Dear Comrade Foster," *American Communist History* 4 (2005): 85–93.

57. Kamarakafego, *Me One*, 87.

58. Ibid.; Year: *1955*; Arrival: *Idlewild Airport, Idlewild, New York*; Microfilm Serial: *T715,*

1897–1957; Microfilm Roll: *Roll 8557*; Line: *6*; Page Number: *210*; Ancestry.com, *New York, Passenger and Crew Lists (including Castle Garden and Ellis Island), 1820–1957*.

59. Kamarakafego, *Me One*, 87.

60. Carol B. Barker, "Meet Jim Clyburn," *Times and Democrat*, January 5, 2007.

61. Kamarakafego, *Me One*, 87.

62. Ibid.

63. "Gloster Current to NAACP Branch Officers in the State of New York," December 9, 1955, Reprisals South Carolina, II:A508, Records of the National Association for the Advancement of Colored People (NAACP), Manuscript Division, Library Of Congress, Washington, DC.

64. "Unknown Subject, Rev. J. A. De Laine," October 10, 1955, Government Document, 1955, 1956, (Washington, DC), Rev. Joseph A. De Laine, Sr., File # HQ 9–28873, Federal Bureau of Investigation; Digital Collections, Joseph A. De Laine Papers, South Caroliniana Library, University of South Carolina, Columbia, South Carolina.

65. "S.C. Whites Burn Church to Chase Minister," *Jet*, October 20, 1955, 3–4; "Negro Postmaster Murdered," *Yorkville Enquirer*, February 22, 1898, 1; "The Assassination of Postmaster Baker," *Democrat and Chronicle*, February 26, 1898, 1.

66. "The Rev. Delaine Case," *Bermuda Recorder*, November 30, 1955, 4; "Hoover, Air-Tel to SAC," Government Document, 1955, 1956; Accessed May 18, 2017; "J. Edgar Hoover to J. DeLaine, 12 September 1955," Government Document, 1955, 1971, 1973, Rev. Joseph A. De Laine, Sr., File # HQ 44–9481; Accessed May 18, 2017; Joseph De Laine Papers.

67. "DeLaine to J. Edgar Hoover," October 13, 1955, Government Document, 1955, 1956; *Jet*, October 3, 2000, 30; "S.C. Minister forced to use shotgun," *Jet*, October 27, 1955, 6–7; "Septima Clark to Elizabeth Waring," October 6, 1955, Box 110–4, Folder 53, Julius Waties Waring Papers, MSRC.

68. "Gloster Current to NAACP"; "Confidential," Essay, 1955, Confidential, Joseph A. De Laine Papers.

69. Modjeska M. Simkins, "DeLaine Home Repeatedly Fired At," Reprisals South Carolina, II:A508, Records of the NAACP, LOC.

70. "Gloster Current to NAACP"; "Clark to Waring," November 7, 1955. Julius Waties Waring Papers.

71. "WLIB receives over 10,000 pieces of mail," December 12, 1955, Reprisals South Carolina, II:A508, Records of the NAACP, LOC; *The State*, October 19, 1955; Elton Bean, "So This Is New York," *Bermuda Recorder*, October 19, 1955; "Speech, 1956 May 30, (Brooklyn, NY), Joseph A. De Laine, Sr., to Brooklyn College audience," Joseph De Laine Papers.

72. "To Chief of Police from Mary Anis," March 20, 1936, Marcus Garvey, Part 10 of 12, FBI Records: The Vault, accessed April 20, 1917.

73. Simkins, "The Orangeburg-Elloree story—2nd installment," Reprisals South Carolina, II:A508, Records of the NAACP, LOC.

74. Ibid.; Ted Poston, "Special to the New York Post," January 20, 1955, Reprisals South Carolina, II:A508, Records of the NAACP, LOC; "They're Trying to Run Us Out . . . We Don't Plan to Leave," *Bermuda Recorder*, December 12, 1955; Robert Ratcliffe, "Ain't Scared of Nothing," *Pittsburgh Courier*, November 13, 1954, 11.

75. "Threatened South Carolina Leader Refuses To Leave," *Atlanta Daily World* (1932–2003); December 13, 1955; ProQuest Historical Newspapers: Atlanta Daily World, 2; John

McCray, "NAACP Leader Dares Klan by Showing up at Meeting," *Baltimore Afro-American*, December 17, 1955; John McCray, "Tired of Starving to be White, Carolina Merchant Quits Area," *Afro-American* (1893–1988); December 24, 1955; ProQuest Historical Newspapers: The Baltimore Afro-American, 5.

76. "KKK Threat Fails to Scare Negro Contractor in Elloree," *Florence Morning News*, December 7, 1955, 1; Katherine Mellen Charron, *Freedom's Teacher*, 237; *Baltimore Afro-American*, December 17, 1955.

77. "Threatened South Carolina Leader Refuses To Leave," *Atlanta Daily World*, 2; McCray, "NAACP Leader Dares Klan," *Baltimore Afro-American*, December 17, 1955.

78. McCray, "Tired of Starving," *Baltimore Afro-American*, December 24, 1955, 17.

Chapter 2. Twenty-One-Gun Salute: Armed and Dangerous in Orangeburg

1. Kamarakafego, *Me One*, 87; "Brooklyn Student Boycotter Expelled by S.C. State College," *New York Amsterdam News (1943–1961)*, July 14, 1956, 19; *Bulldog SCSC Yearbook*, 1955–1956, 103, SC State Historical Collection & Archives, Miller F. Whittaker Library, SC State University, Orangeburg, South Carolina; "Negro Youth Becomes Eagle Scout," *Times and Democrat*, February 11, 1956, 5.

2. Rudolph Pyatt, interview by author; *Bulldog SCSC Yearbook*, 108; Kamarakafego, *Me One*, 87.

3. "Council Pressure Unites Elloree Squeeze Victims," *Afro-American*, December 15, 1956; Census of Population, 1960: US Department of Commerce, Bureau of the Census, 1961, 41–12; W. E. Solomon, "Desegregation in South Carolina," *The Journal of Negro Education* 25, no. 3 (Summer 1956): 320; William C. Hine, "Civil Rights and Campus Wrongs: South Carolina State College Students Protest, 1955–1968," *The South Carolina Historical Magazine* 97, no. 4 (October 1996): 310–31.

4. Solomon, "Desegregation in South Carolina," 320; Modjeska Simkins, "The Orangeburg-Elloree (S.C.) Story," September 10, 1955, Julius Waring Papers, MSRC; "Mixing Is Impossible Council Says," *Florence Morning News*, September 13, 1955, 10.

5. "Gloster Current to NAACP," II:A508, Records of the NAACP, LOC; "Council Pressure Unites Elloree Squeeze Victims," *Afro-American*, December 15, 1956; Simkins, "The Orangeburg-Elloree (S.C.) Story."

6. Simkins, "The Orangeburg-Elloree (S.C.) Story."

7. Ibid.

8. "Roy Wilkins to H. S. M. Burns, Shell Oil Company," October 5, 1955, II:A508; Records of the NAACP, LOC; Septima Clark, *Champions of Democracy*, Highlander Folk School, Mount Eagle Tennessee [1957], Waring Papers, Box 110–34, MSRC, 1.

9. Elizabeth Geyer, "The 'New' Ku Klux Klan," *Crisis* 63, no. 3, (March 1956): 144–45.

10. "Interview with Modjeska Simkins by Jacquelyn Dowd Hall," July 28, 1976 G-0056-2, in the Southern Oral History Program Collection no. 4007, Southern Historical Collection, Wilson Library, University of North Carolina at Chapel Hill.

11. "South Carolina Plot," *Jet*, October 20, 1955, 8–13.

12. Onetha Bennet, Annie Gibson, Rosa Lee McGainey, Mazie Solomon, James Tindel, Gilbert Henry; "Victims of Economic Reprisal Survey," Reprisals South Carolina, II:A508, Records of the NAACP, LOC; *Afro-American*, December 15, 1956.

13. "Interview with Modjeska Simkins"; "Roy Wilkins to A. C. Redd, South Carolina

State Conference," November 10, 1955, Reprisals South Carolina, II:A508, Records of the NAACP, LOC; Woods, "Modjeska Simkins and the South Carolina Conference of the NAACP, 1939–57," 113; "News From NAACP," *Jet Magazine*, December 8, 1955.

14. Simkins, "Economic Freeze," "Info, South Carolina Conference of NAACP," [nd-1956], Box 110–34, Waring Papers, MSRC; *Crisis* 63, no. 5, (May 1956): 298; "Marion Stewart to John Morsell," May 21, 1956, Tally Sheets, "Aid the NAACP," Fund Raising Raffle Trip to Haiti, Box III: A142, Records of the NAACP, LOC; "Negro Student Strike," *Southern School News* 2, no. 11 (May 1956): 14.

15. Interview with Modjeska Simkins.

16. "Open Letter," [ND 1955], Reprisals South Carolina, II:A508, Records of the NAACP, LOC.

17. "A. C. Redd to Henry Lee Moon," December 29, 1955, Reprisals South Carolina, II:A508, Records of the NAACP, LOC, *Afro-American*, December 15, 1956.

18. Ibid.

19. Simkins, "Economic Freeze"; "Hessie McBride," Reprisals South Carolina, II:A508, Records of the NAACP, LOC; "South Carolina Plot," Jet, October 20, 1955, 8–13.

20. Interview with Modjeska Simkins; "Threatened South Carolina Leader Refuses To Leave," *Atlanta Daily World*, December 13, 1955, 2; Simkins, "Orangeburg-Elloree story—2nd Installment"; Simkins, "Orangeburg-Elloree (S.C.) story"; Hine, "Civil Rights and Campus Wrongs."

21. Interview with Modjeska Simkins; *The Index-Journal*, September 24, 1955, 3; "Nine Games On S. C. State Grid Schedule," *New Journal and Guide*, September 3, 24, 1955, November 12, 1955.

22. Hine, "Civil Rights and Campus Wrongs"; John McCray, "Trade ban Hits 23 Orangeburg Stores," *Baltimore Afro-American*, September 24, 1955, 18; Moore, "School Desegregation"; Simkins, "Orangeburg-Elloree (S.C.) Story."

23. Kamarakafego, *Me One*, 87; McCray, "Trade Ban"; Moore, "School Desegregation," 56.

24. Hine, "Civil Rights and Campus Wrongs," 315; "Septima Clark to Waties Waring," August 30, 1955, J. Waties Waring Papers, Folder 227, Box 110–9, MSRC.

25. Robert Ratcliffe and A. M. Rivera, "Negroes Get New Schools," *Pittsburgh Courier*, November 13, 1954, 11; Hine, "Civil Rights and Campus Wrongs," 312.

26. "Report of Student Protest," Willis Goodwin and Ezra J. Moore to Herbert Wright, April 9, 1956, Claflin College, Orangeburg, 1956–65, Box III:E15, Records of the NAACP, LOC; "Elloree NAACP Hears Claflin Faculty Member," *New Journal and Guide*, April 10, 1954, 1.

27. "Youth and the Challenge of Integration," 2nd Annual National Youth Legislative conference, February 3–6, 1955, Report, Box II:E42, Records of the NAACP, LOC.

28. Kamarakafego, *Me One*, 88; "A. C. Redd to Herbert Wright," October 4, 1955, South Carolina State Conference 1954–55, II:E94, Records of the NAACP, LOC.

29. McCray, "Trade Ban"; Kamarakafego, *Me One*, 88; "Septima Clark to Waties Waring," November 7, 1955, Waring Papers, Folder 227, Box 110–9, MSRC.

30. McCray, "Trade Ban"; "Boycott: Teachers hit back at councils," *Afro-American*, September 24, 1955, 5.

31. "Redd to Wright"; "900 Miss Lucys?: Hang S. C. State Prexy in Effigy," *Baltimore Afro-American*, April 7, 1956, 2, McCray, September 24, 1955.

32. "Peace feelers out to end Orangeburg economic battle," *Baltimore Afro-American*, February 11, 1956, 19; McCray, "Trade Ban."

33. Passenger Manifest, Pan American World Airways, November 7, 1955, Arrival: *La-Guardia Airport, New York, New York*, Ancestry.com, *New York, Passenger and Crew Lists (including Castle Garden and Ellis Island), 18201957* (database on-line), Provo, UT, USA; "Excerpts from address by Thurgood Marshall," November 27, 1955, Reprisals South Carolina, II:A508; "Program, 15th annual meeting of SC NAACP," South Carolina State Conference 1954–55, II:E94, Records of the NAACP, LOC; "Thurgood Marshall to Address 15th NAACP Session," *Independent South Carolina*," November 26, 1955, 1; "Marshall Speaks on Campus," *Claflin Panther* 5, no. 2 (December 1955): 2, Special Collections, Claflin University Library, Claflin University, Orangeburg, South Carolina.

34. "White Council Squeeze Eases," *Afro-American*, October 15, 1955, 3; "Clarence Mitchell to Garland Boone," October 20, 1955, Reprisals South Carolina, II:A508, Records of the NAACP, LOC; Simkins, "Orangeburg-Elloree Story."

35. "Report of Student Protest," "White Council Squeeze Eases," *Afro-American*, October 15, 1955, 3.

36. "Resistance, South Carolina," *Southern School News* 2, no.10 (April 1956): 2; "H2100, A concurrent resolution requesting the Attorney General of the United States to place the National Association for the Advancement of Colored People on the Subversive List," Reprisals South Carolina, II:A508, Records of the NAACP, LOC.

37. "H2100," Reprisals South Carolina, II:A508, Records of the NAACP, LOC.

38. Solomon, "Desegregation in South Carolina," 321–22.

39. "R768.H1900, A Joint Resolution to Provide for the Appointment of a Committee to Investigate the Activity of the National Association for the Advancement of Colored People at the South Carolina State College at Orangeburg," March 16, 1956, II: A508, Records of the NAACP, LOC.

40. "Stand With the NAACP," *Amsterdam News*, March 24, 1956; Solomon, "Desegregation in South Carolina," 315–16; "Resolution of the Faculty and Staff of the South Carolina State College," *The Journal of Negro Education* 25, no. 2 (Spring, 1956): 197–199; "Lucille Black to Branch Officer," August 2, 1955, Orangeburg, 1956–61, III:C143, Records of the NAACP, LOC.

41. "Klan Session Draws 2,000," *Florence Morning News*, March 4, 1956, 1; *Southern School News* 2, no. 10–12, (April–June 1956); "About 85 Robed Klansmen Show Up At Florence," *The Index-Journal*, May 22, 1956, 12; John McCray, "Arrest 4 As Cross Burns At SC State," *Afro-American* (1893–1988); August 4, 1956; ProQuest Historical Newspapers: *The Baltimore Afro-American*, 23.

42. "Klansmen Burn Cross," *El Paso Herald-Post*, February 6, 1956, 26; "Integrated cross-burning rally doused by rainfall," *Baltimore Afro-American*, February 18, 1956; "Klansmen Drew Negro Interest in Meeting," *The Anniston Star*, February 5, 1956, 24; "Fiery Cross," *Southern Illinoisan*, February 7, 1956, 1.

43. Kamarakafego, *Me One*, 88; National Archives of Australia (NAA): A6119, 6125, Maza, Robert Lewis Volume 1, "Roosevelt Browne," "Rose Cuong," Interview with Author, October 10, 2014.

44. Kamarakafego, *Me One*, 88.

45. "Students Strike at Carolina State," *Pittsburgh Courier*, April 14, 1956; "Resolution of the Faculty and Staff of the SCSC," *State College Minutes Book*, SC State Historical Collection, Whittaker Library; "Be A Man, Or Get Out," John McCray, *Afro-American*, March 31, 1956, 1.

46. "Report to the Board of Trustees of Factors Related to the student strike at SCSC," *State College Minutes Book*, SC State Historical Collection; "Bulletin!" *New Journal and Guide*, March 31, 1956, 1.

47. "Report to the Board of Trustees," 1; "Bulletin!" *New Journal and Guide*, 1; "Brooklyn Student Boycotter Expelled," *Baltimore Afro-American*.

48. Hine, "Civil Rights and Campus Wrongs," 316.

49. "Board of Trustees Meeting," March 26, 1956, *State College Minutes Book*, SC State Historical Collection, Whittaker Library.

50. McCray, "Be A Man, Or Get Out," "900 Miss Lucys?," "Hang S. C. State Prexy in Effigy," *Baltimore Afro-American*, April 7, 1956, 1; "Report to the Board of Trustees."

51. McCray, "900 Miss Lucys?"; "Report of Student Protest."

52. Murray Kempton, "Education via Revolt," *New York Post,* March 27, 1956, South Carolina State College, Orangeburg, 1960, III: E15, Records of the NAACP, LOC.

53. "Bulletin!" *New Journal and Guide*; McCray, "900 Miss Lucys?"

54. "Students Strike at Carolina State," *Pittsburgh Courier*; "Claflin students try to avoid trouble," *Afro-American*, April 17, 1956, 3; "Report of Student Protest."

55. "Negro Student Strike Highlight of Month in South Carolina," *Southern School News* 2, no. 11 (May 1956): 14; Moore, "School Desegregation," 57; "Governor orders officers Alert for possible college demonstration," *The State*, April 8, 1956; "Governor puts police at S.C. State," *Baltimore Afro-American*, April 14, 1956, 8.

56. "Report of Student Protest John McCray," "Uneasy at S.C.," *Afro-American*, April 21, 1956; "Students Strike at Carolina State," *Pittsburgh Courier*; Moore, "School Desegregation," 57.

57. *The State,* April 10, 1956; McCray, "Uneasy at S.C."

58. McCray; "Uneasy at S.C."; "Students Strike at Carolina State," *Pittsburgh Courier*; "State College demonstration fails to come off yesterday," April 9, 1956, *Times and Democrat*.

59. McCray; "Uneasy at S.C."

60. "Brooklyn Student Boycotter Expelled Bulletin!" *New Journal and Guide*; Moore, "School Desegregation"; Hine, "Civil Rights and Campus Wrongs," 316; "On-Again-Off-Again Negro Students Strike On, Ultimatum Issued," *The Index-Journal*, April 13, 1956, 1, 10.

61. "Student Body, South Carolina State College to W. C. Bethea," April 12, 1956, *State College Minutes Book*, SC State Archives, Whittaker Library.

62. "On-Again-Off-Again"; McCray, "900 Miss Lucys?," "Uneasy At S.C."

63. "Negro Students Strike On," *The Index-Journal*; "Ask 15 students at State College to Remain Away," *Gaffney Ledger*, June 28, 1956, 4.

64. Louis Lomax, "Aid Ousted S.C. Senior," *Afro-American*, May 19, 1956, 1; "Negro Student Head Expelled," *Index-Journal*, April 26, 1956, 1; "SCSC Board Meeting Minutes," April 25, 1956.

65. John McCray, "Jeer S. C. President," *Baltimore Afro-American*, May 5, 1956.

66. Ibid.

67. "In the Colleges," *Southern School News* 2, no. 12 (June 1956): 14; "S. C. Students Again Assail B. C. Turner," *Afro-American*, May 26, 1956, 5.

68. John McCray, "S. C. Students Now On Dance And Party Strike," *Afro-American*, May 12, 1956, 1.

69. "S. Car. State under Fire!" *Pittsburgh Courier*, July 7, 1956, 3; "Strike Over Segregation Brings Dismissals for 15," *Kansas City Times*, June 26, 1956, 21; John McCray, "Unrest Mounts At S.C. State: Students Erect Arrow Pointing to Campus Uncle Tom's Cabin," *Afro-American*, October 6, 1956, 3.

70. "S. Car. State Under Fire!" *Pittsburgh Courier*; "3 Ousted S.C. State Coed Given Grant," *Afro-American*, August 4, 1956, 5.

71. McCray, "Uneasy At S.C." "Septima Clark to Waties Waring," May 3, 1956, Folder 228, Box 110–9, Waring Papers, MSRC.

72. "Septima Clark to Roy Wilkins," June 6, 1956, Reprisals South Carolina, II:A508, Records of the NAACP, LOC; "Septima Clark to Elizabeth Waring," October 6, 1955, Folder 53, Box 110–4, Waring Papers, MSRC.

73. "Clark to Waring," May 3, 1956; "Clark to Wilkins," June 6, 1956.

74. "Septima Clark to Elizabeth Waring," June 8, 22, 1956, Folder 53, Box 110–4; "Septima Clark to Waring," March 20, 1957, Folder 229, 110–9, Waring Papers, MSRC.

75. "Roy Wilkins to Septima Clark," June 15, 1956, Reprisals South Carolina, II:A508, Records of the NAACP, LOC; "Septima Clark to Waring," June 22, 1956; September 16, 27, 1956; March 20, 1957, Folder 229, Box 110–9, Waring Papers, MSRC; "Ousted S.C. State student leader enrolls at Allen U," *Afro-American*, September 29, 1956, 5.

76. "Brooklyn Student Boycotter Expelled."

77. Kamarakafego, *Me One*, 89–90.

78. "A 1 Million Dollar Donation," *Jet*, December 6, 2004.

79. "Mary McLean to Robert July," October 18, 1952, "Mary McLean," July 1951, "James Lee to George Kyle," May 20, 1954, "Alphonso Elder to Mary McLean," July 6, 1964, McLean to Elder, September 16, 1954, Folder 190, Alphonso Elder Papers, James E. Shepard Memorial Library at North Carolina Central University, Durham, North Carolina.

80. Kamarakafego, *Me One*, 89–90.

81. Ibid.; "Riddick to Howard Wright," October 9, 1957; October 10, 1957, Herman H. Riddick-Biology, Football Coach, Alphonso Elder Papers, James E. Shepard Memorial Library.

82. Kamarakafego, *Me One*, 89–90.

83. Ibid.

84. Year: *1957*; Arrival: *LaGuardia Airport, New York, New York*; Microfilm Serial: *T715, 1897–1957*; Microfilm Roll: *Roll 8863*; Line: *3*; Page Number: *197*, Ancestry.com, *New York, Passenger and Crew Lists (including Castle Garden and Ellis Island), 1820–1957*; "Move to Crack Color Line in Durham Play Facilities," *Atlanta Daily World*, June 21, 1957, ProQuest Historical Newspapers: Atlanta Daily World, 1; "Fight Discrimination in Durham, NC. Ball Park," *The Chicago Defender*, May 4, 1957, ProQuest Historical Newspapers: Chicago Defender, 23; "Ball Park Bias Assailed," *New York Times*, April 19, 1957, 22; "Desegregation," 21 May 1957, 1, "Trespassing case opens in Durham," July 18, 1957, 16, *Rocky Mount Telegram*.

85. Kamarakafego, *Me One*, 89–90.

86. *Passenger and Crew Manifests of Airplanes Arriving in Bermuda*. Series A3925, NAI:

2681636, Records of the Immigration and Naturalization Service, 1787–2004, Record Group 85, the National Archives at Washington, DC, Ancestry.com, *Bermuda, Passenger and Crew Manifests*, 1957–1969; Kamarakafego, *Me One*, 92.

87. Kamarakafego, *Me One*, 92.

88. Ibid.

89. Ibid.

90. Ibid.

91. Ibid., 101–3.

92. "Form letter from W. E. B. Du Bois and Linus Pauling. July 26, 1949 "Statement of the Federation of Atomic Scientists," 1945; Excerpts from "U.S. Signatures to the Appeal by American Scientists to the Governments and People of the World," January 15, 1958, Linus Pauling and the International Peace Movement Papers, Special Collections & Archives Research Center, Oregon State University Libraries, Corvallis, OR.

93. Linus Pauling, "The Dead Will Inherit the Earth," November 1961, *Frontier* 13, no. 1 (November 1961): 5–8; "The Best Interests of the United States," May 24, 1952; "Statement by Linus Pauling," July 14, 1950; "Notes by Linus Pauling re: the likely effects of the persecution of scientists," 1956 Linus Pauling, Interviewed by John L. Greenberg, May 10, 1984, 28; Linus Pauling Papers, Oregon State University Libraries.

94. Kamarakafego, *Me One*, 92.

Chapter 3. Liberia: First-Class Africa

1. Kamarakafego, *Me One*, 101–3.

2. W. E. B. Du Bois, "Liberia, the League and the United States," *Foreign Affairs* 11, no. 4 (July 1933): 628–95.

3. Von Eschen, *Race Against Empire*, 39.

4. "Letter from E. Frederic Morrow to Wilton B. Persons on Liberian relations with the U.S." White House, October 3, 1960. *US Declassified Documents Online*, http://tinyurl.galegroup.com/tinyurl/8ropm9. Accessed January 23, 2019.

5. Lawler and Mahan, *Foreign Relations of the United States*, https://history.state.gov/historicaldocuments/frus1958-60v14/d27; "Charles Bowles' report of his mission to African on 10/15/62 to 11/9/62, US Department of State, November 13, 1962. *US Declassified Documents Online*, http://tinyurl.galegroup.com/tinyurl/8rpEL8, GALE/CK2349108445, Wilson International Center.

6. Von Eschen, *Race Against Empire*, 165.

7. Kamarakafego, *Me One*, 16.

8. Ibid., 102.

9. Ibid., 103.

10. Ibid.

11. Ibid., 104–5.

12. The National Archives at Washington, DC; NAI Number: *2848504*; Record Group Title: *Records of the Immigration and Naturalization Service, 1787–2004*; Record Group Number: *85*; Series Number: *A3998*; NARA Roll Number: *309*, Ancestry.com. *New York State, Passenger and Crew Lists, 1917–1967.*

13. See Gaines, *American Africans in Ghana*; George Houser, "A Report on the All African People's Conference Held in Accra, Ghana," December 8–13, 1958, American Commit-

tee on Africa, African Activist Archive Project, Michigan State University Libraries Special Collections, Michigan State University, Lansing, Michigan; Edwin Munger, "First Pan African Student Conference, A Letter from Edwin S. Munger," American Universities Field Staff, July 7, 1958, African Studies Pamphlet Collection, Indiana University Library, Indiana University, Bloomington, Indiana.

14. Munger, "First Pan African Student Conference."

15. Ibid.

16. "Test for Missions," *The Living Church* 140, no. 20 (May 15, 1960): 8.

17. Ibid.

18. John Gay, email correspondence with author, May 12–13, 2013.

19. Gay, *Africa*, 1.

20. Gay, email correspondence with author; Kamarakafego, *Me One*, 103.

21. "L.U.-Cuttington Sports Series Begins Tomorrow," *Liberian Age*, May 26, 1961, 12; Kamarakafego, *Me One*, 103.

22. See Gay, *Long Day's Anger*.

23. Kamarakafego, *Me One*, 103; Gay, email correspondence.

24. "Franchise Debate Moves To St David's Island Tonight," *Bermuda Recorder*, September 7, 1960, 1; "Notes on Bermuda, The Colored Community in Bermuda," Racial Discrimination in Bermuda, CO/1031/1044, Bermuda Government Archives (BGA), Hamilton, Bermuda.

25. Manning, *Bermudian Politics in Transition*, 125–26; Hodgson, *Second Class Citizens*, 138–39; "Glasgoine to British Secretary of State for the Colonies," September 9, 1960; "Note for meeting with the Hon. W. L. Tucker of Bermuda"; "Ambler Thomas (Antigua) to Sir Hilton Poynton," October 21, 1960, CO/1031/3078, House of Assembly, Franchise, Bermuda, BGA.

26. "Notes on Bermuda, 1952," CO/1031/1043, Representations From the Colored Community in Bermuda, 1952, BGA.

27. "Note for Meeting with the Hon. W. L. Tucker," CO/1031/3078, BGA.

28. "Franchise Support Gets Favorable Reception in House of Assembly," *Bermuda Recorder*, May 11, 1960, 1–2, 6.

29. Ibid.

30. Ibid.

31. Ibid.

32. Ibid.

33. Ibid.

34. "One Man, One Vote" Posters in Circulation, *Bermuda Recorder*, May 11, 1960, 1.

35. "Note for Meeting with the Hon. W. L. Tucker," CO/1031/3078, BNA.

36. Ibid.

37. "Letter to the Editor," *Bermuda Recorder*, March 31, 1962, 2.

38. "Franchise Debate Moves to St. David's"; Glenn Fubler, "A salute to Rosalind Williams, Stalwart of the Progressive Group," *Bermuda Sun*, February 6, 2009, http://bermudasun.bm/Content/NEWS/News/Article/A-salute-to-Rosalind-Williams-stalwart-of-The-Progressive-Group/24/270/40393. This also speaks to the covert nature of black insurgency in Bermuda and its twenty-two miles of concrete jungle accented with hubs of foliage, intense surveillance orchestrated by British colonial officials and their "news carrying

dreads"—Bermudian informants. In this context, secrecy is important, but it is not everything. Such proximity warrants that insurgency must also have a public face—an alter ego of innocence and *visible invisibility* that allows it to not be seen even while being looked at. In a colloquial sense of Bermuda, such political shape shifting is referred to as a "ninja move." In fact, the island's black architects of resistance were perhaps so good at performing such "ninja moves" that Bermuda's black radical tradition remains relatively hidden in popular historical narratives. It is also true that Bermuda's colonial education system sought to downplay Bermuda's radical invisible. That the members of the Progressive Group were not publicly revealed until the mid-1990s is testimony to this phenomenon.

39. Kim Bindley, "Still Dreaming the Dream," *New York Times*, February 13, 2009; Fubler, "A salute to Rosalind Williams."

40. Kamarakafego, *Me One*, 113.

41. Ibid., 115.

42. "Tonight's Franchise Meeting Again at Devonshire Hall," *Bermuda Recorder*, October 5, 1960, 1; "Franchise Debate Moves to St. David's," *Bermuda Recorder*, September 7, 1960, 1.

43. Kamarakafego, *Me One*, 115, 117; "Question of 'Tomcatting' and Illegitimacy Now Enters Franchise Debate," *Bermuda Recorder*, October 1, 1960, 1

44. "Two Speakers at Franchise Take Dismal View of Universal Suffrage," *Bermuda Recorder*, September 21, 1960, 1.

45. Ibid., 1.

46. Ibid., 2.

47. Ibid., 5.

48. "Question Time at Franchise Meetings Proves to Be Most Interesting," *Bermuda Recorder*, September 24, 1960, 1.

49. Ibid., 3, 5.

50. Ibid., 3.

51. "Racialism Bitterly Injected in Franchise Meeting," *Bermuda Recorder*, October 12, 1960, 1.

52. Ibid.

53. "Women Have Their Own Franchise Meeting—And a Hot One Too," *Bermuda Recorder*, October 15, 1960, 1

54. "Franchise Committee Chairman Threatened," *Bermuda Recorder*, November 5, 1960, 1.

55. "Report of the Local Intelligence Committee October 1960," CO/1031/3078, BGA.

56. "The Week in Brief," *Bermuda Recorder*, November 19, 1960, 2, "Political Rally To Be under Lights," December 7, 1960, 1, *Bermuda Recorder*.

57. Kamarakafego, *Me One*, 115; See Butler, *Music on the Rock*; "Quiet ferment amongst Negroes," *Scotsman*, January 24, 1961.

58. Anonymous, *Bermuda and Its Social Problems*, reprinted in Kamarakafego, *Me One*, 390.

59. Kamarakafego, *Me One*, 390.

60. "Report of the Local Intelligence Committee October 1960," CO/1031/3078, BGA.

61. "Referendum Demanded on Universal Franchise," *Bermuda Recorder*, November 2, 1960, 1.

62. "The Week in Brief," *Bermuda Recorder*, November 5, 1960, 3; "Report of the Local Intelligence Committee," CO/1031/3078, BGA.

63. Kamarakafego, *Me One*, 119; "Chairman Threatened," *Bermuda Recorder*, November 5, 1960, 1.

64. "Mass Political Rally at Devonshire Rec Field Next Friday," *Bermuda Recorder*, December 3, 1960; "Political Rally to be under Lights," *Bermuda Recorder*, December 7, 1960; "Referendum Demanded on Universal Franchise," *Bermuda Recorder*, November 2, 1960.

65. "Church of England Can't Understand Why Race Question Enters Franchise Debate," *Bermuda Recorder*, November 5, 1960, 3.

66. "Julian Gascoigne to Colonial Secretary," "Ambler Thomas (Antigua) to Sir Hilton Poynton," October 21, 1960, CO/1031/3078, BGA.

67. "Minute from the Colonial Secretary, Bermuda," October 15, 1960, CO/1031/3078, BGA.

68. "Thomas to Poynton," CO/1031/3078, BGA.

69. "Report of the Intelligence Committee," CO/1031/3078, BGA.

70. Ibid.; "Gascoigne to Colonial Secretary," CO/1031/3078, BGA.

71. Kamarakafego, *Me One*, 120.

72. "Gascoigne to Colonial Secretary," CO/1031/3078, BGA.

73. Ibid.

74. Kamarakafego, *Me One*, 121.

75. "The Week in Brief," *Bermuda Recorder*, December 3, 1960, 3.

76. "Report of the Intelligence Committee," CO/1031/3078, BGA.

77. "Governor of Bermuda to Secretary of State," November 12, 1960, CO/1031/3078, BGA.

78. "Ambler Thomas, MacKintosh Minutes," November 14, 1960; "Ambler Thomas to CO," February 14, 1961, CO/1031/3078, BGA.

79. "Ambler Thomas to CO," February 14, 1961, CO/1031/3078, BGA.

80. Ibid.

81. "Note for Meeting with the Hon. W. L. Tucker of Bermuda," CO/1031/3078, BGA.

82. "W. F. Dawson to CO," November 30, 1960; "Representation of Minority Communities with Special Reference to Bermuda," "Bermuda Franchise," A. M. Mackintosh, December 19, 1960, CO/1031/3078, BGA.

83. "Gascoigne to British Secretary of State," September 9, 1960, CO/1031/3078, BGA.

84. See Hodgson, *Second Class Citizens*; "MCP Gives Impressions of Life," *Bermuda Recorder*, February 4, 1961.

85. "Roosevelt Browne returns to Africa, Sees equalization as Means Towards United Bermuda," *Bermuda Recorder*, February 4, 1961, 1.

86. "Immediate Universal Franchise Proposed by Committee," *Bermuda Recorder*, June 14, 1961, 1.

87. "Crucial Vote to be Taken on Franchise Bill," "Universal Suffrage," *Bermuda Recorder*, June 24, 1961, 1–2, .

88. Ibid.

89. "New Era Portends as House Debates Universal Franchise Bill," *Bermuda Recorder*, June 21, 1961, 1.

90. Ibid.

91. Ibid.

92. "MCP Gives Reason for Committee's Reversal, *Bermuda Recorder*, June 21, 1961, 1.

93. "Assembly Votes in Favor of 38 Single Seat Constituencies," *Bermuda Recorder*, June 28, 1961, 1; "Protest Decision to Give Vote to Britishers Here While Denying It to All Bermudians," *Bermuda Recorder*, July 5, 1961, 1.

94. "W. G. Brown, Letter to the Editor," *Bermuda* Recorder, August 5, 1961, 2; "CUAF Members Explain Their Behind-the Scene Activities," *Bermuda Recorder*, July 22, 1961, 2–3, 8.

95. "CUAF Members Explain," *Bermuda Recorder.*

96. "Bitter Debate Marks Passage of Franchise Bill by Assembly," *Bermuda Recorder*, December 22, 1962; "Extract from Intelligence Report," CO/1031/3078, BGA.

Chapter 4. Kenya: All of Africa Is on Our Backs

1. "Pharaoh Nkongo to Dr. Kwame Nkrumah," March 20, 1966, Kwame Nkrumah Papers, MSRC.

2. Kamarakafego, *Me One*, 104.

3. "They are engaged," *Liberian Age*, May 19, 1961, 1.

4. "When Business Stood Still," *Liberian Age*, September 15, 1961, 6–7.

5. *Listener*, September 12, 1961; "When Business Stood Still," *Liberian Age*, September 15, 1961, 6–7.

6. "African Unity Electrifies Monrovia Talks," May 11, 1961, 1; "Low Wages Spark Two Hour Strike at Ducor Palace," *Liberian Age*, August 11, 1961, 1; Dew Tuan-Wleh Mayson and Amos Sawyer, "Capitalism and the Struggle of the Working Class in Liberia," *Liberian Research Association Journal* 9, no. 2 (1979): 140–58.

7. "Evidence of Underground Movement," *Liberian Age*, September 18, 1961, 1–2; Mayson and Sawyer, 140–143; see Alhaji Kromah, "Capital Inflow & Sovereignty, Performance of Firestone in Liberia 1926–1977," July 4, 2008, http://alhajikromahpage.org/alhajifirestone.htm; Du Bois, "Liberia, the League and the United States."

8. See Johnson, *Reflections of an African Diplomat.*

9. "Evidence of Underground Movement," *Liberian Age*, 1–2.

10. Ibid.; "Emergency Laws," *Liberian Age*, September 22, 1961, 6, 8.

11. "Civil Servants," *Liberian Age*, September 18, 1961, 2.

12. Mayson and Sawyer, 140–43.

13. "Evidence of Underground Movement," *Liberian Age*, 1–2.

14. "Thirteen Arrested," *Liberian Age*, September 29, 1961, 1–2.

15. Ibid.

16. Kamarakafego, *Me One*, 104.

17. Gay, interview with author.

18. Kamarakafego, *Me One*, 106–7.

19. Horne, *Mau Mau in Harlem.*

20. Campbell, *Rasta and Resistance.*

21. "The Mau Mau," *Bermuda Recorder*, October 11, 1952, 2.

22. "50 in Kenya Tribe Rituals Are Seized," November 5, 1952, 1, "Kenya and South Africa," *Bermuda Recorder*, December 13, 1952, 4.

23. "African Mothers Charge Forced Labor," *Bermuda Recorder*, April 1, 1953, 1; "Behind Rise of Africans: Rude Whites," *Bermuda Recorder*, April 22, 1961, 6–7.

24. "Earl Cameron Stars in Film on Mau Mau," *Bermuda Recorder*, November 6, 1954, 1; *Killers of Kilimanjaro*, *Bermuda Recorder*, June 1, 1957, June 22, 1957, December 31, 1960.

25. Kamarakafego, *Me One*, 129.

26. See Stutts Njiiri, "Kenya and North America"; Jomo Kenyatta, "Statement of the Prime Minister in Parliament–17th September 1964; Clarification of Government Policy on Africanization," September 17, 1964; "Statement on the Government's Policy of Africanization by the Prime Minister," December 18, 1964; Kenyatta, Jomo, Public Speeches, 1965–1970, 5/9830, "Kenyan Secondary Schools and their addresses," R2/9/52, Kenya National Archives (KNA), Nairobi, Kenya.

27. "University of East Africa, Royal College, Nairobi, Calendar 1963–64." MES/115/9/14, KNA.

28. Nyanza African Teachers Union, "A Memorandum on 7 ½% House Rent From NATU to Government with reference to Primary School Teachers," April 1951, AV/1/25, KNA.

29. P. J. Westley, "The Teaching of Science in Kenya," Meeting of Experts on the Teaching of Science in Tropical Africa, Abidjan, December 1960, NS/ST/1960/11, WS/1060.105, November 14, 1960; UNESDOC, UNESCO Digital Library.

30. Ibid., 3; Kenya Polytechnic Prospectus, 1964. R2/9/51. KNA.

31. See Harper, *Western-Educated Elites in Kenya*.

32. Kamarakafego, *Me One*, 129.

33. Joseph E. Harris, "African Diaspora Studies: Some International Dimensions," *Issue: A Journal of Opinion* 24, no. 2, African [Diaspora] Studies (1996): 6; Ogot, *My Footprints on the Sands of Time*, 137–38; Harriet Jackson Scarupa, "Joseph E. Harris: Forging Links On the Diaspora Trail," *New Directions* 13, no. 4, article 3 (1986):6–17; Joseph and Rosemarie Harris, conversation with author, April 27, 2012.

34. Horne, *Mau Mau in Harlem*, 205; Edwin Munger, "Kikuyu Village Hall Democracy," *American Universities Field Staff Report* 5, no. 3 (August 1959): 3, Box 18, Joseph Jones Papers, Harry Ransom Center for Humanities, University of Austin-Texas, Austin, Texas.

35. John Kamau, "Kenya: Ernestine Kiano—the Minister's Wife Whom Moi Deported," *Daily Nation*, October 26, 2015, https://mobile.nation.co.ke/news/The-minister-s-wife-whom-Moi-deported-/1950946-2930560-format-xhtml-f8ic1i/index.html.

36. "Nairobi to Secretary of State," January 15, 1962. Kenya, Box 127, National Security Files, John F. Kennedy Presidential Library, Boston, Massachusetts.

37. Kamau, "Kenya."

38. "I'm An African Now, Says Roosevelt Brown," *Bermuda Recorder*, August 31, 1963, 4.

39. Kamarakafego, *Me One*, 136.

40. See Horne, *Mau Mau in Kenya*; Stutts Njiiri, "Kenya and North America."

41. "Summary of Malcolm X's Meeting and Speech 10/22/64 in Nairobi, Kenya," Central Intelligence Agency, n.d. *US Declassified Documents Online*, http://tinyurl.galegroup.com/tinyurl/8rqioX, accessed January 23, 2019, GALE|CK2349304208; "Intelligence Special Report Entitled: "Leftist Activity in Kenya," Central Intelligence Agency, July 31, 1964, *US Declassified Documents Online*, http://tinyurl.galegroup.com/tinyurl/8rrqFn1, GALE|CK2349663935, Wilson International Center.

42. "Gazette Notice No. 4317," *Kenya Gazette* 66, no. 61, December 22, 1964; Liner notes, Cathy Mbathi, *My Favorite Negro Spirituals*, Crown V Recordings, 1980.

43. See Marable, *Malcolm X*; Malcolm X Little, File 100–399321, 6–15, FBI files, Washington, DC; Kamarakafego, 157.

44. Kamarakafego, *Me One*, 157.

45. "Summary of Malcolm X's Meeting," CIA; Kamarakafego, *Me One*, 157.

46. "Summary of Malcolm X's Meeting," CIA.

47. "CIA sends FBI information on Malcolm X," Central Intelligence Agency, December 23, 1964, *US Declassified Documents Online*, http://tinyurl.galegroup.com/tinyurl/8rrFK7, accessed January 23, 2019.

48. Ibid.

49. Malcolm X, "Malcolm X Introduces Fannie Lou Hamer (December 20, 1964)," http://malcolmxfiles.blogspot.com/2013/07/malcolm-x-introduces-fannie-lou-hamer.html.

50. Ibid.; see also Mickie Mwanzia Koster, "The Legacy of Malcolm X: Black Nationalism, Internationalism, and Transnationalism," *The Journal of African American History* 100, no. 2 (Spring 2015): 250–71.

51. Kamarakafego, *Me One*, 129.

52. Ibid. For further details of Kamarakafego's experiences in Bermuda between 1968 and 1969, see Swan, *Black Power in Bermuda*.

53. Kamarakafego, *Me One*, 129, 132.

54. Ibid., 400–1, 132.

55. Ibid., 132; "Just Back From Africa," *Bermuda Recorder*, August 18, 1967, 1–2.

56. See Stutts Njiiri, "Kenya and North America."

57. J. E. Anderson, "The Kenya Education Commission Report: An African View of Educational Planning," *Comparative Education Review* 9, no. 2 (June 1965): 202.

58. Kamarakafego, *Me One*, 132.

59. "Do You Want to be a Science Teacher?" Kenya Science Teachers College, Nairobi, Kenya, 1968, 1, http://chotai.org/My%20education.html#KSTC.

60. Kamarakafego, *Me One*, 132.

61. Kamarakafego, *How to Build a Watertank with Bamboo and Cement*, 3.

62. Williams, *Lois*, 56, 97, 331.

63. Kamarakafego, *Me One*, 141.

64. "Just Back From Africa," *Bermuda Recorder*.

65. "PLP's Pembroke Branch Gets New Leader," *Bermuda Recorder*, August 25, 1967, 1; "PLP Appoints Organizer," *Bermuda Recorder*, October 13, 1967, 9; "PLP's Steamroller Begins to Roll," *Bermuda Recorder*, September 8, 1967, 1.

66. "PLP Policy Outlined," *Bermuda Recorder*, January 27, 1967; see Swan, *Black Power in Bermuda*.

67. TNA: FCO 44/195, August 11, 1967, "Visitors of Black Power to Bermuda."

68. *Black Power Conference Reports*, 3.

69. Ibid., 4; "Members of the 1969 Planning Committee, NCBP," National Conference on Black Power, 1968, Black Power Conference, 1969–1970, Chuck Stone Papers, David M. Rubenstein Rare Book and Manuscript Library, Duke University, Durham, NC; TNA: FCO 63/380, June 1970 "Black Power in the Caribbean"; "Intelligence analysis of the Third National Conference on Black Power, which was held in Philadelphia, Pennsylvania, from

8/29–9/1/68," FBI, October 2, 1968 *U.S. Declassified Documents Online*, http://tinyurl.gale-group.com/tinyurl/A5EVi4, accessed May 19, 2019, Wilson International Center.

70. "Yes, I invited Black Power Group to Confer in Bermuda," *Bermuda Recorder*, January 10, 1969, 1–5.

71. Kamarakafego, *Me One*, 144.

72. From Manning to US Department of State, Airgram A-29, May 9, 1969, POL 23 BER, CFPF, 1967–69, RG 59: The Department of State Records at the National Archives, College Park, Maryland (MD:NACP).

73. Swan, *Black Power in Bermuda*; TNA: FCO 44/202, West Indies and Caribbean Area, Monthly Intelligence Summary, July 1969.

74. TNA: FCO 44/199, "Bermuda: Black Power Conference," May 16, 1969; "Bermuda," *Izvestia* 102–50, *Current Digest of the Russian Press* 21, no. 28, August 6, 1969, 47, https://dlin.eastview.com/browse/doc/13654523.

75. TNA: FCO 44/199, "Bermuda: Black Power Conference"; Kamarakafego, 159.

76. Pauulu Kamarakafego, Lecture, tape recording, March 12, 2002, Cedarbridge Academy, Bermuda; Kamarakafego, *Me One*, 159.

77. *Royal Gazette*, April 5, 1969; "Roosevelt Brown Gives More Data On Regional Black Power Conference in Bermuda," *Bermuda Recorder*, April 5, 1969, 1.

78. See Swan, *Black Power in Bermuda*.

79. C. L. R. James, "Open Statement to Black Power Conference," Black Power Conference, First Regional, Box 11, Folder 12, CLR James Papers, 1933–2001, Rare Book & Manuscript Library Collections, Columbia University Libraries, Columbia University, New York, NY.

80. Ibid.

81. Ibid.

82. Ibid.

83. Kamarakafego, *Me One*, 189, 415.

84. Ibid., 415–17.

85. Stokely Carmichael, "Black Power Conference, Bermuda," July 11, 1969, Kwame Nkrumah Papers, Folder 7, Box 154–12, MSRC.

86. Kwame Nkrumah, "Black Power Conference, Bermuda," July 11, 1969, Kwame Nkrumah Papers, Folder 7, Box 154–12, MSRC.

87. Kamarakafego, interview by author; Michelle Khaldun interview by author, October 10, 2004; Swan, *Black Power in Bermuda*, 102–4.

88. *Black Beret* 14, February 20, 1971.

89. Swan, *Black Power in Bermuda*, 102–4.

90. *Manifesto, Black Beret Cadre*, December 10, 1970.

91. TNA: FCO 44/541, Bermuda Intelligence Report, April 1–April 29, 1971; Kamarakafego, Lecture, Cedarbridge Academy.

92. Kamarakafego, interview by author.

93. Jeanna Knight, interview by author.

94. Swan, *Black Power in Bermuda*, 124–125.

95. CIA, "Interrelationships of Black Power Organizations in the Western Hemisphere II," 1971.

96. TNA: FCO 44/408, "A. J. Fairclough to FCO," April 17, 1970; FCO 63/946, Intelligence Report, November 5, 1973.

97. TNA: FCO 44/406, f13; FCO 44/404, "Martonmere to FCO," March 25, 1970; FCO 44/408, E. Wynne, "A Note on the Structure of Society in Bermuda and Some of Its Peoples," November 13, 1970.

98. TNA: PRO FCO 63/380, "BIC Report, 3 June–7 July"; PRO FCO 44/409, "Governor to FCO," October 20, 1970; FCO 63/379, "BICR January–April 1970," "Martonmere to FCO, April 1, 1970; FCO 63/380, "BIC Report, June 1970."

99. "Black Beret Cadre Make Demands," *Bermuda Recorder*, August 8, 1970, 3.

100. Sinclair Swan, interview with author.

101. Swan, *Black Power in Bermuda*, 138–40.

102. "Dudley Thompson to Nkrumah," January 24, 1969; July 11, 1970; Kwame Nkrumah Papers, MSRC.

103. Knight, interview.

104. George Buchanan, "The Black Beret Cadre and its Manifesto," August 10, 1971; "Minutes of the Race Relations Council Meeting," March 1, 1971, May 11, 1971, Race Relations Council Working Papers, December 1970–December 1972, BGA.

105. "Minutes of the Race Relations Council Meeting," March 1, 1971, March 23, 1971, April 13, 1971, February 8, 1972, Race Relations Council Working Papers, BGA.

106. "Minutes of the Race Relations Council Meeting," July 13, 1971; November 9, 1971; December 14, 1971, Race Relations Council Working Papers, BGA.

107. Chair Reverend George Buchanan, "Malcolm X Liberation School," August 10, 1971; "Minutes of the Race Relations Council Meeting," February 8, 1972, Race Relations Council Working Papers, BGA.

108. CIA, "Interrelationships of Black Power Organizations, 1971."

109. "American Consulate to Department of State, London," June 6, 1972, POL 19 BER, CFPF, 1967–69, RG 59: MD: NACP.

Chapter 5. Anansi's Revolution

1. "Prohibited Books Seized," *Bermuda Recorder*, March 7, 1970, 9; CIA, "Interrelationships of Black Power Organizations in the Western Hemisphere II."

2. Lux, "Black Power in the Caribbean."

3. IEC, Interrelationships of Black Power Organizations in the Western Hemisphere," 42; TNA: PRO FCO 44/403, St. Vincent to Foreign and Commonwealth Office, April 17, 1970, St. Lucia to Foreign and Commonwealth Office, April 17, 1970, Bridgetown to Foreign and Commonwealth Office, May 11, 1970; Manning to US Department of State, June 18, 1969; POL 23 BER, file A-29; CFPF; RG 59; MD: NACP.

4. TNA: FCO 44/202, West Indies and Caribbean Area, Monthly Intelligence Summary, July 1969; TNA: FCO 63/608, "Black Power," St. Lucia to FCO, April 17, 1970; FCO 44/202, Monthly Intelligence Summary, July 1969; FCO 44/403, St. Vincent to Foreign and Commonwealth Office, April 17, 1970, Bridgetown to Foreign and Commonwealth Office, 11 May 1970; "Government Lifts Entry Ban on 19 Radicals," Bridgetown, CANA, Daily Report, Latin America (FBIS-LAM-85-060), March 28, 1985, 52, Foreign Broadcast Information Service (FBIS) Daily Report, Wilson Center.

5. "Office of Current Intelligence (OCI) Director Richard Lehman Comments on Oci's Tracing of Caribbean Black Radicalism since 1968," May 7, 1973, *U.S. Declassified Documents Online*, http://tinyurl.galegroup.com/tinyurl/A5ESK4; Central Intelligence Agency, "Intelligence Memorandum: Black Radicalism in the Caribbean," August 6, 1969, July 6, 1970, 2; 1; "Black Radicalism in the Caribbean—Another Look (June 12, 1970)"; Records of the Central Intelligence Agency, MD: NACP.

6. CIA, "Black Radicalism in the Caribbean," July 6, 1970, 2; August 6, 1969, 1, MD: NACP.

7. IEC, "Interrelationship of Black Power Organizations in the Western Hemisphere." Wilson Center.

8. Ibid., 12.

9. CIA, "Black Radicalism in the Caribbean," July 9, 1970; MD: NACP.

10. CIA, "Black Radicalism in the Caribbean—Another Look," 1, MD: NACP.

11. TNA: PRO FCO 63/380, D.M. Kerr to Thomas Sewell, May 22, 1970, "Black Power in the Caribbean," April 1970.

12. IEC, "Interrelationships of Black Power Organizations," 4.

13. Ibid.

14. Horace Sutton, "The Palm Tree Revolt," *Saturday Review*, February 27, 1971, 15.

15. See CIA, "Black Radicalism in the Caribbean," 1969, 5, MD: NACP; Meeks, *Narratives of Resistance*; Palmer, "Identity, Race, and Black Power in Independent Jamaica"; and Rupert Lewis, "Jamaican Black Power in the 1960s," in Kate Quinn, *Black Power in the Caribbean*, 59.

16. CIA, "Black Radicalism in the Caribbean, 1969, 5, MD: NACP; TNA: FCO 63/380, "Black Power in the Caribbean," June 1970; Rodney, *Groundings With My Brothers*, 28.

17. CIA, "Black Radicalism in the Caribbean," 1970, 6, MD: NACP; TNA: FCO 63/380, "Black Power in the Caribbean," June 1970; See Bogues, "Black Power"; Lewis, "Walter Rodney's Intellectual and Political Thought"; Lux, "Black Power in the Caribbean," 213.

18. *Daily Gleaner*, October 18, 1968; CIA, "Black Radicalism in the Caribbean," 1969, 6.

19. CIA, "Jamaica, Special Report," February 14, 1969, Records of the Central Intelligence Agency, MD: NACP; CIA, "Black Radicalism in the Caribbean," 1970, A-6-A-7, 6; TNA: FCO 63/380, "Black Power in the Caribbean," June 1970.

20. Lewis, "Jamaican Black Power in the 1960s," 70; CIA, "Black Radicalism in the Caribbean," 1969, 5.

21. CIA, "Black Radicalism in the Caribbean, 1969," 5, MD: NACP.

22. Bogues, "The Abeng Newspaper," in Quinn, *Black Power in the Caribbean*; Lewis, "Jamaican Black Power in the 1960s," 70; Walter Rodney, "The Rise of Black Power in the West Indies," *Abeng* 1, no. 6 (March 8, 1969): 3.

23. CIA, "Black Radicalism in the Caribbean, 1969," 5, MD: NACP; "Education Ministry Plans to Ban Abeng," (May 3, 1969), 1; Patrick Keatley, "Listing Black Power Agents," (July 26, 1969), 1; *Abeng* 1, nos. 14, 26.

24. "Garvey Journal," *Abeng* 1, no. 15 (May 10, 1969): 3.

25. "Black Power Literature," *Abeng* 1, no. 16 (May 17, 1969): 2; TNA: FCO 63/380, "Black Power in the Caribbean," June 1970.

26. CIA, "Black Radicalism in the Caribbean, 1969," 5, MD: NACP.

27. "In Town and Country, Birthday of Garvey in Action," *Abeng* 1, no. 30 (August 23, 1969): 1.

28. *Hustler*, August 31, 1968, 2–4, Box 24-15, Caribbean, Joseph Jones Papers, Harry Ransom Center.

29. See Austin, *Fear of A Black Planet*.

30. Ibid.

31. "Racial Inquisition Claimed at Trial of Students in Canada," *Bermuda Recorder*, May 30, 1969, 7, 12.

32. See Austin, *Fear of A Black Planet*.

33. TNA: PRO FCO 44/202, Monthly Intelligence Summary, August 15, 1969; *Black Power Conference Reports*, 68–70.

34. "Students Fight Racism in Canada," (February 22, 1969): 4, "Canada's White Lies," (March 15, 1969): 2, *Abeng* 1, nos. 4, 7.

35. TNA: FCO 63/380, "Black Power in the Caribbean," June 1970; PRO FCO 44/406, 30–31 March, Governor Martonmere to Foreign and Commonwealth Office; *Royal Gazette*, April 1, 1970.

36. IEC, "Interrelationships of Black Power Organizations in the Western Hemisphere," 5–9; "Revolution Time! Remembering the Black United Front and the Meeting That Launched it," *The Signal*, November 30, 2018, https://signalhfx.ca/revolution-time-remembering-the-black-united-front-and-the-meeting-that-launched-it/.

37. CIA, "Black Radicalism in the Caribbean—Another Look," June 1970, A-12-13, MD: NACP.

38. Ibid.; Gabriel Christian, "In Times Crucial: Radical Politics in Dominica 1970–1980," http://da-academy.org/radpol.html.

39. Ibid.

40. Ibid.

41. Ibid.

42. CIA, "Black Radicalism in the Caribbean, 1969," 11, MD: NACP; Buhle, *Tim Hector*, 219–20.

43. CIA, "Interrelationships of Black Power Organizations, 1971."

44. TNA: FCO 63/380, "Black Power in the Caribbean, June 1970"; FCO 63/379, "Black Power: Canadian Exercise in Jamaica," March 3, 1970.

45. "Grenada Declaration," *Outlet* 1, no. 5, November 1971.

46. TNA: FCO 63/691, Black Power Movement Antigua 1971, J. H. Reiss, "Crime and Black Power Thinking," September 3, 1971; "Black Power in Antigua," July 10, 1971.

47. Conway, "Domestic Warfare."

48. Elmer Smith, "Black Power: Caribbean Style," Special Report Grenada: Twenty Years After the Invasion. *Institute for Advanced Journalism Studies* (2003): 4–6.

49. TNA: FCO 63/570, "Black Power in St. Lucia," Memorandum, R. W. Newham, June 5, 1970.

50. TNA: FCO 63/570, D.M. Kerr, "Black Power in St. Lucia," March 19, 1970; "Labor Party Supports Black Power," *Crusader*, May 10, 1970.

51. TNA: FCO 63/570. D.M. Kerr, "Black Power in St. Lucia."

52. TNA: FCO 63/570. D.M. Kerr, "Black Power in St. Lucia," April 1, March 19, 1970.

324 · NOTES TO PAGES 136–142

53. TNA: FCO 63/570. D.M. Kerr, "Black Power in St. Lucia," March 19, 1970.

54. Ibid.

55. CIA, "Black Radicalism in the Caribbean," 1969, 11, MD: NACP.

56. Layne, Kingsley C. A., "George Richardson/An Appreciation," January 27, 2007, http://www.vincytoronto.com/pdf/2007/GEORGE%20RICHARDSON%20-%20AN%20 APPRECIATION.pdf; "The Constitution of SVGA Montreal Inc.," St. Vincent And Grenadines Association Of Montreal, accessed July 1, 2015, http://www.svgamontreal.com/ constitution-of-svga-montreal-inc/; TNA: FCO 63/608. D. G. Mitchell, "St. Vincent: Black Power," Black Power St Vincent 1970, May 8, 1970.

57. TNO: FCO 63/379, "The Monitoring Report," British Broadcasting Company, 17 April 1970; TNA: FCO 63/608, "Black Power," St. Lucia to FCO, April 17, 1970.

58. TNA: FCO 63/608, "Black Power," St. Vincent to FCO, April 21, 1970; CIA, "Black Radicalism in the Caribbean," 1969, 3; Smith, "Black Power: Caribbean Style."

59. CIA, "Black Radicalism in the Caribbean," 1969, 12, MD: NACP.

60. TNA: PRO FCO 44/403, St. Vincent to FCO, April 17, 1970, St. Lucia to FCO, 17 April 1970, Bridgetown to FCO, May 11, 1970; TNA: PRO FCO 36/379, "British Virgin Islands Intelligence Report, December 1969," January 15, 1970; Island Sun, April 18, 1970.

61. Anthony Lukas, "The Plaint of the Virgin Islands: We Have Been Encroached On, Invaded, Engulfed," New York Times, April 18, 1971.

62. CIA, "Interrelationships of Black Power Organizations"; Lukas, "The Plaint of the Virgin Islands."

63. CIA, "Black Radicalism in the Caribbean—another look," 1970, A-1, NARA: MD; IEC, "Interrelationships of Black Power Organizations."

64. TNA: FCO 63/433. "Black Power on the Rampage," Economist, May 21, 1970; TNA: FCO 63/380, "Black Power in the Caribbean," June 1970; CIA, "Black Radicalism in the Caribbean—another Look," A-12, NARA: MD.

65. See Dew, The Difficult Flowering of Surinam; IEC, "Interrelationships of Black Power Organizations," 23.

66. Lux, 211–12.

67. See Gonzalez, "The Unified Black Movement"; Hanchard, Orpheus and Power.

68. Lee, "Belizean Racial Project," 27.

69. Ibid.

70. "Black challenge to British in S. America," Bay State Banner, February 15, 1973, 1; TNA: FCO 44/706, "UBAD's Treasurer Found Guilty—Extract from Belize Times, 1972" Black Power British Honduras 1972, November 27, 1972; Lee, 27.

71. "Black challenge to British in S. America," Bay State Banner; TNA: FCO 44/706, "UBAD's Treasurer Found Guilty," Black Power British Honduras 1972, November 27, 1972.

72. TNA: FCO 44/706, "Dangriga Cultural Association," July 21, 1972; TNA:FCO 44/706, "Michek Charles Mawema," August 2, 1972.

73. TNA: FCO 44/706, "Michek Mawema," August 24, 1972.

74. "Curacao!" Abeng 1, no. 19, June 8, 1969, 1.

75. CIA, "Black Radicalism in the Caribbean," 11, NARA: MD; CIA, "Interrelationships of Black Power Organizations in the Western Hemisphere, 1971."

76. TNA: FCO 36/379. "Black Power in the Caribbean," Canadian Embassy, Caracas, to Ottawa, March 6, 1970.

77. "Black Power in the Caribbean," *Race Today* 1, no. 8, (December 1969): 232–33; See Sarah Seidman, "Tricontinental Routes of Solidarity: Stokely Carmichael in Cuba," *Journal of Transnational American Studies* 4, no. 2 (2012); TNA: FCO 63/380, "Black Power in the Caribbean," June 1970.

78. TNA: FCO 63/380, "Black Power in the Caribbean," June 1970.

79. "26 arrested in Puerto Rico under ex-aide of J. Edgar Hoover," "Colonialism in Puerto Rico," *Liberacion*, 1968, Ana Livia Cordero Papers, Schlesinger Library, Harvard University, Cambridge, MA.

80. TNA: FCO 36/379. "Black Power in the Caribbean. Canadian Embassy, Caracas, to Ottawa," March 6, 1970; Gregory Wilpert, "Racism and Racial Divides in Venezuela," *Venezuelanalysis*, January 21, 2004. http://venezuelanalysis.com/analysis/322. See David Guss, "The Selling of San Juan," in *Blackness in Latin America and the Caribbean*, ed. Norman Whitten, Jr., and Arlene Torres (Bloomington: Indiana University Press, 1998), 244–77.

81. CIA, "Interrelationships of Black Power Organizations, 1971."

Chapter 6. Black Power in the Caribbean, Signed Stokely Carmichael

1. Kamarakafego, *Me One*, 181.

2. TNA: PRO FCO 44/403, St. Vincent to Foreign and Commonwealth Office, April 17, 1970; St. Lucia to Foreign and Commonwealth Office, April 17, 1970; Bridgetown to Foreign and Commonwealth Office, May 11, 1970.

3. "Black Power in the Caribbean," *Race Today* 1, no. 8, (December 1969): 232–33.

4. TNA: FCO 63/443. "Black Power," May 15, 1970.

5. Ibid.

6. Ibid.

7. Ibid.; Kamarakafego, *Me One*, 181.

8. Roosevelt Brown, "Barbados Black Power Conference Canceled," *Bermuda Recorder*, May 23, 1970, 4.

9. Ibid.

10. CIA, "Intelligence Memorandum: Black Radicalism in the Caribbean," August 6, 1969, MD: NACP, 12.

11. Kamarakafego, *Me One*, 194.

12. Ibid.

13. "James 34 X to Kwame Nkrumah," n.d. Box 154–5, 2, Kwame Nkrumah Papers, MSRC.

14. "Obi Egbuna to Kwame Nkrumah," May 21, 1968, Box 154–4, 2, Nkrumah Papers, MSRC.

15. TNA: MEPO 2/11409, "Detective K. Thompson, Criminal Investigation Department, to Scotland Yard to Detective Chief Superintendent," August 1, 1968, Benedict Obi Egbuna.

16. TNA: MEPO 2/11409, Obi Egbuna, "What to do when cops lay their hands on Black men at the Speakers Corner," Benedict Obi Egbuna.

17. TNA: MEPO 2/11409, "Thompson to Scotland Yard to Detective Chief Superintendent."

18. "Message to the Black People of Britain, introduced by Obi Egbuna," July 9, 1968, 154–49, 8–9, Nkrumah Papers, MSRC.

19. "Message to the Black People of Britain," July 9, 1968, 154–18, 10, Nkrumah Papers, MSRC.

20. Ibid.

21. Egbuna to Nkrumah, August 19, 1970; Nkrumah to Egbuna, September 21, 1970, 154–4, 21, Nkrumah Papers, MSRC.

22. See Swan, "Caveat of an Obnoxious Slave."

23. Grace and James Boggs to Nkrumah, September 11, 1968, 154–2, 35, Nkrumah Papers, MSRC.

24. Grace and James Boggs to Nkrumah, October 9, 1968, 154–2, 35, Nkrumah Papers, MSRC.

25. Nkrumah to Grace and James Boggs, December 9, 1968, Box 154–2, 35, Nkrumah Papers, MSRC.

26. Jacques Garvey, Black Power, 4; "Nkrumah to Grace Boggs," September 24, 1968, Box 154–2, 35, Nkrumah Papers, MSRC; Nkrumah, The Struggle Continues, 35–42.

27. Nkrumah, The Struggle Continues, 40.

28. Roosevelt Brown to Kwame Nkrumah, September 8, 1969, Box 154–2, 52, Nkrumah Papers, MSRC; Kamarakafego, Me One, 164.

29. "Barbados Premier Due Monday for PLP Banquet," October 17, 1969, 1; "No Shame to Be Opposition Barbados M.P. Progressive Labor Party," October 24, 1969, 1, Bermuda Recorder.

30. Kamarakafego, Me One, 166.

31. James Cheek to Chuck Stone, November 28, 1969, Black Power Conference, Chuck Stone Papers, David M. Rubenstein Library.

32. "Barbados-Site for Conference," March 21, 1970, 1; "Black Power Conference in Barbados," May 9, 16, 1970, 10, Bermuda Recorder.

33. "Black Power Conference '70," African-American Teachers Forum 3, no. 4 (March-April 1970): 7, Chuck Stone Papers, David M. Rubenstein Library.

34. Kwame Nkrumah to Roosevelt Browne, March 30, 1970. Reprinted in Kamarakafego, Me One.

35. CIA, "Black Radicalism in the Caribbean," 1969, 9, MD: NACP.

36. Ibid., 7.

37. Ibid., 8.

38. See Thomas, Black Power in the Caribbean; CIA, "Black Radicalism in the Caribbean," June 1970, A-8-9, MD: NACP; TNA: FCO 63/380, "Black Power in the Caribbean," June 1970; Walters, 304.

39. TNA: FCO 63/380, "Black Power in the Caribbean," June 1970.

40. Ibid.

41. CIA, "Black Radicalism in the Caribbean," 1969, 12, MD: NACP.

42. CIA, "Black Radicalism in the Caribbean," June 1970, A-8-9, MD: NACP.

43. TNA: FCO 63/380, "Black Power in the Caribbean," June 1970; Rickford, 70–71.

44. CIA, "Black Radicalism in the Caribbean," 1969, 8, MD: NACP; See also Meeks, Narratives of Resistance; Pasley, "The Black Power Movement in Trinidad"; Johnson, "Guerrilla Ganja Gun Girls"; TNA: FCO 63/380, "Black Power in the Caribbean," June 1970.

45. TNA: FCO 63/379, "Stokely Carmichael," April 13, 1970; TNA: FCO 63/380, "Black Power in the Caribbean," June 1970.

46. CIA, "Black Radicalism in the Caribbean," 1969, 8, MD: NACP; Nigel Westmaas, "An

Organic Activist: Eusi Kwayana, Guyana, and Global Pan-Africanism," in *Black Power in the Caribbean,* ed. Kate Quinn, 166.

47. TNA: FCO POL 13–10 Guyana, "Black Power in Guyana," A-59, April 3, 1969; "Biographic Report: Eusi Kwayana," POL 6 Guyana, A-70, April 17, 1969, MD: NACP.

48. TNA: FCO POL 13–10 Guyana, "Black Power in Guyana."

49. Ibid; Westmaas, 166; CIA, "Black Radicalism in the Caribbean," 1969, 22, MD: NACP.

50. TNA: FCO, POL 13–10 Guyana, "Black Power in Guyana."

51. "Ascria's Plan or Guyana," *Sunday Graphic,* March 3, 1969; See Kate Quinn, "Sitting on a Volcano," 136-58, in *Black Power in the Caribbean,* ed. Kate Quinn; CIA, "Black Radicalism in the Caribbean," 1969, 8, MD: NACP.

52. TNA: FCO POL 13–10 Guyana, "Black Power in Guyana."

53. Ibid.

54. NARA: MD, POL 6 Guyana, A-70, "Biographic Report: Eusi Kwayana"; CIA, "Black Radicalism in the Caribbean," 1969, 8, MD: NACP.

55. Lux, "Black Power in the Caribbean," 213, 217.

56. CIA, "Black Radicalism in the Caribbean," June 1970, A-4, MD: NACP.

57. Ibid.

58. TNA: FCO 63/463, "Black Power," K. G. Ritchie, April 2, April 25, 1970.

59. CIA, "Black Radicalism in the Caribbean," June 1970, A-4, 22; TNA: FCO POL 13–10 Guyana, "Black Power in Guyana."

60. TNA: FCO 63/463, "Black Power Call for Violence to Win Freedom."

61. TNA: FCO 63/463, "Stokely Carmichael," May 9, 1970.

62. Ibid.

63. Ibid.

64. TNA: FCO 63/463, "Stokely Carmichael," "K. G. Ritchie to TRM Sewell," May 9, 1970.

65. TNA: FCO 63/463, "Stokely Carmichael," May 9, 1970.

66. TNA: FCO 63/463, "Radio Demerara," BBC, May 6, 1970.

67. TNA: FCO 63/463, K. G. Ritchie, "Stokely Carmichael," May 15, 1970.

68. Ibid.

69. Ibid.

70. TNA: FCO 63/463, K. G. Ritchie, "Black Power: Ratoon Group," May 22, 1970; "Ratoon Men Earn 4-Figure Salaries," *New Nation,* May 17, 1970.

71. TNA: FCO 63/463, "Stokely Carmichael," May 9, 1970.

72. TNA: FCO 63/463, "K. G. Ritchie to TRM Sewell," May 8, 1970.

73. Ibid.

74. Ibid.

75. CIA, "Black Radicalism in the Caribbean," 1969, A1, MD: NACP.

76. Ibid., A1, 6, 10; CIA, "Black Radicalism in the Caribbean," June 1970, A-2, MD: NACP.

77. CIA, "Black Radicalism in the Caribbean," June 1970, A-2, MD: NACP.

78. TNA: FCO 63/433, "Will the Wash From Trinidad Rock Barbados," May 22, 1970.

79. Ibid.

80. Ibid.

81. Ibid.

82. TNA: PRO FCO 44/403, St. Vincent to FCO, 17 April 1970; St. Lucia to FCO, April 17, 1970; Bridgetown to FCO, May 11, 1970.

83. Errol Barrow to Mr. Browne, May 4, 1970, reprinted in Kamarakafego, *Me One*, 181.

84. "Chuck Stone to Executive Committee for the National Conference on Black Power," April 18, 1970, Roosevelt Brown to Chuck Stone, May 4, 1970, Black Power Conference, 1969–70, Chuck Stone Papers, David M. Rubenstein Library.

85. Hayward Henry Jr. to Members of the Planning Committee of the World Congress of African Peoples, May 28, 1970; Black Power Conference, 1969–70, Chuck Stone Papers, David M. Rubenstein Library.

86. Ibid.; Kamarakafego, interview by author; Garrett, 6.

Chapter 7. Aborigine—Not Puerto Rican!

1. NAA: A9626, 444, Bruce McGuinness, M/82/32 photos, "Bruce McGuinness, photograph"; NAA: A6119, 90, Bruce McGuinness, Vol 1., "Aborigines Advancement League," August 23, 1968.

2. Bellear, interview by author.

3. Atlanta, September 3, 1970, http://farmersalmanac.com/weather-history/search-results/; "Proposed Ideological Statement of the Congress of African People," in Abschol, *Aborigines Visit the US*, 9, AIATSIS, Canberra.

4. Baraka, *African Congress*, vii–ix.

5. Ibid.

6. Kamarakafego, 160.

7. Gerald Frape, "Black Power in Australia," *Broadside*, June 12, 1969, 4–5.

8. Ibid.

9. Ibid.; Korowa, interview by author.

10. "The Work of the Aborigines' Advancement League," *Smoke Signals* 4, no. 1 (April-June 1964): 12.

11. Korowa, Interview.

12. Ibid.

13. "Roosevelt Browne Meets the Press," *Smoke Signals* 8, no. 2 (September 1969): 5, AIATSIS, Canberra.

14. Korowa, Interview.

15. Ibid.

16. NAA: A463, 1969/2306, Roosevelt Browne to Prime Minister, Telegram, August 25, 1969, W.G.N. Orr, Mr. R. Brown, Member of Bermuda Parliament, August 28, 1969, R Brown MP [Member of Parliament]—Bermuda—Visit to Australia 1969.

17. Kamarakafego, *Me One*, 162; NAA: A9626, 444, Photos, McGuinness, Bruce, M/82/32, "Arrival of R.O. Brown at Essendon Airport, Victoria," "Arrival of R.O Brown Victoria Old Bulla Rd," "R.O Brown leaving 434 Punt Road," "R.O Brown Leaving 434 Koori Club."

18. NAA: A6119, 6125, Maza, Volume 1, IOB (Robert Louis) Maza, August 28, 1969.

19. Kamarakafego, *Me One*, 162; "Roosevelt Brown," August 26, 1969.

20. Kamarakafego, *Me One*, 163; Richard Broome, "Why Use Koori?" *La Trobe Journal* 11, no. 43 (Autumn 1989): 5.

21. Kamarakafego, 163.

22. "Roosevelt Browne Meets the Press," 4–11.

23. Ibid.

24. Ibid.

25. Ibid., 11.

26. Korowa, interview.

27. NAA: A9262, 711, M/82/59, Photos, Robert Lewis Maza, "Departure of Roosevelt Browne," October 27, 1969; Kamarakafego, *Me One*, 164; See Teaiwa, *Consuming Ocean Island*.

28. Roosevelt Brown to Kwame Nkrumah, September 8, 1969, Box 154-2, 52, Nkrumah Papers, MSRC.

29. NAA: A6119, 6125, "Roosevelt Brown," August 26, 1969; Korowa, interview by author; Foley, interview by author; Foley, "Black Power in Redfern."

30. Noonuccal, interview by Hazel de Berg.

31. "Prince William Takes up Search for Lost Aboriginal Skull," *Times*, April 2, 2010. https://www.thetimes.co.uk/article/prince-william-takes-up-search-for-lost-aboriginal-skull-9232bvq5rzs; See Maynard, *Fight For Liberty and Freedom*; Foley, interview.

32. NAA: 2547, 3/2/818, FCAATSI Papers, Vol. 5, "Communist Party of Australia Interest and Influence in Aboriginal Affairs," November 23, 1962.

33. "Aborigines Advancement League (Victoria) Constitution," Records of FCAATSI, MS 3759, 6, AIATSIS, Canberra; NAA: A6119, 2768, Kath Walker Papers, Vol. 8, "Report of FCAATSI Conference," September 1969.

34. Kath Walker, "Political Rights for Aborigines," *Smoke Signals* 8, no. 1 (June 1969): 9–11; Korowa, interview.

35. "Meagher Hits Back at Black Power leader," *Ballarat Courier*, August 30, 1969.

36. Foley, interview.

37. "Black Power IS Here, Native Leader Says," *Herald*, August 29, 1969.

38. Korowa, interview.

39. "The AAL Statement on Black Power," *Smoke Signals* 8, no. 2 (September 1969): 3.

40. Ibid.

41. "Roosevelt Browne Meets the Press"; "International Contacts Force Thinking on Black Power," *AAL Newsletter* 25 (October 1969): 2.

42. NAA: A6119, 6125, "Black is Beautiful," *Newsday*, October 6, 1969.

43. NAA: A6119, 6125, "Robert Louis Maza," November 14, 1969, "Aborigines Advancement League," August 8, November 28, 1969.

44. NAA: A6119, 6125, "Black Power and the Aborigines Advancement League," November 18, 1970.

45. Ibid.

46. "Proposal to Fund 1st Congress of African Peoples," Congress of African Peoples, B. 33, 1, Larry Neal Papers, Schomburg Institute, New York Public Library, NY, New York.

47. "Schedule," "Report of the program committee," Congress of African Peoples, Larry Neal Papers, Schomburg Institute.

48. Alex Poinsett, "Congress of African Peoples," *Ebony* 26, no. 2 (December 1970): 99–104.

49. "FBI Memo-Black Power Conference," June 19, 1970, FBI FOIA Case File 157-RH-2933, v1., RG 65, MD: NACP.

50. "Black Power Conference—Roosevelt Brown," June 23, 1970, 14, "CAP," 267, FBI CF 157-RH-2933 v1, MD: NACP.

51. "BPC-Roosevelt Brown," June 23, 1970, FBI CF 157-RH-2933, v1, 14, MD: NACP.

52. "Conference of July 3, 1970," 23, "CAP," August 14, 1970, 38, FBI CF 157-RH-2933 v1, MD: NACP.

53. "CAP," 35, August 5, "CAP," 38, August 14, "CAP," 277, September 9, 1970, FBI CF 157-RH-2933, v1, MD: NACP.

54. "CAP," August 12, 1970, FBI CF 157-RH-2933 v1, 41–43, MD: NACP.

55. "Racial Informants, Racial Matters," September 2, 1970, "Congress of African Peoples, Racial Matters," June 19, 1970, 30–31, "CAP," 116, FBI CF 157-RH-2933 v1, MD: NACP.

56. NAA: A9262, 711, "Robert Maza," August 18, 1970.

57. ABSCHOL, *Aborigines Visit the US*, 1.

58. NAA: A6119, 6125, "Black Power Conference," August 3, September 2, 1970, "Black Power," September 8, 1970; ABSCHOL, *Aborigines Visit the US*, x.

59. NAA: A446, 1970/77635, Jack Leonard Davis, Vol. 1, J. B. Mackay, "Visit to USA of Mr Jack Davis, President of the Aboriginal Advancement Council—WA," August 20, 1970; "Liaison with the Office of Aboriginal Affairs"; NAA: A6119, 6125, "Congress of African People," August 25, 1970.

60. ABSCHOL, *Aborigines Visit the US*, x.

61. Ibid., 9.

62. "CAP," 173, FBI CF 157-RH-2933 v1, MD: NACP; Queen Audley Moore, *Black Women Oral History Project*, 47.

63. ABSCHOL, *Aborigines Visit the US*, 15.

64. NAA: A6119, 6198, Jack Davis, Vol. 1, Jack Davis, "Fact and Findings on Pan-African Conference"; ABSCHOL, *Aborigines Visit the US*, 9.

65. ABSCHOL, *Aborigines Visit the US*, 9; Poisnett, "Congress of African Peoples," 99–104.

66. "CAP," 167, 267, 271, FBI CF 157-RH-2933 v1, MD: NACP; NAA: A9262, 711, "Robert Louis Maza," n.d.

67. Deborah Garland, "Patsy Wants to Learn how to start a thought rebellion," *Australian*, September 12, 1970; "CAP," 102, 191, FBI CF 157-RH-2933 v1, MD: NACP.

68. "CAP," 109, 118, 125, FBI CF 157-RH-2933 v1, MD: NACP; IEC, "Interrelationships of Black Power Organizations, 1972."

69. Bellear, interview.

70. Charlayne Hunter, "'Third World' Seeks Unity at Conference," *New York Times*, September 6, 1970.

71. "CAP," 214, FBI CF 157-RH-2933 v1, MD: NACP.

72. "CAP," 209–211, 214, FBI CF 157-RH-2933 v1, MD: NACP; Hunter, "'Third World' Seeks Unity"; IEC, "Interrelationships of Black Power Organizations, 1972."

73. "CAP," 89, 128, 175, 183, FBI CF 157-RH-2933 v1, MD: NACP.

74. Roosevelt Douglas, "Speech," in *African Congress*, ed. Amiri Baraka, 83.

75. Ibid.

76. IEC, "Interrelationships of Black Power Organizations, 1972."

77. Ibid.

78. Kamarakafego, *Me One*, 169; "Suggestions," Congress of African People, Larry Neal Papers, Schomburg Library; "CAP," 100, FBI CF 157-RH-2933 v1, MD: NACP; ABSCHOL, *Aborigines Visit the US*.

79. "CAP," 115, 123, 143, FBI CF 157-RH-2933 v1, MD: NACP; Kamarakafego, *Me One*, 169.

80. Bellear, interview; Kamarakafego, *Me One*, 169.

81. Bellear, interview; ABSCHOL, *Aborigines Visit the US*.

82. Ibid.

83. ABSCHOL, *Aborigines Visit the US*, 16.

84. Ibid., 16, 19, 23–24.

85. NAA: A6119, 6198, Jack Davis, "Fact and Findings."

86. Ibid.

87. Ibid.

88. ABSCHOL, *Aborigines Visit the US*, 3.

89. Ibid.

90. NAA: A9262, 711, "Robert Louis Maza," n.d.; A6119, 6125, "Aboriginal Rights," October 15, 1970; A6119, 6198, "Jack Leonard Davis," 57, January 28, 1971.

91. ABSCHOL, *Aborigines Visit the US*, 9; NAA: A6119, 6125, "Bruce McGuinness," April 15, 1971.

92. ABSCHOL, *Aborigines Visit the US*, 23, 27.

93. Ibid., 31.

94. Ibid., 32–34.

95. National Archives of Vanuatu (NAV): New Hebrides Collection, Box NH 026, Résidence de France Synthèses Juillet à Décembre, 1970; NAA: A6119, 6090, Patsy Kruger, Vol. 1, "External Influences, Black Power," 37, 45.

96. NAV: NHC, Box NH 026, "Synthèse Mensuelle," November 1970; "Jimmy Stephens to Roosevelt Brown," August 24, 1970, SPAC NA Pauulu Kamarakafego, Box 6, folder 37, Sixth Pan-African Congress Records, MSRC.

Chapter 8. Minecrafting a Black World: The Sixth Pan-African Congress

1. See Nelson, *Body and Soul*; and Rickford, *We Are an African People*.

2. "Report to President Nyerere, Courtland Cox," June 19–27, 1974, Pan-African Congress, Box One, Cox Papers, David M. Rubenstein Library.

3. "6PAC meeting, Atlanta, Georgia," February 22, 1974, FBI FOIA Case File, 157-WFO-5211, Vol. 1, MD: NACP.

4. Ibid.; Garrett, "A Historical Sketch"; Sylvia Hill, "From the Sixth Pan-African Congress to the Free South Africa Movement," in No Easy Victories, eds. William Minter, Gail Hovey, and Charles Cobb Jr.

5. Cox, interview by author.

6. Ibid.; Kamarakafego, *Me One*, 162, 213.

7. Cox, interview by author.

8. Brindly Benn to Shirley Graham Du Bois, January 10, 1973; Shirley Graham Du Bois to Brindly Benn, January 21, 1973; Graham Du Bois to Bill, March 7, 1873; Graham Du Bois to Courtland Cox, March 27, 1973, Box 21-6, Shirley Graham Du Bois Papers, Schlesinger Library.

9. Graham Du Bois to Cox, March 27, 1973, Graham Du Bois Papers.

10. C. L. R. James to Browne, November 14, 1970, in Kamarakafego, *Me One*, 222–23, 193; IEC, "Interrelationships of Black Power Organizations," 1972.

11. "Kamarakafego, *Me One*, 194.

12. Ibid., 192, 194; Garrett, "A Historical Sketch," 8.

13. "Proposal for contingency funding, 1972–73," Collection 41.G-C.81, Goddard-Cambridge Graduate Program in Social Change Records, 1969–79, Joseph P. Healey Library, Archives and Special Collections, University of Massachusetts-Boston, Boston, MA.

14. "Biographical Summary," Box 6, SPAC NA Pauulu Kamarakafego, SPAC Records, MSRC; "Roosevelt Brown, Student Evaluations," Third World Studies Program, Archives of Goddard College, Plainfield, VT.

15. Roosevelt Brown to Phillip Littlejohn, March 17, 1972, Collection 41.G-C.55, Joseph P. Healey Library.

16. Cox, interview with author, September 24, 2013.

17. Kamarakafego, *Me One*, 194, 226; Garrett, "A Historical Sketch," 5.

18. Kamarakafego, *Me One*, 195, 214; Garrett, "A Historical Sketch," 9.

19. Garrett, "A Historical Sketch."

20. Ibid.

21. Ibid.; Walters, *Pan Africanism*, 80.

22. Augusto, interview, "Internationalism: Organizing 6PAC"; Kamarakafego, *Me One*, 196–99.

23. "The Sixth Pan African Congress: A Briefing Paper," June 1974, FBI CF 157-WFO-5211, Vol. 1, MD: NACP.

24. "Dr. CLR James Talks to Geri Stark, Information Officer, Sixth Pan African Congress," n.d., PAC, Box 1, Cox Papers, Rubenstein Library; Courtland Cox, "Sixth Pan-African Congress: Black Technology," *African Affairs* 1, no. 26, (October 1973): 14–15, Box 6, SPAC records, MSRC.

25. "The Sixth Pan African Congress," June 1974, FBI CF 157-WFO-5211, Vol. 1, RG 65, MD: NACP; "Working Paper for an Association of African Scientists and Technologists," Box 5, SPAC NA Science and Technology, SPAC records, MSRC.

26. Memorandum: Society of Scientists and Technologists for African Development (SSTAD), FBI CF 157-WFO-5211, Vol. 1, MD: NACP; "Working Paper for an Association of African Scientists and Technologists," Box 5, SPAC records, MSRC.

27. "Planning Proposal for SSTAD," Box 5, SPAC records, MSRC.

28. "Tentative Agenda for 6PAC," Box 5, SPAC records, MSRC.

29. Cox, "Sixth Pan-African Congress," 14–15.

30. Abdulkadir Said, "The Sixth Pan-African Congress: Black Unity: Coming of Age in Dar-es-Salaam," *New Directions* 1, no. 4, article 3 (June 1, 1974): 1; "Southern Forum of the 6PAC Congress," "North American Steering Committee," February 23, 1974, FBI CF 157-WFO-5211, MD: NACP.

31. "Science and Technology Meeting," Box 5, SPAC records, MSRC.

32. From American Embassy, Dar es Salaam to Secretary of State, Washington, DC, Telegram 1974NAIROB04127, May 20, 1974, "Journalist Visits To Diego Garcia," CFPF, RG 59, MD: NACP; See David Vine, "Taking on Empires," in Mullings, *New Social Movements in the African Diaspora*, 171–92.

33. "Sixth Pan-African Conference," May 9, 1973, Box 294, Classification 157 (Civil Unrest), 1957–1978, New York, 157-7836, Vol. 1, FBI Field Office Case Files, General Records of FBI, Record Group 65, MD: NACP; Lerone Bennett, Jr., "Stokely Carmichael: Architect of Black Power," *Ebony* 21, no. 11 (September 1966): 26; Peniel Joseph, "Stokely Carmichael and American Democracy in the 1960s," CSPAN, http://www.c-spanvideo.org/program/310669-1.

34. "Sixth Pan-African Conference," May 9, 1973; May 2, 1972, Box 294, FBI FOCF 157-7836, Vol. 1, MD: NACP.

35. "Sixth Pan-African Conference," May 9, 1973, September 18, 1972, Box 294, FBI FOCF 157-7836, Vol. 1, MD: NACP.

36. "Memo, Sixth Pan African Congress," May 17, 1974, FBI CF 157-WFO-5286, Vol. 1; "CBE Forum," March 25–27, 1974, FBI CF 157-WFO-5286, Vol. 2, MD: NACP.

37. "CBE Forum," March 25–27, 1974, FBI CF 157-WFO-5286, Vol. 2, MD: NACP.

38. Ibid.; "The Struggle of Black people in Australia and the South Pacific Islands," Box 6, SPAC NA Pauulu Kamarakafego, SPAC records, MSRC.

39. "The Jamaican Planning Conference," "Domiabra," Box 7, Sixth PAC NA Misc. Documents undated, SPAC records, MSRC; "General Report of the Caribbean and South American Regional Planning Conference of the Sixth Pan African Congress," 1973; 26, Box 294, FBI FOCF New York, 157-7836, Vol. 2; RG 65; MD: NACP.

40. "News Pictorial," Daily Gleaner, February 22, 1973, 14.

41. "Convention to Plan Pan African Congress Here," *Daily Gleaner*, February 20, 1973, 18; "General Report of the Caribbean and South American Conference," Box 294, FBI FOCF 157-7836, Vol. 2, MD: NACP.

42. Vincent William de Roulet to Secretary of State, Washington, DC, February 15, 1973, Box 294, FBI FOCF 157-7836, Vol. 2, MD: NACP.

43. "General Report of the Caribbean and South American Conference," "Sixth PAC Congress," August 29, 1973, Box 294, FBI FOCF 157-7836, Vol. 2, MD: NACP.

44. NAA: A6119, 4229, Roberta Barkley Sykes, Vol. 2, Bobbi Sykes, February 15, 1973.

45. NAA: A6119, 4229, Roberta Sykes, Vol. 2, "Concerned Convener, Dear Friends," November 23, 1972.

46. "General Report of the Caribbean and South American Conference," Box 294, FBI FOCF 157-7836, Vol. 2, MD: NACP.

47. Roberta Sykes, "Open Letter to the Planning Conference of the Secretariat of the Sixth Pan African Congress," February 1, 1973, Box 6, SPAC Papers, MSRC.

48. Ibid.

49. Ibid.

50. See Sykes, *Snake Dreaming*; NAA: A6119, 4229, Roberta Sykes, Vol. 2, "The Conditions of the Black People of Australia."

51. Ibid.

52. *Daily Gleaner*, February 20, 1973, 16; See Sykes, *Snake Dreaming*.

53. Bobbi Sykes, "World From Down Under," *Black World* 22, no. 8 (June 1973): 46–48; "Australia sends greetings to the Fourth International," *Negro World*, August 2, 1924, 1; Sis Bobbi Sykes, "Black Australia," *Black News* 2, no. 2 (April 15, 1973): 26.

54. Kasisi Adeyemi Al-Muqaddim, "Black Bermuda," *Black News* 2, no. 2 (April 15, 1973): 36–37; "Governor of Bermuda and Aide Are Assassinated," *New York Times*, March 12,

1973, 1; Minutes of the Race Relations Council Meeting, December 12, 1972, Race Relations Council Working Papers, BGA; See Swan, *Black Power in Bermuda*; Donald McCue to US Department of State, March 22, 1973, POL 19 BER, Subject Numeric Files, 1970–73, RG 59, MD: NACP.

55. Kamarakafego, *Me One*, 246; "Rumblings of Discontent Under the Calm," *Guardian*, March 13, 1973, 4.

56. "Foreign Political Matters," April 16, 1974, Box 284, FBI FOCF 157-7836, Vol. 5, Serials 84–211, RG 65, MD: NACP.

57. "Letter to Bob Brown," PAC, Box 2, Cox Papers, Rubenstein Library.

58. "Geri Augusto to all Members of the Working Committee for 6th PAC," July 15, 1973, Memorandums on Sixth Pan-African Congress, PAC, Box 2, Cox Papers, Rubenstein Library.

59. Owusu Sadaukai to Courtland Cox, October 16, 1973, Box 284, FBI FOCF 157-7836, Vol. 2, MD: NACP.

60. "Sixth Pan-African Congress: The Canada Group," "Sixth Pan-African Congress: The Toronto Group," Box 284, FBI FOCF 157-7836, Vol. 2, MD: NACP.

61. "Sixth Pan African Congress," November 15, 1973, Box 284, FBI FOCF 157-7836, Vol. 2, MD: NACP.

62. Courtland Cox to Owusu Sadaukai, October 18, 1973, Box 284, FBI FOCF 157-7836, Vol. 2, MD: NACP.

63. "6PAC Caribbean Report," May 1974, Box 284, FBI FOCF 157-7836, Vol. 6, Serials 212–241, MD: NACP; "Caribbean Steering Committee," May 28, 1974, PAC, Box 2, Cox Papers, Rubenstein Library.

64. "Steering Committee Meeting Minutes," May 11, 1974, PAC, Box 2, Cox Papers, Rubenstein Library.

65. From American Embassy, Georgetown, Guyana to Secretary of State, Washington, DC, Telegram 1974GEORGE00501, April 2, 1974, "Caribbean Black Power Militants Meet In Georgetown Amidst Evidence Of Government Concern," CFPF, MD: NACP.

66. "Steering Committee Meeting Minutes," Cox Papers, Rubenstein Library; Garrett, "Historical Sketch," 20.

67. "Courtland Cox to CLR James," July 12, 1974, PAC, Box 2, Cox Papers, Rubenstein Library.

68. "Memo, Sixth Pan African Congress," May 17, 1974; "We were betrayed," Labour Reporter, June 13, 1974, FBI CF 157-WFO-5286, Vol. 2, MD: NACP.

69. "Transcription," May 24, 1974, FBI CF 157-WFO-5286, Vol. 2, MD: NACP.

70. "CLR James to Courtland Cox," June 9, 1974, "CLR James to Brother J.S. Malecela," June 5, 1974, Box 2, PAC, Cox Papers, Rubenstein Library.

71. "Courtland Cox to CLR James," July 12, 1974, PAC, Box 2, Cox Papers, Rubenstein Library.

72. Pan-African Congress, Resolutions and Selected Speeches.

73. "Declaration of the Jamaican Delegation," PAC, Box 2, Cox Papers, Rubenstein Library.

74. Pan-African Congress, Resolutions and Selected Speeches; Notes from the Editor, Pan African Notes 4, no. 2 (Spring-Summer 1974): 50; African Studies Pamphlet Collection, Indiana University Library.

75. Neville Parker, "Pan-African Imperative for Increased Emphasis on Science and Technology," PAC, Box 1, Cox Papers, Rubenstein Library.

76. "Science and Technology, Committee Preamble," PAC, Box 1, Cox Papers, Rubenstein Library; See Pan-African Congress, Resolutions and Selected Speeches.

77. Courtland Cox to Kamarakafego, March 18, 1974, Kamarakafego, *Me One*, 227, 309.

78. Kamarakafego, *Me One*, 202.

79. Ibid.

80. Ibid.

81. "Ujamaa Safari," *Risk* 10, no. 4 (1974): 13.

82. NAV: Vanua'aku Pati Archives, Vanuaàku Party's Constitution, 1971–1980, "Vanuaaku Pati Constitution"; Sope, interview with author, October 5, 2014.

83. NAV: Vanua'aku Pati Archives, Box VP 16, Telegram, Kamarakafego to Lini, April 20, 1974; TNA: FCO 32/1231, Roosevelt Brown (leading Black Power figure in Bermuda): Arrest and Deportation From New Hebrides, "Roosevelt Oris Nelson Brown, nd."

84. Sope, interview; NAV: Vanua'aku Pati Archives, Box VP 16, Telegram, Baraka to Lini, June 3, 1974.

85. John Bani and Baraka Sope, "The Struggle Against Anglo-French Colonialism in the New Hebrides," Box 7, SPAC Papers, MSRC.

86. Ibid.; From American Embassy, Dar es Salaam, Tanzania to US State Department, Washington, DC, Telegram 1974DARES02115, June 26, 1974, "New Hebrides Group Active At Sixth Pan African Congress," CFPF, MD: NACP.

87. NAA: A1838, 155/20 Part 2, Africa—Pan African Conferences—General, "Sixth Pan African Congress," August 27, 1974; "Sixth Pan African Congress," August 1, 1974.

88. NAA: A1838, 155/20 Part 2, A R H Kellas to James Callaghan, July 20, 1974.

89. "Report to President Nyerere by Courtland Cox," June 19–27, 1974, Box One, PAC, Cox Papers, Rubenstein Library.

90. Ibid.

91. "Cox to Kamarakafego," August 13, 1974, in *Me One*, 228; Photo, "Roosevelt Brown of Bermuda," Cox Papers, Rubenstein Library.

Chapter 9. Les Nouvelles-Hébrides sont le pays des noirs

1. Sope, interview; Kamarakafego, *Me One*, 204.

2. NAV: NHC, Box NH 034, "Parti National Néo-Hébridais: Visite de Monsieur le Professeur Jimmy Garett, 1974."

3. Ross, *Prospects for Crisis Prediction*, 67; Gayleatha Cobb, "An Interview with Roosevelt Browne," *Black World* 25, no. 5 (March 1976): 36.

4. NAV: NHC, Box NH 034, "Synthèse mensuelle de Mai 1974."

5. "Fiery Rumors, and Fact, in Vila," *Pacific Islands Monthly* 46, no. 2 (February 1975): 46.

6. NAV: NHC, Box NH 034, "Synthèse mensuelle de Juillet 1974."

7. Ibid.

8. Ibid.

9. NAV: NHC, Box NH 034, "Synthèse mensuelle de Août 1974," "Traduction du rapport sure les activities du Parti National Neo-Hebrides"; Vanua'aku Pati Archives, Box VP 016, "National Party Rally—Sunday July 14, Tagabe Mission Grounds."

10. NAV: NHC, Box NH 034, "Synthèse mensuelle de Novembre 1974," "Les Néo-Hébridais Power."

11. NAV: NHC, Box NH 034, "Synthèse mensuelle de Août 1974," "Les activities du Parti National Neo-Hebrides."

12. Ibid.

13. Ibid.

14. Ibid; NAV: NHC, Box NH 034, "Synthèse mensuelle de Juillet 1974."

15. NAV: NHC, Vanuaʼaku Pati Archives, Box VP 003, Miscellaneous Loose Papers, 1973–1997, "Resolutions of the New Hebrides National Party Governing Council, November, 8–11, 1974," 3.

16. NAV: NHC, Box NH 034, "Visite de Monsieur le Professeur Jimmy Garett, 1974."

17. Ibid.

18. Ibid.

19. Ibid.

20. Ibid.

21. Nato, interview by author; VNA: Vanuaʼaku Pati Archives, Box VP 016, Miscellaneous Papers, 1975–1986; 1989, Telegram to Lini and Kalkot, April 4, 1975.

22. Nato, interview by author.

23. NAV: NHC, Box NH 048, *one talk*, June 1968.

24. NAV: Vanuaʼaku Pati Archives, Box VP 003, Miscellaneous Loose Papers 1973–97, Walter Lini to Port Moresby Community Develop Group, January 6, 1975.

25. NAV: Vanuaʼaku Pati Archives, Box VP 002, Miscellaneous and Correspondence, World Council of Churches, "World Council of Churches Program to Combat Racism, Special Fund," Geneva August 18, 1976, 5, Box VP 003, Milton McMahon to Father Thomas Butu, November 14, 1974.

26. TNA: FCO 32/1231, "Roosevelt Oris Nelson Brown," Vila to FCO, May 29, 1975.

27. Ibid.; TNA: FCO 32/1231, K. Woodard to R. Eilbeck, FCO, March 6, 1975, May 5, 1975, J H Mallett to Chief Immigration Officer, Bermuda, May 19, 1975, J.H. Mallett to Miss O. Goodinson, May 19, 1975.

28. TNA: FCO 32/1231, "Roosevelt Oris Nelson Brown," May 29, 1975, CM Dumper, "Black Power—Roosevelt Oris Nelson Brown," May 13, 1975.

29. TNA: FCO 32/1231, "Roosevelt Brown," May 29, 1975.

30. TNA: FCO 32/1231, "Secret," May 22, 1975.

31. Kamarakafego, *Me One*, 241.

32. TNA: FCO 32/1231, "Black Power," May 29, 1975.

33. Ibid.

34. NAV: Vanuaʼaku Pati Archives, Box VP 003, "School Leavers for Longana People Center Ambae."

35. NAV: Vanuaʼaku Pati Archives, Box VP 003, "To Sub-Committee Round the Group," "Proposed Course for Longana Centre."

36. Kamarakafego, *Me One*, 240; Cobb, "An Interview with Roosevelt Browne," 5, 32.

37. Lini, interview by author; Mala, interview by author.

38. TNA: FCO 32/1231, "Du Boulay to FCO," May 29, 1975.

39. TNA: FCO 32/1231, "Roosevelt Brown," May 29, 1975.

40. NAV: Vanuaʼaku Pati Archives, Box VP 003, A. R. Worner to Hayde, May 14, 1971; TNA: FCO 32/1231, "Black Power," May 29, 1975.

41. TNA: FCO 32/1231, "Activités d'un agent du Black Power," May 15, 1975.

42. TNA: FCO 32/1231, "Mr. Roosevelt Brown," May 20, 1975.

43. Ibid.

44. Ibid.; TNA: FCO 32/1231, "Roosevelt Brown," May 29, 1975.

45. Lini, interview.

46. Sope, interview.

47. TNA: FCO 32/1231, Du Boulay to FCO, June 11, 1975.

48. NAV: Vanua'aku Pati Archives, Box VP 003, Walter Lini to Boulay, June 19, 1975.

49. Ibid.

50. TNA: FCO 32/1231, De Boulay to Walter Lini, June 24, 1975.

51. TNA: FCO 32/1231, De Boulay to FCO, June 26, 1975.

52. Ibid.

53. Ibid.

54. TNA: FCO 32/1231, Callaghan to Flash Vila, June 27, 1975.

55. TNA: FCO 32/1231, Maclehose to FCO, June 30, 1975.

56. Ben Lowings, "Documents Show Britain Thought About Sending Soldiers into Vanuatu in 1975 To Prevent Unrest," April 18, 2013, Radio New Zealand International, https://www.radionz.co.nz/international/pacific-news/211574/documents-show-britain-thought-about-sending-soldiers-into-vanuatu-in-1975-to-prevent-unrest.

57. TNA: FCO 32/1231, Du Boulay to FCO, June 30, 1975.

58. Lini, interview; Mala, interview.

59. TNA: FCO 32/1231, "Roosevelt Brown," June 30, 1975; Kamarakafego, *Me One*, 245–46.

60. TNA: FCO 32/1231, Boulay to AEW Bullock; Boulay to FCO, July 1, 1975; Mataskelekele, interview by author.

61. Mataskelekele, interview; Swan, 2014; Taurakoto, interview, September 27, 2014.

62. Ibid.

63. TNA: FCO 32/1231, Mataskelekele to De Boulay, June 30 1975.

64. NAV: NHC, Box NH 034, "Synthèse Mois de June 1975;" TNA: FCO 32/1231, Boulay to Bullock, Boulay to FCO, July 1, 1975.

65. TNA: FCO 32/1231, "Bauerfueld Incident," August 18, 1975; Taurakoto, interview.

66. "French Accuse Subversives," *Pacific Islands Monthly* 46, no. 8 (August 1975): 10; "The Brown Affair," *New Hebridean Viewpoints* 1, no. 14 (August 1975): 20–21, Special Collections, Library of the University of the South Pacific (Emalus), Vila, Vanuatu.

67. "Twenty Arrests," *New Hebridean Viewpoints* 1, no. 14 (August 1975): 21.

68. "Du Boulay," *New Hebridean Viewpoints* 1, no. 12 (June 1975): 23.

69. Mataskelekele, interview; Barak Sope, "Editorial," *New Hebrides Viewpoints* 1, no. 12 (June 1975): 2; Taurakoto, interview.

70. "NHNP 4th Congress, 30 January 1976," *New Hebrides Viewpoints* 1, no. 16, January 1976"; "Non-payment of fines-Peter Taurakoto," January 26, 1976, note in possession of Peter Taurakoto.

71. "Man Removed," *New Hebrides News*, July 18, 1975, Special Collections, Library of USP (Emalus); TNA: FCO 32/1231, De Boulay to FCO, July 2, 1975.

72. TNA: FCO 32/1231, "New Hebrides: Immigration Control," July 24, 1975.

73. "Aborder L'Avenir," "Incidents a Bauerfield lors de l'Expulsion d'un Ressortissant

338 · NOTES TO PAGES 240–248

Britannique," "Black Power," *Nabanga* 1, no. 6 (July 4, 1975): 1, 3, Special Collections, Library of USP (Emalus).

74. NAV: NHC, Box NH 034, "Synthèse Mois de June 1975"; Vanua'aku Pati Archives, Box VP 003, "W. Hayde Lini to Kalkot Mataskelekele," July 11, 1975.

75. TNA: FCO 32/1231, "New Hebrides: Roosevelt Brown," July 8, 1975; "For Dumper From Mcallum's Secretary, July 15, 1975.

76. Kamarakafego, *Me One*, 245–46.

77. "University of California, Register, 1958–59 with announcements for 1959–1960," Vol. 2, Los Angeles: University of California, 1959, 28; Larry Aubry, "Ode to My Niece," *Los Angeles Sentinel,* March 2012. http://search.proquest.com.ezp-prod1.hul.harvard.edu/docv iew/1024273300?accountid=11311.

78. Griffen, *Women Speak Out*, 120–33; Lini, interview; Mala, interview.

79. Kamarakafego, *Me One*, 245–46.

80. Jeff Donaldson to Toni Cade Bambara, February 11, 1976, Box 12, Professional Files Funds Raised for New Hebrides Islands 1976, Jeff Donaldson Papers, Archives of American Art, Smithsonian Institution, Washington, DC.

81. Ibid.

82. Ibid.

83. Arnold to Donaldson, March 2, 1976, Catlett to Donaldson, March 16, 1976, Brooks to Donaldson, Box 12, Jeff Donaldson Papers.

84. Cobb, "Interview with Browne," 32–40.

85. Carole Park, "Blacks in Africa . . ." *Black World* 25, no. 5 (March 1976): 41–42.

86. Ibid.

87. NAV: Vanua'aku Pati Archives, Box VP 007, NHNP/VP Secretary-General Barak Sope, "Claire Slatter to Walter Lini and Barak Sope," February 2, 1976. "

88. Mataskelekele, interview.

89. NAV: Vanua'aku Pati Archives, Box VP 004, NHNP/Vanua'aku Pati: Nuclear Free Pacific Issues, *NFPC Action Bulletin* 1, No. 9, October 3, 1975,

90. See Swan, "Blinded by Bandung?" *Radical History Review* 2018, Issue 131 (May 1, 2018): 58–81.

91. Chris Plant, "New Hebridean National Party Fights Against Uneven Odds," December 12, 1975, Box 12, Jeff Donaldson Papers.

92. "Thanks to you and sixteen others," Box 12, Jeff Donaldson Papers.

93. NAV: Vanua'aku Pati Archives, Box VP 007, Barak Sope, Letter from Barak Sope, May 8, 1976.

94. Ibid.

95. Ibid.

Chapter 10. Papua New Guinea: A House for Every Family

1. Max Quanchi, "The Waigani Seminars and Other Talk-Fests," *Pacific Science Association Inter-Congress,* 2–6, March 2009, Tahiti, French Polynesia.

2. Leo Hannett, "The Niugini Black Power Movement," in *Tertiary Students and the Politics of Papua New Guinea* (Lae: Papua New Guinea Institute of Technology, 1971), UPNG Library, Papua New Guinea Collection, Port Moresby, Papua New Guinea; Leo Hannett, "Niugini Black Power," *Lott's Wife* 11, no. 4 (September 1971): 9.

3. See *Kovave: A Magazine of New Guinea Literature* (1969), and *Modern Poetry From Papua New Guinea* (1972).

4. Kasaipwalova, *The Reluctant Flame*; "Arthur Jawodimbari," *Papua New Guinea Writing* 13 (March 1974): 12.

5. Epeli Hau'ofa, "Anthropology and Pacific Islanders," *Oceania* 45, no. 4 (June 1975): 285–86.

6. Griffen and Slatter, interview by author.

7. NAA: A1838, 338/1/3 Part 1, New Hebrides—Political Personalities, "Roosevelt Oris Nelson Brown-Pacific People's Action Front," September 27, 1976.

8. Kamarakafego, *Me One*, 247; Griffen and Slatter, interview.

9. C. L. R. James to Roosevelt Brown, October 5, 1976, in *Me One*, 283.

10. Griffen, interview.

11. Ibid.

12. Kamarakafego, *Me One*, 247–48.

13. UNESCO, *Bulletin of the UNESCO Regional Office for Science and Technology For Africa*, 9, no. 1 (January-March 1979): 6–7, INF/13/33, KNA.

14. United Nations, *United Nations Conference on Desertification*, UNEP/GC.6/9/Add.2 (April 19, 1978), https://digitallibrary.un.org/record/750897.

15. Pauulu Kamarakafego, "This Project was Prepared for the Science and Technology On-Going Committee of the 6th Pan-African Congress," Box 25, Folder 15, CLR James Papers, Rare Book and Manuscript Library Collections, Columbia University.

16. Anthony Sacardi and William W. Seifert, "A Tragedy of the Commons in the Sahel," *Technology Review* 78, no. 6 (May 1976): 42–49; Kamarakafego, *Me One*, 303.

17. Antony G Tasker, "The Commonwealth Fund For Technical Co-Operation: A Unique Mechanism For Mutual Assistance." *Journal of the Royal Society of Arts* 126, no. 5258 (1978): 93–105.

18. Kamarakafego, *Me One*, 285.

19. Ibid., 248; H. E. Charles Lepani, interview by Jonathan Ritchie and Ian Kemish, May 20, 2015, https://www.pngspeaks.com/charles-lepani; Tasker, "The Commonwealth Fund For Technical Co-Operation."

20. Kamarakafego, *Me One*, 248, 281, 284; Griffen, interview.

21. Griffen, interview; Carr, *Intermediate Technology in Papua New Guinea*, 8.

22. Pauulu Kamarakafego, "The Office of Village Development," *Yumi Kirapim* 1, no. 4 (December 1977), Box 25, and Folder 27, CLR James Papers, Rare Book & Manuscript Library Collections, Columbia University.

23. O'Collins, *Social Development in Papua New Guinea 1972–1990*, 34; "A Message From the Prime Minister for 'Yumi Kirapim,'" *Yumi Kirapim* 1, no. 4 (December 1977), 11, C. L. R. James Papers; Rare Book and Manuscript Library, Columbia University.

24. Kamarakafego, "The Office of Village Development," *Yumi Kirapim* 1, no. 4 (December 1977); "Development Fellowship Scheme," *Yumi Kirapim* 1, no. 3 (October 1977), 5, Box 25, Folder 27, C. L. R. James Papers, Rare Book and Manuscript Library, Columbia University.

25. "Plitty Aid Post Report," *Me One*, 251; "West's Medicine Bows to Rediscovered Magic," *The Age*, November 4, 1978, 21.

26. David Holdsworth and Benedict Wamoi, "Medicinal Plants of the Admiralty Is-

lands, Papua New Guinea, Part I," *International Journal of Crude Drug Research* 20, no. 4, (1982): 169–81; Ryan Case, Guido F. Pauli, and D. Doel Soejarto, "Factors in Maintaining Indigenous Knowledge Among Ethnic Communities of Manus Island," *Economic Botany* 59, no. 4 (2005): 357.

27. Kamarakafego, *Me One*, 251; *The Age*, November 4, 1978, 21.

28. See Holdsworth and Wamoi, "Medicinal Plants."

29. Samore, "A Message From the Prime Minister," *Yumi Kirapim* 1, no. 4.

30. Ibid.

31. Ibid.

32. Office of Village Development, *Proposal: South Pacific Appropriate Technology Foundation*, 14, PNG collection, National Library of Papua New Guinea.

33. Ibid., 15, 26.

34. Ibid., 16–19.

35. Ibid., 14, 22.

36. Samore, "A Message From the Prime Minister," *Yumi Kirapim*, 4.

37. South Pacific Appropriate Technology Foundation (SPATF), *National Women's Network on Appropriate Technology*. PNG collection, National Library of Papua New Guinea, 5.

38. SPATF, *How to make an . . . Oil Drum Stove; Discussion Paper: Technology for Papua New Guinea For 'Science & Society Unit;'* SPATF, "Energy Changes," *New Nation* 3, no. 10 (November-December 1979): 14; Sandy Kalmakoff, "Putting the Pacific in SPATF," *New Nation* 3, no. 3 (April 1979): 8; Sandy Kalmakoff, "Appropriate Technology in Papua New Guinea," *South Pacific Bulletin* 29, no. 4, (4th Quarter, 1979): 13–16.

39. Kamarakafego, *Me One*, 248, 282.

40. Griffen, interview.

41. Ibid.

42. Carr, *Intermediate Technology in Papua New Guinea*.

43. Kamarakafego, *A House For Every Family*.

44. Ibid.

45. Kamarakafego, *How to Make Water Tank, Point* 5, PNG Collection, National Library of Papua New Guinea; Griffen, interview.

46. Vanessa Griffen. *Knowing and Knowing How*; T. Tongatule to Kamarakafego, January 18, 1983, reprinted in Kamarakafego, *Me One*, 291–92.

47. "Coconut-Oil Soap," *UNIDO Newsletter*, no. 150 (October 1980): 4–5.

48. Kamarakafego, *Me One*, 294–96, 298–300, 302.

49. Penelope Murphy to Kamarakafego, August 11, 1978, *Me One*, 288; VNA: NHC, Miscellaneous Files & Loose Papers, 1965–76; 1978–81, Box NH 048, Clem Wright to Pauulu Kamarakafego, November 5, 1979.

50. VNA: NHC, Box NH 048, Knox Tull to Pauulu Kamarakafego, October 11, 1979.

51. Griffen, interview.

52. Baizum Kamarakafego, interview by author.

53. F. C. Kawonga to Kamarakafego, July 10, 1979, Kamarakafego, *Me One*, 301.

54. Sam Roystone Neverson to Kamarakafego, August 6, 1979, Kamarakafego, *Me One*, 286; Nyamekye and Premdas, *The Colonial Origins of the Organisasi Papua Merdeka*.

55. Kamarakafego, *Me One*, 286; "Black Studies," Henry Olela to Walter Burford, June 27, 1975, Box 2, Folder 37: Oleila, Henry, Assistant Professor of Afro-American Studies,

1970–75, Department of African and African American Studies records, Duke University Archives, David M. Rubenstein Rare Book & Manuscript Library.

56. Narokobi, *The Melanesian Way*; Olela, *From Ancient Africa to Ancient Greece in 1981*; Yosef Ben-Jochannan, "We, the Sons and Daughters of 'Africa's' Great Sperms and Ovum, Let Us This Day of 6086 N.Y. / 1986 C.E. Speak as One Voice, Academically," *Africology: The Journal of Pan African Studies* 8, no. 10 (February 2016).

57. Ben-Jochannan, *They All Look Alike: All of Them? From Egypt to Papua New Guinea*.

58. Ibid.; Papua New Guinea *Post Courier*, July 20, 1979.

59. Ben-Jochannan, *They All Look Alike*, 265, 313.

60. Ibid., 289.

61. Ibid., 439; Griffen, interview; Lini, interview.

62. Ben-Jochannan, *They All Look Alike*, 289, 323, 417.

63. Ibid., 242, 265.

64. Ibid., 359.

65. Ibid., 361; "Popondetta Village Development," *New Nation* 3, no. 7 (August 1979): 20–21.

66. Melvin Bolton and Miao Laufa, "The Crocodile Project in Papua New Guinea," *Biological Conservation* 22, no. 3 (March 1982): 169–79.

67. Ben-Jochannan, *They All Look Alike*, 379, 450.

68. Ibid., 323, 380.

69. Merz Tate, "The War Aims of World War I and World War II and Their Relation to the Darker Peoples of the World," *Journal of Negro Education* 12, no. 3 (Summer 1943: 521), Merz Tate Papers, MSRC; http://drrunoko.com; "Declaration of Black Intellectuals and Scholars in Support of the People's Struggle of West Papua New Guinea and East Timor Against Indonesian Colonialism," undated; TAM 187; 2; 34; Tamiment Library/Robert F. Wagner Labor Archives, Elmer Holmes Bobst Library, New York, New York University Libraries.

70. Ben-Jochannan, *They All Look Alike*; Maev O'Collins to editor, *Koorier* 1, no. 10 (1969): 14.

71. NAA: A138, 338/1/3 Part 1, "New Hebrides: National Party," August 26, 1976.

72. NAA: A138, 338/1/3 Part 1, W. N. Fisher to D. Richardson, August 26, 1976. Mataskelekele served as President of Vanuatu from 2004 to 2009.

73. Mataskelekele, interview; Lini, interview.

74. Mataskelekele, interview.

75. Lini, interview.

76. Ibid.

77. Ibid.

78. Lini, interview; Griffen, interview; Kamarakafego, *Me One*, 13.

79. Policy Paper, "The Problem of West New Guinea (West Irian)," October 12, 1960, Papers of John F. Kennedy, Presidential Papers, National Security Files, Box 205, "West New Guinea General, 2/61-3-61," John F. Kennedy Presidential Library.

80. "Memorandum of Conversation," May 28, 1963, Papers of John F. Kennedy, Presidential Papers, National Security Files, Box 143, "Netherlands General 1963 and Indonesia," John F. Kennedy Presidential Library.

81. Ayamiseba, interview by author; Sope, interview; Mataskelekele, interview.

82. Kamarakafego, *Me One*, 253.

83. "M. J. Cayer to Kamarakafego," June 30, 1981, in Kamarakafego, *Me One*, 350.

84. Lini, *Beyond Pandemonium*, 30–31; National Planning and Statistics Office, *Review of Vanuatu's First Development Plan, 1984*, i.

85. Office of Prime Minister to Pauulu Kamarakafego, September 16, 1981, in Kamarakafego, *Me One*, 289, 252–55; National Planning Office, *République de Vanuatu*, iii; "Mario Gonzalez to Pauulu Kamarakafego," August 31, 1981, *Me One*, 290.

86. Nato, interview, Mataskelekele, interview.

87. Cuong, interview; Bresnihan and Woodward, *Tufala Gavman*, 40.

88. Baizum Kamarakafego, interview.

89. Cuong, interview.

90. Sope, interview.

91. Sope, interview; Ayamiseba, interview.

Chapter 11. Environmental Justice: A Global Agenda for Pan-Africanism

1. "PLP Veteran Pays Tribute to Political Role Model," *Bermuda Sun*, June 16, 1989.

2. Kamarakafego, *Me One*, 222, 329.

3. *A Celebration of the Life of Dr. Pauulu Kamarakafego*, Obituary, April 20, 2007, 7.

4. "PLP Veteran Pays Tribute," *Bermuda Sun*, June 16, 1989; 7th Pan-African Congress," February 4, 1990, Pan-African Foundation (PANAF), Pan-African Congress, Wole Soyinka papers, Houghton Library, Harvard University, Cambridge, MA; "Alvin Williams and Roosevelt Brown Featured in 'Third World First,'" *Worker's Voice* 17, no. 12 (February 21, 1992): 3.

5. Naiwu Osahon to Roosevelt Brown, October 27, 1988, personal archive of Vanessa Griffen.

6. Kamarakafego, *The 7th Pan African Congress Discussion Paper and Recommendations*, personal archive of Griffen.

7. Ibid.

8. Ibid.

9. Ibid.

10. Ibid.

11. Ibid.

12. Ibid.

13. Ibid.

14. "Resolutions of The Plenary of The 7th Pan African Congress, Kampala, 1994," *African Journal of Political Science* 1, no. 1; Pan-Africanism in the 21st Century (June 1996): 113–33.

15. Ibid.

16. Ibid.

17. Ibid.

18. Kamarakafego, *Me One*, 326.

19. "Roosevelt Brown and his Contribution to the Rio Earth Summit," *Worker's Voice* 17, no. 21 (June 3, 1992): 4.

20. Kamarakafego, *Me One*, 321; United Nations, Department of Public Information, Briefing Papers, "Earth Summit," May 23, 1997; United Nations, General Assembly, *Report of the United Nations Conference On Environment And Development (Rio De Janeiro, 3–14 June 1992)*, A/Conf.151/26, Vol. 1 (August 12, 1992), undocs.org/A/Conf.151/26.

21. "Rio's poor make their point," *New Scientist* 1, no. 1826 (June 20, 1992), https://www.newscientist.com/article/mg13418260-600-rios-poor-make-their-point/.

22. Ibid.; Andrew Garton, "Voices Not Heard at the Earth Summit," *Greenleft Weekly* 1, no. 65 (August 5, 1992), https://www.greenleft.org.au/content/voices-not-heard-earth-summit.

23. Freire-Medeiros, *Touring Poverty*, 79; Kamarakafego, *Me One*, 321.

24. "Oppressed by Life March Brings 50,000 Demonstrators Together," *Terra Vira*, June 11, 1992, 6.

25. UN, *Report of the UN Conference*, A/Conf.151/26, Vol. 3 (August 12, 1992), 38, undocs.org/A/Conf.151/26.

26. United Nations, *Earth Summit, Press Summary of Agenda 21*, 22.

27. "Male Declaration on Global Warming and Sea Level Rise," November 18, 1989, b. 83, f. 14, Sea Level Rise, 1989–93, Robert Van Lierop Papers, Schomburg Institute.

28. AOSIS, "Alliance of Small Island States," https://aosis.org/25-years-of-leadership-at-the-united-nations.

29. United Nations, *Report of the UN Conference*," A/Conf.151/26, Vol. 3, 9–14.

30. Ibid., 14.

31. Ibid., 55.

32. Ibid.

33. Ibid.

34. Ibid., 9–14

35. Ibid., 93.

36. Dodd, Strauss, and Strong, *Only One Earth*, xiv; "Roosevelt Brown," *Worker's Voice* 17, no. 21 (June 3, 1992): 4.

37. "Prepcom Highlights," no. 6 (September 7, 1993): 1; "NGOs," no. 3 (September 1, 1993): 2, *Earth Negotiations Bulletin* 8.

38. Kamarakafego, *Me One*, 310–11; "NGO activities," *Earth Negotiations Bulletin* 8, no. 11 (December 21): 4.

39. Lopeti Senituli to Kamarakafego, November 24, 1993, *Me One*, 310–11, 375.

40. "Pan-African Movement," *Earth Negotiations Bulletin* 8, no. 26 (May 5, 1994): 1.

41. "NGO Influence," "Barbados Declaration," *Earth Negotiations Bulletin* 8, no. 28 (May 9, 1994): 10.

42. "NGO Action Plan," *Earth Negotiations Bulletin* 8, no. 26 (May 5, 1994): 1; Kamarakafego, "Paper by Pauulu Kamarakafego."

43. Kamarakafego, "Paper by Pauulu Kamarakafego."

44. Hazel Brown, "Implementing Agenda 21: The Caribbean NGO Experience," in *Implementing Agenda 21: NGO Experiences From Around the World*, eds. Leyla Alyanak and Adrienne Cruz (Geneva: UN Non-Governmental Liaison Service, 1997).

45. Pauulu Kamarakafego, "Sustainable Community, Created by Arts Project," *Outreach/ECO* 1, no. 18 (April 11, 1997): 17.

46. Ibid.

47. "Re: NGO Speakers at Official Meetings," *Outreach* 1, no. 19 (April 14, 1997): 13; United Nations Press Release, Department of Public Information, *Sustainability Should Be Promoted for Inclusion in Government Fiscal Policy, Under-Secretary-General Tells Commission on Sustainable Development*, ENV/DEV/360, May 1, 1996, https://www.un.org/press/en/1996/19960501.envde360.html; "Commission on Sustainable Development Concludes

Fourth Session," ENV/DEV/365, May 6, 1996, https://www.un.org/press/en/1996/19960506.envdev.365.html; United Nations Commission on Sustainable Development, "Report on the Fourth Session, April 18-May 3, 1996," June 27, 1996, Economic and Social Council Official Records, 1996, No. 8, E/1996/28, E/CN.17/1996/38, http://www.un.org/documents/ecosoc/docs/1996/e1996-28.htm, UN Digital Library.

48. Kamarakafego, *Me One*, 312.

49. Kamarakafego, *Me One*, 312–13; "SIDS NGOS," *Earth Negotiations Bulletin* 5, no. 57 (May 6, 1996): 11.

50. "Pauulu Kamarakafego, Interview with Amy Goodwin," April 22, 1997, *Democracy Now*, https://www.democracynow.org/1997/4/22/earth_day_talks_on_environment.

51. Ibid.

52. NGO Steering Committee to the UN Commission on Sustainable Development, "1997–1998 Directory," June 9, 1997; http://information-habitat.net/csd-97/steering.html; Kamarakafego, *Me One*, 314; Phillip Wells, "Stirring the Pot," http://philwells.typepad.com/latest_news/2004/06/stirring_the_po.html. Accessed June 20, 2018.

53. Jenson, *Proceedings from the Global Conference on Renewable Energy*, i.

54. Ibid., iii.

55. Ibid., 21–22.

56. Ibid.

57. Ibid.

58. Ibid.

59. Ibid.

60. Ibid.

61. "Bermuda Workshop," *Earth Negotiations Bulletin* 5, no. 147 (March 13, 2000): 4; UNESCO, Commission on Sustainable Development, 9th Session, *Report of the 3rd Alliance of Small Island States (AOSIS) Workshop on Climate Change, Energy and Preparations*, E/CN.17/20001/11, February 7, 2001, https://unfccc.int/resource/docs/2001/un/eng/ecn17200111.pdf.

62. Susan Thomson to Kamarakafego, August 6, 1995, *Me One*, 356–359; "Building of Water Tank and House Using Indigenous Materials," http://mirror.unhabitat.org/bp/bp.list.details.aspx?bp_id=3709.

63. "Dr. Pauulu Kamarakafego Recognized for His UN Work," *Worker's Voice* 20, no. 21, (July 5, 1996): 7.

64. Brondo, *Land Grab*, 106; "Organización Negra Centroamericana Oneca," http://www.afrocubaweb.com/oneca.htm, accessed 10 July 2018.

65. Langworthy, *Language Planning in a Trans-National Speech Community*, 45–46; Kamarakafego, *Me One*, 325.

66. List of accredited NGO representatives," *World Conference Against Racism, Racial Discrimination, Xenophobia and Related Intolerance, Durban, 31 August–8 September, 2001*; "Bermudians at Conference Against Racism," *Worker's Voice* 27, no. 2 (September 21, 2001): 5.

67. Kamarakafego, *Me One*, 422–23.

68. African/African Descendants Caucus, "Proposal for the Draft Declaration and Program of Action for the Second International Prepcom of the World Conference on Racism," May 25, 2001, http://www.icare.to/prepcom3/; accessed July 2018.

69. UN, General Assembly, *WCAR Preparatory Committee Second Session, Geneva, 21 May-June 1, 2001,* A/CONF.189/PC.2/L.1, May 31, 2001, https://undocs.org/A/CONF.189/PC.2/L.1; *WCAR Preparatory Committee Third Session, Geneva, 30 July-August 10, 2001,* A/CONF.189/PC.3/L.1, August 9, 2001, https://undocs.org/A/CONF.189/PC.3/L.1; *Report Of The World Conference Against Racism, Racial Discrimination, Xenophobia and Related Intolerance, Durban, 31 August-8 September 2001,* A/CONF.189/12, 11–12, 28–30; https://undocs.org/A/CONF.189/12, UN Digital Library.

70. *A Celebration of the Life of Pauulu Kamarakafego,* 8.

71. "South NGOs Summit in Algiers," *Ecoflash* 1, no. 19 (January–March 2002): 12, http://www.nesda-redda.org/wp-content/uploads/2017/10/ecoflash_en19.pdf.

72. "Algiers Declaration," Southern NGO Summit, Algiers, Algeria, March 17, 2002, http://www.staff.city.ac.uk/p.willetts/NGOS/WSSD/ALG-DECL.HTM, accessed July 23, 2018.

73. Civil Society Secretariat, WSSD, *A Sustainable World is Possible,* 7, 10, 63, 132, http://www.staff.city.ac.uk/p.willetts/NGOS/WSSD/GPFOUTCM.PDF.

74. Ibid., 7, 10, 63, 132.

75. "Daily Earth Negotiations Bulletin Photo Coverage," Sixth Session of the UN Commission on Sustainable Development (CSD-6), April 20–May 1, 1998, enb.iisd.org/csd/csd-6photo.html; "Locals attending United Nations CSD Workshops," *Worker's Voice* 21, no. 39 (April 24, 1998): 1; Kamarakafego, *Me One,* 12.

76. "Dr. Kamarakafego is Keynote Speaker," *Worker's Voice* 25, no. 21 (June 16, 2000): 1; Kamarakafego, *Me One,* 336; Kamarakafego, Lecture, Cedarbridge Academy; "Pan-Africanism Lives: Dr. Pauulu Kamarakafego," March 14, 2003, Howard University, Washington, DC, private collection of author; "Butler's Heart Beats Series Continues," *Worker's Voice* 29, no. 22 (October 1, 2004): 19.

77. "Why Universal Suffrage Was Such a Priority for Me and Others," *Worker's Voice* 21, no. 38 (April 10, 1998): 10–11.

78. Ibid.

79. Ibid.

80. Kamarakafego, "Recommendations for Independence in Bermuda," November 3, 2004.

81. Kamarakafego to Baizum Kamarakafego, September 18, 1995, private collection of author.

82. "Rodriquez at BIU," *Worker's Voice* 28, no. 19 (June 20, 2003): 1; "Eight Students Receive Cuban Scholarships," *Worker's Voice* 31, no. 3 (September 9, 2005): 1–2.

83. Kamarakafego, Rronniba, interview by author; Mohammad and Worrell, interview by Colwyn Burchall.

84. *A Celebration of the Life of Pauulu Kamarakafego,* 2.

85. Ibid.

86. Ibid.

87. *Bernews,* "National Hero Profile," April 30, 2011, www.bernews.com, http://bernews.com/2011/04/national-hero-profile-roosevelt-brown/.

BIBLIOGRAPHY

Primary Sources

Abeng. University of Florida Digital Collections, George A. Smathers Library, Gainesville, FL.

"A Celebration of the Life of Dr. Pauulu Roosevelt Osiris Nelson Brown Kamarakafego." Obituary, April 20, 2007. Private collection of author.

African Activist Archive Project. Michigan State University Libraries Special Collections, Lansing, MI.

African Studies Pamphlet Collection. Indiana University Library, Bloomington, IN.

Alliance of Small Island States, *Alliance of Small Island States: 25 Years of Leadership at the United Nations*. Malé: AOSIS, 2015.

Augusto, Geri. "Internationalism: Organizing 6PAC," SNCC Digital Gateway, 3; https://snccdigital.org/our-voices/internationalism/part-4/.

Australian Security Intelligence Organization Files. National Archives of Australia, Canberra, Australia.

Ayamiseba, Andy. Interview by author. Digital recording. Vila, Vanuatu. October 5, 2014.

Ball, Jared. "Defining Black Power." Accessed May 12, 2018. https://imixwhatilike.org/2010/03/25/defining-black-power-dr-jared-ball-debates-peniel-joseph/.

Bellear, Sol. Interview by author. Digital recording. Sydney, Australia. November 4, 2014.

Bermuda Recorder. Bermuda National Library Digital Collection, Hamilton, Bermuda.

Bin-Wahad, Dhoruba al-Mujahid. "Assata Shakur, Excluding the Nightmare after the Dream." Accessed November 17, 2013. http://imixwhatilike.org/2013/10/15/dhoruba2/.

Black Power Conference Reports, Philadelphia August 30–September 1, 1968; Bermuda, July 13, 1969. New York: Action Library, 1971.

Black Women Oral History Project. Interviews, 1976–81. Schlesinger Library, Radcliffe Institute, Harvard University, Cambridge, MA.

Brown, R. MP [Member of Parliament], Bermuda, Visit to Australia 1969 File. Australian Security Intelligence Organization Files. National Archives of Australia, Canberra, Australia.

Civil Society Secretariat, World Summit on Sustainable Development. *A Sustainable World is Possible, Outcomes of the Global Peoples Forum at the World Summit on Sustainable Development*, 2002.

Claflin University Library Special Collections, Orangeburg, SC.

Colonial Office Papers. Bermuda Government Archives, Hamilton, Bermuda.

Cordero, Ana Livia papers. Schlesinger Library, Radcliffe Institute, Harvard University, Cambridge, MA.

Cox, Courtland. Interview by author. Digital recording. Washington, DC.

Cox, Courtland. Papers. David M. Rubenstein Rare Book and Manuscript Library, Duke University, Durham, NC.

Cruse, Harold. Papers. Tamiment Library/Robert F. Wagner Labor Archives. Elmer Holmes Bobst Library, New York University Libraries.

Cuong, Rose. Interview by author. Digital recording. Vila, Vanuatu, October 7, 2014.

Davis, Jack Leonard. Australian Security Intelligence Organization Files. National Archives of Australia, Canberra, Australia.

De Laine, Joseph A. Papers. Digital Collections, South Caroliniana Library. University of South Carolina, Columbia, SC.

Digital National Security Archive. Woodrow Wilson Center for International Scholars. Washington, DC.

Donaldson, Jeff. Papers. Archives of American Art, Smithsonian Institution. Washington, DC.

Dubois, Shirley Graham. Papers. Schlesinger Library, Radcliffe Institute, Harvard University, Cambridge, MA.

Du Bois, W. E. B. Papers. Special Collections and University Archives, University of Massachusetts Amherst Libraries.

Duke University Archives. David M. Rubenstein Rare Book and Manuscript Library, Duke University, Durham, NC.

Earth Negotiations. International Institute for Sustainable Development Reporting Services.

Earth Summit, Press Summary of *Agenda 21.* New York: Department of Public Information, United Nations, 1992.

Eastview Information Services. Woodrow Wilson Center for International Scholars, Washington, DC.

Elder, Alphonso. Papers. James E. Shepard Memorial Library, North Carolina Central University, Durham, NC.

FBI FOIA Case File 157-RH-2933, v1, 2017. Records of the Federal Bureau of Investigation. US National Archives and Records Administration (NARA), College Park, MD.

FBI FOIA Case File, 157-WFO-5211, Vol. 1, 2017. Records of the Federal Bureau of Investigation. US National Archives and Records Administration (NARA). College Park, MD.

Federal Council for the Advancement of Aborigines and Torres Strait Islanders. Australian Security Intelligence Organization Files. National Archives of Australia, Canberra, Australia.

Foley, Gary. Interview by author. Digital recording. Melbourne, Australia. November 8, 2014.

Foreign Broadcast Information Service. Woodrow Wilson Center for International Scholars, Washington, DC.

Frazier, E. Franklin. Papers. Moorland-Spingarn Research Center, Howard University, Washington, DC.

Garvey, Marcus. Papers. Federal Bureau of Investigation Records: The Vault, Federal Bureau of Investigation, Washington, DC.

General Records of the Department of State. US National Archives and Records Administration (NARA), College Park, MD.

Goddard-Cambridge Graduate Program in Social Change, Records, 1969–1979. Joseph P. Healey Library, Archives and Special Collections. University of Massachusetts, Boston, Boston, MA.

Griffen, Vanessa. Interview by author. Digital recording. Suva, Fiji. November 12, 2014.

Griffen, Vanessa, and Claire Slatter. Interview by author. Digital recording. Suva, Fiji. November 11, 2014.

Hazel de Berg Collection. National Library of Australia. Canberra, Australia.

James, C. L. R. Papers, 1933–2001. Rare Book and Manuscript Library Collections, Columbia University, New York.

Jones, Joseph. Papers. Harry Ransom Center for Humanities, University of Texas, Austin, Austin, Texas.

Kamarakafego, Baizum. Interview by author. Digital recording. Vila, Vanuatu, October 19, 2014.

Kamarakafego, Pauulu. Interview by author. Digital recording. Hamilton, Bermuda. October 12, 2004.

———. "Interview with Amy Goodwin." April 22, 1997, *Democracy Now*. https://www.democracynow.org/1997/4/22/earth_day_talks_on_environment.

———. Lecture. Tape recording by author. Cedarbridge Academy, Bermuda. March 12, 2002.

———. "Recommendations for Independence in Bermuda." November 3, 2004. Private collection of author.

———. "The 7th Pan African Congress Discussion Paper and Recommendations." Private collection of Vanessa Griffen.

Kamarakafego, Rronniba. Interview by author. Transcript. Lahey, MA. March 2007.

Kennedy, John F. Papers, National Security Files. John F. Kennedy Presidential Library. Boston, MA.

Kenya National Archives, Nairobi, Kenya.

Khaldun, Michelle. Interview by author. Digital recording. Hamilton, Bermuda. October 10, 2004.

Knight, Jeanna. Interview by author. Telephone. Washington, DC, March 20, 2019.

Korowa, Patricia. Interview by author. Digital recording. Sydney, Australia. November 2, 2014.

Kruger, Patsy. Australian Security Intelligence Organization Files. National Archives of Australia. Canberra, Australia.

Lee, Devon. "Belizean Racial Project: A Preliminary Exploration of a Black Racial Project," PhD diss., University of Kansas, 2012.

Levy, La TaSha. "Remembering Sixth-PAC: Interviews with Sylvia Hill and Judy Claude, Organizers of the Sixth Pan-African Congress." *Black Scholar* 37, no. 4 (Winter, 2007): 39–47.

Liberia Collections. Indiana University Library, Bloomington, IN.

Lini, Hilda. Interview by author. Digital recording. Ambae, Vila, Vanuatu, October 3, 12, 2014.

Mala, Edison. Interview by author. Digital recording. Ambae, Vanuatu, October 13, 2014.

Manifesto. Black Beret Cadre, December 10, 1970.

Mataskelekele, Kalkot. Interview by author. Digital recording. Vila, Vanuatu, September 26, 2014.

Maza, Robert Lewis. Australian Security Intelligence Organization Files. National Archives of Australia, Canberra, Australia.

McGuinness, Bruce. Australian Security Intelligence Organization Files. National Archives of Australia, Canberra, Australia.

Mid-Term Review of Vanuatu's First Development Plan. National Planning and Statistics Office. Port Vila: National Planning Office of Vanuatu, 1984.

Mohammad, Sofia, and Lucinda Worrell. Interview by Digital recording. Colwyn Burchall, Bermuda. 2014.

Moore, Audley. Black Women Oral History Project. Interviews, 1976–81. Audley Moore. OH-31. Schlesinger Library, Radcliffe Institute, Harvard University, Cambridge, MA.

Nato, Daniel. Interview by author. Digital recording. Malekula, Vanuatu, October 3, 2014.

Neal, Larry. Papers. Schomburg Institute, New York Public Library. New York, NY.

New Hebrides Collection. National Archives of Vanuatu. Port Vila, Vanuatu.

New York, Passenger and Crew Lists, 1820–1957. Ancestry.com.

NGO Forum Documents. Internet Center Anti-Racism Europe.

Nkrumah, Kwame. Papers. Moorland-Spingarn Research Center, Howard University. Washington, DC.

Noonuccal, Oodgeroo (Kath Walker). Interview by Hazel de Berg. Sound Recording. Minjerribah, Australia. March 10, 1976.

Outreach. Information Habitat.

Pacific Collection. Library of the University of the South Pacific (Laucala), Suva, Fiji.

Papua New Guinea Collection. National Library of Papua New Guinea, Port Moresby, Papua New Guinea.

Papua New Guinea Collection. University of Papua New Guinea Library, Port Moresby, Papua New Guinea.

Pauling, Linus and the International Peace Movement Papers. Special Collections and Archives Research Center, Oregon State University Libraries, Corvallis, OR.

Pauulu Kamarakafego Grassroots Collective. Program, "Reversing Sail: Honoring Pauulu Kamarakafego and the Black Power Conference of 1969." 2009.

PEN Records. Harry Ransom Center for Humanities, University of Texas, Austin, Austin, Texas.

Place, Brownlow (former juvenile member of the Universal Negro Improvement Association's Bermuda Division). Interview by author. Tape recording. Hamilton, Bermuda, August 12, 2000.

Print Media Collection. Australian Institute of Aboriginal and Torres Strait Islander Studies, Canberra, Australia.

ProQuest Historical Newspapers. ProQuest.

Pyatt, Rudolph. Interview by author. Telephone. Washington, DC. April 23, 2015.

Records of the Central Intelligence Agency. US National Archives and Records Administration (NARA). College Park, MD.

Records of the Federal Council for the Advancement of Aborigines and Torres Strait Islanders. Australian Institute of Aboriginal and Torres Strait Islander Studies. Canberra, Australia.

Records of the Foreign and Commonwealth Office. The National Archives of the UK (TNA), London, United Kingdom.

Records of the Metropolitan Police Office. The National Archives of the UK (TNA), London, United Kingdom.

Records of the National Association for the Advancement of Colored People. Manuscript Division, Library of Congress, Washington, DC.

République de Vanuatu: Premier Plan National De Développement, 1982–1986. National Planning Office. Port-Vila: National Planning Office, 1982.

Simkins, Modjeska. Interview by Jacquelyn Dowd Hall, July 28, 1976 G-0056-2, in the Southern Oral History Program Collection #4007, Southern Historical Collection, Wilson Library, University of North Carolina at Chapel Hill.

Sixth Pan-African Congress Records. Moorland-Spingarn Research Center, Howard University, Washington, DC.

Sope, Barak. Interview by author. Digital Recording. Vila, Vanuatu, October 5, 2014.

South Carolina State Historical Collection and Archives. Miller F. Whittaker Library, South Carolina State University, Orangeburg, SC.

Southern Historical Collection. Wilson Library, University of North Carolina at Chapel Hill, Chapel Hill, NC.

Southern School News Collection. Tennessee Virtual Archive, Tennessee State Library and Archives, Nashville, TN.

Soyinka, Wole. Papers. Houghton Library. Harvard University, Cambridge, MA.

Special Collections. Library of the University of the South Pacific (Emalus), Vila, Vanuatu.

Stone, Chuck. Papers. David M. Rubenstein Rare Book and Manuscript Library, Duke University, Durham, NC.

Swan, Sinclair. Interview by author. Digital recording. Hamilton, Bermuda. October 9, 2004.

Sykes, Roberta Barkley. Australian Security Intelligence Organization Files. National Archives of Australia, Canberra, Australia.

Tate, Merz. Papers. Moorland-Spingarn Research Center, Howard University, Washington, DC.

Taurakoto, Peter. Interview by author. Digital recording. Vila, Vanuatu, September 26, 2014.

Third World Studies Program. Archives of Goddard College, Plainfield, VT.

UK, Outward Passenger Lists, 1890–1960. Ancestry.com

UNESDOC. UNESCO Digital Library.

United Nations Conference on Desertification; Round-up, Plan of Action and Resolutions. New York: United Nations, 1978.

United Nations Digital Library, https://undocs.org/ and https://digitallibrary.un.org.

US Declassified Documents Online. Woodrow Wilson Center for International Scholars. Washington, DC.

US National Archives and Records Administration (NARA), College Park, MD.

Van Lierop, Robert. Papers. Schomburg Institute, New York Public Library, New York, NY.

Vanua'aku Pati Archives. National Archives of Vanuatu. Port Vila, Vanuatu.

Walker, Kath. Australian Security Intelligence Organization Files. National Archives of Australia, Canberra, Australia

Waring, Julius Waties. Papers. Moorland-Spingarn Research Center, Howard University, Washington, DC.

Worker's Voice. Bermuda National Library Digital Collection, Hamilton, Bermuda.

World Conference Against Racism, Racial Discrimination, Xenophobia and Related Intolerance, Durban, August 31–September 8, 2001. New York: WCAR Secretariat, 2001.

X Little, Malcolm. Papers. Federal Bureau of Investigation Records: The Vault, Federal Bureau of Investigation, Washington, DC.

Secondary Sources

Abu-Jamal, Mumia. *We Want Freedom.* Brooklyn, NY: Common Notions, 2016.

Adi, Hakim. *Pan-Africanism: A History.* London: Bloomsbury Press, 2018.

———. *Pan-Africanism and Communism: The Communist International, Africa and the Diaspora, 1919–1939.* Trenton, NJ: Africa World Press, 2013.

Agarwal, Anil, and Sunita Narain. *Global Warming in an Unequal World: A case of Environmental Colonialism.* New Delhi: Centre for Science and Environment, 1991.

Ahmad, Muhammad. *We Will Return in the Whirlwind: Black Radical Organizations, 1960–1975.* Chicago: Charles Kerr, 2007.

Allen, Robert. *Black Awakening in Capitalist America.* New York: Anchor Day Books, 1969.

Alyanak, Leyla, and Adrienne Cruz, eds. *Implementing Agenda 21: NGO Experiences from Around the World.* Geneva: UN Non-governmental Liaison Service, 1997.

Anderson, Carol. *Bourgeois Radicals: The NAACP and the Struggle for Colonial Liberation, 1941–1960.* New York: Cambridge University Press, 2014.

———. *Eyes off the Prize: The United Nations and the African American Struggle for Human Rights, 1944–1955.* New York: Cambridge University Press, 2003.

Asher, Kiran. *Black and Green: Afro-Colombians, Development and Nature in the Pacific Lowlands.* Durham, NC: Duke University Press, 2009.

Austin, Curtis. *Up against the Wall: Violence in the Making and Unmaking of the Black Panther Party.* Fayetteville: University of Arkansas Press, 2008.

Austin, David. *Fear of a Black Nation: Race, Sex, and Security in Sixties Montreal.* Toronto: Between the Lines, 2013.

Ball, Jared, and Tod Burroughs. *A Lie of Reinvention: Correcting Manning Marable's Malcolm X.* Baltimore: Black Classic Press, 2012.

Banivanua Mar, Tracey. *Decolonisation and the Pacific: Indigenous Globalisation and the Ends of Empire.* Cambridge, UK: Cambridge University Press, 2016.

Baraka, Amiri, ed. *African Congress: A Documentary of the First Modern Pan-African Congress.* New York: William Morrow, 1972.

Bedasse, Monique. *Rastafarians, Tanzania, and Pan-Africanism in the Age of Decolonization.* Chapel Hill: University of North Carolina Press, 2017.

Ben-Jochannan, Yosef. *They All Look Alike: All of Them? From Egypt to Papua New Guinea.* New York: Alkebulan Books and Educational Materials Association, 1980.

Bennett, Herman. "The Black Power February (1970) Revolution in Trinidad." In *Caribbean*

Freedom: Economy Society from Emancipation to the Present, edited by Hilary Beckles and Verene Shepherd, 548–56. Kingston: Ian Randle Publishers, 1993.

Benson, Richard. *Fighting for Our Place in the Sun: Malcolm X and the Radicalization of the Black Student Movement, 1960–1973*. New York: Peter Lang, 2015.

Biko, Steve. *I Write What I Like: A Selection of His Writings*. London: Bowerdean, 1996.

Biondi, Martha. *The Black Revolution on Campus*. Berkeley: University of California Press, 2012.

Blain, Keisha N. *Set the World on Fire: Black Nationalist Women and the Global Struggle for Freedom*. Philadelphia: University of Pennsylvania Press, 2018.

Blain, Keisha N., and Tiffany Gill, eds. *To Turn the World Over: Black Women and Internationalism*. Urbana: University Press of Illinois, 2019.

Bloom, Joshua, and Waldo Martin. *Black against Empire: The History and Politics of the Black Panther Party*. Berkeley: University of California Press, 2013.

Blyden, Edward Wilmont. "The Call of Providence to the Descendants of Africa in America." In *Liberia's Offering: Being Addresses, Sermons, etc.*, 67–94. New York: John A. Gray, 1862.

Bradley, Stefan. *Harlem vs. Columbia University: Black Student Power in the Late 1960s*. Urbana: University of Illinois Press, 2009.

———. *Upending the Ivory Tower: Civil Rights, Black Power, and the Ivy League*. New York: New York University Press, 2018.

Bresnihan, Brian, and Keith Woodward. *Tufala Gavman: Reminiscences from the Anglo-French Condominium of the New Hebrides*. Suva: Institute of Pacific Studies, 2002.

Brondo, Keri Vacanti, *Land Grab: Green Neoliberalism, Gender, and Garifuna Resistance in Honduras*. Tucson: University of Arizona Press, 2013.

Broome, Richard. *Fighting Hard: The Victorian Aborigines Advancement League*. Canberra: Aboriginal Studies Press, 2015.

Brown, Scot. *Fighting for Us: Maulana Karenga, the US Organization, and Black Cultural Nationalism*. New York: New York University Press, 2005.

Buhle, Paul. *Tim Hector: A Caribbean Radical's Story*. Jackson: University Press of Mississippi, 2006.

Bukhari, Safiya. *The War Before: The Truth Life Story of Becoming a Black Panther, Keeping the Faith in Prison and Fighting for Those Left Behind*. New York: Feminist Press, 2010.

Butler, Dale. *Music on the Rock*. Bermuda: Atlantic Publishing House, 2009.

Butler, Kim. *Freedoms Given, Freedoms Won: Afro-Brazilians in Post-Abolition Sao Paulo and Salvador*. New Brunswick, NJ: Rutgers University Press, 1998.

Cabral, Amilcar. "Connecting the Struggles: An Informal Chat with Black Americans." In *Return to the Source: Selected Speeches*, edited by Africa Information Services, 75–92. New York: Monthly Review Press, 1973.

———. *Unity and Struggle: Speeches and Writings of Amilcar Cabral*. New York: Monthly Review Press. 1979.

Caldwell, Kia. *Health Equity in Brazil, Intersections of Gender, Race, and Policy*. Urbana: University of Illinois Press, 2017.

Campbell, Horace. *Rasta and Resistance: From Marcus Garvey to Walter Rodney*. New Jersey: African World Press, 1985.

Carmichael, Stokely. *Stokely Speaks: From Black Power to Pan-Africanism*. New York: Lawrence Hill Books, 2007.

Carmichael, Stokely, and Charles Hamilton. *Black Power: The Politics of Liberation in America*. New York: Vintage Books, 2003.

Carmichael, Stokely, and Michael Ekwueme Thelwell. *Ready for Revolution: The Life and Struggles of Stokely Carmichael (Kwame Ture)*. New York: Scribner, 2003.

Carr, Marilyn. *Intermediate Technology in Papua New Guinea: A Review of SPATF*. London: Intermediate Technology Development Group, 1984.

Césaire, Aimé. *Discourse on Colonialism*. New York: Monthly Review Press, 2000.

Chambers, Glenn. *Race, Nation, and West Indian Immigration to Honduras, 1890–1940*. Baton Rouge: Louisiana State University Press, 2010.

Charron, Katherine Mellen. *Freedom's Teacher: The Life of Septima Clark*. Chapel Hill: University of North Carolina Press, 2009.

Chinweizu. *The West and the Rest of Us: White Predators, Black Slavers and the Western Elite*. New York: Random House, 1975.

Churchill, Wade. *The COINTELPRO Papers: Documents from the FBI's Secret Wars Against Dissent in the United States*. Boston: South End Press Classics Series, 2001.

Churchill, Wade, and Jim Vander Wall. *Agents of Repression: The FBI's Secret Wars against the Black Panther Party and the American Indian Movement*. Boston: South End Press, 1998.

Cleaver, Kathleen, and George Katsiaficas, eds. *Liberation, Imagination, and the Black Panther Party: A New Look at the Panthers and Their Legacy*. New York: Routledge, 2001.

Clemons, Michael, and Jones Charles. "Global Solidarity; The Black Panther Party in the International Arena." In *Liberation, Imagination, and the Black Panther Party: A New Look at the Panthers and Their Legacy*, edited by Kathleen Cleaver and George Katsiaficas, 20–40. New York: Routledge, 2001.

Cobb, Gayleatha. "An Interview with Roosevelt Browne: Black Nationalism in the South Pacific." *Black World* 25, no. 5 (March 1976): 32–43.

Congress of African Peoples and National Union of Australian University Students Aboriginal Scholarship Scheme and Congress of African Peoples. *Aborigines Visit the US: Report on Trip by Five Aborigines to Congress of African Peoples and United Nations*. Atlanta, GA, 1971.

Conway, Marshall. "Domestic Warfare: A Dialogue." In *Warfare in the American Homeland: Policing and Prison in a Penal Democracy*, edited by James Joy, 99–100. Durham, NC: Duke University Press, 2007,

Conway, Marshall, and Dominque Stevenson. *Marshall Law: The Life & Times of a Baltimore Black Panther New York*. Chico, CA: AK Press, 2011.

Coombs, Orde, ed. *Is Massa Day Dead? Black Moods in the Caribbean*. New York: Anchor Books, 1974.

Daulatzai, Sohail. *Black Star, Crescent Moon: The Muslim International and Black Freedom Beyond America*. Minneapolis: Minnesota University Press, 2012.

Davenport, Christian. *Media Bias, Perspective, and State Repression: The Black Panther Party*. Cambridge, UK: Cambridge University Press, 2010.

Davies, Carol Boyce. *Caribbean Spaces: Escapes from Twilight Zones*. Urbana: University of Illinois Press, 2013.

———. *Left of Karl Marx: The Political Life of Black Communist Claudia Jones*. Durham, NC: Duke University Press, 2007.

Dew, Edward. *The Difficult Flowering of Surinam Ethnicity and Politics in a Plural Society*. Leiden: Martinus Nijhoff, 1978.

Diouf, Sylviane, Komozi Woodard, and Khalil Gibran Muhammad. *Black Power 50*. New York: The New Press, 2016.

Dodd, Felix, Michael Strauss, and Maurice Strong. *Only One Earth: The Long Road via Rio to Sustainable Development*. New York: Routledge, 2012.

Drake, St. Clair. "Diaspora Studies and Pan-Africanism." In *Global Dimensions of the African Diaspora*, edited by Joseph E. Harris, 451–515. Washington, DC: Howard University Press, 1993.

Du Bois, W. E. B. "Liberia, the League and the United States." *Foreign Affairs* 11, no. 4 (July 1933): 628–95.

Edwards, Brent Hayes. *The Practice of Diaspora: Literature, Translation, and the Rise of Black Internationalism*. Cambridge, MA: Harvard University Press, 2003.

Egbuna, Obi. *Destroy This Temple*. New York: William and Morrow, 1971.

———. *The ABC of Black Power Thought*. Lagos: Di Nigro Press, 1978.

Esedebe, Olisanwuche. *Pan-Africanism: The Idea and Movement, 1776–1991*. Washington, DC: Howard University Press, 1994.

Fanon, Frantz. *Black Skin, White Masks*. New York: Grove Press, 1982.

Farmer, Ashley. *Remaking Black Power: How Black Women Transformed an Era*. Chapel Hill: University of North Carolina Press, 2017.

Fenderson, Jonathan. *Building the Black Arts Movement: Hoyt Fuller and the Cultural Politics of the 1960s*. Urbana: University of Illinois Press, 2019.

Fisbach, Michael. *Black Power and Palestine: Transnational Countries of Color*. Redwood City, CA: Stanford University Press, 2018.

Foley, Gary. "Black Power in Redfern, 1968–1972." http://www.kooriweb.org/foley/essays/essay_1.html.

Ford, Tanisha. *Liberated Threads: Black Women, Style, and the Global Politics of Soul*. Chapel Hill: University Press of North Carolina, 2015.

Frazier, Robeson Taj. *The East Is Black: Cold War China in the Black Radical Imagination*. Durham, NC: Duke University Press, 2014.

Freire-Medeiros, Bianca. *Touring Poverty*. New York: Routledge, 2013.

Fujino, Diane. *Samurai among Panthers: Richard Aoki on Race, Resistance, and a Paradoxical Life*. Minneapolis: University of Minnesota Press, 2012.

Gaines, Kevin. *American Africans in Ghana: Black Expatriates and the Civil Rights Era*. Chapel Hill: University of North Carolina Press, 2008.

Garrett, James. "A Historical Sketch, the Sixth Pan-African Congress." *Black World* 26, no. 5 (March 1975): 4–20.

Gay, John. *Africa: A Dream Deferred*. Porter Ranch, CA: New World African Press, 2004.

———. *Long Day's Anger*. Porter Ranch, CA: New World African Press, 2004.

Gibbons, Arnold. *The Legacy of Walter Rodney in Guyana and the Caribbean*. Lanham, MD: University Press of America, 2011.

Glaude, Eddie, ed. *Is It Nation Time? Contemporary Essays on Black Power and Black Nationalism*. Chicago: University of Chicago Press, 2001.

Glave, Dianne. *Rooted in the Earth: Reclaiming the African American Environmental Heritage.* Chicago: Chicago Review Press, 2010.

Gomez, Michael. *Reversing Sail: A History of the African Diaspora.* Cambridge, UK: Cambridge University Press, 2005.

Gonzalez, Lélia. "The Unified Black Movement." In *Race, Class & Power in Brazil*, edited by Pierre-Michel Fontaine, 120–134. Los Angeles: UCLA Center for Afro-American Studies, 1985.

Gore, Dayo. *Radicalism at the Crossroads: African American Women Activists in the Cold War.* New York: New York University Press, 2012.

Gott, Richard. *Cuba: A New History.* New Haven: Yale University Press, 2005.

Griffen, Vanessa, *Knowing and Knowing How: A Self Help Manual on Technology for Women in the Pacific.* Suva: Center for Applied Studies in Development, University of the South Pacific, 1981.

———, ed. *Women Speak Out.* Suva: The Pacific Women's Conference, 1976.

Guillén, Nicolás. *El Gran Zoo.* Buenos Aires: Quetzal, 1967.

Guridy, Frank Andre. *Forging Diaspora: Afro-Cubans and African Americans in a World of Empire and Jim Crow.* Chapel Hill: University of North Carolina Press, 2010.

Hanchard, Michael. *Orpheus and Power: The Movimento Negro of Rio de Janeiro and São Paulo, Brazil 1945–1988.* Princeton, NJ: Princeton University Press, 1994.

Harms, Robert. *Games against Nature: An Eco-cultural History of the Nunu of Equatorial Africa.* Cambridge: Cambridge University Press, 1987.

Harper, Jim C. *Western-Educated Elites in Kenya, 1900–1963: The African American Factor.* New York: Routledge, 2005.

Harris, Joseph, ed. *Global Dimensions of the African Diaspora.* Washington, DC: Howard University Press, 1993.

Hass, Jeffrey. *The Assassination of Fred Hampton: How the FBI and the Chicago Police Murdered a Black Panther.* New York: Lawrence Hill Books, 2009.

Higashada, Cheryl. *Black Internationalist Feminism: Women Writers of the Black Left, 1945–1995.* Chicago: University of Illinois Press, 2011.

Hill, Lance. *The Deacons for Defense: Armed Resistance and the Civil Rights Movement.* Chapel Hill: University of North Carolina Press, 2004.

Ho, Fred, and Bill Mullen. *Afro Asia: Revolutionary Political and Cultural Connections between African Americans and Asian Americans.* Durham: Duke University Press, 2008.

Hodgson, Eva. *Second Class Citizens, First Class Men.* Hamilton, Bermuda: The Writers Machine, 1997.

Holdsworth, David, and Benedict Wamoi, "Medicinal Plants of the Admiralty Islands, Papua New Guinea, Part I," *International Journal of Crude Drug Research* 20, no. 4, (1982): 169–81.

Horne, Gerald. *End of Empires: African Americans and India.* Philadelphia: Temple University Press, 2008.

———. *Fire This Time: The Watts Uprising and the 1960s.* New York: Da Capo Press, 1997.

———. *Mau Mau in Harlem? The U.S. and the Liberation of Kenya.* New York: Palgrave Macmillan, 2009.

———. *Race Woman: The Lives of Shirley Graham Du Bois.* New York: New York University Press, 2002.

——. *Red Seas: Ferdinand Smith and Radical Black Sailors in the United States and Ja-maica*. New York University Press, 2005.

——. *White Pacific: US Imperialism & Black Slavery in the South Seas After the Civil War*. Honolulu: University of Hawaii Press, 2007.

Howard, Philip A. *Black Labor, White Sugar: Caribbean Braceros and Their Struggle for Power in the Cuban Sugar Industry*. Baton Rouge: Louisiana State University Press, 2015.

Jackson, George. *Blood in My Eye*. Baltimore: Black Classic Press, 1996.

Jacques Garvey, Amy. *Black Power in America: Marcus Garvey's Impact on Jamaica and Africa; The Power of the Human Spirit*. Kingston: Amy Jacques Garvey, 1968.

James, Joy. *Imprisoned Intellectuals: America's Political Prisoners Write on Life, Liberation, and Rebellion*. New York: Rowman & Littlefield, 2003.

——, ed. *Warfare in the American Homeland: Policing and Prison in a Penal Democracy*. Durham, NC: Duke University Press, 2007.

James, Winston. *Holding Aloft the Banner of Ethiopia: Caribbean Radicalism in Early Twentieth-Century America*. New York: Verso, 1999.

James, Winston, and Clive Harris. *Inside Babylon: the Caribbean Diaspora in Britain*. New York: Verso, 1993.

Jeffries, Hassan. *Bloody Lowndes: Civil Rights and Black Power in Alabama's Black Belt*. New York: New York University Press, 2009.

Jeffries, Judson. *Comrades: A Local History of the Black Panther*. Bloomington: Indiana University Press, Party 2007.

——. *On the Ground: The Black Panther Party in Communities Across America*. Jackson: University Press of Mississippi. 2011.

Jenson, Lynge, ed. *Proceedings from the Global Conference on Renewable Energy Islands*. Ærø: Forum for Energy and Development, 1999.

Johnson, Cedric. *Revolutionaries to Race Leaders: Black Power and the Making of African American Politics*. Minneapolis: University of Minnesota Press, 2007.

Johnson, Martinus. *Reflections of an African Diplomat*. Bloomington, IN: Authorhouse, 2012.

Johnson-Odim, Cheryl, and Nina Emma Mba. *For Women and Nation: Funmilayo Ransome-Kuti of Nigeria*. Urbana: University of Illinois Press, 1997.

Jones, Charles, ed. *The Black Panther Party Reconsidered*. Baltimore: Black Classic Press, 1998.

Jones, Claudia. "An End to the Neglect of the Problems of the Negro Woman!" In *Daughters of Africa: An International Anthology of Words and Writings by Women of African Descent*, edited by Margaret Busby, 261–62. New York: Vintage 1993.

Jones, Meta. *The Muse Is Music: Jazz Poetry from the Harlem Renaissance to Spoken Word*. Urbana: University Press of Illinois, 2011.

Joseph, Peniel. *Neighborhood Rebels*. New York: Palgrave Macmillan, 2010.

——. *Stokely: A Life*. New York: Civitas Books, 2016.

——. *The Black Power Movement: Rethinking the Civil Rights-Black Power Era*. New York: Routledge, 2006.

——. *Waiting 'Til the Midnight Hour: A Narrative History of Black Power in America*. New York: Henry Holt, 2006.

Kamarakafego, Pauulu. *A House for Every Family*. Boroko: Hebamo Press, 1979.

———. *How to Make Watertank, Point 5*. Port Moresby: Hebamo Press, 1980.

———. *How to Build a Watertank with Bamboo and Cement*. Vila: Pauulu Kamarakafego, 1983.

———. *Me One: The Autobiography of Pauulu Kamarakafego*. Bermuda: PK Publishing, 2001.

———. "Paper by Pauulu Kamarakafego." In *Proceedings from the Global Conference on Renewable Energy Islands*, edited by Lynge Jenson, 21–22. Ærø: Forum for Energy and Development, 1999.

Kasaipwalova, John. *The Reluctant Flame*. Port Moresby: Papua Pocket Poets, 1971.

Kendi, Ibram X. *The Black Campus Movement: Black Students and the Racial Reconstitution of Higher Education, 1965–1972*. New York: Palgrave Macmillan, 2012.

Kuti, Fela, and Africa 70. "Sorrow Tears and Blood." Track 1 on *Sorrow Tears and Blood*. Kalakuta, 1977, record.

Langworthy, Geneva. *Language Planning in a Trans-National Speech Community*. Washington, DC: ERIC Clearinghouse, 2002.

Lawler, Daniel J., and Erin R. Mahan, eds. *Foreign Relations of the United States, 1958–1960*, Vol. 14, *Africa*. Washington, DC: Government Printing Office, 2010.

Lazerow, Jana. *In Search of the Black Panther Party: New Perspectives on a Revolutionary Movement*. Durham, NC: Duke University Press, 2006.

Leach, Melissa and Robert Mears. *The Lie of the Land: Challenging Received Wisdom on the African Environment*. Oxford: James Currey, 1996.

Lemelle, Sidney, and Robin Kelley, eds. *Imagining Home: Class, Culture and Nationalism in the African Diaspora*. London: Verso, 1994.

Levy-Hinte, Jeff. *Soul Power*. DVD. Directed by Jeff Levy-Hinte. Toronto: Sony Pictures Classic, 2009.

Lewis, Rupert Charles. *Walter Rodney's Intellectual and Political Thought*. Detroit: Wayne State University Press, 1998.

Lini, Walter. *Beyond Pandemonium: From the New Hebrides to Vanuatu*. Wellington: Asia Pacific Books, 1980.

Maathai, Wangari. *The Greenbelt Movement: Sharing the Approach and the Experience*. New York: Lantern Books, 2003.

Mackenzie, Fiona. *Land, Ecology and Resistance in Kenya, 1880–1952*. Edinburgh: Edinburgh University Press, 1998.

Makalani, Minkah. *In the Cause of Freedom: Radical Black Internationalism from Harlem to London, 1917–1939*. Chapel Hill: University of North Carolina Press, 2011.

Maloba, W. A. *African Women in Revolution*. New Jersey: African World Press, 2010.

Manning, Frank. *Bermudian Politics in Transition: Race, Voting and Public Opinion*. Hamilton: Island Press, 1978.

Marable, Manning. *Malcolm X: A Life of Reinvention*. New York: Penguin Press, 2011.

Markle, Seth. *A Motorcycle on Hell Run: Tanzania, Black Power, and the Uncertain Future of Pan-Africanism*. East Lansing: Michigan State University Press, 2017.

Matera, Mark. *Black London: The Imperial Metropolis and Decolonization in the Twentieth Century*. Berkeley: University of California Press, 2015.

Maynard, John. *Fight for Liberty and Freedom: The Origins of Australian Aboriginal Activism*. Canberra: Aboriginal Studies Press, 2007.

Mayson, Dew Tuan-Wleh and Amos Sawyer. "Capitalism and the Struggle of the Working Class in Liberia." *Liberian Research Association Journal* 9, no. 2 (1979): 140–58.

M'Baye, Babacar. *The Trickster Comes West: Pan-African Influence in Early Black Diasporan Narratives.* Jackson: University Press of Mississippi, 2009.

McDuffie, Erik S. *Sojourning for Freedom: Black Women, American Communism and the Making of Black Left Feminism.* Durham, NC: Duke University Press, 2011.

McGillivray, Gillian. *Blazing Cane: Sugar Communities, Class, and State Formation in Cuba, 1868–1959.* Durham, NC: Duke University Press, 2009.

Meeks, Brian. *Narratives of Resistance: Jamaica, Trinidad, the Caribbean.* Jamaica: University of West Indies Press, 2000.

———. "The Rise and Fall of Caribbean Black Power." In *From Toussaint to Tupac: The Black International Since the Age of Revolution*, edited by Michael West, William Martin, and Fanon Che Wilkins, 197–214. Chapel Hill: University of North Carolina Press, 2009.

Meriwether, James. *Proudly We Can Be Africans: Black Americans and Africa, 1935–1961.* Chapel Hill: University of North Carolina Press, 2002.

Minter, William, Gail Hovey, and Charles Cobb Jr., eds. *No Easy Victories: African Liberation and American Activists over a Half Century, 1950–2000.* Trenton, NJ: Africa World Press, 2007.

Mokhtefi, Elaine. *Algiers, Third World Capital: Freedom Fighters, Revolutionaries, Black Panthers.* New York: Verso, 2018.

Moore, Fred. "School Desegregation." In *The Angry Black South: Southern Negroes Tell Their Own Story*, edited by Glenford Mitchell and William Peace III, 52–72. New York: Corinth Books, 1962.

Mortimore, Michael. *Adapting to Drought: Farmers, Famines and Desertification in West Africa.* Cambridge, UK: Cambridge University Press, 1989.

Mullings, Leith, ed. *New Social Movements in the African Diaspora: Challenging Global Apartheid.* New York: Palgrave Macmillan, 2009.

Muntaqim, Jalil. *We Are Our Own Liberators: Selected Prison Writings.* Binghamton, NY: Arissa Media Group, 2010.

Murch, Donna. *Living for the City: Migration, Education, and the Rise of the Black Panther Party in Oakland, California.* Chapel Hill: University of North Carolina Press, 2010.

Narokobi, Bernard. *The Melanesian Way.* Boroko: Institute of Papua New Guinea Studies, 1980.

Nelson, Alondra. *Body and Soul: The Black Panther Party and the Fight Against Medical Discrimination.* Minneapolis: University of Minnesota Press, 2011.

Nkrumah, Kwame. *The Struggle Continues.* London: Panaf Books Ltd., 1973.

Nyamekye, Kwasi, and Ralph Premdas. *The Colonial Origins of the Organisasi Papua Merdeka (OPM) or the Free Papua Movement.* Port Moresby: Institute of Papua New Guinea Studies, 1979.

O'Collins, Maev. *Social Development in Papua New Guinea 1972–1990: Searching for Solutions in a Changing World.* Canberra: Department of Political and Social Change Research School of Pacific Studies, Australian National University, 1993.

Office of Village Development, *Proposal: South Pacific Appropriate Technology Foundation.* Boroko: Papua New Guinea, 1970.

Ogbar, Jeffrey. *Black Power: Radical Politics and African American Identity*. Baltimore: University of Johns Hopkins Press, 2005.

Ogot, Bethwell A. *My Footprints on the Sands of Time: An Autobiography*. Bloomington, IN: Trafford Publishing, 2003.

Olela, Henry. *From Ancient Africa to Ancient Greece in 1981: An Introduction to Philosophy*. Atlanta: Black Heritage Productions, 1981.

Onishi, Yuichiro. *Transpacific Antiracism: Afro-Asian Solidarity in Twentieth-Century Black America, Japan, and Okinawa*. New York: New York University, 2013.

Pan-African Congress, *Resolutions and Selected Speeches from the Sixth Pan African Congress*, Dar es Salaam: Tanzania Publishing House, 1976.

Penn, Steve. *Case for Pardon: The Pete O'Neal Story*. Shawnee, PA: Penn Books, 2013.

Perry, Kennata Hammond. *London is the Place for Me: Black Britons, Citizenship and the Politics of Race*. Oxford: Oxford University Press, 2015.

Philip, Ira. *Freedom Fighters: From Monk to Mazumbo*. London: Akira Publishers, 1987.

Plummer, Brenda. *In Search of Power: African Americans in the Era of Decolonization. 1956–1974*. Cambridge. UK: Cambridge University Press, 2012.

Prashad, Vijay. *Everybody was Kung Fu Fighting: Afro-Asian Connections and the Myth of Cultural Purity*. Boston: Beacon Press, 2002.

Putnam, Lara. *Radical Moves: Caribbean Migrants and the Politics of Race in the Jazz Age*. Chapel Hill: University of Chapel Hill Press, 2013.

Quinn, Kate, ed. *Black Power in the Caribbean*. Gainesville: University Press of Florida, 2014.

Ransby, Barbara. *Eslanda: The Large and Unconventional Life of Mrs. Paul Robeson*. New Haven: Yale University Press, 2013.

Reij, Chris and Ian Scoones and Camilla Toulmin, editors. *Sustaining the Soil: Indigenous Soil and Water Conservation in Africa*. London: Earthscan, 1996.

Rickford, Russell. *We Are an African People: Independent Education, Black Power, and the Radical Imagination*. Oxford: Oxford University Press, 2016.

Robinson, Cedric. *Black Marxism: The Making of the Black Radical Tradition*. Chapel Hill: University of North Carolina Press, 2000.

Rodney, Walter. *The Groundings with My Brothers*. London: Bogle-L'Ouverture Publications, 1990.

Rojas, Fabio. *From Black Power to Black Studies: How a Radical Social Movement Became an Academic Discipline*. Baltimore: Johns Hopkins University Press, 2010.

Ross, Ken. *Prospects for Crisis Prediction: A South Pacific Case Study*. Canberra: Strategic and Defense Studies Center, 1990.

Ryan, Selwyn. "Politics in an Artificial Society: The Case of Bermuda." In *Size, Self Determination and International Relations: The Caribbean*, edited by Vaughn Lewis, 180–202. Kingston: University of West Indies Institute of Social and Economic Research, 1976.

Ryan, Selwyn, and Taimoon Stewart, eds. *The Black Power Revolution 1970: A Retrospective*. Trinidad: ISER, University of the West Indies, 1995.

Samanga, Michael. *Amiri Baraka and the Congress of African Peoples: History and Memory*. New York: Palgrave Macmillan, 2015.

Sawyer, Mark. *Racial Politics in Post-Revolutionary Cuba*. Cambridge, UK: Cambridge University Press, 2005.

Scott, Clovis. "Islander." In *Bite in 3*, edited by Cecil Gray, 178–79. Cheltenham, UK: Thomas Nelson and Sons, 1972.

Self, Robert. *American Babylon: Race and the Struggle for Postwar Oakland*. Princeton, NJ: Princeton University Press, 2003.

Sharpley-Whiting, Tracey. *Negritude Women*. Minneapolis: University of Minnesota Press, 2002.

Shayne, Julie D. *The Revolution Question: Feminisms in El Salvador, Chile, and Cuba*. New Jersey: Rutgers University Press, 2004.

Sherwood, Marika. *Claudia Jones: A Life in Exile*. London: Lawrence & Wishart Ltd, 2000.

———. *Malcolm X: Trips Abroad*. London: Tsehai Publishers, 2011.

Shilliam, Robbie. *The Black Pacific: Anti-Colonial Struggles and Oceanic Connections*. London: Bloomsbury Publishing, 2015.

Shoatz, Russell Shoatz. *Maroon the Implacable: The Collected Writings of Russell Maroon Shoatz*. Oakland, CA: PM Press, 2013.

Singh, Nikhil Pal. *Black is a Country: Race and the Unfinished Struggle for Democracy*. Cambridge, MA: Harvard University Press, 2004.

Slate, Nico. *Black Power Beyond Borders: Global Dimensions of the Black Power Movement*. New York: Palgrave, 2012.

Smith, Kimberly. *African American Environmental Thought Foundations*. Lawrence: University of Kansas Press, 2007.

South Pacific Appropriate Technology Foundation. *Discussion Paper: Technology for Papua New Guinea For "Science & Society Unit."* Boroko: UPNG, 1979.

———. *How to Make an Oil Drum Stove*. Port Moresby: SPATF, 1980.

———. *National Women's Network on Appropriate Technology*. Boroko: SPATF, 1978.

Spencer, Robyn. *The Revolution Has Come: Black Power, Gender, and the Black Panther Party in Oakland*. Durham, NC: Duke University Press, 2016.

Springer, Kimberly. *Living for the Revolution: Black Feminist Organizations, 1968–1980*. Durham, NC: Duke University Press, 2005.

Stutts Njiiri, Ruth. "Kenya and North America: Educational Comparisons of their Black Populations." PhD diss., University of Massachusetts Amherst, 1974.

Suliman, Mohamed. *What Does It Mean to be Green in Africa?* London: Institute for African Alternatives, 1993.

Swan, Quito. "Bermuda Looks to the East: Marcus Garvey, the UNIA, and Bermuda." *Wadabegei: A Journal of the Caribbean and Its Diaspora* 13, no. 1 (2010), 30–33.

———. *Black Power in Bermuda and the Struggle for Decolonization*. New York: Palgrave MacMillan Press, 2010.

Sykes, Roberta. *Snake Dancing*. London: Allen and Unwin, 1998.

Taketani, Etsuko. *The Black Pacific Narrative: Geographic Imaginings of Race and Empire between the World Wars*. Lebanon, NH: Dartmouth College Press, 2015.

Taylor, Ula Yvette. *The Promise of Patriarchy: Women and the Nation of Islam*. Chapel Hill: University of North Carolina Press, 2017.

———. *The Veiled Garvey: The Life and Times of Amy Jacques Garvey*. Raleigh-Durham: University of North Carolina Press, 2002.

Teaiwa, Katerina Martina. *Consuming Ocean Island: Stories of People and Phosphate from Banaba*. Bloomington: Indiana University Press, 2014.

Terborg-Penn, Rosalyn, and Sharon Harley, eds. *Women in Africa and the African Diaspora*. Washington: Howard University Press, 1994.

Theoharis, Jeanne, and Komozi Woodard, eds. *Groundwork: Local Black Freedom Movements in America*. New York: New York University Press, 2005.

———. *Want to Start a Revolution? Radical Women in the Black Freedom Struggle*. New York: New York University Press, 2009.

Thomas, Tony. *Black Power in the Caribbean: The Upsurge in Trinidad*. New York: Pathfinder Press, 1971.

Tinson, Christopher. *Radical Intellect: Liberator Magazine and Black Activism in the 1960s*. Chapel Hill. NC: University of Chapel Hill Press, 2017.

Tolbert, Emory, ed. *Perspectives on the African Diaspora*. Vol. 1. Boston: Houghton-Mifflin, 2001.

Trew, Winston. *Black for a Cause . . . Not Just Because . . . : The case of the "Oval 4?" and the Story it Tells of Black Power in 1970s Britain*. Derbyshire: Derwent Press, 2010.

Ture, Kwame, and Charles Hamilton. *Black Power: The Politics of Liberation*. New York: Random House, 1967.

Tyson, Timothy. *Radio Free Dixie: Robert F. Williams and the Roots of Black Power*. Chapel Hill: University of North Carolina Press, 2001.

Umoja, Akinyele Omowale. "Repression Breeds Resistance: The Black Liberation Army and the Radical Legacy of the Black Panther Party." In *Liberation, Imagination, and the Black Panther Party: A New Look at the Panthers and Their Legacy*, edited by Kathleen Cleaver and George Katsiaficas, 3–20. New York: Routledge, 2001.

———. *We Will Shoot Back: Armed Resistance in the Mississippi Freedom Movement*. New York: New York University, 2013.

Van DeBurg, William. *New Day in Babylon: The Black Power Movement and American Culture, 1965–1975*. Chicago: University of Chicago Press, 1992.

Von Eschen, Penny. *Race Against Empire: Black Americans and Anticolonialism, 1937–1957*. New York: Cornell University Press, 1997.

Walters, Ronald. *Pan Africanism in the African Diaspora: An Analysis of Modern Afrocentric Political Movements*. Detroit: Wayne State University Press, 1993.

West, Michael. "Seeing Darkly: Guyana, Black Power, and Walter Rodney's Expulsion from Jamaica." *Small Axe* 25, no. 1 (February 2008): 93–104.

West, Michael, William Martin, and Fanon Che Wilkins, eds. *From Toussaint to Tupac: The Black International in the Age of Revolution*. Chapel Hill: University of North Carolina Press, 2009.

White, Derrick. *The Challenge of Blackness: The Institute of the Black World and Political Activism in the 1970s*. Gainesville: University Press of Florida, 2011.

Wilkins, Fanon Che. "A Line of Steel: The Organization of the Sixth Pan-African Congress and the Struggle for International Black Power, 1969–1974." In *The Hidden 1970s: Histories of Radicalism*, edited by Dan Berger, 97–114. New Brunswick, NJ: Rutgers University Press, 2010.

———. "The Making of Black Internationalists: SNCC and Africa Before the Launching of Black Power, 1960–1965." *Journal of African American History* 92, no. 4 (fall 2007): 467–90.

Williams, Jakobi. *From the Bullet to the Ballot: The Illinois Chapter of the Black Panther Party and Racial Coalition Politics in Chicago.* Chapel Hill: University of North Carolina Press, 2013.

Williams, J. Randolph. *Lois: Bermuda's Grand Dame of Politics.* Bermuda: Camden Editions, 2001.

Williams, Rhonda Y. *Concrete Demands: The Search for Black Power in the 20th Century.* New York: Routledge, 2014.

Williams, Yohuru. *Black Politics/White Power: Civil Rights, Black Power and the Black Panthers in New Haven.* Hoboken, NJ: Wiley-Blackwell, 2000.

Williams, Yohuru, and Jama Lazerow. *Liberated Territory: Local Perspectives on the Black Panther Party.* Durham, NC: Duke University Press, 2008.

Wilson, Amos. *Blueprint for Black Power: A Moral, Political and Economic Imperative for the Twenty-First Century.* New York: Afrikan World InfoSystems, 1998.

Woodard, Komozi. *A Nation Within a Nation: Amiri Baraka (LeRoi Jones) and Black Power Politics.* Chapel Hill: North Carolina Press, 1999.

Woods, Barbara. "Modjeska Simkins and the South Carolina Conference of the NAACP, 1939–1957." In *Women in the Civil Rights Movement: Trailblazers and Torchbearers, 1941–1965,* edited by Vicki L. Crawford, Jacqueline Anne Rouse, and Barbara Woods, 99–120. Bloomington: Indiana University Press, 1990.

X, Malcolm. "Message to the Grassroots." In *Malcolm X Speaks, Selected Speeches and Statements,* edited by George Breitman, 3–17. New York: Grove Press, 1965.

Young, Cynthia. *Soul Power: Culture Radicalism, and the Making of a U.S. Third World Left.* Durham, NC: Duke University Press, 2006.

INDEX

QUITO J. SWAN is professor of Africana studies and director of the William Monroe Trotter Institute at the University of Massachusetts–Boston. The author of *Black Power in Bermuda*, his scholarship is focused on black internationalism, African Diasporic social and environmental justice movements, and the Black Pacific. He is the recipient of several national awards, including fellowships from the National Endowment for the Humanities, the American Council of Learned Societies and Harvard University's Radcliffe Institute, and the Wilson International Center for Scholars.